FREEDOM *versus* ORGANIZATION
1814–1914

FREEDOM *versus*

ORGANIZATION

1814-1914

BY BERTRAND RUSSELL, M.A., F.R.S.

> Chaos umpire sits
> And by decision more embroils the fray
> By which he reigns: next him high arbiter
> Chance governs all. MILTON

W·W· NORTON & COMPANY, INC.

PUBLISHERS · NEW YORK

PRINTED IN THE UNITED STATES OF AMERICA
FOR THE PUBLISHERS BY THE VAIL-BALLOU PRESS
DESIGNED BY ROBERT JOSEPHY

CONTENTS

Part Three. Democracy and Plutocracy in America

SECTION A. DEMOCRACY IN AMERICA

SECTION B. COMPETITION AND MONOPOLY IN AMERICA

Part Four. Nationalism and Imperialism

PREFACE

THIS book is an attempt to trace the main causes of political change during the hundred years from 1814 to 1914. These causes appear to me to have been of three kinds: economic technique, political theory, and important individuals. I do not believe that any one of these three can be ignored, or wholly explained away as an effect of causes of other kinds. Economic technique would not have changed as it did but for the existence of certain remarkable inventors. Belief in nationality, and advocacy of democracy by large sections of the governing classes, powerfully influenced the course of events, and cannot themselves be traced, in their entirety, to economic sources. Free competition, which was accepted whole-heartedly as the main incentive to progress by British and American Radicals, was, no doubt, recommended chiefly by economic considerations, but had also an obvious connection with Protestantism. While, therefore, economic technique must be regarded as the most important cause of change in the nineteenth century, it cannot be regarded as the sole cause; in particular, it does not account for the division of mankind into nations.

The part played in history by individuals, which was over-emphasized by Carlyle, and is still exaggerated in our day by his reactionary disciples, tends, on the other hand, to be unduly minimized by those who believe themselves to have discovered the laws of sociological change. I do not believe that, if Bismarck had died in infancy, the history of Europe during the past seventy years would have been at all closely similar to what it has been. And what is true in an eminent degree of Bismarck is true, in a somewhat lesser degree, of many of the prominent men of the nineteenth century.

Nor can we ignore the part played by what may be called chance, that is to say, by trivial occurrences which happened to have great effects. The Great War was made probable by large causes, but not inevitable. Down to the last moment, it might have been postponed by minor events which did not take place, though nothing that we know

vii

of made them impossible; and if it had been postponed, the forces making for peace might have become predominant.

History, in short, is not yet a science, and can only be made to seem scientific by falsifications and omissions.

It is possible, however, to trace the effects of large causes without over-simplification, provided it is remembered that other causes have also been operative. The purpose of this book is to trace the opposition and interaction of two main causes of change in the nineteenth century: the belief in *freedom* which was common to Liberals and Radicals, and the necessity of *organization* which arose through industrial and scientific technique.

Throughout the writing of this book, the work has been shared by my collaborator, Peter Spence, who has done half the research, a large part of the planning, and small portions of the actual writing, besides making innumerable valuable suggestions.

May 1934

PART ONE

THE PRINCIPLE OF LEGITIMACY

A REPUBLICAN ON THE FALL OF BONAPARTE

> . . . I know
> Too late, since thou and France are in the dust,
> That virtue owns a more eternal foe
> Than Force or Fraud: old Custom, legal Crime,
> And bloody Faith the foulest birth of Time.
>
> SHELLEY

CHAPTER I

NAPOLEON'S SUCCESSORS

IDEALISM is the offspring of suffering and hope, and therefore reaches its maximum when a period of misfortune is nearing its visible termination. At the end of a great war, men's hopes fasten upon one among the victors as a possible champion of their idealistic aims. After the fall of Napoleon, this rôle was offered by popular acclamation to the Tsar Alexander, and was by him accepted with alacrity. It must be said that his competitors for ethical supremacy were not morally very formidable. They were, among sovereigns, the Emperor Francis of Austria, Frederick William of Prussia, the Prince Regent, and Louis XVIII; among statesmen, Metternich, Castlereagh, and Talleyrand.

Of these men, Francis had been the last of the Holy Roman Emperors, a title which had descended to him from Charlemagne, and of which he had been deprived by Napoleon, who considered himself the true heir of that barbarian conqueror. Francis had become accustomed to defeat by Napoleon, and had at last given his daughter Marie Louise to be the wife of the "Corsican upstart," hoping thereby to break him of the habit of making war on Austria. When, after the Russian disaster of 1812, Napoleon began to seem no longer invincible, Francis was the last of the great monarchs to join the coalition against him. Throughout all the years of trouble, Austria had always been willing to profit by any bargain that Napoleon cared to propose, and as the result of a policy that aimed at expediency rather than heroism, the Austrian army, though large, had distinguished itself less than that of Prussia in the campaigns of 1813 and 1814. This policy was due, not to Francis, but to his minister, Metternich, who, having entered the service of his Emperor at an early age, was left in charge of foreign affairs as soon as he had taken well to heart that all change was unwelcome to his master. Relieved of external responsibility, Francis was free to concentrate upon the more congenial task of regulating the in-

3

ternal administration of his Empire. The judicial system was so centralized that the details of the most trivial prosecutions came to his notice, and, having a taste for such matters, he interested himself even in the conduct of executions. He rarely revised a sentence, and never exercised the prerogative of mercy. Even in his closest associates he inspired no affection, and to the rest of the world he was practically unknown.

Frederick William, though his troops had distinguished themselves, had won even less personal respect than the Emperor of Austria. While Austria was being battered in 1805, Prussia remained a vacillating spectator, to be crushed in the following year at Jena, where all the prestige derived from Frederick the Great was dissipated in a day. The poor king was compelled to take refuge in the extreme eastern corner of his dominions, and when, in 1807, Alexander and Napoleon made friends at Tilsit, he sent his beautiful Queen to intercede for him with the two Emperors. Napoleon was unmoved, but the gallant Alexander liked to think of himself as the champion of beauty in distress. The result was a treaty in which Napoleon declared that, out of deference to the wishes of Alexander, he permitted Frederick William to retain a portion of his former kingdom. Frederick William's gratitude to Alexander was warm and lasting, but to the very end he continued to be unreliable owing to his hesitating temperament, and thereby earned the contempt even of his closest allies.

George III, after losing the American colonies and forbidding Pitt to introduce Catholic Emancipation, had been belatedly certified as insane, but was still King of England. His functions were executed by the Prince Regent, an elderly beau, much ashamed of his corpulence, but too greedy to take any steps to cure it. Politically, the Prince Regent stood for all that was most reactionary; privately, for all that was most despicable. His treatment of his wife had been such that he was hissed when he appeared in the streets of London; his manners, to which the English Court had grown accustomed, were such as foreign ladies found unendurable. Throughout his whole life, so far as is known, he never succeeded in acquiring the respect of any single human being.

Louis XVIII, whom united Europe restored to the throne of his ancestors, and on whose behalf, in a sense, the twenty-two years of warfare had been waged, had few vices but still fewer virtues. He was old, fat, and gouty, practically a stranger to France, which he had left as a young man nearly a quarter of a century ago. He was not without shrewdness, and he was more good-natured than most of his friends. But he had spent the years of his exile among the enemies of France, hoping for the defeat of his country as the only means to his own restoration. His *entourage* consisted of princes and aristocrats who had fled from the Revolution, and who knew nothing of the France created by the Convention and Napoleon. As the *protégé* of foreign enemies, he could hardly be respected in his own country, and foreign governments, while they placed him on the throne, did so because his weakness gave them hopes of that security of which they had been robbed by Napoleon's strength.

Such were Alexander's royal competitors for popular favor. His competitors among statesmen were abler, but hardly such as to inspire general enthusiasm. The most powerful among them, throughout the years of the Great Peace, was Metternich, who remained the ruler of Austria and almost the arbiter of Europe until he was dislodged by the revolutions of 1848, which his policy had rendered inevitable. Throughout the whole period from 1814 to 1848, he was the prop of reaction, the bugbear of liberals, and the terror of revolutionaries. His fundamental political principle was simple, that the Powers that be are ordained of God, and must therefore be supported on pain of impiety. The fact that he was the chief of the Powers that be gave to this principle, in his eyes, a luminous self-evidence which it might otherwise not have possessed.

Born in 1773, of an ancient noble family in the Rhineland, Metternich represented a type intermediate between the eighteenth and nineteenth centuries. His father lost a large part of his estates as a result of the invasion of Germany by French revolutionary armies, and this circumstance did nothing to increase Metternich's love of revolutions. The Austrian diplomatic service, in which his father had a meritorious but not distinguished career, was the obvious profession for the young man, and his prospects were promoted by marriage with the rich granddaughter of the famous Kaunitz, who brought about the Franco-Austrian Alliance at the time of the Seven Years' War. Metternich had at no time any sympathy with German nationalism, or indeed with any other nationalism. States were, for him, the personal estates of monarchs, and required no other principle of cohesion. Western Germany was traditionally pro-French, and Austria, whose territory comprised Germans, Magyars, Slavs, and Italians, was the chief enemy of nationalism throughout the whole of the nineteenth century. In this respect, Metternich, like Austria, carried on the traditions of the pre-revolutionary age. The same is true of his attitude towards the Church, for, though a pious Catholic, he showed little reverence for the Pope in his temporal capacity, and was often politically anti-clerical.

There were other traits in Metternich's character, however, which make him worthy to rank as a Victorian. (When he died, Queen Victoria had been twenty-two years on the throne.) Conceit is not peculiar to any one period, but Metternich's special brand of pompous priggery belongs to the epoch between the Napoleonic wars and the Great War. If we are to believe his memoirs, he was totally devoid of ambition, and remained in public life solely from a sense of duty and the painful realization that others lacked his abilities. Metternich is indeed almost unique; since Little Jack Horner there has been no one to equal him. So persuaded was he of his own moral grandeur that he thought it must be equally obvious to others. Late in 1813, when, having at last seen which way the cat would jump, he had terminated the double game of Austria between France and Russia, he wrote to his daughter: "I am certain Napoleon thinks of me continually. I must seem to him a sort of conscience personified." His statement of the reasons which led him to overcome his shrinking from worldly glory is most impressive:

That a public career was distasteful to me I have already mentioned. Convinced that everyone ought to be prepared to answer for the deeds of his own life; penetrated by the consciousness of the enormous difficulties of propping up a society which was falling to pieces on every side; disapproving, before the tribunal of my own conscience, of almost all the measures which I saw adopted for the salvation of the social body, undermined as it was by the errors of the eighteenth century; lastly, too diffident to believe that my mind was of so powerful a stamp that it could improve whatever it undertook: I had determined not to appear on a stage on which the independence of my character rebelled against playing a subordinate part, though I did not consider myself capable of taking the part of a reformer.

The care with which my education had been directed to the wide field of politics had early accustomed me to contemplate its vast extent. I soon remarked that my mode of thinking of the nature and dignity of this sphere was essentially different from the point of view from which all this was regarded by the enormous majority of those who are called to play great political parts.

The great names in diplomacy, both of past times and of his own day, did not, so he tells us, inspire him with respect.

Resolved not to walk in their steps, and despairing of opening a path in harmony with my own conscience, I naturally preferred not to throw myself into those great political affairs, in which I had far more prospect of succumbing materially than of succeeding: I say materially, for I have never been afraid of failing morally. The man who enters public life has always at command a sure resource against this danger, that is—retirement.

To the onlookers, Austria, in Napoleon's day, did not seem to be playing a very glorious part. This, however, was not the way matters presented themselves in Metternich's memory. "Under the load of enormous responsibility," he says, "I found only two points on which it seemed possible to rest, the immovable strength of character of the Emperor Francis, and my own conscience."

From Metternich's Memoirs one would hardly be able to discover what he was like as a social being, although it was to his social arts that he owed his success. He was at no time profound; he was clever in carrying out his schemes, but scarcely exceptional in conceiving them. He was gay and pleasant; only those whom he was actively thwarting disliked him. Like most of the diplomatists of the period, but with more success than the others, he mixed politics with love affairs. Ladies from whom political secrets were to be learnt received from him attentions which they usually found irresistible. Sometimes the game was played on both sides. For many years he was on intimate terms with Napoleon's sister Caroline Murat; he learnt from her sometimes Napoleon's secrets, sometimes what Fouché thought it well for him to hear. When Austria befriended Murat in 1814, Talleyrand, in his letters to Louis XVIII, roundly accused Metternich of being influenced by love for Queen Caroline; but at first there were sound political motives for Austria's attitude, and when these motives failed the Queen's charms lost their potency.

Metternich may have been sometimes outwitted in his gallantries with political ladies, but he cannot justly be accused of having ever been led astray by the heart.

Above all else, Metternich was an aristocrat—not of a territorial aristocracy, such as those of England and Russia, but of that type of Court aristocracy that the world owed to Louis XIV. Great affairs were for sovereigns and their ministers, who had no need to consider the interests of the vulgar. The people, for Metternich, scarcely exist, except when he is forced to contemplate with disgust the dirt and raggedness of French revolutionaries. When, later, the populace begins again to be intrusive, his instinct is to tread on it as one would on a black beetle. A very polished gentleman—almost the last before the democratic deluge.

Castlereagh, the British Foreign Secretary, was a man of estimable private character, personally disinterested, and impartial in diplomacy. He was not brilliant, and foreigners laughed at him (as they did later at Wilson) for his ignorance of Continental geography.[1] But he had sound good sense, and less predisposition to trickery than most of his contemporaries. Without being showy, he was shrewd. At the Congress of Vienna, the Austrian Government succeeded in placing its spies as housemaids in almost all the embassies, where the contents of waste-paper baskets were pieced together and sent to the police; Castlereagh, however, brought his own maidservants, and caused the secret police difficulties of which they complain bitterly in their reports. He was a man who seldom deceived others, but was himself not easy to deceive. From his correspondence one would judge him to be a man without emotions and without bias except that of his class and nation: personal likings and antipathies seem to play no part in the formation of his opinions. He had a thoroughly British suspicion of foreigners. On January 30, 1815, he writes to Lord Bathurst: "I beg you will not give any money at present to any of the Continental Powers. The poorer they are kept, the better, to keep them from quarrelling." After Napoleon's fall, he sincerely desired peace. The Austrian Minister Gentz, speaking of the Congress of Vienna, says: "England wished for peace, peace before everything, peace—I am sorry to say it—at any price and almost on any condi-

[1] Talleyrand, in this connection, quotes the remark of Kaunitz: "It is prodigious how much the English don't know."

tions." In foreign affairs Castlereagh had considerable merit. He was, however, an important member of one of the worst and most cruel governments with which England has ever been cursed, and deserves his full share of reprobation on this account. It is psychologically surprising that this cold precise mind succumbed finally to a form of madness leading to suicide. Greville rightly says that his "great feature was a cool and determined courage, which gave an appearance of resolution and confidence to all his actions, and inspired his friends with admiration and excessive devotion to him, and caused him to be respected by his most violent opponents." In his correspondence as foreign secretary it is surprising to find with what authority he can write to ambassadors without causing resentment; even the Duke of Wellington is not above receiving instruction from him. But although, as Greville says, those who were brought into close contact with him by their work were devoted to him, his colorless personality could not inspire any wide-spread enthusiasm. This also appears from what Greville says about the news of his death: "When I got to town I met several people who had all assumed an air of melancholy, a *visage de circonstance*, which provoked me inexpressibly, because it was certain that they did not care; indeed, if they felt at all, it was probably rather satisfaction at an event happening than sorrow for the death of the person." A vain man would not like to know that this was to be his epitaph, but I doubt whether Lord Castlereagh would have minded.

Of the important personages at the Congress of Vienna, the only one remaining is Talleyrand, who represented Louis XVIII and the interests of Bourbon France. Born in 1754, of a family of the highest French aristocracy, he had time, after he grew up, to enjoy the *ancien régime*, and always maintained afterwards that those born too late for this did not know the true delight of living. Owing to an accident in early childhood, he was debarred from the career of arms; his parents therefore destined him for the Church, and made his younger brother the heir of the family estates. He became Bishop of Autun, but no great piety was expected of aristocratic Church dignitaries, so that he was able to enjoy life in the company of dissolute, liberal-minded, and highly intelligent friends. His dislike of an ecclesiastical career, as well as his genuine convictions, made him throw in his lot with the Revolution, and support the civil constitution of the clergy. At the beginning of the Reign of Terror, however, he found it necessary to fly. He escaped to England, where the Government suspected him of being a French spy and refused to let him stay. From England he went to America, where he made many friends, the most important of whom was Alexander Hamilton, the Secretary of the Treasury. Finally, when the storm had abated, he returned to France.

As Napoleon's foreign minister, he at last found scope for his talents. He was not heroic, and always avoided sharp conflicts when he could; when he disagreed with Napoleon, he would submit sooner than resign office. He was never above taking a bribe for what he meant to do in any case, and in this way he amassed an enormous fortune; but there is no evidence that bribes ever influenced his policy. He had the virtues belonging to unheroic intelligence: he was good-natured, had few hatreds, disliked war, and did all he could to promote free commercial intercourse between nations. He endeavored, but without success, to restrain Napoleon's ambitions; when he failed, foreseeing Napoleon's fall, he began to intrigue with the Bourbons. At Erfurt, in 1808, when Napoleon and the Tsar Alexander met to partition the world, he warned Alexander against Napoleon, in whose service he still was. When his treachery was discovered, he was dismissed from office, but not disgraced; and as soon as Napoleon fell, he came into power again, though not for long, owing to the hostility of the clericals and ultra-royalists whom the Restoration again brought into prominence.

There were some surprising things about Talleyrand. Though a priest, he married; though an aristocrat, he married a woman of no pretence to birth or breeding, who lived an openly irregular life both before and after the marriage. But he retained through everything his imperturbable good manners, which Napoleon found infuriating. On one occasion, when the Emperor scolded him in public, Talleyrand's apparent indifference led to greater and greater violence on the part of Napoleon, who finally taunted him with his lameness and his wife's infidelities. Talleyrand smiled unmoved, and when the tirade had at last ended he turned to the bystanders and remarked, with a shrug: "What a pity that such a great man should be so ill bred."

Few men have lived through such changes as occurred during the life-time of Talleyrand. He was born under Louis XV; he died during the reign of Queen Victoria. He had innumerable love-affairs, many of them marked by genuine affection; indeed affection is one of the key-notes of his character. In his old age, free thought and free love had gone out of fashion; Victorian virtue had become the thing, in France as in England. He adapted himself to the changing times, assuming as much virtue as the new code of manners demanded,[2] and reconciling himself with the Church on his death-bed in the most dramatic fashion imaginable. Almost his last words were to remind the officiating priest that he must receive extreme unction after the manner prescribed for bishops.

At heart, throughout his life, he retained the outlook which was common among liberal aristocrats of the time of Louis XVI. Most men of this type were guillotined, or were killed in the wars, or became reactionaries from fright during the Reign of Terror. Talleyrand escaped all these disasters through his suppleness, his philosophic calm, and the dominating force of his intellect. His conversation had such charm that even in old age he could captivate the prudish ladies of a morally regenerated but intellectually enfeebled century: beginning by regarding him as a reprobate, they would soon come under the spell of his wit, his culture, his breadth of outlook, and his very real kindliness. Undeniably he was a scamp, but he did less harm than many men of impeccable rectitude.

The Emperor Alexander, who was his own foreign minister, was quite a match for these able men. Metternich, Castlereagh, and Talleyrand all unsuccessfully tried to influence him; the King of Prussia followed him blindly, even against the advice of his own Ministers. In after years, it is true, Metternich acquired an ascendancy over the opinions of Alexander, but that belongs to a later phase of his character; in 1814 he still retained complete independence of judgment. He had learned diplomacy in a hard school. His grandmother was the enlightened and dissolute Catherine the Great; his father was the mad Tsar Paul. His grandmother took him away from his parents at birth, and saw to his education herself. Seeing that Paul was not going to make a good Emperor, she wished to pass him over and make Alexander her successor. When he was not yet quite eighteen, his

[2] Writing to Louis XVIII in 1815, he speaks of "that sentiment of religious indifference which is the malady of the times in which we live."

grandmother communicated this project to him in writing, and it was necessary for him to reply by letter. Placed thus between an aged autocrat and a frenzied psychopath, many boys would have had difficulty in finding a suitable epistolary style. Not so Alexander. He wrote:

24 September 1796.

Your Imperial Majesty!

I could never express my gratitude for the confidence with which your Majesty has been willing to honour me and the goodness which you have deigned to have in making by your own hand a writing serving as explanation of the other papers. I hope that your Majesty will see, by my zeal in deserving your precious favours, that I feel all their value. I could not, it is true, ever pay sufficiently, even by my blood, for all that you have deigned and still intend to do for me. These papers evidently confirm all the reflections which your Majesty has been good enough to communicate to me recently, and which, if it is permitted to me to say so, could not be more just. It is in placing once more at the feet of Your Imperial Majesty the sentiments of my most lively gratitude that I take the liberty of being, with the most profound respect and the most inviolable attachment,

of Your Imperial Majesty the very humble and very submissive subject and grandson

Alexander

Truly a model grandson! At the same time, if the letter was seen by his father (as some maintain), there was nothing in it to show that as a son he was less dutiful than as a grandson. After such a training, he need not fear to be hoodwinked by either Metternich or Talleyrand.

From a scholastic point of view, Alexander's education was much better than that of most princes. In the middle of the campaign of 1812, he would converse with silly young ladies about Kant and Pestalozzi. Catherine had him indoctrinated with eighteenth-century enlightenment, and even with political liberalism; nor did she change the principles of his education after the French Revolution had turned her into a reactionary. His tutor was a virtuous Swiss named La Harpe, who filled his conscious mind with rational benevolence while his father and grandmother were poisoning his unconscious. La Harpe believed in democracy, admired (within reason) the French Revolution, and

at first thought well of Napoleon. His rectitude was of a somewhat pedantic kind: on purely legalistic grounds he opposed Catherine's scheme for passing over Paul, although Paul hated him and
Alexander loved him, and although it was evident that Paul could do
nothing but harm to Russia. This led Catherine to dismiss La Harpe,
although her intention to disinherit Paul was never carried out. She
took, however, certain preliminary steps. She declared Alexander's
education finished, and compelled him to marry at the age of sixteen,
in order that he might seem grown up.

Paul reigned for four years, which, for Alexander as for all Russia,
were years of terror. At last a plot was formed by his immediate entourage for his assassination. Alexander was informed of the plot, and
begged the conspirators, if possible, to dethrone his father without
killing him. This would have been difficult and dangerous; they therefore murdered Paul and left Alexander to make the best of it. Those
most obviously implicated were banished from Court, but as little as
possible was done in the way of punishment. All Russia heaved a sigh
of relief, and welcomed Alexander with joy; his complicity was hushed
up, and, though suspected, was not known for certain until more than
a century later. This incident made a wound in his conscience which
never healed, and had much to do with the curious and rather sinister forms of his later religiosity. This effect, however, was scarcely
visible before the year 1815; from then until his death in 1825,
Alexander sank into an ever-deepening gloom, until at last he became a perfect example of a modern Orestes.

What the world saw of Alexander during the first half of his
reign was something very different. He was gay and gallant, rather
too well dressed, liberal in his politics, and anxious that his reign
should be associated with the furtherance of idealistic aims. He had
a principal mistress of whom he was very fond and by whom he had
several children. His affection for his sister Catherine was more passionate than is customary. He was never too busy to write to her,
and his letters to her show a complete unreserve which makes them
very valuable historically. He was grateful to her for making friends
with his mistress, and was in an alliance with her against their mother.
He enjoyed showering upon her hyperbolic expressions of affection,
such as "Adieu, charm of my eyes, adoration of my heart, lustre of
the age, phenomenon of Nature, or, better than all that, Bisiam

Bisiamovna with the flattened nose." (This was written just before
the battle of Austerlitz.) Catherine was a lively and tactless young
lady, and on at least one occasion (when Alexander visited England in
1814) her influence led him astray politically, with important consequences for the affairs of Europe. They were always on the best of
terms except during Napoleon's advance in 1812, when she joined in
the patriotic outcry against her brother's apparent lack of success.

When Alexander came to the throne in the year 1801, he was only
twenty-two years old, and had little knowledge of affairs. He recalled
La Harpe, and endeavored to introduce reforms by the help of a
Council composed of his personal friends. He succeeded in undo-
ing the evils wrought by Paul, relaxed the censorship, and improved
education. But when it came to such matters as the emancipation of
the serfs or the introduction of a constitution, he found the difficulties
too formidable. As regards foreign affairs, he at first made friends
with Napoleon, whom La Harpe still admired. But when Napoleon
bullied Switzerland and made himself Emperor, which offended
La Harpe both as patriot and as democrat, Alexander turned against
him, and fought the unfortunate campaigns of 1805 and 1806, in
which the Russians, in alliance first with Austria and then with Prussia, suffered the defeats of Austerlitz and Friedland. This led to the
Peace of Tilsit, and to a sudden friendship between the Eastern and
Western Emperors. At first there was a honeymoon atmosphere, and
each believed the other to be sincere. But as soon as they had parted, disputes began. Alexander, who had been fighting the Turks, wanted to
keep Moldavia and Wallachia; Napoleon did not wish to offend the
Turks, for fear of throwing them into the arms of the English. He
therefore demanded a *quid pro quo* at the expense of Prussia, to
which Alexander could not agree on account of his promises to the
beautiful Queen Louise. At last Napoleon endeavoured to dazzle
Alexander by a grandiose project of the partition of Turkey leading
on to the joint conquest of India. The boyish part of Alexander,
which enjoyed the Arabian Nights, was fascinated, and responded as
Napoleon had hoped. But his shrewdness could not be put to sleep.
He stipulated that he should have not only Moldavia and Wallachia,
but also Constantinople. After that, he would be prepared to help
Napoleon in Syria; but he must secure his own gains first. As agreement by letter proved impossible, the two sovereigns agreed to meet

at Erfurt, where Napoleon hoped to prevail by personal influence. He underestimated Alexander, however, who wrote to his sister: "Bonaparte gives out that I am only a fool. He laughs best who laughs last, and for my part I put all my hope in God." The mere fact that he spoke of "Bonaparte" instead of "Napoleon" implied a feeling of hostility, and would have made all friendship impossible if it had been known.

Meanwhile Alexander employed the period of apparent friendship with France to conquer Finland, which belonged to Sweden. That done, he bought the friendship of Sweden by promising to help the Swedes to acquire Norway, which belonged to Denmark, which was friendly to France. After this, since Napoleon still would not help him to get Moldavia and Wallachia, he felt that the friendship of France served no further purpose. When Napoleon complained that six hundred British ships had sailed up the Gulf of Finland and landed British goods in Russia, Alexander contented himself with a blunt denial. The Grand Army marched to Moscow and perished in the retreat; Europe greeted Alexander as her saviour, and the triumphant Allies marched to Paris. In all this Alexander saw the hand of God, since he could not attribute the victory to himself or his generals. The Prussians saw the victory of moral force against the corruption and atheism of France. The Austrians saw the vindication of ancient right. The English saw the victory of sea power and cheap manufactures. The world in general saw the hope of peace. Such was the situation at the opening of our epoch.

CHAPTER II

THE CONGRESS OF VIENNA

ALEXANDER, Frederick William, Metternich, and Castlereagh held collectively the power to decide the map of Europe and to establish whatever form of government they chose, both internationally and in the several countries of the Continent. Certain treaties limited their freedom. During 1813, first Russia, then England, then Austria, had promised Prussia that she should again become as great as before Napoleon defeated her in 1806. The Treaty of Paris (May 30, 1814) assigned to France the limits of 1792; all the conquests of the revolutionary and Napoleonic epoch were renounced, and the right to dispose of them to new owners was one from which France was to be excluded in the deliberations of the Congress. In view of the fact that France was completely at the mercy of the Allies after twenty-two years of war, during which almost every Continental country had suffered invasion, the mildness of the Treaty of Paris was surprising; it was largely due to the magnanimity of Alexander. He had marched into Paris at the head of the armies, had declared that the enemy was Napoleon, not France, and had accepted the semi-voluntary restoration of the Bourbons by the French Provisional Government as a ground for not depriving France of any of the territory previously possessed by the legitimate kings.

Alexander's generosity was vehemently resisted by his closest allies, the Prussians, and was a cause of anxiety to the English. On January 30, 1814, Castlereagh wrote to the Prime Minister Lord Liverpool:

I think our greatest danger at present is from the *chevaleresque* tone in which the Emperor Alexander is disposed to push the war. He has a *personal* feeling about Paris, distinct from all political or military combinations. He seems to seek for the occasion of entering with his magnificent guards the enemy's capital, probably to display, in his clemency and forbearance, a contrast to that desolation to which his own was devoted.

In this wish Alexander was fully gratified, and the people of Paris displayed, in consequence, all the enthusiasm for him that he could desire. The other Allies remarked that, if France had been compelled to cede more territory, it would not have been acquired by Russia, and that the Emperor was less generous in matters nearer home, such as Poland. But these reflections were made only by the initiated, and did not affect the warmth of popular demonstrations.

The territorial questions to be decided at the Congress of Vienna were many and complex. It was felt that perhaps it might be a help to have some sort of principle by which the decisions arrived at could be made to seem just. Metternich's colleague, Gentz, who had the reputation of being the hardest worker at the Congress, stated his impressions in a memorandum of February 12, 1815:

Those who at the time of the assembling of the Congress at Vienna had thoroughly understood the nature and objects of this Congress, could hardly have been mistaken about its course, whatever their opinion about its results might be. The grand phrases of "reconstruction of social order," "regeneration of the political system of Europe," "a lasting peace founded on a just division of strength," &c., &c., were uttered to tranquillize the people, and to give an air of dignity and grandeur to this solemn assembly; but the real purpose of the Congress was to divide amongst the conquerors the spoils taken from the vanquished.

But this could hardly be openly avowed; moreover, on most questions there were some Powers whose interests were not involved, and who might therefore be influenced by arguments of principle. In this situation, it was Talleyrand who discovered the only moral appeal to which the Congress was not deaf. For this purpose, he invented the "principle of legitimacy," which governed Europe until the year 1830. This he expounded in the instructions which he instructed Louis XVIII to give him for his own guidance. Having suffered military defeat, France was obliged to rely upon moral force; this Talleyrand supplied, no doubt to his own secret amusement.

The principle of legitimacy asserts, speaking broadly, that territories ought to belong to their hereditary sovereigns, unless voluntarily parted with in exchange for some compensation. On this ground, France, if governed by the Bourbons, had a right to all territory that was French in the time of Louis XVI. But the principle had to be carefully stated. It would not do, for example, to suggest that the English ought to restore the Stuart dynasty. Then there was Genoa, which had been an independent republic before it was conquered by France, and which was now to be given to the King of Sardinia. The Genoese might have invoked the principle of legitimacy, but unfortunately invoked instead one belonging to a later Congress, namely the right of self-determination; and what was even worse, they were in favor of a democratic constitution. This was dangerous. Talleyrand says:

The Genoese had presented the project of a constitution which, owing to its democratic spirit, could not be admitted. But the capitulation is all the more necessary because the Genoese feel a singular reluctance to this act of submission, and because it is good to remove everywhere as much as is possible the germs of bitterness and discord which are multiplied at all points on the occasion of the union of the Belgians to the Dutch, the Saxons to the Prussians, and the Italians to the Austrians.

Legitimacy could not, therefore, be invoked by populations against princes. It would be too much to say that the principle could never be invoked by republics: it could be invoked by Switzerland, because of Alexander's affection for La Harpe. It could not be invoked by Poland, because Poland no longer had a legitimate king, and because the partition was not due to the French. Roughly speaking, territory was treated as we still treat landed estate: we do not think that the tenants of a landowner can acquire a right to own the land on which they live by merely deciding that they would like to do so. This would seem absurd to most men at the present day; and the principle of self-determination as regards government would have seemed equally absurd to the negotiators at Vienna. If a king had a hereditary right to a piece of territory, that gave him a claim of which the Congress was bound to take notice; if not, the territory could be assigned by bargaining among the Powers.

As we have seen in the case of Genoa, the Congress had a very definite dislike to anything that savored of democracy. The British constitution was allowed to survive because it was traditional, and the French were given a constitution for a variety of reasons. Alexander was liberal outside Russia. The British thought that a constitution would reconcile France to the Bourbons and give stability to the dynasty. The Austrians and Prussians, after some hesitation, became persuaded that a constitution, being inherently pernicious, would weaken France, and prevent a recurrence of what had been suffered at the hands of Louis XIV and Napoleon. But constitutions elsewhere were not to be encouraged. In this matter, the Whigs in England were opposed to the Tory Government. In Italy, Lord William Bentinck, a high-spirited Whig, and too important to be summarily dismissed, had caused his government much trouble by encouraging the Genoese and protesting against the atrocities committed by the King of Sicily. Castlereagh writes to him on May 7, 1814:

It is impossible not to perceive a great moral change coming on in Europe, and that the principles of freedom are in full operation. The danger is, that the transition may be too sudden to ripen into anything likely to make the world better or happier. We have new constitutions launched in France, Spain, Holland, and Sicily. Let us see the result before we encourage farther attempts. The attempts may be made, and we must abide the consequences; but I am sure it is better to retard than accelerate the operation of this most hazardous principle which is abroad.

In Italy, it is now the more necessary to abstain, if we wish to act in concert with Austria and Sardinia. Whilst we had to drive the French out of Italy, we were justified in running all risks; but the present state of Europe requires no such expedient; and, with a view to general peace and tranquillity, I should prefer seeing the Italians await the insensible influence of what is going on elsewhere, than hazard their own internal quiet by an effort at this moment.

It may be said, in passing, that the constitutions of Spain and Sicily were quickly suppressed.

In contradistinction to the illiberality of the Western Powers, Alexander decided to give a constitution to Poland, or rather to that part of Poland which he finally obtained from the decisions of the Congress. The history of this constitution, however, shows that his liberalism was hardly more than a matter of phrases. The legislature was composed of two Houses, the Lower House consisting of seventy-one representatives of the land-owning nobility and fifty-one representatives of the towns. The Upper House consisted of the Imperial Family, some bishops, and a few officials. The Parliament was to sit for thirty days once every two years; it could accept or reject measures proposed by the Government, but could not itself propose measures. At the first meeting of the Parliament, in 1818, all went well; both Houses accepted Alexander's measures, with the exception of one about divorce, as to which he made a gracious speech saying that he respected their principles and rejoiced in the proof of their independence. In 1820, however, they rejected all his proposals. He was furious, and decided, in spite of the constitution, that Parliament should not meet again till 1825. After this, it met only once, in 1829; in 1830 the Polish insurrection occurred, and from that time until the Great War, Russian Poland was governed autocratically by the Tsar. Nevertheless, at Vienna Alexander made a great parade of his liberal intentions towards Poland, and of the advantages which that country would derive from being united under his rule.

The principle of legitimacy, suggested by Talleyrand, was thoroughly congenial to Metternich. There was, however, a difficulty in regard to Naples: Murat, its King, had been induced to abandon his brother-in-law Napoleon by a treaty in which Austria promised to maintain him on his throne. With Napoleon gone, this treaty no longer served any purpose, and Talleyrand strongly urged the claims of the legitimate Bourbon King Ferdinand. Fortunately this delicate problem was solved by Murat's indiscretions: when Napoleon returned from Elba, Murat repented of his previous treachery, and therefore fell when Napoleon fell. This left Metternich free to embrace the principle of legitimacy without reserve.

The attitude of the English to the principle was one of benevolence, so long as it was not allowed to conflict with any British interest. It could not, of course, apply to colonies: the British insisted upon acquiring permanently certain important Dutch colonies, which the Dutch had lost through their enforced alliance with France. The Prince of Orange was given Belgium in compensation, and was quite grateful, though he lost it in 1830. Outside Europe, and on the high seas, the British attitude was decided by British interests; but on the Continent, the principle of legitimacy would do well enough, since all questions of importance to England had been settled before the Congress began.

Prussia and Russia offered more opposition. The opposition of Russia was due in part to Alexander's vague liberalism, but in the main to the fact that his territorial ambitions were related in a complicated way to those of Prussia. He had promised the King of Prussia as fine a domain as he had had before 1806. But before 1806 Prussia owned certain parts of Poland which Alexander wished to keep; therefore, said Alexander, Prussia must be compensated elsewhere. The most convenient plan was to give Saxony to Prussia, since the King of Saxony had failed to abandon Napoleon at the proper moment. But the King of Saxony was a legitimate sovereign: Louis XVIII and Talleyrand were outraged at the thought of his being dispossessed. Austria feared both Russia and Prussia, and therefore sided with France. England wished to strengthen Prussia and weaken Russia; therefore Castlereagh at first supported Prussia's claim to Saxony but opposed Russia's claim to practically the whole of Poland. When he found that it was impossible to support Prussia without supporting Russia, he decided against both, and joined Austria and France. This question absorbed most of the time of the Congress.

At the very beginning, on October 1st, Talleyrand had an interview with Alexander, in which he maintained the ethical importance of the principle of legitimacy against what he represented as the Tsar's unscrupulousness. Alexander did not like Talleyrand, partly, no doubt, because he regarded him as a cynic, but more because, when the Russian Government protested against Napoleon's murder of the Duc d'Enghien, Talleyrand replied by a hint that it was not as bad as murdering one's father. On that occasion, as on this, he had been in a position of moral superiority to the highly religious Emperor, which must have amused him, but his amusement is not allowed to appear in the account which he gives in his *Mémoires* of the interview on October 1st:

A. At present let us speak of our affairs. We must finish them here.

T. That depends upon Your Majesty. They will finish quickly and happily if Your Majesty brings to them the same nobility and the same greatness of soul as to those of France.

A. But each must find his interests (*convenances*) in the settlement.

T. And each his rights.

A. I shall keep what I occupy.

T. Your Majesty will only wish to keep what will be legitimately yours.

A. I am in agreement with the Great Powers.

T. I do not know whether Your Majesty counts France amongst these Powers.

A. Yes, certainly. But if you do not wish each to find his interests, what do you intend?

T. I put justice first, and interests afterwards.

A. The interests of Europe are justice.

T. This language, Sire, is not yours; it is foreign to you, and your heart disallows it.

A. No, I repeat, the interests of Europe are justice.

At this point Talleyrand turned to the wall, hit his head against it, and cried: "Europe, Europe, unhappy Europe! Shall it be said that you have destroyed it?" Alexander replied: "Rather war than renounce what I occupy." Talleyrand continues:

I let my arms fall, and, in the attitude of a man afflicted but decided, who seemed to be saying "the fault will not be ours," I kept silence. The Emperor remained some instants without breaking it, then he repeated: "Yes, rather war." I kept the same attitude. Then, raising his hands and agitating them as I had never seen him do, in a manner which recalled to me the passage that terminates the eulogium of Marcus Aurelius, he shouted rather than said: "The time for the theatre is come. I must go; I promised the Emperor [of Austria]; they are waiting for me." And he went away; then, coming back, he took me in his two hands, pressed my body, and said in a voice which was no longer his own: "Adieu, adieu, we shall see each other again."

In spite of this affecting scene, the opposition between the two men continued throughout the Congress, and the points in dispute were finally decided by a compromise. Alexander got less of Poland than he had claimed, and Prussia got only half of Saxony, the other half being left to the legitimate King. This compromise was only reached after Napoleon's return from Elba compelled the Powers to compose their differences. But for this event, they might have continued to wrangle down to the present day.

The attitude of Prussia was superficially similar to that of the other Powers, but fundamentally very different. The Chancellor Hardenburg was, in the main, friendly to Austria; the King was entirely devoted to Alexander. But there existed in Prussia a powerful nationalist movement, German rather than purely Prussian, and therefore viewed with sympathy by many people in other parts of Germany. After 1806, Prussia had embarked upon reforms, so far as Napoleon would permit. The patriotic Minister Stein, having incurred Napoleon's displeasure, had been forced to leave the country, and was, at the time of the Congress of Vienna, in the service of Alexander. But the Prussian army was filled with sentiment for Germany, and with a passionate hatred for the French. Ever since the time of Louis XIV, Western Germany, composed of a number of small weak States, had been at the mercy of France; Prussia had, under Frederick the Great, successfully withstood Louis XV, but had not been able to resist Napoleon. It had become clear to all patriotic Germans that some degree of unity was necessary if future French invasions were to be made impossible; but to all projects of unity the tenacious princelings offered an obstacle.

Thus German patriotism combined with hatred of the French to produce throughout the educated classes, and especially among the young, a feeling in favor of Prussia, as the most effective bulwark of Germany against France. This feeling was, of course, hostile to the principle of legitimacy, which would perpetuate the petty principalities that made Germany weak. German patriotism was thus compelled to be in some degree revolutionary, and, in this respect, was suspect to governments, even to that of Prussia; but it was encouraged by Prussia in so far as it stood for Prussian greatness. Opposition to the Princes gave a democratic tinge to Teutonic nationalism, which had caused the King of Prussia, during the height of the struggle in 1813, to promise a constitution as the reward of victory. The hope that this promise might be fulfilled had to be kept alive until Frederick William had derived all possible advantage from the warlike exertions of his subjects, but it had to be kept alive discreetly, so as not to alarm the other autocrats. After Waterloo, of course, little more was heard of it.

Talleyrand, on arriving in Vienna, was astonished by the new German patriotism. France, he confesses, had behaved as an insolent conqueror, and had overwhelmed the conquered with contributions. (It was Napoleon's principle to make his victims pay for his wars.) They were indignant at the mildness of the Treaty of Paris, and, as Talleyrand puts it, "very *blasé* to the delights to be derived from generosity." The nationalism of Germany appears to him as Jacobinism. He says that Jacobinism dominates not the middle and lower classes, but the highest and richest nobility, with whom conspire, he says, the men of the universities, and the young men imbued with their theories, who deplore the division of Germany into small States. "The unity of the German Fatherland is their cry, their dogma, their religion exalted up to fanaticism, and this fanaticism has gained even princes actually reigning." German unity, he thinks, would not have been dangerous to France while she possessed the left bank of the Rhine and Belgium, but would now be very serious for her. It was accordingly his business to combat all approaches to German unity, and in this respect the principle of legitimacy was useful. Metternich, from fear of Prussia, was at one with him in this.

Prussia thus became the more or less half-hearted champion of a new principle, that of nationality, which appeared to the older diplomats to be full of revolutionary danger. It cannot be said that the older diplomats were wrong. What Talleyrand calls the "Jacobinism" of the German patriots led straight on to the Great War, by a movement which, in retrospect, acquires a perhaps fallacious appearance of inevitability. At the Congress of Vienna, the German patriots were ahead of their time; but from 1848 onward their point of view increasingly dominated the world.

There were in this new doctrine of German nationalism various distinct elements. There was the purely German element: the belief in the superior virtue and virility of the German race. There was the belief that the boundaries of States should be the boundaries of nations. And there was the democratic belief that populations should have a right to choose their own form of government. All these were anathema to the orthodoxy of 1815.

The right of populations to choose their own form of government was upheld by the Tsar as regards France, at the time of Napoleon's fall in 1814. Gentz, expressing the view of the Austrian Government, said that if the French were allowed to appoint another ruler this would involve "a recognition of the principle which in our times can hardly be uttered without trembling, that it depends upon the people whether they shall or shall not tolerate the actual ruling sovereign. This principle of popular sovereignty is the very pivot of all revolutionary systems."

The belief that the boundaries of States should be the boundaries of nations was necessarily abhorrent to Austria. If this principle were to be victorious, a small part of the Emperor Francis's dominions would become incorporated in a United Germany, Galicia would become part of a reunited Poland, while Bohemia and Transylvania would be independent. As a result of nationalism, all this has happened since the Great War, except, of course, the part favorable to Germany. It is not to be wondered at, therefore, that the Austrian Government was opposed to German nationalism.

The belief in the superior virtue and virility of the German race was generated by the struggle with Napoleon, and especially by the campaign of 1813, which plays the same part in German popular history as the Spanish Armada plays in that of the English, or the War of Liberation in that of the Americans. The generation that was young in the Germany of 1813, and those older men whom it recognized as its leaders, would have nothing to do with cosmopolitanism, and reacted in every way against the classicism of the eighteenth century. The romantic movement in Germany, unlike that in England, was in close touch with actual politics, and had realizable ideals; indeed its ideals were realized by Bismarck. During the romantic movement, men admired excitedly, and more than reason could warrant. Shelley admired Greek rebels against the Turks and Spanish rebels against the Bourbons, but the German romanticists admired Blücher, that stern man of God, who occupies in German legend the place occupied by Drake in that of England.

Since Blücher became a German national hero, it is worth while to dwell for a moment upon his character. He was a great soldier, an ardent patriot, and a completely loyal servant of his King. His religion was sincere and profound. His attitude to France was one of moral reprobation. During the Waterloo campaign, while the issue was still in doubt, he wrote: "I hope that this war will be concluded in such a way that in the future France will no longer be so dangerous to Germany. Alsace and Lorraine must be surrendered to us." In this connection, Treitschke, the standard historian of nineteenth-century Germany, speaks of Blücher as "a cosmopolitan in the noblest sense of the word," who possessed "a reckless self-forgetfulness which was possible only to German idealism."

Very characteristic was Blücher's attitude to the Saxon mutineers in his army of 1815. Part of Saxony was being restored to the King of Saxony, part was being given to Prussia; accordingly part of the Saxon army was incorporated with the army of Prussia. A sentiment of loyalty to their own King and country led some of these Saxon troops to refuse to take orders from Blücher. He suppressed the mutiny with extreme severity, and on this occasion wrote as follows to King Frederick Augustus of Saxony:

Your Majesty,

By your earlier proceedings your majesty has brought the profoundest disaster upon your subjects, a respected branch of the German nation.

It may result from your subsequent conduct that this branch will be overwhelmed with shame.

The rebellion in the army, which has been organised from Friedrichsfelde and Pressburg, has broken out, has broken out at a time when the whole of Germany is rising against the common enemy. The criminal offenders have openly proclaimed Bonaparte as their protector, and have forced me, who during five-and-fifty years of active service have been in the fortunate position of never shedding any blood but that of my enemies, for the first time to carry out executions in my army.

By the enclosure, your majesty will see what I have hitherto done in the hope of saving the honour of the Saxon name, but it is the last attempt.

If my voice is not heard, I shall be compelled, not without pain, but with the repose of my own good conscience and sense of duty fulfilled, to restore order by force, and, if it should be necessary, to have the entire Saxon army shot down.

The blood that has been spilled will one day at God's judgment-seat be visited upon him who is responsible: and before the throne of the Almighty to have given commands, and to have allowed commands to be given, will be regarded as identical.

Your majesty is well aware that an old man of seventy-three can no longer have any other earthly desire than to make the voice of truth audible and to make the right prevail.

For this reason your majesty will have to receive this letter.

BLÜCHER.

Headquarters at Liège,
  May 6, 1815.

His ways of expressing affection were peculiar. When his wife died, he observed: "Yes, the toad was beautiful like the deuce, and she had the feeling of a thousand devils." A rather similar type of sentiment is shown in a remark he made to Metternich in the grand gallery of Napoleon's palace at Saint Cloud, which he and his hussars were occupying after Waterloo. "That man," he said, "must have been a regular fool to have all this and go running after Moscow." He was disappointed that the "regular fool" was allowed such an easy fate as exile to St. Helena, and had tried to get him put to death. Wellington would have nothing to do with this plan, as appears in a letter he wrote on June 28th, when Napoleon was still at large:

The Parisians think the Jacobins will give him [Napoleon] over to me, believing that I will save his life. Blücher writes to kill him; but I have told him that I shall remonstrate, and shall insist on his being disposed of by common accord. I have likewise said that, as a private friend, I advised him to have nothing to do with so foul a transaction—that he and I had acted too distinguished parts in these transactions to become executioners—and that I was determined that, if the Sovereigns wished to put him to death, they should employ an executioner, who should not be me.

Those who remember the Hang-the-Kaiser election at the end of the Great War, the popular feeling at that time, and the speeches of our leading statesmen, will realize how much Prussia was ahead of the world in 1815, and how antiquated scruples such as the Duke's were to seem to a later generation.

Whatever may be thought of the political ideas associated with the German renaissance of the early nineteenth century, it must be admitted that, as regards the contributions of great individuals to culture, Germany at that time led the world. Kant and Hegel, Goethe and Schiller, are hard to match among their non-German contemporaries. Kant and Goethe, it is true, owed their greatness in part to their freedom from German nationalistic excitement, and some of their best qualities were felt to be regrettable by subsequent generations of Germans. Kant admired Rousseau, and liked the French Revolution; he wrote a treatise advocating "the unmanly dream of perpetual peace," as it is called by Treitschke. As for Goethe, the sound of the guns at the battle of Jena roused in him philosophic, not patriotic, emotions, and he could subsequently visit the battlefield in the company of Frenchmen without a qualm. Kant and Goethe were great men, but they would not have liked the use to which they have been put by German nationalism. Most of the great Germans subsequent to them have, it is true, been filled with patriotism, and not without justification. Throughout the whole period from the fall of Napoleon to the Great War, Germany retained its supremacy in science and in almost all forms of learning. Not only in science, but in many other respects also, Germany's outlook in 1815 was more akin to that of the next hundred years than was that of any other country. As Treitschke says:

For the first time since the days of Martin Luther, the ideas of Germany once more made the round of the world, and now found a more willing acceptance than of old had the ideas of the Reformation. Germany alone had already got completely beyond the view of the world-order characteristic of the eighteenth century. The sensualism of the days of enlightenment had been replaced by an idealist philosophy; the dominion of reason by a profound religious sentiment; cosmopolitanism by a delight in national peculiarity; natural rights by a recognition of the living growth of the nations; the rules of correct art by free poesy, bubbling up as by natural energy from the depths of the soul; the preponderance of the exact sciences by the new historico-aesthetic culture. By the work of three generations, those of the classical and of the romanticist poets, this world of new ideas had slowly attained to maturity, whereas among the neighbor nations it had hitherto secured no more than isolated disciples, and only now at length made its way victoriously through all the lands.

At the same period, as Treitschke also points out, the Inquisition and the Index were re-introduced by the Pope, and Bible societies were declared to be the work of the devil, while in Southern France at the Restoration "the Catholic mob stormed the houses of the Protestants and murdered the heretics to the cry of 'Let us make black puddings of Calvin's blood!' "

The statesmen assembled at the Congress of Vienna, while personally enlightened and civilized, did nothing to discourage such black reaction, but were terrified by the new ideas in Germany. Metternich, in particular, set himself to prolong the eighteenth century in Germany, and succeeded in suppressing all overt liberalism until 1848.

The Congress of Vienna was eighteenth-century in tone, and German democratic nationalism, where it intruded, seemed to belong to a later age. Another question that was discussed at Vienna seems equally out of the picture, namely the slave trade. This subject, which was the first to rouse nineteenth-century philanthropy, was brought up by England, and was viewed with complete cynicism by all the other Powers. In England the sentiment for the abolition of the slave trade was overwhelming, and Castlereagh, whatever he may have privately thought, was obliged to listen with respect to Wilberforce and Clarkson, the champions of abolition. The British had abolished their own slave trade, and endeavoured to induce other Powers to undertake that they would abolish theirs within five years. To the amazement of such men as Talleyrand, it was found that for such an undertaking the British Government was willing to give a solid *quid pro quo* in territory or cash, while a refusal was likely to lead to unfriendly commercial discrimination. The following letter, from Castlereagh to the British Ambassador at Madrid, is typical of many:

St. James's Square, August 1, 1814.

My dear Sir,

. . . You must really press the Spanish Government to give us some more facilities on the subject of the Slave Trade, else we can do nothing for them, however well inclined: the nation is bent upon this object. I believe there is hardly a village that has not met and petitioned upon it; both Houses of Parliament are pledged to press it; and the Ministers must make it the basis of their policy. It is particularly important that Spain and Portugal should not separate from all Europe upon it, else prohibitions against the import of their colonial produce will be the probable result. Urge, therefore, the French engagement for five years, and prevail upon them to instruct Labrador [the representative of Spain at Vienna] accordingly.

With respect to the immediate abolition north of the Line, if you cannot confine them to the southward of Cape Lopez, or Lope Gonsalves, press Cape Formoso, or even three points a little to the westward of Cape Coast Castle; but Lopez is the best, as ships having cargoes may from thence keep at once free of the coast.

You will recollect that Spain had no Slave Trade of her own, previous to our abolition; and it now appears that she imports few really for her own colonies. The greatest proportion of those carried in the first instance to Cuba and Porto Rico, are re-shipped on American account, and smuggled into the United States, principally up the Mississippi, in defiance of the American laws of abolition. A mutual right of search is of great importance to check abuse.

The English attitude about the Slave Trade is a psychological curiosity, since the very men who did most for its abolition opposed every attempt to mitigate the horrors of English industrialism. The only concession that such men as Wilberforce were prepared to make on the subject of child labor was that children should have time on Sundays to learn the truths of the Christian religion. Towards English children they were pitiless; towards negroes they were full of compassion. I do not care to suggest an explanation, since the only ones that occur to me are intolerably cynical. But the fact deserves to be noticed, as an outstanding example of the complexity of human sentiment.

Until 1919, it was customary to regard the Congress of Vienna as a failure, but the world has now acquired a higher standard of failure. In spite of its shortcomings, there were two important respects in which the decisions arrived at deserved the gratitude of Europe. The first of these was the tolerant attitude towards France. After the hundred days, it is true, a somewhat greater severity was felt to be necessary. An indemnity was imposed, and Allied troops were left in occupation of important posts in France. But within a few years the indemnity was paid and the troops were withdrawn, with the result that France felt no lasting bitterness towards the victors.

The second advantage which Europe derived from the Congress was the establishment of an international government as a means of preserving peace. It is true that the government was temporary and that its measures were bad; nevertheless, it gave Europe a breathing space after the twenty-three years of warfare. Russia, Prussia, Austria and England—to whom France was afterwards joined—agreed to meet in Congresses from time to time to regulate the affairs of the world. Partly as a result of this arrangement, no important war occurred for thirty-nine years.

CHAPTER III

THE HOLY ALLIANCE

TO repeat a successful performance is always risky. When the Allies entered Paris in 1814, the foremost place belonged to Alexander; but when they entered Paris in 1815, his glory was eclipsed by that of Wellington and Blücher, who, without his help or that of Austria, had finally defeated the greatest military genius of modern times. However, if earthly glory failed, heavenly glory was still attainable. About this time, Alexander became much more religious than he had been.

From various ladies of his acquaintance, he had heard much of a remarkable prophetess, the Baroness Krüdener. This excellent lady, now in her fifty-second year, had not always devoted herself to the religious life. She had had a gay and checkered youth, although she assures us that her higher nature never wholly slept, and that, amid all the luxury and senseless pleasures of Copenhagen, she remained single and true, and always in harmony with nature. In 1789 she decided to leave Copenhagen (where her husband was the Russian Ambassador), in order to live in harmony with nature in Paris. In a few months, however, she ran up a bill of £800 with Marie Antoinette's dressmaker, which, together with other causes, led her to move to Montpellier.

After the King's flight to Varennes, as he had made use of the passport of a friend of hers, she felt it prudent to leave France, which she did in the company of her lover disguised as a valet. She presented him to her husband with a frank explanation, but the experiment was not a success. "M. de Krüdener," she remarks on a later occasion, "appreciates no sort of domestic happiness; he is more bent than ever on dinners, visits, theatricals, etc." In spite of this insensibility on his part, she lived with him in Berlin, where he was now Ambassador. She believed that she brought him good fortune, and that "God has wished to bless my husband since my return to him. . . . Why should I not believe that a pious heart, which prays to

31

God with simplicity and confidence for grace to contribute to the happiness of another, obtains that for which it asks?" Nevertheless, in 1801 she finally left the worthy Baron, and if God blessed him after that, it must have been in other ways.

Her conversion occurred in 1805, when she was staying with her mother in Riga. A young man who was in love with her took off his hat to her, and instantly dropped dead. This made her profoundly unhappy, from the thought that it might have happened to her. Before long, however, noticing that her shoemaker looked happy, she asked him why, and he said it was because he was a Moravian Brother and given to reading the Bible. She tried his recipe and found it a success. "You have no notion," she writes, "of the happiness which I gain from this holy and sublime faith. . . . Love, ambition, success, seem to me mere folly; exaggerated affections, even when lawful, seem to me as nothing compared to the pure and celestial happiness which comes from on high."

The opportunity which gave her a place in history came after she had been living a religious life for ten years. Having a premonition that she was destined to meet her Tsar, she settled, in the spring of 1815, in a village on the road from Vienna to the Russian army. At last, on the fourth of June, as Alexander was hurrying from the Congress to place himself at the head of his troops, he found himself one evening at Heilbronn, close to where she was staying. He had heard much of her, but did not know that she was in the neighborhood. Too weary to read, too troubled to sleep, he remembered what he had been told about her, and wished for an opportunity to make her acquaintance. At this moment she was announced.

She wasted no time. She told him that he was a sinner, that he had not yet sufficiently humbled himself before God, that she also had been a great sinner, but that she had found pardon for her sins at the foot of the Cross of Christ. Alexander replied: "You have made me discover things in myself which I had never seen. I give thanks for it to God; but I feel the want of many such conversations, and I beg of you not to go far away." She obeyed the Imperial commands, and throughout the succeeding months was never far distant from her august penitent.

The offspring of their virtue was the Holy Alliance. This curious document was drawn up by Alexander in September, 1815, and was intended to embody the application to politics of the great religious truths which he had learnt from the Baroness. He submitted the draft to her, accepted respectfully her suggested emendations, and then took it at once to the Emperor of Austria and the King of Prussia. The signatures of other European sovereigns were to be obtained as soon as possible. (The Sultan, however, not being a Christian, could not be asked to sign.)

The following is the text of the Holy Alliance as signed by Alexander, Francis, and Frederick William on September 26th:

In the Name of the Holy and Undivided Trinity.

Their Majesties the Emperor of Austria, the King of Prussia, and the Emperor of Russia, in consequence of the great events which have occurred in Europe in the course of the last three years, and especially in consequence of the benefits which a divine Providence has been pleased to confer on those states whose governments have placed their confidence and hope solely in it, having become profoundly convinced that it is necessary to base the principles of conduct to be adopted by the Powers in their mutual relations on the sublime truths contained in the eternal religion of Christ our Saviour; declare solemnly that the present act has for its sole object to manifest, in the face of the universe, their unalterable determination to adopt as their rule of conduct, whether in the administration of their respective states or in their political relations with all other governments, no other principles than those of their holy religion, precepts of justice, of charity, and of peace, which, far from being exclusively applicable to private life, ought, on the contrary, directly to influence the resolutions of princes and guide all their decisions, as offering the only means of consolidating human institutions and remedying their imperfections.

In consequence their Majesties have adopted the following articles:—

Art. I. In accordance with the words of Holy Scripture, which command all men to regard one another as brothers, the three contracting monarchs will remain united by the bonds of a true and indissoluble brotherhood, and, regarding each other as compatriots, they will lend one another aid and succour in all places, and under all circumstances; believing themselves to be placed towards their subjects and their armies in the position of a father towards his children, they will direct them in a similar spirit of brotherhood, for the protection of religion, peace, and justice.

Art. II. As a result, the only principle in operation, either between the said governments or between their subjects will be that of rendering reciprocal service; to display to one another, by an unalterable good-will, the mutual affection with which each should be animated; to regard one another without exception as members of one and the same Christian nationality; the three allied princes themselves only considering themselves as delegated by Providence to govern three branches of one and the same family, to wit:—

Austria,
Prussia,
Russia;

thus confessing that the Christian nation of which they and their people form a part has really no other sovereign than Him to whom alone supreme power belongs, because in Him alone are contained all the treasures of love, of knowledge, and of infinite wisdom, that is to say in God, our divine Saviour Jesus Christ, the incarnate Word.

Their Majesties consequently recommend to their people with the most earnest solicitude, as being the only means of enjoying that peace that is born of a good conscience, and which alone is lasting, daily to fortify themselves more and more in the principles and practice of those duties which our divine Saviour imposed on mankind.

Art. III. All the Powers that may wish solemnly to avow the sacred principles by which this act is inspired, and that recognise how important it is to the happiness of nations so long distracted that in future these truths should exercise their due influence over the destinies of man, will be received with much ardour and affection into this Holy Alliance.

Signed in Paris in the year of grace 1815 the 14 (26) September.

(Signed)   François.
Frédéric-Guillaume.
Alexandre.

The other sovereigns and statesmen had no very high opinion of the Holy Alliance. It was decided that, while the affairs of Europe should still be regulated by the Four-Power Alliance inaugurated at Chaumont, Louis XVIII should be allowed to join the Holy Alliance, since its significance was religious and not of this world. Metternich's view, as he told Castlereagh, was that Alexander's mind was affected; the Emperor Francis, taking this view, thought it wiser to humor him by signing. The British Government refused to join the Holy Alliance, but the Prince Regent—that earnest Christian— wrote a letter to the Tsar expressing sympathy with his sentiments.

When Alexander came to speak to Castlereagh about the Alliance, it happened that Wellington was present. Both of them (so Castlereagh wrote to Lord Liverpool) had difficulty in preserving becoming gravity while the Emperor was explaining the matter. It is interesting to note that Alexander's conversion was universally recognized as a victory for the reactionaries, and that the reactionaries themselves, all of whom professed Christianity, regarded the proposal to live according to its principles as a proof of insanity.

Formally, the Holy Alliance itself had no influence on the course of events, which were regulated by the Congresses of the Great Powers provided for in the Final Act of the Congress of Vienna. But in fact, during the fifteen years of black reaction from 1815 to 1830, popular sentiment did not go astray in regarding all the suppression of liberty that took place as the work of the Holy Alliance. Alexander, as a result of his conversion, ceased to be liberal, and consequently fell more and more under the influence of Metternich. Metternich's power in Europe would have been less but for the timely intervention of Madame Krüdener. The Tsar, it is true, tired of her before long, but replaced her by other religious mentors who were even more pernicious. There is a similarity between the relation of Alexander to Madame Krüdener and that of Nicholas II to Rasputin. There is also a difference: the one is comedy and the other tragedy. But the comedy ceases when we pass from the person of the Tsar to the world at large. Neapolitan patriots died or suffered life-long imprisonment, Russian soldiers were flogged to death, Greeks were impaled, because Alexander's tender conscience demanded these sacrifices. Before he found salvation he was humane; afterwards, he sank gradually into greater and greater depths of cruelty.

The Congresses that carried on the system inaugurated by Vienna were: Aix-la-Chapelle, in 1818; Troppau and Laibach (which were virtually one), in 1820–1; and Verona, in 1822.

Aix-la-Chapelle, which Metternich described as "a very pretty little Congress," was largely concerned with the affairs of France. It was agreed that within two months the foreign troops should evacuate French territory. Russia, Austria, Prussia and England renewed the treaty of Chaumont, by which, in 1814, they had bound themselves to oppose any government in France which was a menace to other countries. But, that done, France was admitted to the Concert of the Great Powers, and ceased to be regarded with suspicion. A secret protocol decided that any one of the five Powers could, in the event of any revolutionary disturbance, appeal to the other four, which should not fail to give their help. Congresses were to meet periodically, and also on occasion of any crisis. Thus the international government had its legislative and its executive; its constitution was the principle of legitimacy.

The Congresses of Troppau and Laibach had occasion to make important practical applications of the principles agreed upon at Aix-la-Chapelle. Various alarming occurrences had been disturbing the peace of mind of the sovereigns and their ministers. In Spain, the army had mutinied and forced the King to renew the constitution of 1812. This was the occasion which inspired Shelley's Ode to Liberty, beginning:

> A glorious people vibrated again
> The lightning of the nations, Liberty.

But lightning is a dangerous thing, and Russia, Prussia and Austria decided that it should be prevented. This, however, was no simple matter. Portugal followed the example of Spain. Naples, which concerned Metternich more nearly, rebelled against Ferdinand, and made him swear to observe the new constitution which was extorted from him. England, which had from the first viewed with suspicion the reactionary politics of the Eastern Powers, refused to co-operate in suppressing the revolutions. France, which had been compelled by the Allies to accept a parliamentary régime, was not at all sure that Spain ought not to have a Parliament, and was quite sure that, if there was to be intervention in Spain, it should be a purely French intervention. The Eastern Powers feared that, if French troops came in contact with Spanish revolutionaries, their own revolutionary traditions might revive. The English vetoed all action in Portugal. Metternich was determined that only Austrian troops should go to Naples, which caused fears of Austrian aggrandizement in the minds of others.

In spite of these difficulties, the work of reaction was accomplished, except in Portugal. A change of ministry in France gave power to the extreme conservatives, who caused French troops to invade Spain in 1822 and restore the absolute government of the King. In Naples the matter was accomplished more quickly. Ferdinand escaped to the Papal States, and invoked the help of the Austrians; his irresponsible power was restored, with all the usual atrocities of a White Terror. These incidents were a lesson to liberals, and kept them quiet on the Continent for some years.

The part played by Alexander, who had been himself a liberal, is psychologically interesting. It was fortunate for Metternich that, at the crucial moment, a mutiny occurred in the Semionovsky regiment, of which Alexander had, till then, thought very highly. It was a very mild mutiny, occasioned by the intolerable brutality of a new Colonel. The Emperor, while letting it appear as if he were leaving the matter to his minister Arakcheev, in fact concerned himself personally with the punishment of the mutineers, and insisted upon sentences of incredible severity under a hypocritical form of clemency. For example: "H.M. the Emperor, in consideration both of the long preventive detention of the undermentioned men, and of their record of service under fire, deigns to spare them the degrading penalty of the knout, and to cause to be inflicted upon each of them six thousand strokes of the rod, after which they shall be sent to forced labour in the mines."

At practically the same moment he was writing to his religious friend Prince Golitzin:

I abandon myself completely to *His direction*, to *His determinations*, and it is *He* who *ordains* and *places* matters; I merely follow in complete abandonment, persuaded as I am in my heart that this can only lead to the goal which His economy has decided for the common good.

These pious reflections, written at the time of the Congress of Laibach, occur in a long letter justifying his policy towards Naples, which the Prince had ventured to criticize. Alexander professes himself at a loss to imagine the reason for criticism, which cannot spring "from a belief on your part that the disorganizing principles which, in less than six months, have revolutionized three countries, and which threaten to spread and embrace all Europe, should be quietly endured." For these principles, he continues, are directed not only against thrones, but against the Christian religion. He then proceeds to compare the King of Naples to Judith and the Neapolitan revolutionaries to Holofernes, in order to prove that God can give the victory to the weaker party; and he quotes letters from Ferdinand saying that his sole trust is in God. (Ferdinand was running no risk unless he chose to commit perjury, since the constitutionalists wished him to remain their King.) After this come several pages of worldly argument, shrewd and to the point. But presently he returns to sacred themes. The Liberals, revolutionaries, and Carbonari of the whole world, he says, are part of one general conspiracy, aimed not so much against governments as against the Religion of the Saviour. "Their motto is to crush the Inf— [Voltaire's motto, *Ecrasez l'infame*]. I do not dare even to write this horrible blasphemy, only too well known through the writings of Voltaire, Mirabeau, Condorcet, and so many others of the like sort." His beliefs, he says, are in agreement with St. Paul:

At this moment, I have opened the Scriptures to look for the passage bearing on what I have just been saying to you, and, in opening the book, my eyes fell on the Epistle to the Romans, Chap. VIII. from v. 22 to the end of the Chapter. This is not the quotation that I was looking for, but as what opened appeared so striking and analogous to what I was writing to you, I urge you to read it.

The quotation on which I rest what I said to you about *faith* is in the Epistle to the Romans, Chap. XIV, in the last verse 23: "He is damned because he doeth not of faith: for whatsoever is not of faith is sin." [1]

I feel that I am the depository of a sacred and holy work; I neither must nor can compromise it; I must even less be a cause of scandal.

St. Paul says, Epistle to the Romans, Chap. XIV:

V. 13: Let us not therefore judge one another any more: but judge this rather, that no man put a stumbling block or an occasion to fall in his brother's way.

V. 16: Let not then your good be evil spoken of.

V. 18: For he that in these things serveth Christ is acceptable to God, and approved of men.

V. 19: Let us therefore follow after the things which make for peace, and things wherewith one may edify another.

V. 21: It is good not to do anything whereby thy brother stumbleth, or is offended, or is made weak.

---

[1] Where I have departed from the Authorized Version, I have done so in order to conform to the Emperor's text.

V. 22: Hast thou a clear faith? Have it to thyself before God. Happy is he whose conscience condemneth him not in that which he doth.

V. 23: For whatsoever is not of faith is sin.

From these texts it apparently followed that it was right to imprison the best people in Naples, and restore a cruel tyrant to absolute rule. Alexander commanded the largest army in the world, and had power to make his will prevail. Metternich, it is true, thought him mad, but regarded that as a matter of no consequence, so long as the madman could be made to carry out the wishes of the Austrian Foreign Office.

Alexander's religion went through many phases. At first, while orthodox, he did not trouble himself much about it. Then, partly under his sister Catherine's influence, he became interested in the Free Masons, whom the more orthodox regarded with aversion. Madame Krüdener, following the advice of the Moravian cobbler, laid stress on the Bible, and led Alexander to study the Scriptures. He encouraged the British and Foreign Bible Society to distribute Bibles in Russia, and Prince Golitzin was associated with him in this work. Koshelev, a friend of Golitzin, was another of Alexander's religious coadjutors. These two men endeavored to prevent him from becoming wholly reactionary, and were, in their religious views, not in agreement with the fanatical orthodoxy of the Russian Church dignitaries. One of the most prominent of the latter was the Archimandrite Photius, who, after the death of Koshelev, acquired considerable influence over the Emperor. When Koshelev died, Photius pronounced a somewhat singular funeral prayer:

In the depth of silence and solitude, I pray the Lord to employ in His works, when He shall judge it suitable, the man of God, to destroy the Satanic vaults, hidden in mysterious resorts, secret societies of Voltaireans, freemasons and martinists, and to decapitate the seven-headed hydra, that thrice cursed illuminism, of which the High Priest or magus, quite recently, on St. George's Day, the 26th of November, was summoned to appear before the tribunal of the Lord.

In international affairs, Alexander's policy had still one step to take; this was taken in 1822, at the Congress of Verona and in the preliminary conversations at Vienna. The revolt of the Greeks against Turkish tyranny was gathering force, and was rousing passionate enthusiasm, not only among liberals, but also among those who retained the outlook of the Crusades, and disliked the subjection of Christians to Mohammedans. In Russia there was, in addition, a nationalistic motive for sympathy with Greece, since Turkey was the hereditary national enemy, and Russia had territorial ambitions which could only be satisfied at the expense of the Turks. To Austria the matter presented itself in a different light: the break-up of Turkey was likely to strengthen Russia unduly. Metternich succeeded in persuading Alexander not to take up the cause of the Greeks, on the ground that they were rebels against lawful authority. Metternich was well aware that Alexander was sacrificing important Russian interests; he wrote to the Emperor Francis: "The Russian Cabinet has ruined with one blow the great work of Peter the Great and of his successors." From that time onward, the Concert of Europe took cognizance of Russia's dealings with the Porte, which had not previously been the case. Metternich congratulated himself on his achievement; "the *tour de force* that I have accomplished is an uncommon one," he notes complacently.

To Alexander, it seemed that he was merely carrying out the principles of the Holy Alliance. Chateaubriand, who was one of the French plenipotentiaries at the Congress of Verona, relates what the Tsar said to him on this subject:

There can no longer be English, French, Russian, Prussian, Austrian policies; there is no longer anything but one general policy, which must, for the good of all, be adopted in common by the peoples and by the kings. It is for me to show myself convinced by the principles upon which I based the Alliance. An occasion presented itself: the revolt of Greece. No doubt nothing appeared more in my interests, in those of my peoples, in accordance with the opinion of my country, than a religious war with Turkey; but I thought I observed the revolutionary mark in the troubles of the Peloponnesus. Consequently, I abstained. . . . No, I will never separate myself from the monarchs with whom I am united; it must be permitted to kings to have public alliances to defend themselves against secret societies. What could tempt me? What need have I to increase my Empire? Providence has not placed eight hundred thousand soldiers under my orders to satisfy my ambition, but to protect religion, morality, and justice, and to cause to reign the principles of order upon which human society rests.

By these reflections the Imperial introvert preserved his virtue while the Greeks continued to be impaled.

In home affairs, during his last years, Alexander was no better than in the affairs of Europe. He made the censorship very strict, curtailed education, severely limited academic freedom, and devoted most of his attention to the "military colonies," which were attempts to subject peasants to army discipline without taking them away from their labor as serfs. His minister Arakcheev was his dark angel, playing upon his remorse, encouraging him in despair leading to cruelty. Arakcheev had been a faithful servant of the Emperor Paul, and did not fail to remind Alexander of this fact. In 1823, on the anniversary of Paul's birthday, Arakcheev wrote to Alexander: "After having expressed in the Divine temple my sentiments of profound gratitude for the memory of him whose name we celebrate to-day, and who, from the place which he occupies near the throne of God, certainly sees the sincere affection and devotion which are felt for his August Successor by that one among his subjects whom it pleased him, while he still lived, to place near his son, ordering him to be to him a faithful servant, I execute this order with entire sincerity and I thank God every day for the favor that Your Majesty shows me."

The Emperor owed gratitude to Arakcheev for protection from the furies of Paul, which were often dangerous even to his own family. Alexander left many things in home affairs to Arakcheev; others he pretended to leave to him while in fact regulating them himself. For example, there exists in the Emperor's handwriting the draft of a letter from Arakcheev to an official who wished to retire, stating that he (Arakcheev) had thought it best not to submit this demand to the Emperor, and professing to refuse the demand without the Emperor's knowledge.

It is a debated question how far Arakcheev was cruel on his own account, and how far he was merely a screen for Alexander; but I do not think it can be doubted that he nourished Alexander's remorse, which, in the end, made him sick of life, and incapable of staying long in any one place. To his darkened mind, standing on the edge of madness, grim bigots such as the Archimandrite Photius became congenial. Since 1815, he had eschewed gaiety and love; his sister Catherine was dead. Bit by bit, the real world became obscured by the mists of his own troubles, until, oppressed by gloom, he died.

Alexander's character, apart from the touch of Romanov madness, was compounded of vanity and peasant shrewdness. His shrewdness failed in the end, but was remarkable in his heyday. From Erfurt, where he was pretending friendship with Napoleon, he writes to his mother to say "we shall see his fall with serenity, if such is the will of Providence," and to give sound reasons for expecting his fall, while explaining that meanwhile his friendship is preferable to his enmity. His vanity demanded every one's approval. Gentz, reporting on the Congress of Vienna, says: "The Emperor of Russia has come to Vienna, in the first place to be admired, which is always the principal thing in his thoughts." One can see the Emperor, in his early days, as a handsome young peasant, alternately dancing at village festivals so as to win the hearts of maidens, and swindling his neighbors over the sale of cows. A considerable part of his religion might be described as vanity towards God, Who, he feared, disapproved of the way he had acquired the throne. In exercising tyranny, he felt that he was pleasing God, Whom he evidently imagined as resembling his father.

Such was the author of the Holy Alliance, who for a period of ten years caused the international affairs of Europe to be regulated in accordance with his conception of the Christian religion. It was an interesting experiment, but the results were perhaps not entirely satisfactory.

CHAPTER IV

THE TWILIGHT OF METTERNICH

AT the time of the Congress of Verona, in 1822, Metternich's power was at its height. Various fortunate circumstances had helped him. First and foremost, the firm support of the Emperor Francis, who was, if anything, even more reactionary than his minister, and objected to education on the ground that "obedient subjects are more desirable than enlightened citizens." A second support of Meternich's power was his success in securing the supremacy of Austria and Austrian principles in Germany. Some of the German Princes were inclined to grant constitutions, as almost all had promised to do in 1813. The universities were full of liberalism, aiming not only at democracy, but at German unity. "Some men," says Metternich in a report to the Emperor Francis "(and it is noticeable that they are nearly all persons engaged in teaching), . . . direct their eyes to the union of all Germans in one Germany. . . . The systematic preparation of youth for this infamous object has lasted already more than one of these [student] generations. A whole class of future State officials, professors, and incipient literary men, is here ripened for revolution." In dealing with this situation, he had a stroke of luck. In March, 1819, just before the Conference of Carlsbad, which had been summoned to deal with such matters, a reactionary writer, Kotzebue, a Pole much admired by the Emperor Alexander, was murdered by a theological student named Karl Sand. Many of those whom Metternich regarded as his enemies considered this murder meritorious, and made a hero of the assassin. In these circumstances it was not difficult to persuade both Alexander and the German Princes that liberalism was dangerous. Decrees were passed at Carlsbad imposing more severe restrictions on the Press and the professors; and Kotzebue's death did as much as the mutiny in the Semionovsky regiment to win for Metternich the support of Russia. The policy of France, throughout this period, was growing steadily more reactionary. Finally Castlereagh, who had learnt to co-operate

43

with Austria at the Congress of Vienna, continued the same policy in subsequent years except where British interests made it impossible. On hearing of his death in 1822, Metternich wrote that he "was the only man in his country who had gained any experience in foreign affairs; he had learned to understand me." This was high praise indeed!

Throughout the years from 1814 to 1822, Metternich's power was continually on the increase, until it came to seem as if his will were omnipotent throughout Europe. It is no wonder if he came to have a good opinion of himself. Shortly before the Congress of Aix-la-Chapelle, in 1818, he writes to his wife:

I am more and more convinced that affairs of importance can only be properly conducted by oneself. . . . I have become a species of moral power in Germany, perhaps even in Europe—a power which will leave a void when it disappears: and nevertheless it will disappear, like all belonging to poor frail human nature. I hope Heaven will yet give me time to do some good; that is my dearest wish.

A year later, finding himself in the same room in which he signed the Quadruple Alliance in 1813, solemn reflections concerning his importance to the world are forced upon him:

My mind conceives nothing narrow or limited; I always go, on every side, far beyond all that occupies the greater number of men of business; I cover ground infinitely larger than they can see or wish to see. I cannot help saying to myself twenty times a day: "Good God, how right I am, and how wrong they are! And how easy this reason is to see—it is so clear, so simple, and so natural." I shall repeat this till my last breath, and the world will go on in its own miserable way none the less.

After 1822, however, he was no longer omnipotent. Canning, who succeeded Castlereagh, opposed the Austrian policy, not only in details, but in its broad outlines. In 1823, Metternich writes sadly about England:

What a pity it is that the Queen of the Sea and the sometime ruler of the world should lose her salutary influence. What has become of the great and noble British Empire? What has become of its men and its orators, its feeling for right and duty, and its ideas of justice? This is not the work of a single individual, of one weak and feeble man; Canning is but the personification of the symptoms of the terrible malady which runs through every vein of the fatherland—a malady which has destroyed its strength and threatens the weakened body with dissolution.

Why this lamentation? Chiefly because England would not help Spain to reconquer Spanish America, or Turkey to reconquer Greece. On this latter question, there was worse to follow.

If the death of Castlereagh was a misfortune for Metternich, the death of Alexander was perhaps even more of a disaster to his policy. He was proud of his achievement in persuading Alexander that, as regards Greece, the principle of legitimacy must be put above Russian interests. But after Alexander's death in 1825, his brother Nicholas reverted to the natural Russian policy of hostility to the Porte. In 1827, England, France, and Russia, combined, destroyed the Turkish fleet at the battle of Navarino, after which the recognition of Greek independence by all the Powers could not be long delayed.

The collapse of the system of international government inaugurated at the Congress of Vienna was made still more complete by the Revolution of 1830. France got rid of Charles X and substituted Louis Philippe, who had no legitimate claim to the throne; Belgium refused to remain united with Holland, and had to be recognized as a separate kingdom; there were revolutionary movements in Italy and Germany; and Russian Poland rebelled against the Tsar. Except in France and Belgium, however, no success attended these movements; even in France, it was soon found that the new King was not so very different from the legitimate Bourbons.

In the end, while Metternich's system never again controlled Europe, his personal position was improved by the events of 1830. The Tsar Nicholas, who loved Charles X, and was alarmed by the Polish insurrection, decided that the reactionary Powers must stand by each other, and that it was unsafe to quarrel with Austria. The movements of revolt in Germany, though rather mild, became a source of strength to the reaction after they had been suppressed. Within Austria, while a party of reform existed, Metternich, now grown very deaf, was able to ignore its programme, and did in fact remain largely unaware of it.

What, in the end, defeated him was the growing force of nationalism. "By the help of God," he wrote in 1819, "I hope to defeat the German Revolution just as I vanquished the conqueror of the world." This hope proved delusive, in spite of his most earnest efforts to realize it. The censorship did what it could to prevent even the most indirect encouragement of national feeling. "A band of youthful heroes who flocked around the glorious standard of their country" was altered by the Censor to "a considerable number of young men who voluntarily enlisted themselves for the public service." [1] Metternich forbade Austrian students to study in foreign universities, objected to young men learning history or philosophy or politics, and preferred that Austrian writers should publish their books abroad rather than in their own country. In 1834 he harangued a Conference of German Ministers on the evils of Liberalism, speaking of "the misguided attempts of factions to supersede the monarchical principle by the modern idea of the sovereignty of the people," and of the Liberal party as one that "corrupts the youth, deludes even those of riper years, introduces trouble and discord into all the public and private relations of life, deliberately incites the population to cherish a systematic distrust of their rulers, and preaches the destruction and annihilation of all that exists." The assembled Ministers applauded; nevertheless "the distrust of rulers" continued to increase.

In the last years of Metternich's power, there was trouble in Italy, trouble in Bohemia, trouble in Galicia, and trouble in Hungary—in each case from the awakening sense of nationality. The most serious of these was the trouble in Hungary. Hungary had a constitution which had come down from the middle ages, which gave power to the aristocracy in local affairs, though not in the central government. In theory there was a Diet which was supposed to be summoned on great occasions, but in practice it was becoming obsolete when Hungarian nationalism revived it. In 1825, it demanded the substitution of the Magyar language for Latin, in which its debates were traditionally conducted; and after a long struggle it obtained, in 1827, a promise that it should be summoned every three years. From this time onwards, the Government made a series of concessions to the Magyars, resisting only sufficiently to encourage nationalist feeling. The patriot Kossuth was arrested, but was released when the Diet, in 1839, refused to grant either money or soldiers until he was set free. A feeble effort at repression in the years 1844 to 1847 stimu-

[1] Sandeman, *Metternich*, p. 263.

lated national feeling, and led, in 1847, to the election of a Diet in which the majority was passionately anti-governmental. This was the situation in Hungary on the eve of the Revolution of 1848.

The other non-German portions of the Hapsburg Empire had no constitutional means of expressing their discontent, but they employed such means as they possessed. National feeling revived in Bohemia, and among the South Slavs; the Galician Poles prepared to rebel. Everywhere the situation was threatening, but Metternich's long tenure of power had made him fatuous.

The French Revolution of 1848 gave occasion for the discontents of the whole of the Continent to break loose. Revolts had already begun in Italy even before Louis Philippe had to fly from Paris, but after this event they spread to the whole peninsula, with the exception of the dominions of the King of Sardinia, who was himself a somewhat timid liberal. Throughout Germany the democrats rose; in Hungary Kossuth proclaimed freedom; in Galicia, the Polish aristocrats raised a nationalist revolt, and were quelled only by means of a jacquerie encouraged, or at least tolerated, by the Austrian Government. For a moment, the champions of legitimacy were routed everywhere except in the dominions of the Tsar.

In German Austria, meanwhile, the Liberals were demanding a constitution, but were demanding still more earnestly the fall of Metternich. The streets of Vienna were in an uproar, and Metternich, to his amazement, found himself opposed, not only by the rabble, not only by the doctrinaire Liberals, but by many hitherto conservative aristocrats and by a powerful faction at Court. He agreed to all the demands of the revolutionaries except his own retirement, but this concession did nothing to quiet them. At last, intimidated by the mob, the Imperial family, who had been divided in their opinions, all agreed that Metternich must go. With some difficulty, he made his escape, taking refuge in England, where he handed on the torch to Disraeli.

Metternich was not a great man; his talents did not entitle him to the place that he occupied on the European stage. He had agreeable manners and a persuasive tongue; he was pleasing to women; he was adroit in taking advantage of the personal idiosyncrasies of those with whom he had to negotiate. His principles were those of his Emperor, and circumstances gave Austria a commanding position after the fall of Napoleon. France had been crushed by defeat; England was determined to preserve peace at all costs; Alexander was willing to sacrifice Russia to religion; the King of Prussia was feeble and vacillating. To these factors is to be added Austria's peculiar interest in the legitimist anti-nationalist principles which inspired all the Great Powers while fear of the Revolution and Napoleon still dominated their political thought. But as the years went by the Powers, one by one, abandoned Metternich's creed: England in 1822, Russia in 1825, France in 1830, while his hold on Germany gradually weakened. His passion was for immobility—not unnaturally, in view of the many years during which revolutionary France had kept the world in turmoil. In 1815 there were many to sympathize with immobility as the basis of statecraft, but the long peace generated new energy, and new energy made immobility intolerable. In this new mood, the world saw Metternich as he was: pompous, vain, vapid, incapable of stating his own principles interestingly, and closed to all new ideas from the moment of Napoleon's disappearance. In his immediate *entourage* the eighteenth century survived as in a museum, and he refused to believe that the rest of the world had adopted new ways of living and thinking. Gradually his admiring audience, which had embraced all the leading men of Europe, grew less, but he continued to act the same part. Before he was hissed off the stage, his style had long been antiquated. Deaf and garrulous, nothing remained for him but an old age of reminiscent monologue. In that rôle, at last, he had become harmless.

PART TWO

THE MARCH OF MIND

"GOD bless my soul, sir!" exclaimed the Reverend Doctor Folliott, bursting, one fine May morning, into the breakfast-room at Crotchet Castle, "I am out of all patience with this march of mind. Here has my house been nearly burned down, by my cook taking it into her head to study hydrostatics, in a sixpenny tract, published by the Steam Intellect Society, and written by a learned friend who is for doing all the world's business as well as his own, and is equally well qualified to handle every branch of human knowledge."

THOMAS LOVE PEACOCK

SECTION A   THE SOCIAL BACKGROUND

ENGLAND in the first part of the nineteenth century has a special importance in history, owing to the development of industrialism, at that time virtually non-existent elsewhere. Industrialism generated certain habits of thought, and certain systems of political economy, in which features peculiar to the England of that time were inextricably interwoven with the essentials of the new method of production. The modern outlook had to force its way, with difficulty, against older ways of thinking and acting. It was only in a small part of England that modern factories and mines existed; they had almost no effect upon the minds of most men of education, including almost all the possessors of political power. To understand the new ideas of that time it is, therefore, necessary to take account of the social *milieu* in which they grew up, and of the ignorance concerning industrial problems which the governing classes had derived from a classical education and a pre-occupation with sport.

At the end of the Napoleonic wars, the English were sharply divided into different classes and different kinds of occupation. Industrial life, both that of employers and that of wage-earners, was practically unknown to the rest of the community. In the country there were the three classes of landlords, farmers, and laborers. The smaller landlords were country gentry; the larger landlords formed the aristocracy. Political power, ever since the Revolution of 1688, had been almost wholly concentrated in the aristocracy, which, by means of the system of rotten boroughs, controlled the House of Commons as well as the House of Lords. Since about 1760, the aristocracy, by a shameless use of the power of Parliament, had considerably lowered the standard of life among wage-earners. It had also impeded the progress of the middle-class manufacturers, partly from ignorance, partly from jealousy of new power, partly from a desire for high rents. But most of this had been done in a semi-

51

conscious, almost somnambulistic fashion, for the legislators of those days did not take their duties very seriously. With the beginning of our period, however, a new strenuousness comes into vogue, and the easy-going eighteenth-century spirit gradually gives way to the earnestness and virtue of the Victorians.

CHAPTER V

THE ARISTOCRACY

THE Whigs and Tories, the two parties into which the aristocracy was divided, had originally been composed, respectively, of the enemies and the friends of the Stuarts, with the result that, after the fall of James II, the Whigs held almost uninterrupted power for nearly a century. But the Tories crept back into office under the aegis of George III, consolidated their rule by opposition to the French Revolution, and kept the Whigs in opposition until 1830. The division between Whigs and Tories was social as well as political: there were Whig houses where one met Whigs, and Tory houses where one met Tories. As a rule, Whigs married Whigs, and Tories married Tories. While both were equally aristocratic, they differed considerably in their traditions and in their attitude to the rising middle class.

In the early nineteenth century, the Tories were, on the whole, less intelligent than the Whigs. Their leading principle, opposition to France and to all French ideas, was one which neither demanded nor stimulated intellectual thought. They felt that all had been well before the Jacobins put their poison into men's minds, and that, now that Napoleon was safely interned in St. Helena, the only thing necessary was to suppress at once every tendency to a recrudescence of revolutionary nonsense whether at home or abroad. They were loyal to Church and King, though they found George IV something of a strain. They believed in the divinely appointed hierarchy of social grades, and in the importance of respect from inferiors to superiors. They were friends to the agricultural interest, and anxious to keep England self-supporting in the matter of food. They were, of course, opposed to popular education, freedom of the Press, and seditious oratory. For the rest, they drank their port from loyalty to our ancient ally Portugal, and accepted the consequent gout as a price paid for the performance of patriotic duty. Their politicians, since the death of Pitt, were men of mediocre ability. Their one great man was the Duke of Wellington, and he had been more successful in war than he subsequently proved in statesmanship. Tom Moore in 1827 expressed the general view of Wellington in the lines:

> Great Captain who takest such pains
> To prove—what is granted—*nem. con.*
> With how moderate a portion of brains
> Some heroes contrive to get on.

There was, it is true, one man of great political ability in the Tory party, namely Canning. But he was unpopular among the Tories; on one occasion when Canning went out of office a Tory gentleman was heard thanking God that "they would have no more of these confounded men of genius."

The Whigs were more interesting and more complex. Owing their position to successful revolution against a King, they never adopted the unquestioning loyalty of the Tories. Having imported the Hanoverians, they felt towards them, in some degree, as towards hired servants, who could be dismissed if they proved unsatisfactory. Lord John Russell, being asked by Queen Victoria if it was true that he held resistance to sovereigns justifiable in some circumstances, replied: "Madam, speaking to a sovereign of the House of Hanover, I think I may say that I do." At the time of the French Revolution, while most of the Whigs followed Burke in condemnation, Fox, who remained the official leader of the party, was as pro-French as was possible in view of the Reign of Terror. Throughout the long years from 1793 to 1815, when all friendship to French ideas was regarded as criminal, and men suspected of Jacobin tendencies were sentenced to long terms of imprisonment, some of the most prominent Whigs continued freely to express opinions which would have landed humbler folk in jail, such as belief in liberty and advocacy of drastic parliamentary reform. They supported the war against Napoleon, whom they regarded as a tyrant. But they were never as enthusiastic for the war as the Tories were, and when Napoleon returned from Elba in 1815 many of them thought that he ought to be given another chance. Even after Waterloo, Lord John Russell expressed regret in the House of Commons that this policy had not been adopted.

The Whigs believed in monarchy, as a useful element in the defence of order; but they never pretended to have any respect for royal personages. Greville in 1829 remarks:

"There have been good and wise kings, but not many of them. Take them one with another, they are of an inferior character, and this [George IV] I believe to be one of the worst of the kind."

Writing of the building of Buckingham Palace in the reign of William IV, Creevey says:

"Never was there such a specimen of wicked, vulgar profusion. It has cost a million of money, and there is not a fault that has not been committed in it. Raspberry-coloured pillars without end, that quite turn you sick to look at; but the Queen's paper for her own apartments far exceed [sic] everything else in their ugliness and vulgarity. . . . Can one be surprised at people becoming Radical with such specimens of royal prodigality before their eyes? to say nothing of the characters of such royalties themselves." [1]

The sufferings of the aristocracy were, unlike those of royalty, a matter for sympathy. When William IV comes to the throne, Creevey (who calls him "Billy") makes fun of him for having bad eyesight. But when he finds Lord Holland (who was Fox's nephew) hard up, he regards it as a grave matter:

"I was at Lord Holland's yesterday. . . . They both looked very ill. They are evidently most sorely pinched—he in his land, and she still more in her sugar and rum.[2] So when I gave it as my opinion that, if things went on as they did, *paper* must ooze out again by connivance or otherwise [England had not long before returned to the gold standard], she said she wished to God the time was come, or anything else to save them. He said that he never would consent to the return of paper, but he thought the standard might be altered: *i.e.* a sovereign to be made by law worth one or two or three and twenty shillings."

Lord and Lady Holland were the social centre of Whig society. If a man had brains and the right principles, he did not need to be an aristocrat in order to be admitted to their dinners. Sydney Smith and (later) Macaulay were frequent visitors. Greville (February 6, 1832) describes his first meeting with Macaulay at Holland House:

[1] *Creevey Papers*, 1903, II, pp. 307–8.
[2] Lady Holland was the daughter and heiress of a Jamaica planter.

February 6th.—Dined yesterday with Lord Holland; came very late, and found a vacant place between Sir George Robinson and a common-looking man in black. As soon as I had time to look at my neighbour, I began to speculate (as one usually does) as to who he might be, and as he did not for some time open his lips except to eat, I settled that he was some obscure man of letters or of medicine, perhaps a cholera doctor. In a short time the conversation turned upon early and late education, and Lord Holland said he had always remarked that self-educated men were peculiarly conceited and arrogant, and apt to look down upon the generality of mankind, from their being ignorant of how much other people knew; not having been at public schools, they are uninformed of the course of general education. My neighbour observed that he thought the most remarkable example of self-education was that of Alfieri, who had reached the age of thirty without having acquired any accomplishment save that of driving, and who was so ignorant of his own language that he had to learn it like a child, beginning with elementary books. Lord Holland quoted Julius Caesar Scaliger as an example of late education, saying that he had been married and commenced learning Greek the same day, when my neighbour remarked "that he supposed his learning Greek was not an instantaneous act like his marriage." This remark, and the manner of it, gave me the notion that he was a dull fellow, for it came out in a way which bordered on the ridiculous, so as to excite something like a sneer. I was a little surprised to hear him continue the thread of conversation (from Scaliger's wound) and talk of Loyola having been wounded at Pampeluna. I wondered how he happened to know anything about Loyola's wound. Having thus settled my opinion, I went on eating my dinner, when Auckland, who was sitting opposite to me, addressed my neighbour, "Mr. Macaulay, will you drink a glass of wine?" I thought I should have dropped off my chair. It was MACAULAY, the man I had been so long most curious to see and to hear, whose genius, eloquence, astonishing knowledge, and diversified talents have excited my wonder and admiration for such a length of time, and here I had been sitting next to him, hearing him talk, and setting him down for a dull fellow. I felt as if he could have read my thoughts, and the perspiration burst from every pore of my face, and yet it was impossible not to be amused at the idea. It was not till Macaulay stood up that I was aware of all the vulgarity and ungainliness of his appearance; not a ray of intellect beams from his countenance; a lump of more ordinary clay never enclosed a powerful mind and lively imagination. He had a cold and sore throat, the latter of which occasioned a constant contraction of the muscles of the thorax, making him appear as if in momentary danger of a fit. His manner struck me as not pleasing, but it was not assuming, unembarrassed, yet not easy, unpolished, yet not coarse; there was no kind of usurpation of the conversation, no tenacity as to opinion or facts, no assumption of superiority, but the variety and extent of his information were soon apparent, for whatever subject was touched upon he evinced the utmost familiarity with it; quotation, illustration, anecdote, seemed ready in his hands for every topic. Primogeniture in this country, in others, and particularly in ancient Rome, was the principal topic, I think, but Macaulay was not certain what was the law of Rome, except that when a man died intestate his estate was divided between his children. After dinner Talleyrand and Madame de Dino came in. Macaulay was introduced to Talleyrand, who told him that he meant to go to the House of Commons on Tuesday, and that he hopes he would speak, "qu'il avait entendu tous les grands orateurs, et il desirait à présent entendre Monsieur Macaulay."

Melbourne was a frequent visitor at Holland House, and his conversation, as reported by Greville, is incredibly cultivated. Take this as a sample, on September 7, 1834: "Allen spoke of the early reformers, the Catharists, and how the early Christians persecuted each other; Melbourne quoted Vigilanutius's letter to Jerome, and then asked Allen about the 11th of Henry IV, an Act passed by the Commons against the Church, and referred to the dialogue between the Archbishop of Canterbury and the Bishop of Ely at the beginning of Shakespeare's *Henry V,* which Lord Holland sent for and read, Melbourne knowing it all by heart and prompting all the time."

Creevey, who had tendencies to Radicalism, sometimes turned against the Hollands. On one occasion, during a quarrel about Fox's epitaph, he wrote: "As for the wretched dirt and meanness of Holland House, it makes me perfectly sick" (July 24, 1820). But on another occasion his impression was quite different: "Never was so much struck with the agreeableness of Lord Holland. I don't suppose there is any Englishman living who covers so much ground as he does—biographical, historical, and anecdotical" (November 23, 1833). Intermediate in sentiment is a third entry: "I dined with Madagascar [nickname for Lady Holland] at Holland House, a small party, and for once, to my delight, plenty of elbow-room. . . . Whilst Holland House *can* be as agreeable a house as any I know, it is quite as much at other times distinguished for *twaddle,* and so it was on this occasion" (April 23, 1836). The overcrowding at Holland House dinner parties was notorious. My grandmother used to tell how, on one occasion when she was present, an unexpected guest had arrived, and Lady Holland had called the length of the table "Make room, my dear," to which Lord Holland replied "I shall have to make it, for it does not exist."

Lady Holland displayed on occasion all the insolence of a great lady. Creevey (July 6, 1833) gives the following instance:

I met Lady Holland again on Thursday at Lord Sefton's. She began by complaining of the slipperiness of the courtyard, and of the danger of her horses falling; to which Sefton replied that it should be gravelled the next time she did him the honor of dining there. She then began to sniff, and, turning her eyes to various pots filled with beautiful roses and all kinds of flowers, she said: 'Lord Sefton, I must beg you to have those flowers taken out of the room, they are so much too powerful for me.'— Sefton and his valet Paoli actually carried the table and all its contents out of the room. Then poor dear little Ly. Sefton, who has always a posy as large as life at her breast when she is dressed, took it out in the humblest manner, and said:—'Perhaps, Lady Holland, this nosegay may be too much for you.'—But the other was pleased to allow her to keep it, tho' by no means in a very gracious manner. Then when candles were lighted at the close of dinner, she would have three of them put out, as being too much and too near her. Was there ever?

When she died, Greville took the opportunity to sum up the importance of Holland House (November 24, 1845):

Though she was a woman for whom nobody felt any affection, and whose death therefore will have excited no grief, she will be regretted by a great many people, some from kindly, more from selfish motives, and all who had been accustomed to live at Holland House and continued to be her *habitués* will lament over the fall of the curtain on that long drama, and the final extinction of a social light which illuminated and adorned England and even Europe for half a century. The world never has seen and never will again see anything like Holland House, and though it was by no means the same thing as it was during Lord Holland's life, Lady Holland contrived to assemble round her to the last a great society, comprising almost everybody that was conspicuous, remarkable, and agreeable.

It must not be supposed that all Whig society was as intellectual as the Holland House dinner parties. But on the whole the leading

Whigs were people of considerable culture, which they took lightly, and combined with an eighteenth-century freedom of morals. Lady Holland had left a previous husband for Lord Holland, and they had lived together for some time before she was divorced. Melbourne's wife, as all the world knew, had been madly in love with Byron, and had pursued him even more than he liked. Lady Oxford also loved Byron, and *her* affection was reciprocated. Sir Francis Burdett was another of Lady Oxford's lovers, and her children were known as the Oxford Miscellany.

Whig society was tolerant of Radical aberrations, provided they were accompanied by wit, learning, or a combination of birth and fortune. Byron at first fitted in quite easily. When he made his one and only speech in the Lords, in defence of the Luddite rioters who were being punished with extreme ferocity, no one thought the worse of him, partly, of course, because it was known that his speech could have no influence. But in the end he went too far, not in political ways, but in matters of private morals. It was not so much his sins that were condemned as his habit of flaunting them. At last he was dropped even by old Lady Melbourne, the statesman's mother, who had been his confidante, and had, in her day, carried eighteenth-century freedom to the extreme limit permitted by good manners.

Polite skepticism was common among the Whigs. But their middle-class supporters were mostly earnest nonconformists, and therefore infidel opinions were only to be avowed in conversation: to state them in a form accessible to the lower orders was vulgar. For this reason, Shelley, whose talents would otherwise have made him eligible, was an outcast from the first. For an undergraduate to try to convert the Master of his College to atheism, while it may not have been wicked, was certainly bad form. Moreover, he had abandoned his wife, and what was worse, he had run away with the daughter of that old reprobate Godwin, a Jacobin who had only escaped the just penalty of his crimes by publishing his book at a prohibitive price. And not only was the young lady's father a hoary revolutionary, but her mother had advocated the rights of women, and had lived an openly immoral life in Paris, not for fun merely, but in obedience to a theory. This was beyond a joke. The Whigs remembered that even liberal aristocrats had had their heads cut off by Robespierre. They always knew where to draw the line, and they drew it, emphatically, at Shelley. The prejudice persisted down to my own day, and, I am told, still persists in certain circles. When, at the age of sixteen, I became interested in Shelley, I was informed that Byron could be forgiven because, though he had sinned, he had been led into sin by the unfortunate circumstances of his youth, and had always been haunted by remorse, but that for Shelley's moral character there was nothing to be said, since he acted on principle, and therefore he could not be worth reading.

CHAPTER VI

COUNTRY LIFE

THROUGHOUT the Napoleonic wars, and for some time afterwards, the life of the country gentry was quiet and prosperous. Wars were not, in those days, so disturbing as they have since become, and few squires bothered their heads about public affairs. The value of land was increasing, and rents were going up: the demand for agricultural produce grew as the population grew, and Great Britain still provided for almost the whole of its own consumption of food. In Jane Austen's novels, which deal with the lives of small rural landowners, there is, so far as I remember, only one allusion to the war: the hero of *Persuasion* has been a naval officer, and there is some prize money due to him, which is expected to facilitate his marriage. Of his valiant feats of arms we hear not a word, and apparently they would not have increased his attractiveness to the heroine. Newspapers are rarely mentioned, and only once, I think, in connection with politics. Generally they are introduced to throw sidelights on her characters. Mr. Darcy picked up a newspaper to conceal his embarrassment when he called to propose to Elizabeth Bennett. Mr. Palmer, when he had been reluctantly persuaded by his wife to pay a call, as soon as he had said how-do-you-do, picked up a newspaper. "Is there anything in the newspaper?" asked Mrs. Palmer. "Nothing whatever," said Mr. Palmer, and went on reading. Perhaps the newspaper contained an account of the mutiny at the Nore or the extinction of the Venetian Republic. If so, Mr. Palmer did not think such events worth mentioning.

There have been periods when religion disturbed men's minds. Indeed, at the very time when Jane Austen was writing, Methodism was producing a profound transformation of the middle and lower classes. But in her novels religion appears only under one aspect: as providing parsonages for younger sons. All the richer characters in her books have livings in their gift; sometimes they bestow them upon absurdities, sometimes upon the virtuous hero, but in either case it is the economic aspect that interests her.

The larger farmers were, in their way, as comfortable as the landowners, though they grumbled about the tithe and the poor-rate. They aped the manners of "gentlefolk," hunted and drank and gambled. The traditional figure of John Bull is derived from this period; it is curious that he should have been accepted, down to the present day, as the type of an overwhelmingly urban nation.

There was a dreadful moment, in 1815, when the country gentry and the farmers feared that their pleasant manner of life was to be brought to an abrupt end. The war was over, and it was possible to import grain from abroad. The harvest at home was bad, and foreigners were offering wheat at a price with which British produce could not compete. There was acute distress in the industrial regions, because foreign nations were erecting tariffs against British manufactures. But Parliament listened to the complaints of landowners and farmers, and imposed a heavy duty on foreign grain. As a result, the richer classes in the country remained rich—at what cost to the rest of the nation we shall see.

The life of the rural wage-earners in England in the early nineteenth century presented such an extreme contrast to the prosperity of the gentry that it is difficult to understand the bland complacency of the upper classes. The Continental peasantry, except in France, and in some parts of Germany, were wretched enough, but their misery was of long standing and was, on the whole, in process of amelioration. But in England from 1760 onwards there had been a steady deterioration in the condition of the rural poor, though the change was silent and almost unnoticed. The landless class, which hardly existed on the Continent, was greatly augmented, and supplied the human material essential to the rapid rise of British industrialism. Most historians did not adequately realize the miseries which resulted from the altered position of the rural wage-earner until the publication, in 1911, of *The Village Labourer*, by J. L. and Barbara Hammond, a massive and horrifying indictment of upper-class greed.

The instruments of spoliation of the poor by the rich were various; the two most important were enclosures and the Poor Law.

The history of enclosures, apart from its intrinsic interest, is important as showing the influence of politics on economic progress. In the first half of the eighteenth century, the rural poor enjoyed a state of tolerable comfort. At that time probably half of the cultivated land in England was worked on the old strip system, and divided up into holdings of all sizes, from very large to very small. Most laborers on farms rented strips of land and cottages which carried with them rights of grazing and firewood on the commons. In many cases these common rights existed, or were taken for granted, independently of the holding of a cottage. Thus the lalaborer got his firewood free, could keep fowls, a cow, or a pig on the common, and, if he were thrifty, could save his wages and lay strip to strip until he became a well-to-do farmer.

But throughout the eighteenth century and the first half of the nineteenth, first the open fields and then the waste lands were, at an increasing speed, enclosed and redistributed by Acts of Parliament. A few, or sometimes only one, of the local landowners would petition for such an Act, a Bill would be introduced and a Committee appointed. When the Bill had been passed the land could be redistributed at the discretion of the appointed Commissioners. The lion's share went to the principal landowner, who was often either a peer or a Member of Parliament: there was a system of log-rolling by which a great man could safely leave his interests in the hands of his friends. The larger farmers would secure a substantial share, but the smaller farmers and cottagers, as a rule, obtained nothing, or, if they were given their share, were unable to take it because of the expense of the necessary fencing. "The small farmer either emigrated to America or to an industrial town, or became a day laborer." The cottager was often reduced to a state of starvation. This was considered highly satisfactory by the landlords, who regretted the demoralizing effects on the laborer of the partial independence which his ancestors had enjoyed for centuries, considering that it made him lazy, and that, until he became completely dependent on his employer, he could not be relied upon to give all his energy to his employer's interests. Enclosures deprived the laborers, not only of land and valuable rights, but also of bargaining power in their dealings with farmers and landlords: they were therefore doubly impoverished, first, by the loss of sources of livelihood outside their wages, and second, by a fall of wages. The total amount of agricultural produce was increased, but the laborers had to put up with not merely a smaller proportion, but an absolute diminution in their earnings. The degradation of the peasantry which ensued was a heavy price to pay for more scientific agriculture.

The second mechanism for depressing the condition of the laborers was one nominally designed for their benefit, namely, the Poor Law. This dated from the time of Queen Elizabeth, and is said (though this seems scarcely credible) to have had philanthropic motives. The Poor Law decreed that every parish was responsible for seeing that none of its poor perished from hunger. If any man, woman, or child became destitute, it was the duty of the parish in which he or she was born to provide a bare maintenance. It was possible, if a man obtained work at a distance from his birthplace, for his new parish to take over the obligation of his support in case of necessity, but this was seldom done. A man was said to have a "settlement" in the parish which was responsible for him. His own parish was unwilling to let him go, since it might become responsible for the expense of bringing him back from the other end of the kingdom. Even if his own parish would let him go, no other parish was likely to admit him unless he brought a certificate from his original parish admitting responsibility; but the parish officers were under no obligation to grant such certificates, which were, in practice, very difficult to obtain. There were, in theory, various methods of acquiring a new "settlement," but ways were found of preventing the poor from profiting by them. It was thus exceedingly difficult for a poor man to move away from his birthplace, however little need it might have for his labor.

An important step in the development of the Poor Law was taken by the inauguration of what is called the "Speenhamland" system in 1795. At that time fear of revolution was in the air, as the Reign of Terror in France had only just come to an end. The harvest was bad, and there was great distress throughout England, leading to wide-spread food riots, in which women took the chief part. The governing classes became alarmed, and decided that they could not secure their own safety by repression alone. They tried to make the poor eat brown bread and potatoes and drink soup, but the poor, to the surprise of well-meaning persons, refused to depart from the best wheaten bread. Subsequent experience proved that they were right from an economic point of view: the Irish were persuaded to eat potatoes, with the result that, during the famine of 1845–7, they died in large numbers. Some men, more enlightened than their contemporaries, advocated a minimum wage, and Whitbread brought in a Bill for that purpose in Parliament, but was defeated by the opposition of Pitt. The plan actually accepted, not universally, but throughout the greater part of England, was the system of supplementing a man's wages out of the poor rate, if they seemed insufficient to afford a bare living to himself and his family. A number of Berkshire magistrates assembled at Speenhamland (where the system was first introduced) estimated that a man needed three gallon loaves a week, while a woman or a child needed one and a half. If his wages were insufficient to purchase this amount of bread, they were to be supplemented from the poor rate to the necessary extent, which would, of course, fluctuate with the price of bread.

The relevant words of the original resolution are:

When the gallon loaf of second flour, weighing 8 lbs. 11 oz., shall cost one shilling, then every poor and industrious man shall have for his own support 3s. weekly, either produced by his own or his family's labour or an allowance from the poor rates, and for the support of his wife and every other of his family 1s. 6d. When the gallon loaf shall cost 1s. 4d., then every poor and industrious man shall have 4s. weekly for his own, and 1s. 10d. for the support of every other of his family. And so in proportion as the price of bread rises or falls (that is to say), 3d. to the man and 1d. to every other of the family, on every penny which the loaf rises above a shilling.[1]

This system, with unimportant alterations, persisted until the reformed Parliament passed the new Poor Law in 1834. Whether the new Poor Law was any better than the old is a matter as to which debate is still possible; but as to the badness of the old system no debate is possible.

The natural result of the Speenhamland system was that employers paid low wages in order that part of the expense of the labor employed by them should be borne by the poor rate. In large numbers of rural parishes, most of the wage-earning population were paupers. There was a great development of a system, which already existed in 1795, by which laborers were wholly paid by the parish

[1] Quoted from Hammond, *Village Labourer*, 4th ed., p. 139.

authorities, and were by them hired out to any one who had work to be done; such laborers were called "roundsmen" because they went the rounds of the parish.

The Speenhamland scale of living was not lavish; nevertheless it was higher than the scale adopted in many places after the end of the Napoleonic wars. It seems that the decline continued so long as the old Poor Law lasted, and that in 1831 the usual allowance for a family was one loaf a week per person and one over. As the Hammonds say:

In thirty-five years the standard had dropped, according to McCulloch's statement, as much as a third, and this not because of war or famine, for in 1826 England had had eleven years of peace, but in the ordinary course of the life of the nation. Is such a decline in the standard of life recorded anywhere in history? [2]

From the standpoint of the upper classes, the system had many merits. They felt that what was paid out of the poor rate was charity, and therefore a proof of their benevolence; at the same time, wages were kept at starvation level by a method which just prevented discontent from developing into revolution. In France, revolution had immensely benefited the peasant, whose standard of life was much higher in 1815 than in 1789, in spite of the long wars and final defeat. It was probably the certainty, derived from the old Poor Law, that actual death would be averted by the parish authorities, which induced the rural poor of England to endure their misery patiently. It would have been difficult to devise a cheaper scheme for keeping the poor quiet. There were, it is true, occasional disturbances, more particularly the "Last Revolt" in 1830. But they caused the government little trouble to suppress, and gave opportunities for savage sentences. The Poor Law impoverished the laborers and sapped their self-respect; it taught them respect for their "betters," while leaving all the wealth that they produced, beyond the absolute minimum required for subsistence, in the hands of the landowners and farmers. It was at this period that landowners built the sham Gothic ruins called "follies," where they indulged in romantic sensibility about the past while they filled the present with misery and degradation.

[2] *Village Labourer*, p. 161. This was written before the Great War.

CHAPTER VII

INDUSTRIALISM

IN rural life there were three classes, but in industrial life there were only two. The landowner, as a rule, did not choose to live amid the grime and smoke and squalor of factories or mines; even if, for a while, he lingered in a neighborhood which had been rural in his father's time, he had little contact with the rising class of industrial employers, whom he regarded as vulgar and uneducated. The relations of the landowning class with the mill-owners were, for the most part, political rather than social. They had a common interest in suppressing disturbances, but on most points their interests diverged. There was an import duty on raw cotton which the manufacturers resented. The duty on grain increased the price of bread, and therefore the cost of keeping a laborer alive; the extra wages which this obliged the manufacturer to pay ultimately found their way into the pocket of the landowner in the shape of rent for agricultural land. The manufacturer desired free trade, the landowner believed in protection; the manufacturer was often a nonconformist, the landowner almost always belonged to the Church of England; the manufacturer had picked up his education as best he could, and had risen from poverty by thrift and industry, while the landowner had been at a public school and was the son of his father.

The upper classes, when they stopped to think, were aware that the new industrial life of the North had its importance. They knew that our manufacturers had helped to beat Napoleon; some of them had heard of James Watt, and had a hazy impression that there were processes in which steam had been found useful. But this sort of thing seemed to them new-fangled and rather unpleasant; moreover, if it spread, it might interfere with the foxes and partridges. My grandfather, at one period of his education, had for his tutor Dr. Cartwright, the inventor of the power loom, which introduced machinery and the factory system into the weaving trade. His pupil, in later life, observed: "From Dr. Cartwright, who was a man of

much learning and great mechanical ingenuity, I acquired a taste
for Latin poetry, which has never left me." His reminiscences go on
to give some examples of the pedagogue's "mechanical ingenuity,"
but not a word is said about the power loom, of which, for aught that
appears, my grandfather never heard, although its inventor addressed to him " a volume of letters and sonnets on moral and other
interesting subjects." Abroad England was known for its machinery,
but upper-class England resented this view, and put the emphasis on
agriculture. Even so late as 1844, this feeling is amusingly expressed
by Kinglake in *Eothen,* in an imaginary interview between an English
traveller and a Turkish Pasha:

Pasha: . . . . whirr! whirr! all by wheels!—whizz! whizz! all by
steam!

Traveller (to the Dragoman): What does the Pasha mean by
that whizzing? he does not mean to say, does he, that our Government will ever abandon their pledges to the Sultan?

Dragoman: No, your excellency, but he says the English talk by
wheels and by steam.

Traveller: That's an exaggeration; but say that the English really
have carried machinery to great perfection. Tell the Pasha (he'll
be struck with that) that whenever we have any disturbances to put
down, even at two or three hundred miles from London, we can
send troops by the thousand to the scene of action in a few hours.

Dragoman (recovering his temper and freedom of speech): His
Excellency, this Lord of Mudcombe, observes to your Highness,
that whenever the Irish, or the French, or the Indians rebel against
the English, whole armies of soldiers and brigades of artillery are
dropped into a mighty chasm called Euston Square, and, in the
biting of a cartridge, they rise up again in Manchester, or Dublin, or
Paris, or Delhi, and utterly exterminate the enemies of England
from the face of the earth.

Pasha: I know it—I know all; the particulars have been faith-
fully related to me, and my mind comprehends locomotives. The
armies of the English ride upon the vapours of boiling caldrons,
and their horses are flaming coals;—whirr! whirr! all by wheels!—
whizz! whizz! all by steam!

Traveller (to his Dragoman): I wish to have the opinion of an unprejudiced Ottoman gentleman as to the prospects of our English commerce and manufactures; just ask the Pasha to give me his views on the subject.

Pasha (after having received the communication of the Dragoman): The ships of the English swarm like flies; their printed calicoes cover the whole earth, and by the side of their swords the blades of Damascus are blades of grass. All India is but an item in the ledger-books of the merchants, whose lumber-rooms are filled with ancient thrones!—whirr! whirr! all by wheels!—whizz! whizz! all by steam!

Dragoman: The Pasha compliments the cutlery of England, and also the East India Company.

Traveller: The Pasha's right about the cutlery: I tried my scimitar with the common officers' swords belonging to our fellows at Malta, and they cut it like the leaf of a novel. Well (to the Dragoman), tell the Pasha I am exceedingly gratified to find that he entertains such a high opinion of our manufacturing energy, but I should like him to know, though, that we have got something in England besides that. These foreigners are always fancying that we have nothing but ships and railways, and East India Companies; do just tell the Pasha that our rural districts deserve his attention, and that even within the last two hundred years there has been an evident improvement in the culture of the turnip; and if he does not take any interest about that, at all events you can explain that we have our virtues in the country—that we are a truth-telling people, and, like the Osmanlees, are faithful in the performance of our promises. Oh! and by-the-by, whilst you are about it, you may as well just say, at the end, that the British yeoman is still, thank God! the British yeoman.

The British yeoman, as we have seen, was not still the British yeoman; Kinglake's traveller and his friends had transformed him into a starving, terrified pauper. But if the evils of rural England were great, those of industrial England were infinitely greater. The abominations in the mills and mines of those days are a trite theme, and yet one that remains all but unbearable. I have scarcely the heart to embark upon it, and yet something must be said.

Napoleon had been defeated by the snows of Russia and the children of England. The part played by the snows of Russia was acknowledged, since it could be attributed to Providence; but the part played by the children of England was passed over in silence, since it was shameful to the men of England. It was Michelet, in his history, who first gave it due prominence in the shape of an imaginary conversation between Pitt and the employers: when they complain of his war taxes, he replies "Take the children." But it was a very long time after the end of the war before they let the children go again.

There were two systems of child labor: the older system, of pauper apprentices, and the newer system, of "free" children. The older system was as follows: in London and in various other places, when a man received poor relief, the parish claimed the exclusive right of disposing of his children up to the age of twenty-one. Until 1767, almost all such children died, so that no problem arose for the authorities. In that year, however, a philanthropist named Hanway got an Act passed which caused the children to be boarded out up to the age of six, instead of being kept in the workhouse. The consequence was that large numbers had the misfortune to survive, and the London authorities were faced with the problem of their disposal. The demand for child labor in the Lancashire mills supplied the solution. The children were apprenticed to some mill-owner, and became virtually his property until the age of twenty-one. If the mill worked continuously, day and night, the children were employed in two shifts of twelve hours each, each bed being shared between a day-child and a night-child. These were the more fortunate children. In mills which closed during the night, there was only one shift, and the children might have to work fifteen or sixteen hours every day.

Sometimes the mill-owners would go bankrupt, and the children would be taken in a cart to a lonely spot, and then turned out to shift for themselves. Unless this happened, the children never left the mill, except to go to church on Sundays if the machinery was cleaned in time. The possibility of insufficient religious instruction was almost the only point on which the general conscience of the time was sensitive; it was, however, somewhat moved by the frequent epidemics of which large numbers of the children died.

In the year 1802, Sir Robert Peel (father of the statesman), who had been himself a far from model employer, introduced and carried through Parliament a Bill "for the better preservation of the Health and Morals of Apprentices and others employed in the cotton and other mills and the cotton and other manufactories." The Bill in fact applied only to apprentices, and only to cotton. Sir Robert Peel thought that it "would render the cotton trade as correct and moral as it was important." It prescribed that apprentices were not to work at night, and no more than twelve hours a day; they were to have some education every day, one new suit of clothes a year, and separate rooms for the boys and girls, with a whole bed for each. Every Sunday they were to be taught the Christian religion, and once a year they were to be examined by a clergyman. What could virtuous children want more?

The employers protested that this Act was going to ruin their business. But it turned out that no one was going to force them to obey the law, and in practice little good resulted. Moreover, the employment of apprentices came to be more and more replaced by what were amusingly called "free" children, i.e. those who went to work at the behest of their parents although they had not been deprived of the legal right to starve. The change was due to the substitution of steam for water power, which led to the removal of mills to the towns, where a local supply of child labor was available. The authorities refused the aid of the Poor Law to parents who refused to send their children to the mill, and owing to the competition of the new machines there were many weavers on the verge of starvation. The result was that many children were forced to begin earning their living at the age of six or seven, and sometimes even sooner. Their life as wage-earners is described by the Hammonds in *The Town Labourer*:

When once children became wage earners, their working life differed little from that of the apprentices already described. They entered the mill gates at 5 or 6 A.M., they left them (at earliest) at 7 or 8 P.M., Saturdays included. All this time they were shut up in temperature varying from 75 to 85. The only respite during the fourteen or fifteen hours' confinement was afforded by meal hours, at most half an hour for breakfast and an hour for dinner. But regular meal hours were privileges for adults only: to the children for three or fours days a week they meant merely a change of work; instead of tending a machine that was running, they cleaned a machine that was standing still, snatching and swallowing their food as best they could in the midst of dust and flue. Children soon lost all relish for meals eaten in the factory. The flue used to choke their lungs. When spitting failed to expel it, emetics were freely given.

The work on which these children were engaged was often described as light and easy, in fact almost as an amusement, requiring attention but not exertion. Three-fourths of the children were "piecers"—that is, engaged in joining together or piecing the threads broken in the various roving and spinning machines. Others were employed in sweeping up the waste cotton, or removing and replacing bobbins. Fielden (1784–1849), the enlightened and humane employer who represented Oldham with Cobbett, and shares the laurels that grace the memory of Shaftesbury and Sadler, made an interesting experiment to measure the physical strain that the children endured. Struck with some statements made by factory delegates about the miles a child walked a day in following a spinning machine, he submitted the statements to a practical test in his own factory, and found to his amazement that in twelve hours the distance covered was not less than twenty miles. There were indeed short intervals of leisure, but no seat to sit on, sitting being contrary to rules. The view that the piecers' work was really light was best given by Mr. Tufnell, one of the Factory Commissioners. Three-fourths of the children, he says, are engaged as piecers at mules, and whilst the mules are receding there is nothing to be done and the piecers stand idle for about three-quarters of a minute. From this he deduces the conclusion that if a child is nominally working twelve hours a day, "*for nine hours he performs no actual labour*," or if, as is generally the case, he attends two mules, then "his leisure is six hours instead of nine."

The fourteen or fifteen hours confinement for six days a week were the "regular" hours: in busy times hours were elastic and sometimes stretched to a length that seems almost incredible. Work from 3 A.M. to 10 P.M. was not unknown; in Mr. Varley's mill, all through the summer, they worked from 3.30 A.M. to 9.30 P.M. At the mill, aptly called "Hell Bay," for two months at a time, they not only worked regularly from 5 A.M. to 9 P.M., but for two nights each week worked all through the night as well. The more humane employers contented themselves when busy with a spell of sixteen hours (5 A.M. to 9 P.M.).

It was physically impossible to keep such a system working at all except by the driving force of terror. The overseers who gave evidence before Sadler's Committee did not deny that their methods were brutal. They said that they had either to exact the full quota of work, or to be dismissed, and in these circumstances pity was a luxury that men with families could not allow themselves. The punishments for arriving late in the morning had to be made cruel enough to overcome the temptation to tired children to take more than three or four hours in bed. One witness before Sadler's Committee had known a child, who had reached home at eleven o'clock one night, get up at two o'clock next morning in panic and limp to the mill gate. In some mills scarcely an hour passed in the long day without the sound of beating and cries of pain. Fathers beat their own children to save them from a worse beating by the overseers. In the afternoon the strain grew so severe that the heavy iron stick known as the billy-roller was in constant use, and, even then, it happened not infrequently that a small child, as he dozed, tumbled into the machine beside him to be mangled for life, or, if he were more fortunate, to find a longer Lethe than his stolen sleep. In one mill indeed, where the owner, a Mr. Gott, had forbidden the use of anything but a ferule, some of the slubbers tried to keep the children awake, when they worked from 5 in the morning to 9 at night, by encouraging them to sing hymns. As the evening wore on the pain and fatigue and tension on the mind became insupportable. Children would implore any one who came near to tell them how many hours there were still before them. A witness told Sadler's Committee that his child, a boy of six, would say to him, " 'Father, what o'clock is it?' I have said perhaps it is seven o'clock. 'Oh, it is two hours to nine o'clock? I cannot bear it.' " [1]

As the circumstances became known, an agitation arose for an Act to prohibit the worst abuses, with which we shall be concerned in a later chapter. For the present, I shall only observe that an Act was passed in 1819, but proved wholly ineffective, as the work of inspection was left to magistrates and clergymen. To the relief of employers, experience showed that magistrates and clergymen had no objection to law-breaking when its purpose was merely the torture of children.

It was not only in cotton mills that children suffered; they were subjected to conditions quite as terrible in the coal mines. There were, for example, the trappers, generally from five to eight years old, who "sat in a little hole, made at the side of the door, holding a string in their hand, for twelve hours. As a rule they were in the dark, but sometimes a good-natured collier would give them a bit of candle." A girl of eight, according to the Report of the Children's Employment Committee in 1842, said: "I have to trap without a light, and I'm scared. I go at four and sometimes at half-past three in the morning and come out at five and half-past (in the afternoon). I never go

[1] *The Town Labourer*, 1932, pp. 157–60.

to sleep. Sometimes I sing when I've light, but not in the dark: I dare not sing then."

It was by the labor of children under such conditions that Lord Melbourne acquired the fortune which enabled him to be civilized and charming. Castlereagh, as Lord Londonderry, was a very important mine-owner. Indeed, the chief difference between mines and cotton was that many of the leading aristocrats of both parties were directly interested in the mines, and they showed themselves quite as callous as the most brutal self-made mill-owners. The agony of tortured children is an undertone to the elegant conversation of Holland House.

I have spoken of the children, because that is the most terrible aspect of industrialism a hundred years ago. But such sufferings for children would have been impossible unless their parents had been in a condition of despair. Hours for adults were almost incredibly long, wages very low, and housing conditions abominable. Industrial workers, many of whom had till recently lived in the country, were herded together in new, ill-built, smoky, and insanitary towns, some even lived in cellars, and cholera and typhus were endemic. Skilled handicraftsmen were reduced to destitution by the new machines; weavers, who had formerly been prosperous, could only earn 6s. 6d. a week. Combinations among wage-earners were illegal until 1824, and though trade unions existed, they were necessarily small and ineffectual so long as they had to be kept secret. The Government employed spies whose business it was to induce poor men to utter revolutionary sentiments. The spies themselves, with great trouble, organized little movements, and their dupes were hanged or transported.

The men guilty of these atrocities were human beings: you and I share their human nature, and might, I suppose, in other circumstances, have done as they did. Meanwhile their grandchildren protest, in the name of humanity, against what is done in Soviet Russia, and inflict savage sentences upon men who attempt to prevent the recurrence of some of the old evils in the young industrialism of India.

SECTION B   THE PHILOSOPHICAL RADICALS

CHAPTER VIII

MALTHUS

THINKING is not one of the natural activities of man; it is a product of disease, like a high temperature in illness. In France before the Revolution, and in England in the early nineteenth century, the disease in the body politic caused certain men to think important thoughts, which developed into the science of political economy. This science, in combination with the philosophy of Bentham and the psychology which James Mill learnt from Hartley, produced the school of Philosophical Radicals, who dominated British politics for fifty years. They were a curious set of men: rather uninteresting, quite without what is called "vision," prudent, rational, arguing carefully from premises which were largely false to conclusions which were in harmony with the interests of the middle class. John Stuart Mill, their last representative, had less brains than Bentham or Malthus or Ricardo, but surpassed them in imagination and sympathy, with the result that he failed to remain orthodox and even allowed himself to coquette with Socialism. But the founders of the sect, like Mr. Murdstone in *David Copperfield*, would tolerate no weakness.

Adam Smith, the founder of British economics, falls outside our period, since the *Wealth of Nations* was published in 1776. He was important because of the doctrine of *laissez faire* which he took over from the French, and because he first set forth the argument in favor of free trade. But he has not the qualities possessed by the founders of sects. He is sensible, moderate, unsystematic; he always admits limitations, as, for example, in his famous argument for the Navigation Acts on the ground that defence is more important than opulence. He is a pleasant old gentleman, with the comfortable eighteenth-century characteristic of holding no doctrine more firmly than a gentleman should. He did, however, believe, within the boundaries of common sense, that the interests of the individual and of society are, broadly speaking, in harmony, and that enlightened self-interest dictates the same conduct as would be dictated by benevolence. This principle was used later to prove that the self-interest of the manufacturer is in accordance with the true interest of the community, and that the interest of the community must be identical with the true interest of the wage-earner. It followed that when the wage-earner resisted the employer, he was foolish.

More important for our period, and indeed for the world, is Malthus, whose *Essay on the Principle of Population* (1st ed. 1798; 2nd ed. 1803) has profoundly affected all subsequent theory and practice. Malthus, though he was born in 1766, seems to have never shared the optimism which was common before 1789. Characteristically, when Pitt, at the age of 24, became Prime Minister in 1783, Malthus was shocked that so young a man should hold so important an office, while his father thought otherwise. His father was a perfectionist, a friend of Rousseau, some say his executor, though this appears to be an error; he was an ardent admirer of Godwin's *Political Justice* and of Condorcet's *Progrès de l'esprit humain*. He was fond of disputation, and used to encourage his family to set up theses and argue them with him. His son, who was temperamentally annoyed by his belief in progress, invented, at first as a mere weapon in argument, what Bagehot describes as "an apparatus for destroying cheerfulness." This weapon turned out so potent that Malthus adopted it for good and all. It was his famous theory of population.

It was true that there was much occasion for gloom in 1797, when Malthus first thought of his theory. The French Revolution had passed, through the Terror, to the corrupt and uninspiring rule of the *Directoire*. Liberal ideas were almost dead in England; taxes and poverty were increasing side by side; patriots had not yet had the satisfaction of Nelson's victories; the Navy was in a state of mutiny; the Radicals had been imprisoned by Pitt, but Ireland was on the threshold of the rebellion of 1798. It was not difficult to foresee a long war, a long tyranny, hunger and periodical famine, the extinction of all the hopes out of which the French Revolution had grown. Gloomy doctrines were the order of the day, and Malthus set to work to supply them.

His Essay, as it first appeared in 1798, was a rather slight work, almost wholly deductive. Between that date and 1803, he travelled extensively in Europe, collecting facts everywhere in support of his thesis. The result, in the second edition, was a book which is impressive by its massiveness, and by the appearance which it presents of inductive support from all the countries of the world. The Table of Contents alone is formidable: "Population in Russia," "Population in Sweden," "Population in Germany," and so on. By this time the reader is already half convinced of whatever may follow.

The essence of Malthus's doctrine is simplicity itself. If nothing checked the growth of population, it would double every twenty years or so; in a hundred years it would be 32 times what it is now, in two hundred years 1,024 times, in three hundred years 32,768 times, and so on. Clearly this sort of thing does not happen, and cannot happen. Why?

There are, says Malthus, only three ways in which the population can be kept down; they are: moral restraint, vice, and misery. Of moral restraint on a large scale he has little hope until all the population shall have been educated in the true principles of political economy. Of "vice" he cannot, as a clergyman, speak otherwise than in terms of reprobation; moreover, while he admits that it may have been an important check to population at certain periods such as that of the Roman Empire, he does not expect it, at most times, to be very effective. He proves that the losses caused by epidemics are soon made good, and he concludes that misery is the chief preventive of excessive population. It is because people die of hunger that the population is not greater than it is.

But, it may be said, if there are more people to work the land, it can be made to produce more food. Why then should an increase of numbers cause any one to starve? At this point, the argument depends upon what was afterwards called the law of diminishing returns. If twice as much labor as before is expended on a given piece of land, and also twice as much capital, the produce will be increased, but it will not be doubled. If the labor and capital are expended upon a piece of land which previously lay waste, the result, in general, will be the same, since it may be assumed that the best land is cultivated first. All this, of course, is not true when the population is very sparse; pioneers in a new country tend to be benefited by the arrival of new settlers. But in an old settled country, such as those of Europe, it is in general true that, if the population is increased without any concomitant progress in the art of agriculture, the amount of food per head will be diminished. There comes at last a point at which, if the population were further increased, one man's labor would produce less than one man's food. At this point, hunger sets a limit to possible increase.

Those who form the poorest class in a society must, so Malthus contends, be as poor as is compatible with survival, since otherwise their numbers would increase until that point had been reached. There may be short exceptional periods, as, for example, after the Black Death, but they cannot last long, since more children will survive until the old condition is restored. It is therefore a good thing that some are richer than others, for, in any system of equality, all would be at the lowest level; on this ground he rejects the schemes of Godwin, Owen, and other reformers. "It is absolutely certain," he says, "that the *only* mode consistent with the laws of morality and religion, of giving to the poor the largest share of the property of the rich, without sinking the whole community in misery, is the exercise on the part of the poor of prudence in marriage, and of economy both before and after it." Malthus thus makes a clean sweep of all schemes of human amelioration which fail to tackle the population problem. And this problem must be tackled by "moral restraint"; other methods, which have become associated with his name, he speaks of with horror as "improper arts."

Malthus, naturally, objects to the Poor Laws, though he does not think they can be abolished suddenly. It is impossible, he says, to prevent poverty; it would be possible to make the poor rich and the rich poor, but some are bound to be poor so long as the present proportion of food to population continues. If the poor rate were made higher, that would not enable each laborer to have his share of meat: the amount of meat in the country would be the same, and since there is not enough for every one, the price would go up.

He does not believe in the possibility of Europe obtaining any considerable part of its food-supply from other continents. "In the wildness of speculation," he says, "it has been suggested (of course more in jest than in earnest) that Europe should grow its corn in America, and devote itself solely to manufactures and commerce, as the best sort of division of the labour of the globe."

There is only one hope for the working classes, and that is education as a means of inculcating moral restraint. It should seem that the process of educating men up to the degree of "moral restraint" demanded by the combination of Malthus's economics and ethics might be somewhat lengthy. Nevertheless, he agreed with almost all the other reformers of his time in regarding popular education as essential to any radical improvement. Some men object to education, he says, on the ground that the poor, if taught to read, would read Tom Paine; but for his part he agrees with Adam Smith that the more they are educated the less likely they are to be led away by inflammatory writings.

There is, he maintains, no *right* to support: if a man cannot live by his own exertions, or if a child cannot live by the exertions of its parents, the community is under no obligation to provide subsistence.

But as it appears clearly, both from theory and experience, that, if the claim were allowed, it would soon increase beyond the possibility of satisfying it; and that the practical attempt to do so would involve the human race in the most wretched and universal poverty; it follows necessarily that our conduct, which denies the right, is more suited to the present state of our being, than our declamations which allow it.

The great Author of nature, indeed, with that wisdom which is apparent in all his works, has not left this conclusion to the cold and speculative consideration of general consequences. By making the passion of self-love beyond comparison stronger than the passion of benevolence, he has at once impelled us to that line of conduct, which is essential to the preservation of the human race.

The advantages to the community which flow from individual selfishness are repeatedly emphasized by Malthus; it is for this reason that a beneficent Providence has made us all such egoists. But the egoism that does good is of a special kind: it is prudent, calculating, and self-restrained, not impulsive or thoughtless. Malthus himself had three children in the first four years of his marriage, and after that no more, owing, one presumes, to "moral restraint." Mrs. Malthus's opinion of the principle of population is not recorded.

Owing largely to Malthus, British Philosophical Radicalism, unlike the Radicalism of all other ages and countries, laid more stress on prudence than on any other virtue; it was cold at heart, and hostile to the life of the emotions. At all points it was the antithesis of romantic mediaevalism. Malthus was, of course, bitterly attacked, but the attacks were all based on sentiment or on orthodox religion. In repelling theological attacks he was in a strong position, being himself a clergyman free from the remotest suspicion of heresy. In repelling attacks based upon sentiment, he had only to appeal to the patent facts as they existed in England at that time. To his contemporaries, no reasoned refutation of his theory appeared possible, with the result that all who were capable of being influenced by argument came to agree with him. For the first eighty years from the publication of his Essay, he profoundly influenced opinion; since then, he has influenced the birth-rate, though in ways which he would have deplored. His influence on opinion declined as his influence on the birth-rate increased, but the latter is even more important than the former. If a man's greatness is to be measured by his effect upon human life, few men have been greater than Malthus.

To judge what was true and what false in the doctrine of Malthus is possible now as it was not in his own day. Great Britain, during the Napoleonic wars, was compelled to rely almost entirely upon home-grown food; there was wide-spread misery, and the population was rapidly increasing. The Poor Law, since it gave relief in proportion to the number of children in a family, appeared to afford a direct incentive to improvident marriages. It was thought, until recently, that the rapid increase of population [1] at that time was due to an increase in the birth-rate, but it is now generally held that the main cause was a diminution in the death-rate. It may seem strange that the death-rate should have diminished during so painful a period, but the fact seems indubitable. The causes enumerated by Clapham [2]

---

[1] The first census of Great Britain (without Ireland) was in 1801. The figures of the first four censuses were:

| 1801 | .... | 10,943,000 | 1821 | .... | 14,392,000 |
| 1811 | .... | 12,597,000 | 1831 | .... | 16,539,000 |

[2] Clapham, *Economic History of Modern Britain* (1926), Vol. I, p. 55.

are: "The conquest of small-pox, the curtailment of agueish disorders through drainage, the disappearance of scurvy as a disease of the land, improvements in obstetrics leading to a reduction in the losses both of infant and of maternal life in childbed, the spreading of hospitals, dispensaries and medical schools." The birth-rate was slightly less in 1811 than in 1790, and neither the Poor Law nor child labor in factories appears to have affected it.

Whatever may have been the cause of the increase of population, the fact of the increase became undeniable as soon as the results of the second census, that of 1811, were known. Now Malthus is unquestionably in the right in maintaining that, apart from technical improvements in agriculture, a limited area, such as that of Great Britain, which has already a considerable population, cannot produce the food needed for a larger population without a lowering of the standard of life, and must, if population continues to increase, soon reach the point where a further increase is impossible from lack of food. Ultimately, this proposition is true not only of Great Britain, but of the world. There are parts of the world—China, for instance— where its truth is evident and tragic.

But since Malthus wrote, the limitations to the truth of his theory have turned out to be unexpectedly important. Railways and steamships brought it about that "Europe should grow its corn in America," which Malthus thought a mere jest. Technical improvements in agriculture have proved far more important than he supposed possible. But above all the increased prosperity of wage-earners, so far from leading to a higher birth-rate, led to a very rapid diminution, which was still further accelerated when, after the Great War, the standard of comfort again declined. This is perhaps not a refutation of anything that Malthus said, but it has destroyed the importance of his theory so far as the white races are concerned. In Asia it remains important.

CHAPTER IX

BENTHAM

THE Philosophical Radicals were commonly known as the Benthamites, and most of them regarded Jeremy Bentham as their leader; it is doubtful, however, whether he would ever have occupied this position but for the intervention of James Mill. He is certainly one of the most singular characters in history. Born in 1748, he might have been expected to have belonged to an earlier period than that with which we are concerned. The fact is, however, that his long life (he died in 1832) is divided into three phases, of which the third and most important began when he was already an old man; in fact, he was sixty years old when he became converted to the principle of democracy.

His antecedents were not such as to make it probable that he would be a reformer. His family were Jacobite, but had sufficient prudence not to become involved in either the '15 or the '45. His grandfather made money in business, and his father was well off throughout his life. He took great pains with Jeremy's education, which apparently served, to some extent, as a model for John Stuart Mill's. At the age of seven Jeremy was sent to Westminster School; at the age of twelve he went to Oxford, and at fifteen he took his B.A. His father, who was an arrant snob, wished him to associate with lords and grand people at the university, and was always willing to supply him with the extra pocket money required for gambling when in their society. But Jeremy was a shy boy, and preferred books to play. Like Malthus, though in a different way, he reversed the usual relation of father and son: while the father urged frivolous pleasures, the boy insisted upon industry and sobriety. To please his father, he was called to the Bar; to please himself, he wrote on law reform instead of practising law. He fell in love, but his father, though he had displeased *his* father by a love-match which had turned out perfectly happy, objected to Jeremy's choice because she was not rich. Jeremy gave her up rather than devote himself to money-making, but he suffered severely. His letters to his brother, which were very intimate, show him at this time as assuming a devil-may-care cynicism, something of which, in a pedantic and purely theoretical form, survives in his later philosophy. To those who only knew him in later life, he was a kindly eccentric, almost unbelievably shy, and completely imprisoned in a self-imposed routine; but in this is to be seen, I think, the abiding influence of his conflicts with his father and his renunciation of emotional happiness.[1]

Robert Owen, who made his acquaintance in 1813 in spite of Bentham's aversion to meeting strangers, has left an account of their first meeting:

"After some preliminary communication with our mutual friends James Mill and Francis Place, his then two chief counsellors, and some correspondence between him and myself, it was at length arrived at that I was to come to his hermit-like retreat at a particular hour, and that I was, upon entering, to proceed upstairs, and we were to meet half-way upon the stairs. I pursued these instructions, and he, in great trepidation, met me, and taking my hand, while his whole frame was agitated with the excitement, he hastily said— 'Well! well! It is all over. We are introduced. Come into my study!' "

Fifteen years later he met Owen's son, and at parting said: "God bless you, if there be such a being, and at all events, my young friend, take care of yourself."

In 1814 and the three following years, Bentham spent half his time at an old house called Ford Abbey, in Devonshire, where, by his own account, life was spent in a round of gaieties:

It is the theatre of great felicity to a number of people, and that not very inconsiderable. Not an angry word is ever heard in it. Mrs. S. (the housekeeper) governs like an angel. Neighbours all highly cordial, even though not visited. Music and dancing, though I hate dancing. Gentle and simple mix. Crowds come and dance, and Mrs. S. at the head of them.

But Francis Place's account is, I fear, nearer the truth:

[1] He made an unvarying practice of walking round his garden before breakfast and after dinner. These walks he described as his "ante-jentacular and post-prandial circumambulations."

All our days are alike, so an account of one may do for all. Mill is up between five and six; he and John compare his proofs, John reading the copy and his father the proof. Willie and Clara are in the saloon before seven, and as soon as the proofs are done with, John goes to the farther end of the room to teach his sisters. When this has been done, and part of the time while it is doing, he learns geometry; this continues to nine o'clock, when breakfast is ready.

Mr. Bentham rises soon after seven, and about eight gets to his employment. I rise at six and go to work; at nine breakfast in the parlour— present, Mrs. Mill, Mill, I, John and Colls.

Breakfast ended, Mill hears Willie and Clara, and then John. Lessons are heard under a broad balcony, walking from end to end, the breakfast parlour on one hand and pots of flowers rising one above another as high as your head on the other hand; this place is in the front of the Abbey. All the lessons and readings are performed aloud, and occupy full three hours, say till one o'clock.

From nine to twelve Mr. Bentham continues working; from twelve to one he performs upon an organ in the saloon.

From breakfast time to one o'clock I am occupied in learning Latin; this is also done aloud in the walks, and already I have conquered the substantives and adjectives. During this period Colls, who is a good boy, gets a lesson of Latin from Mill, and of French from me: his is a capital situation for a boy of genius.

At one we all three walk in the lanes and fields for an hour. At two all go to work again till dinner at six, when Mrs. Mill, Mill, Bentham, I, and Colls, dine together. We have soup or fish, or both, meat, pudding, generally fruit, viz. melons, strawberries, gooseberries, currants, grapes; no wine. The first day I came, wine was put upon the table; but as I took none, none has since made its appearance. After dinner, Mill and I take a sharp walk for two hours, say, till a quarter past eight, then one of us alternately walks with Mr. Bentham for an hour; then comes tea, at which we read the periodical publications; and eleven o'clock comes but too soon, and we all go to bed.

Mrs. Mill marches in great style round the green in front of the house for about half an hour before breakfast and again after dinner with all the children, till their bed-time.

The intellectual influences which formed Bentham's mind were mainly French. Hume, it is true, influenced his philosophy, and Hartley, by the principle of association, influenced his psychology. His ethical first principle, almost in his own words, is to be found in Hutcheson's *Inquiry concerning moral good and evil*. The moral evil of a given action, according to Hutcheson, "is as the *Degree* of Misery, and *Number* of Sufferers; so that, *that Action* is *best*, which accomplishes the *Greatest Happiness* for the *Greatest Number*." [2] But it was the French pre-Revolution philosophers who formed the tone of his mind. He admired Voltaire, and was an enthusiastic follower of Helvetius. He read Helvetius in 1769, and immediately determined to devote his life to the principles of legislation. "What Bacon was to the physical world, Helvetius was to the moral. The moral world has therefore had its Bacon; but its Newton is yet to come." It is not hazardous to surmise that Bentham aspired to be the Newton of the moral world.

When he came to know Beccaria *On Crimes and Punishments*, he thought even more highly of him than of Helvetius:

"Oh, my master," he exclaimed, "first evangelist of Reason, you who have raised your Italy so far above England, and I would add above France, were it not that Helvetius, without writing on the subject of laws, had already assisted you and had provided you with your fundamental ideas; you who speak reason about laws, when in France there was spoken only jargon: a jargon, however, which was reason itself as compared with the English jargon; you who have made so many useful excursions into the path of utility, what is there left for us to do?—Never to turn aside from that path." [3]

His journey to Paris in 1770, at the age of twenty-two, served to confirm French influence; indeed he remained throughout his life, in many respects, a French philosopher of the age of Louis XVI. The only other journey which had any effect upon him was his visit to Russia in 1785. His brother Samuel (afterwards General Sir Samuel Bentham) was employed by the Empress Catherine in an attempt to modernize Russian agriculture, a task which proved as difficult then as now. Jeremy had hopes that Catherine would introduce a scientific penal code drawn up by himself: "In Russia," he wrote, "as much pains has been taken to make men think as in some governments to prevent them to think." [4] But unfortunately his brother, who had been doing well at Court, wished to marry

---

[2] Quoted by Halévy, *The Growth of Philosophic Radicalism*, p. 13.
[3] *Ibid.*, p. 21.
[4] Everatt, *The Education of Bentham*, p. 153.

a lady-in-waiting, which Catherine regarded as presumption; he therefore fell into disfavor, and Jeremy and codification along with him.

Wherever Bentham might be, whether on the Black Sea, or in his chambers, or at Queen Square Place, he always wrote voluminously every day. What he had written he put away carefully in pigeon holes, and there it remained unless some kind friend retrieved it. The consequence was that in England he remained obscure, and such work as he did publish attracted little attention. In 1788, however, he met the Genevese Dumont, who became his enthusiastic disciple, secured manuscripts from him, translated them into French, and caused them to become widely known on the Continent. Moreover Dumont supplied the material for the speeches of Mirabeau, who was too busy making love and eluding creditors to have time for research. Long extracts from Bentham were published by Dumont in Mirabeau's paper, the *Courrier de Province*. In 1789, Bentham wrote to Mirabeau:

I am proud, as becomes me, of your intentions in my favour. I look out with impatience for the period of their accomplishment. Meanwhile, in addition to the honour of calling the Comte de Mirabeau my translator and reviewer, permit me that of styling myself his correspondent.

So great was his fame in France that the Assembly elected him a French citizen. But he was still a Tory, and soon became disgusted with the Revolution; and at about the same time, the Revolution forgot him. Elsewhere, however, his reputation increased steadily. Alexander's liberal minister Speransky greatly admired him; Alexander, in 1814, asked him to help in drafting a code. In Spain, and throughout Latin America, he was revered. The Cortes voted that his works should be printed at the public expense. Borrow, in *The Bible in Spain*, tells how he was arrested in a remote part of Galicia for selling the scriptures, but was immediately liberated when the magistrate found he was a countryman of "the grand Baintham." Aaron Burr, former Vice-President of the United States, invited him to come to Mexico, where the one was to be Emperor and the other was to be legislator. (It does not appear what the Mexicans thought of the scheme.) He thought of going to Caracas, to enjoy the climate and make a penal code for Venezuela. There was no end to his fame in distant regions. As Hazlitt says:

Mr. Bentham is one of those persons who verify the old adage, that "A prophet has most honour out of his own country." His reputation lies at the circumference; and the lights of his understanding are reflected, with increasing lustre, on the other side of the globe. His name is little known in England, better in Europe, best of all in the plains of Chili and the mines of Mexico. He has offered constitutions for the New World, and legislated for future times. The people of Westminster, where he lives, hardly dream of such a person; but the Siberian savage has received cold comfort from his lunar aspect, and may say to him with Caliban— "I know thee, and thy dog and thy bush!" The tawny Indian may hold out the hand of fellowship to him across the GREAT PACIFIC. We believe that the Empress Catherine corresponded with him; and we know that the Emperor Alexander called upon him, and presented him with his miniature in a gold snuff-box, which the philosopher, to his eternal honour, returned. Mr. Hobhouse is a greater man at the hustings, Lord Rolle at Plymouth Dock; but Mr. Bentham would carry it hollow, on the score of popularity, at Paris or Pegu. The reason is, that our author's influence is purely intellectual. He has devoted his life to the pursuit of abstract and general truths, and to those studies—

"That waft a *thought* from Indus to the Pole"—

and has never mixed himself up with personal intrigues or party politics. He once, indeed, stuck up a handbill to say that he (Jeremy Bentham) being of sound mind, was of opinion that Sir Samuel Romilly was the most proper person to represent Westminster; but this was the whim of the moment. Otherwise, his reasonings, if true at all, are true everywhere alike: his speculations concern humanity at large, and are not confined to the hundred or the bills of mortality. It is in moral as in physical magnitude. The little is seen best near: the great appears in its proper dimensions, only from a more commanding point of view, and gains strength with time, and elevation from distance!

Mr. Bentham is very much among philosophers what La Fontaine was among poets:—in general habits and in all but his professional pursuits, he is a mere child. He has lived for the last forty years in a house in Westminster, overlooking the Park, like an anchoret in his cell, reducing law to a system, and the mind of man to a machine. He scarcely ever goes out, and sees very little company. The favoured few, who have the privilege of the *entrée*, are always admitted one by one. He does not like to have witnesses to his conversation. He talks a great deal, and listens to nothing but facts.

Bentham, meanwhile, had become involved in the unfortunate project which filled the middle period of his life with bitterness and financial embarrassment. He (or perhaps his brother) invented a new sort of prison, called a "Panopticon," which was to be in the shape of a star, so that a jailer sitting in the middle could see the door of every cell; nay, by a combined system of mirrors and blinds, the jailer is to see the prisoner while the prisoner cannot see the jailer. He thought the same idea could be applied to factories, hospitals, asylums, and schools. There were those who objected to this plan, except in the case of prisons, in the name of liberty. But Bentham believed happiness to be the goal, not liberty, and he was not convinced that liberty is necessary to happiness. "Call them soldiers, call them monks, call them machines, so they were but happy ones, I should not care. Wars and storms are best to read of, but peace and calms are better to endure." [5]

It must not be supposed that Bentham, at any time, confined himself wholly to the *Panopticon;* his activities were always multifarious; for example, in 1800 he invented a *frigidarium.* But for many years the *Panopticon* was his main pre-occupation, and he did everything in his power to induce the British Government to construct at least one prison according to his plans. He secured a half-promise, bought land for the purpose, found that the Government had changed its mind, and lost the bulk of his fortune. He attributed his failure to the personal influence of George III, and there are those who regard this as the cause of his later republicanism. In other times and places his scheme was approved; the Emperor Alexander had a panopticon built in St. Petersburg, and the State of Illinois had one constructed in 1920. But the British Government remained obdurate. At length, in 1813, he was awarded £20,000 to compensate him for expenses incurred as a result of governmental encouragement. But already in 1808 he had entered upon the third and most important phase of his life by his alliance with James Mill.

When Bentham became a Radical, he made no change in his gen-

---

[5] Elie Halévy, *The Growth of Philosophic Radicalism*, p. 84.

eral philosophy, which remained just what it had been in his youth. He was not a profound philosopher, but he was clear and logical and quite sure of his own rightness. His philosophy had two foundations, one psychological, the other ethical. He states these succinctly in a note written only for his own benefit:

Association Principle. Hartley. The bond of connection between ideas and language: and between ideas and ideas. *Greatest Happiness Principle*. Priestley. Applied to every branch of morals in detail, by Bentham: a part of the way previously by Helvetius.

There is something to be said about each of these principles.

The "association principle," which Bentham attributes to Hartley, is the familiar "association of ideas," which caused me, in speaking to Mr. Upton Sinclair, to say: "I hope Mrs. Lewis is well." Sometimes the consequences of the principle are less unhappy, as when the sight of beef makes you think of beer. As every one knows, association gives a method of catching criminals. You are examining, let us say, a man whom you suspect of having cut his wife's throat with a knife. You say a word, and he is to say the first other word that comes into his head. You say "cat" and he says "dog;" you say "politician" and he says "thief;" you say "knife," and he has an impulse to say "throat," but knows he had better not, so after long hesitation he says "fork." The length of time shows his resistance.

So far, the matter is a commonplace. But some have thought that all mental processes could be explained by association, and that psychology could be made scientific by the use of this principle alone. This doctrine Bentham learnt from Hartley. Hume, who was a greater man that any of his British or French successors, had, before Hartley, done what seemed to him possible in the same direction. Hume thought of all the things that his followers thought of, showed what reason there was to think them true, and then proceeded to show that after all they were not quite true. This annoyed his followers, who wished to derive a dogma from skepticism; they therefore always gave Hume less credit than he deserved. What Hartley invented was not the principle of association, but its undue extension to cover all mental phenomena.

It should be observed that, on this question, the situation in psychology is unchanged since the time of Bentham, except for a variation of phraseology. Instead of the "principle of association" we now speak of the "conditioned reflex," and we regard the effects of experience as operating primarily, not upon "ideas," but upon muscles, glands, nerves, and brain. Pavlov has shown that the principle can do much, and Watson has asserted that it can do everything. But until he has explained why the word "pepper" does not make you sneeze, his system must be regarded as uncompleted.

This is one important difference between associationism and behaviorism. The latter concerns, primarily, what is done by the body; the former concerned what was done by the mind. The associationists were inclined to deny the existence of matter, but not of mind. The poet, it is true, has said:

> Stuart Mill both mind and matter
> Ruthlessly would beat and batter,

but he was much less ruthless to mind than to matter. With the behaviorist, the opposite is the case: he believes in matter, but thinks mind an unnecessary hypothesis.

In so far as the principle of the conditioned reflex differs from that of the association of ideas, there has been a definite scientific advance. The new law covers all that was covered by the old, and a good deal more. It cannot be questioned that the old law was true over a certain field, nor that the new law is true over a wider field which includes the field of the old law. It is not the truth of either law, but its scope, that is legitimate matter of debate: some say that all mental phenomena are covered by it, while others maintain that there are kinds of thought of which the laws are different. This controversy remains substantially where it was a hundred and thirty years ago.

There is an important respect in which associationism and behaviorism have exactly similar consequences. Both are deterministic, that is to say, they think that what we do is governed by laws which are, at least in great part, ascertainable, so that our actions in given circumstances can be predicted by a good psychologist. So Bentham, one may suppose, said to himself: "The criminal is the product of circumstances, and if certain circumstances have made him bad, there must be others which would make him good. I need only, therefore, invent the right kind of prison, and it will automatically turn thieves into honest men." In like manner, the behaviorist thinks that the problem of producing virtuous children is merely one of creating the right conditioned reflexes. In the laboratory, when the dog does what you want, you give him food; when he does the opposite, you give him an electric shock. The same method applied to children, we are assured, will soon turn them into models of good behavior. I have not found due credit for this discovery given to Mr. Wackford Squeers.

The "greatest happiness principle" was the most famous formula of the Benthamite school. According to this principle, actions are good when they promote the greatest happiness of the greatest number, and bad when they do not. Why, in the passage quoted above, Bentham should have attributed this principle specially to Priestley, I do not know. As we have seen, it was stated almost exactly in Bentham's words by Hutcheson at a much earlier date, and in one form or another it had come to be accepted by most British and French philosophers. Priestley, as every one knows, was a Unitarian divine, a chemist, and a Radical. He constructed a highly rationalized scheme of theology, he more or less discovered oxygen, and he stood by the French Revolution even in its worst days. On this account, the Birmingham mob wrecked his house, while he, very wisely, fled to America. He was a most praiseworthy citizen, but he had no special claim to be the inventor of the greatest happiness principle.

Between Bentham's ethics and his psychology there was something of a conflict. While a good act is one which furthers the general happiness, it is, according to him, a psychological law that every man pursues his own happiness. Since this is a thing which people cannot help doing, it would be mere waste of breath to blame them for it; it is, however, the business of the legislator to arrange that a man's private happiness shall be secured by acts that are in the public interest. This is the principle which inspires all Bentham's legal work.

There are, however, according to him, various reasons which make this artificial identification of private and public interests less frequently necessary than might have been supposed. As many previous writers had pointed out, there is sympathy, which makes the spectacle of another man's pain painful. But in addition to this, it will be found (so all the economists of that period contended) that, as a general rule, a man can best further the general interest by pursuing his own. This doctrine, which afforded the theoretical justification of *laissez faire*, arose, like some other very sober doctrines, out of a *jeu d'esprit*. Mandeville, in his *Fable of the Bees*, which appeared in 1723, developed, not too solemnly, his doctrine of "private vices, public benefits," in which he maintained that it is by our selfishness that we promote the good of the community. Economists and moralists appropriated this doctrine, while explaining that Mandeville should not have spoken of "private *vices*," since egoism could only be accounted a vice by those who had failed to grasp the true principles of psychology. Thus the doctrine of the natural harmony of interests, not as an absolute truth without exceptions, but as a broad general principle, came to be adopted by all the advocates of *laissez faire*. We shall see, later, how Ricardo unwittingly gave it its death-blow, and laid the foundations for the opposite doctrine of the class war.

The ethic based upon the greatest happiness principle, which came to be known as utilitarianism, was, when taken seriously, somewhat opposed to orthodox moral teaching. It is true that eminent divines, such as Bishop Butler, had adopted the principle, and that, until it became the watchword of the Radicals, no one found it objectionable. But any theory which judges the morality of an act by its consequences can only by a fortunate accident agree with the conventional view, according to which certain classes of acts are sinful without regard to their effects. No doubt the precept "Thou shalt not steal" is, in general, very sound, but it is easy to imagine circumstances in which a theft might further the general happiness. In a utilitarian system, all moral rules of the ordinary kind are liable to exceptions. Bentham was a free-thinker, and so were his leading disciples; it was therefore natural to accuse them of immoral teaching. There was, in fact, much less of such accusation than might have been expected, partly because the leaders of the school were cautious in propounding their doctrines, and partly because their private lives were singularly blameless. Although their teaching was fundamentally subversive, they continued to be regarded as on the whole respectable.

Bentham did not distinguish between pleasure and happiness, and resolutely refused to assign a qualitative superiority to what are called "higher" pleasures. As he put it, "quantity of pleasure being equal, pushpin is as good as poetry." None the less, his doctrine was, in practice, almost ascetic. He held that self-approbation is the greatest of pleasures. Since men tend to value present pleasures more than pleasures in the future, the wise man will exercise prudence and self-restraint. On the whole, he and his disciples sought happiness in hard work and an almost complete indifference to all pleasures of sense. This, no doubt, was a matter of temperament, not to be explained as a deduction from the doctrine; but the result was that their morality was quite as severe as that of their orthodox opponents.

CHAPTER X

JAMES MILL

IT was chiefly through the instrumentality of James Mill that Bentham became a force in English politics, and a great deal of the personality of this hard-headed Scotchman passed into the character of British Radicalism. He was born in 1773, twenty-five years later than Bentham; his father was a small tradesman, and he owed his education to a patron, Sir John Stuart, who was struck by the boy's abilities. It was intended that he should become a minister, but by the time his education was finished he had ceased to believe in the Christian religion. He came to London in 1802, and must have been at that time by no means a Radical, since he contributed to the *Anti-Jacobin*. He lived by journalism, and spent his leisure in educating his son and writing a history of India. His history, begun in 1806, was published in 1818, and led to his being employed by the East India Company throughout the remainder of his life. From 1808 to 1818 he depended largely on Bentham's bounty. In the garden of Queen Square Place, where Bentham lived, there was a small house which had belonged to Milton; for a while, Bentham lent that house to James Mill, but later on he took another house, near his own, on purpose to let it to Mill for half what he himself paid for it. In the summer, if Bentham went away from London, Mill usually came with him.

Mill had become a Radical before he met Bentham; in psychology he was a disciple of Hartley, in economics he accepted Malthus and was a close friend of Ricardo, in politics he was an extreme democrat and a doctrinaire believer in *laissez faire*. He was not an original thinker, but he was clear and vigorous, and had the unquestioning faith of the born disciple, with the disciple's utter contempt for doctrines at variance with the Master's. "I see clearly enough what poor Kant is about," he wrote, after a brief attempt to read that philosopher. Like all his kind, he greatly admired Helvetius, from whom he accepted the current doctrine of the omnipotence of education. His

94

eldest son, John Stuart, born in the year in which he began his history of India, afforded suitable material for exemplifying the truth of Helvetius's theories. The victim's autobiography, one of the most interesting books ever written, tells the result, and incidentally reveals the character of James Mill.

His capacity for work must have been amazing. He would spend the day at his desk writing his History, while his son John, in the same room, was learning his lessons, with the right of asking for explanations whenever it might be necessary. The whole of John's education was conducted by his father. He began Greek, he tells us, at the age of three, "committing to memory what my father termed vocables, being lists of common Greek words, with their signification in English, which he wrote out for me on cards." He did not begin Latin until he was seven. In the same year he read six of Plato's dialogues, but did not fully understand the *Theaetetus*. He learned arithmetic at the same time; also an incredible amount of history. "When I came to the American war, I took my part, like a child as I was (until set right by my father) on the wrong side, because it was called the English side." For amusement, he had such books as *Anson's Voyages*. "Of children's books, any more than of playthings, I had scarcely any, except an occasional gift from a relation or acquaintance: among those I had, *Robinson Crusoe* was pre-eminent, and continued to delight me all through my boyhood. It was no part, however, of my father's system to exclude books of amusement, though he allowed them very sparingly."

From his eighth year onwards, John had not only to learn, but also to teach his younger brothers and sisters, who were numerous. Apart from the *Iliad* and *Odyssey*, Aeschylus, Sophocles, and Euripides, all the best Latin authors, a great deal of history, and a minute study of Roman Government, he had not time for much learning after instructing the younger members of the family; he seems to have mastered little else, before the age of twelve, except algebra and geometry, the differential calculus, and several other branches of higher mathematics.

It must not be supposed that John got no fun out of life. "During this part of my childhood," he says, "one of my greatest amusements was experimental science; in the theoretical, however, not the practical sense of the word; not trying experiments—a kind of discipline which

I have often regretted not having had—nor even seeing, but only reading about them."

At twelve years old he began logic, reading all that Aristotle had to say on the subject, several of the schoolmen, and Hobbes. In his times of recreation he used to walk with his father on Bagshot Heath, being instructed that he must not think the syllogistic logic silly, and taught how to reduce arguments to correct syllogistic form.

It was towards the end of John's thirteenth year that his father began to be employed by the East India Company, but John's education continued as before; in this very year, his father taught him all political economy.

At fourteen, the boy was considered to have reached a point where he ought to see something of the world, and he was sent abroad for over a year. Before he left the parental roof, his father, like Polonius on a similar occasion, gave him some good advice. The *exact* words are not recorded, but they appear to have been roughly as follows:

"John: until this moment, mindful of the fact that over-estimation of one's own merits is a grievous defect, I have carefully concealed from you the extent to which your intellectual attainments surpass those of most boys of your age. Now, however, in view of the year of foreign travel which I have decided to be for your welfare, you are certain to learn this fact from others, if not from me; some may even be so thoughtless as to pay you compliments, and suggest to your mind the erroneous belief that you possess exceptional abilities. In fact, whatever you know more than others cannot be ascribed to any merit in you, but to the very unusual advantage which has fallen to your lot, of having a father able to teach you, and willing to give the necessary trouble and time. That you know more than less fortunate boys, is no matter of praise; it would be a disgrace if you did not."

James Mill was passionately anti-Christian, and maintained that the orthodox God, if He existed, would be a Being of infinite cruelty. He seems, however, to have been unable wholly to divest himself, in his dealings with his son, of some of the God-like attributes of which he disapproved. John, who criticizes him with reluctance, says that he showed insufficient tenderness to his children. He adds immediately that he believes his father to have *felt* tenderness, but to have concealed it from reserve and dislike of emotional display; this, however, the reader feels inclined to doubt. John confesses that he himself had no affection for his father, since "fear of him was drying it up at its source." He adds that this must have been a grief to his father, and that the younger children, who had had John for their tutor, loved their father tenderly. Perhaps.

John, in later life, was perpetually discovering reasons for disagreeing with his father, but hesitating to take the step to actual disagreement; in his books, his father's ghost seems to stand over him whenever he is tempted to feel sentiment, saying: "Now, John, no weakness." James Mill was a good man; he worked hard, and devoted himself to public objects. But he ought not to have been let loose among children.

John's account of his father's outlook on life is interesting, the more so as James Mill, more exactly than any other individual, typified the whole Benthamite school in this respect.

In his views of life he partook of the character of the Stoic, the Epicurean, and the Cynic, not in the modern but the ancient sense of the word. In his personal qualities the Stoic predominated. His standard of morals was Epicurean, inasmuch as it was utilitarian, taking as the exclusive test of right and wrong, the tendency of actions to produce pleasure or pain. But he had (and this was the Cynic element) scarcely any belief in pleasure; at least in his later years, of which alone, on this point, I can speak confidently. He was not insensible to pleasures; but he deemed very few of them worth the price which, at least in the present state of society, must be paid for them. The greater number of miscarriages in life, he considered to be attributable to the over-valuing of pleasures. Accordingly, temperance, in the large sense intended by the Greek philosophers—stopping short at the point of moderation in all indulgences—was with him, as with them, almost the central point of educational precept. His inculcations of this virtue fill a large place in my childish remembrances. He thought human life a poor thing at best, after the freshness of youth and of unsatisfied curiosity had gone by. This was a topic on which he did not often speak, especially, it may be supposed, in the presence of young persons: but when he did, it was with an air of settled and profound conviction. He would sometimes say, that if life were made what it might be, by good government and good education, it would be worth having: but he never spoke with anything like enthusiasm even of that possibility. He never varied in rating intellectual enjoyments above all others, even in value as pleasures, independently of their ulterior benefits. The pleasures of the benevolent affections he placed high in the scale; and used to say, that he had never known a happy old man, except those who were able to live over again in the pleasures of the young. For passionate emotions of all sorts, and for everything which has been said or written in exaltation of them, he professed the greatest contempt. He regarded them as a form of madness. "The intense" was with him a by-word of scornful disapprobation. He regarded as an aberration of the moral standard of modern times, compared with that of the ancients, the great stress laid upon feeling.

The intellectual conviction that pleasure is the sole good, together with a temperamental incapacity for experiencing it, was characteristic of Utilitarians. From the point of view of the calculus of pleasures and pains, their emotional poverty was advantageous: they tended to think that pleasure could be measured by bank-account, and pain by fines or terms of imprisonment. Unselfish and stoical devotion to the doctrine that every man seeks only his own pleasure is a curious psychological paradox. Something not dissimilar was to be found in Lenin and his most sincere followers. Lenin held, apparently, that the good consists in abundance of material commodities; he was very scornful of all appeals to altruism, and believed, as firmly as the Benthamites, that economic self-interest governs men's economic activities. On behalf of this creed, he endured persecution, exile and poverty; when he rose to be the head of a great State he lived with Spartan simplicity; and from worship of material prosperity he plunged his country into many years of abysmal poverty. The Benthamites were not called upon for such heroic action, but their mentality is closely similar.

James Mill was a democrat, not because he felt himself downtrodden (for who would have dared to down-tread such a man?), nor yet from generous sympathy, with which nature had not endowed him in any large measure. He was a democrat, so far as can be judged, from a rational application of the felicific calculus. If you have a shilling to distribute among twelve children, you will, other things being equal, cause most happiness by giving them each a penny. If you gave a shilling to one, and nothing to the other eleven, the one would get ill from a surfeit of sweets, and the other eleven would be filled with envious rage. This, so far as it goes, is an argument for Communism, but Communism was vehemently opposed by all the Benthamites, because they considered competition a necessary spur to activity. No such argument applied to the distribution of political power. In view of the universal egoism, no man's interests could safely be entrusted to another, so that any class destitute of political power was sure to suffer injustice. Moreover, if the spur to useful activity is competition, all men should be exposed to it, and unjust privileges should be abolished. These arguments were such as Bentham could understand; combined with the failure of the *Panopticon*, they decided him to abandon Toryism and become a democrat.

The Utilitarians were unusually rational men, and had a firm belief in the rationality of the mass of mankind. "Every man possessed of reason," says James Mill, "is accustomed to weigh evidence, and to be guided and determined by its preponderance. When various conclusions are, with their evidence, presented with equal care and with equal skill, there is a moral certainty, though some few may be misguided, that the greater number will judge right, and that the greatest force of evidence, wherever it is, will produce the greatest impression." There is a happy innocency about this confession of faith; it belongs to the age before Freud and before the growth of the art of propaganda. Oddly enough, in Mill's day his confidence was justified by the event. The Benthamites, who were learned men and authors of difficult books, aimed solely at appealing to men's reason, and yet they were successful; in almost all important respects, the course of British politics down to 1874 was such as they advocated. In the Victorian era, this victory of reason surprised no one; in our more lunatic period, it reads like the myth of a Golden Age.

Bentham, as soon as he had accepted the argument for democracy, became more democratic than any of his school. He regarded the monarchy and the House of Lords as undesirable institutions, although, on this point, no one ventured publicly to agree with him. He failed even to find any argument against votes for women; on the contrary, he advanced many excellent arguments in favor, though without reaching a definite conclusion in print. He seems privately to have been rather favorable than unfavorable, for John Stuart Mill says, in giving an account of the opinions of the group of young men whom he influenced: "Every reason which exists for giving the suffrage to anybody, demands that it should not be withheld from women. This was also the general opinion of the younger proselytes; and it is pleasant to be able to say that Mr. Bentham, on this important point, was wholly on our side." With Mr. Bentham, however, this opinion remained academic; it was left to John Stuart Mill, in later life, to bring the question to the notice of Parliament as one of practical importance.

James Mill has a two-fold importance in the Benthamite movement. In the first place, he fashioned his son John as Hamilcar fashioned Hannibal. John, by his amiable and kindly disposition, was not designed by nature for such stern doctrine as that of the Philosophical Radicals; indeed, in later life he softened it at various points. But he retained the belief that his father's teaching was sound in the main, and this gave him a greater influence than he could have had if he had had to rely upon confidence in himself.

In the second place, James Mill, by his capacity for discipleship, combined a number of separate eminent men into a single school, and thereby immensely increased their collective influence. Most Radicals, not unnaturally, looked upon Malthus and his theory with suspicion; James Mill accepted the theory, and gave it a new twist. He and his friend Francis Place, the Radical tailor, were not affected by Malthus's clerical scruples, and therefore deduced, from his economic doctrine, the desirability of artificial checks to conception. What is called neo-Malthusianism begins with them. From them it spread, slowly and in spite of persecution, until, in our own day, it has put an end to the increase of population in the most civilized countries.

It was in the year 1812, through the instrumentality of James Mill, that Place was introduced to Bentham, who was thus brought into contact with a social layer and a kind of politics of which he had previously known little. Place treated Bentham with affectionate respect, addressing him in letters as "My dear old Father." Of Bentham's letters to Place, one, quoted by Graham Wallas in his *Life of Francis Place*, may serve as a sample. It concerns the precautions which Bentham took to conceal his hostility to Christianity and his belief (probably as a result of Place's persuasion) in neo-Malthusianism. The word "juggical," which occurs in it means "Christian." It is derived from "Juggernaut," which was used in that set to mean "Christianity," so that the subject could be mentioned before servants without giving occasion for scandal. The letter is as follows:

Queen's Square Place,
April 24, 1831, Sunday.

Dear Good Boy,

I have made an appointment for you; and you must absolutely keep it, or make another. It is to see Prentice, and hear him express his regrets for calling you a "bold bad man." (Oh, but the appointment it is for Tuesday, one o'clock, commencement of my circumgiration time.) I said you were a *bold* man, but denied your being a *bad* one, judging from near twenty years' intimacy. I asked him why he called you a bad man; his answer was because of the pains you had taken to disseminate your anti-over-population (I should have said your over-population-stopping) expedient. The case is, he is juggical; Calvinistic; is descended from two parsonical grandfathers of considerably notoriety. I observed to him that every man is master of his own actions, but no man of his own opinions; that on the point in question he was no less far from you than you from him; and that if every man were to quarrel with every man whose opinions did not on every point whatsoever coincide with his, the earth would not be long burdened with the human race. As to the point in question, I took care not to let him know how my opinion stood; the fat would have been all in the fire, unless I succeeded in converting him, for which there was no time; all I gave him to understand on the score of religion as to my own sentiments was, that I was for universal toleration; and on one or two occasions I quoted scripture. . . .

James Mill brought together Bentham and Malthus and Ricardo and the lower-middle-class Radicalism of Francis Place, who, in turn, was closely associated with the upper-class Radicalism of Sir Francis Burdett. The doctrine of Hartley and Helvetius, with such parts of Hume as could be fitted into a doctrinaire orthodoxy, gave the intellectual respectability of a philosophical basis to the excitement of the mob in the Westminster elections. In all this, James Mill's function was that of mortar, by which the separate bricks were combined into an edifice. It was a strange edifice, containing materials which no one could have expected to see in combination. Most Radical movements have been inspired either by sentiments of sympathy for the oppressed, or by hatred of oppressors. In James Mill's Radicalism, neither of these is prominent. He felt, undoubtedly, a universal benevolence, which appears, for example, in his opposition to what he regarded as cruel in theological orthodoxy. This emotion, however, was not very intense, and would have been pushed aside by stronger passions in any man of more intense feeling. In James Mill, benevolence supplied the emotional stimulus, but remained in the background, and at no point overpowered reason. He accepted without difficulty opinions according to which much suffering is inevitable; where those opinions were sound, this was a strength, but where they were false, a weakness. This strength and weakness characterized the Benthamite school throughout its history.

CHAPTER XI

RICARDO

RICARDO, unlike James Mill, is important through his doctrine alone, not through his personality. He was, by all accounts, a lovable man; John Stuart Mill alludes to him repeatedly as "my father's dearest friend," and says that "by his benevolent countenance, and kindliness of manner, [he] was very attractive to young persons." He entered Parliament in 1818, and was listened to with respect, but his influence was as a writer. His chief work was *The Principles of Political Economy and Taxation*, published in 1817. This book became, in a sense, the canon of economic orthodoxy; at the same time, it was found that the devil could quote scripture: both Socialists and Single-Taxers derived their proposals from his doctrines. The Socialists appealed to his theory of value, the Single-Taxers to his theory of rent. More generally, by discussing the distribution of wealth among the different classes of society, he incidentally made it clear that different classes may have divergent interests. There is much in Marx that is derived from Ricardo. He has thus a two-fold importance: as the source of official economics, and also as the unintentional parent of heresy.

Ricardo's theory of rent is simple, and in suitable circumstances perfectly valid. In considering it, let us, to begin with, confine ourselves to agricultural land. Some land is more fertile, some less; at any given moment, there must be some land on the margin of cultivation, which is only just worth cultivating. That is to say, it just yields a return to the farmer's capital which is equal to what the same capital would yield if otherwise invested. If the landlord were to demand rent for this land, the farmer would no longer find it worth cultivating; such land, therefore, will yield no rent to the landlord. On more fertile land, on the contrary, a given amount of capital yields more than the usual rate of profit; therefore the farmer is willing to pay the landlord for the right to cultivate it. What he is willing to pay is the excess of the produce above what is yielded by the same amount of the worst land in cultivation. Thus the rent of an acre of land is the amount by which the value of the crop that can be raised on it exceeds the value of the crop that can be raised on an acre of the worst land in cultivation.

What applies to agricultural land applies equally to all land. A piece of land in the centre of a big town can be used for such purposes as shops or offices, out of which an immense income can be made. Part of this income is interest on capital, in the shape of buildings etc.; part is profits of business enterprise; but there is a further part, which goes to the owner of the land in the shape of ground-rent. Anything that increases the size of the town, and therefore the income to be made by a shop or office at its centre, increases the rent that the landowner can exact for the right of using the site. It must be understood, of course, that the theory is concerned only with ground-rent, not with that part of the rent which is due to the value of the buildings erected on the site.

In the circumstances of England while the Corn Laws were in force, Ricardo's theory of rent had great practical importance. If it had been possible to import grain, the worst agricultural land in England would have gone out of cultivation. Consequently the difference between the best land and the worst that would have remained in cultivation would have diminished, and rents would have fallen. So much was, of course, obvious to the landowners, who controlled Parliament.

There were, however, further consequences, which were connected with Adam Smith's arguments in favor of free trade. If the importation of grain were to occur as a result of abolishing the import duty, the capital now employed on the worst land would flow into industry, where it would make the exports required to pay for the imported grain. This new employment of capital would necessarily be more profitable than the old, since, if not, it would not pay to import grain instead of producing it at home. There would, therefore, be an increase of the national wealth accompanied by a fall in rents: there would be more to divide, and of the increased total an increased proportion would go to the industrious classes. This perfectly sound argument naturally appealed to manufacturers, but not to landowners. It was only after the Reform Bill had transferred political power to the middle class that the free-traders could obtain control of Parliament. When, in 1846, free trade in corn was introduced, its consequences were found to be such as the economists had predicted.

Ricardo's theory of rent reflects accurately the conflict between middle-class manufacturers and upper-class landowners which dominated English politics from 1815 to 1846. But it was possible to make a much more radical application of the theory than any contemplated by Ricardo or the Manchester men. These men were rich, but wished to be richer; they were the industrious rich, and were not willing to accept a position inferior to that of the idle rich. But they were by no means revolutionaries; they wished the world to remain one in which wealth could be enjoyed. Moreover they had a rooted distrust of the State, owing, no doubt, to the fact that they did not control it. For these reasons, they did not advance from Ricardo to Henry George and the doctrine of the single tax. Yet that is a perfectly logical consequence. Economic rent is not paid to the landowner in return for any service that he performs; it is paid merely for permission to produce wealth on his land. By the labor of others he is enriched, while he need not lift a finger; his economic function is merely to receive rent, without in any way adding to the national wealth. It is no very difficult inference that the private ownership of land should be abolished, and all rent paid to the State. This inference, however, was not drawn, or even considered, by Ricardo.

Ricardo's theory of value, while less true than his theory of rent, has had even more influence. The question of value arises in economics as follows: Suppose you have one pound to spend, you can obtain for it a certain quantity of wheat, or of beer, or of tobacco, or of pins, or of books, or what not. If a certain quantity of wheat and a certain number of pins both cost one pound, they have the same "value." What determines how many pins will have the same value as a given amount of wheat? Ricardo answered: They will have the same value if the same amount of labor has been required to produce them. The value of any commodity, he says, is measured by the work involved in making it.

Up to a point, this doctrine is true. If you are a carpenter, and it takes you twice as long to make a table as to make a chair, you will naturally charge twice as much—apart from the cost of the wood. Different manufactured articles made by men who are all paid the same rate of wages will have a price proportional to the labor that has gone into them—again apart from the cost of the raw material. Ricardo's theory of value, one may say, is approximately true, under conditions of free competition, whenever the value of the commodity is mainly dependent upon the process of manufacture as opposed to the natural fertility of the earth.

But it is easy to see that the theory cannot be wholly correct, if only because it conflicts with Ricardo's own theory of rent. Two bushels of wheat of the same quality are of the same value wherever they have been produced; but a bushel of wheat costs less labor to produce on good land than on poor land. This is the basis of Ricardo's theory of rent, and should have made him see that his theory of value could not be right. There are, of course, more extreme examples. In the early days of a new goldfield, it has sometimes happened that a man has picked up by accident a huge nugget worth as much as £10,000. The value of his labor, at an ordinary rate of wages, would have been about half a crown, but his gold was worth just as much as if he had had to work for it.

I do not wish to weary the reader with the niceties of the theory of value, but the subject proved of such immense importance in the development of Socialism that some discussion of it is unavoidable. In certain cases, Ricardo's theory is quite right, while in certain others it is quite wrong; in the commonest kind of case, it is more or less right, but not wholly. The question turns on the part played by monopoly in the particular case concerned.

Let us take first some instance in which, apart from the rent of land, monopoly plays almost no part—say the manufacture of cotton cloth as it was in Ricardo's day. This was probably the sort of commodity that he had in mind. There were many manufacturers, all keenly competing against each other; the raw material was produced under fairly uniform conditions, and sold by the growers competitively. The labor involved in making the necessary machinery was, of course, part of the labor involved in making the cloth; here, also, there was in that day a plentiful supply of iron ore, belonging to many different mines which were in no way combined, and there were also, as time went on, many firms making textile machinery. There was one element of monopoly, it is true, namely that due to the existence of patents: these represent, in theory, the monopoly value of the inventor's skill. Royalties to inventors formed, however, a very small part of the cost of a given piece of cotton cloth. On the whole, the price would be determined pretty accurately by the amount of labor involved in making it.

Now let us take something at the opposite extreme, say a picture by Leonardo. There was presumably no more labor in it than in some daub that could be bought for five shillings, and yet it may be worth fifty thousand pounds. This is a case of pure monopoly: the supply cannot be increased, and therefore the price depends only upon the demand. The earnings of persons who have a complete or partial monopoly of some kind of skill come under this head; I am thinking of such persons as opera-singers, eminent surgeons and barristers, film stars, and so on.

Most cases are intermediate between these two extremes. In general, the raw material of an industry is either agricultural or mineral. If it is agricultural, the law of rent, as we saw already, modifies Ricardo's law of value: it is the labor cost on the worst land under cultivation, not on average land, that determines value. In the case of minerals, if there are many independent sources of supply, exactly the same reasoning applies as in the case of agricultural produce; but not infrequently there is a combination among the owners of the sources of supply, so that the value of the raw material is determined by the rules governing monopolies. In the later stages, also, monopoly, partial or complete, has been more and more replacing competition. This comes partly through the formation of Trusts, partly through patents, partly through ownership of raw materials.

Where there is monopoly with power to increase supply, the producer has to consider whether it will pay him better to dispose of large quantities at low prices, or of small quantities at high prices. It is obvious that the more he charges the less he will sell, and that there is some price which gives him the maximum profit. But this has nothing to do with cost of production, except that cost of production sets a minimum, below which the producer cannot profitably let the price fall.

Ricardo's theory that value is determined by the amount of labor involved in production is therefore far from being quite true, and has become less true since his time, owing to the diminution of competition. He himself was partially aware of its limitations, but James

Mill and McCulloch seized on it with the zeal of disciples, and refused to admit even the qualifications which Ricardo thought necessary. Orthodox economics thus accepted the theory in an almost unqualified form until a better theory, giving due place to the importance of demand, was invented by Jevons at a much later date.

Ricardo's theory of value, not unnaturally, was welcomed by the champions of labor, and put by them to uses which he had not foreseen. If the whole value of a commodity is due to the labor which has gone into producing it, why, they asked, should not the whole value be paid to the men who have made the commodity? With what right did the landlord and the capitalist appropriate part of the product, if they had added nothing to its value? Economists associated with working-class movements, notably Thomas Hodgskin and William Thompson, basing themselves on Ricardo, argued that no one should receive money except in return for labor, and that the laborer had a right to the whole produce of his own work. These men, as we shall see later, became influential in the Socialist movement connected with Robert Owen. At a later stage, they influenced Marx, who also based his argument on Ricardo's theory of value. At the present day, while Ricardo's influence is much diminished in orthodox economics, it lives on in the economics of the Marxists, who, in this respect as in some others, preserve an outlook belonging to the early nineteenth century.

CHAPTER XII

THE BENTHAMITE DOCTRINE

AS a result of the combined teaching of Malthus, Bentham, and Ricardo, a body of doctrine grew up, which was accepted by a gradually increasing number of progressive people, both in the middle class and among working men—though among the latter, as we shall see, there were rival schools which also had influence. The views accepted by the followers of the Benthamites were, in some respects, more crude than those of the leaders, but in other respects less so. It is worth while to consider what the doctrine became in the minds of its popularizers, since it was through them that it influenced legislation.

The views of the Philosophical Radicals fall naturally under three heads, economic, political, and moral, and of these three the economic was, in their case, the most important.

The economics of the school were dominated by Malthus. Until such time as the working classes could be induced to practise moral restraint, the principle of population made it inevitable that the wages of unskilled labor should barely suffice to enable a man to live and rear a family. Where women and children earned wages, the man's wages would only need to suffice for his own support. There might be moments in the world's history, after a destructive war or a very terrible epidemic, when wages would temporarily rise above subsistence level, but the result would be a diminution of infant mortality until the population, through increasing numbers, returned to its previous low level. There was, therefore, no point in the schemes of well-meaning philanthropists, nor yet in relief by the medium of the Poor Law. Working men who tried to raise wages by means of strikes and trade unions were utterly misguided. Communists, who aimed at economic equality, might drag the rich down, but could not improve the position of the poor, since increase of population would quickly destroy any momentary amelioration.

There was one hope for the working classes, and only one, namely that, from prudence, they would learn to control their procreative instincts. Middle-class Radicals, with a few exceptions, urged that they should do this by "moral restraint"; Place, an ardent Malthusian who yet remembered his working-class origin, urged less painful methods. Meanwhile, the whole school were excused by their doctrines from all participation in humanitarian efforts to diminish the sufferings of the wage-earning classes by what seemed to them superficial methods.

The landlords, at the other end of the social scale, equally had to be kept in their place. Ricardo's theory of rent showed that, in the long run, the whole benefit of the Corn Laws went to the landlords; the farmers were deprived, by higher rents, of whatever benefit might otherwise have come to them. The wage-earners neither gained nor lost, since in any case they would be on the verge of starvation. But the industrial employers lost, because, when bread was dear, they had to pay higher wages to prevent their laborers from dying of hunger. Therefore, for the sake of the factory owners, the import duty on corn ought to be abolished.

Profits represented what was left after paying rent and wages. Therefore the way to increase profits was to lower rent and wages. Wages could only be lowered by making bread cheaper, i.e. by free trade in corn; the same measure, by allowing the worst lands to go out of cultivation, would lower rents, and would, therefore, be doubly advantageous to the class that lived on profits, as opposed to rent and wages. The Benthamites represented this class; they were the first to adopt the modern creed of industrialism and mechanization.

Politically, the creed of the school contained three main articles: *laissez faire*, democracy, and education. *Laissez faire*, as a principle, was invented in France during the *ancien régime*, but it disappeared during the Revolution, and Napoleon had no use for it. In the England of 1815, however, the same conditions existed which had produced it in the France of Louis XVI: an energetic and intelligent middle class politically controlled by a stupid government. There might conceivably be beneficial forms of State control, but the existing State was much more likely to adopt harmful forms. The new men, conscious that they wielded a new power and were creating a new world, asked only to be let alone.

So far, there was much to be said for *laissez faire*, but it became a dogma and was carried to ridiculous extremes. The *Economist*, a periodical which represented the views of the Benthamites, even objected to the Public Health Act of 1848, which was passed as the result of a Commission revealing the most appallingly insanitary conditions in most of the big towns. While the Bill was before the House of Commons, the *Economist* regretted that it was not being more vigorously opposed. "Suffering and evil," the editor wrote, "are nature's admonitions; they cannot be got rid of; and the impatient attempts of benevolence to banish them from the world by legislation, before benevolence has learned their object and their end, have always been productive of more evil than good." [1] The "benevolence" of Parliament was proof against these arguments for not constructing a proper drainage system, because epidemics due to its absence were raging within a stone's throw of the House of Commons. Most of the Philosophical Radicals were opposed to factory legislation, even where the case for it was most indubitable. When, in 1847, the Bill prohibiting children from working more than ten hours a day in cotton factories was passed by both Houses, the *Economist's* head-line was "The Lords leagued with the Commons to prohibit Industry." The principle, the paper said, was the same as in the case of the Corn Law—in each an unwarrantable interference for the sake of one class.[2]

Democracy, which was advocated whole-heartedly by James Mill and (in later life) by Bentham, was accepted with some limitations by most of the school. The importance of property had a large place in their minds, and they did not welcome the idea of great numbers of voters who owned nothing. They all wanted something more far-reaching than the Reform Act of 1832, but few wanted manhood suffrage, and only a handful wanted votes for women. The advocacy of manhood suffrage was taken up by the Chartists, who were working class and less respectable than the Benthamites. Nevertheless, the Benthamites always urged as much extension of the suffrage as was at all within the sphere of practical politics; they were, therefore, quite as effective in furthering democracy as they would have been if their demands had been more extreme.

Belief in democracy was bound up with belief in the power of

[1] Clapham, *op. cit.*, Vol. I, p. 545.   [2] *Ibid.*, p. 577.

reason over men's minds, provided they were sufficiently educated to be able to follow an argument. James Mill, his son says, had

an almost unbounded confidence in the efficacy of two things: representative government, and complete freedom of discussion. So complete was my father's reliance on the influence of reason over the minds of mankind, whenever it is allowed to reach them, that he felt as if all would be gained if the whole population were taught to read, if all sorts of opinions were allowed to be addressed to them by word and in writing, and if by means of the suffrage they could nominate a legislature to give effect to the opinions they adopted. He thought that when the legislature no longer represented a class interest, it would aim at the general interest, honestly and with adequate wisdom; since the people would be sufficiently under the guidance of educated intelligence, to make in general a good choice of persons to represent them, and having done so, to leave to those whom they had chosen a liberal discretion. Accordingly aristocratic rule, the government of the Few in any of its shapes, being in his eyes the only thing which stood between mankind and an administration of their affairs by the best wisdom to be found among them, was the object of his sternest disapprobation, and a democratic suffrage the principal article of his political creed, not on the ground of liberty, Rights of Man, or any of the phrases, more or less significant, by which, up to that time, democracy had usually been defended, but as the most essential of "securities for good government." In this, too, he held fast only to what he deemed essentials; he was comparatively indifferent to monarchical or republican forms—far more so than Bentham, to whom a king, in the character of "corrupter-general," appeared necessarily very noxious.

"All would be gained if the whole population were taught to read." James Mill imagined the working man coming home in the evening and reading Hume or Hartley or Bentham; he did not foresee the literature that would be provided for a population that had learnt to read, but had been taught almost nothing else. The kind of working man that he imagined does exist, but he is not common, and no one less ascetic than the early Benthamites would have expected him ever to become common. With such expectations, however, it was natural to feel a great desire for the spread of education. All the Benthamites took a considerable part in the movements of the time for providing working-class schools. Universal compulsory education did not come in England till 1870, but it would not have come then but for the Philosophical Radicals.

The opposition to popular education at that time was amazingly strong, even in quarters in which it might not have been expected. In the year 1807, a Bill to provide elementary schools throughout England was introduced by Whitbread. It was defeated in the Lords, at the instance of Eldon and the Archbishop of Canterbury. This is quite in order, but it is curious to find that it was vehemently opposed by the President of the Royal Society. "However specious in theory the project might be (so he said), of giving education to the labouring classes of the poor, it would in effect be found to be prejudicial to their morals and happiness; it would teach them to despise their lot in life, instead of making them good servants in agriculture, and other laborious employments to which their rank in society had destined them; instead of teaching them subordination, it would render them fractious and refractory, as was evident in the manufacturing counties; it would enable them to read seditious pamphlets, vicious books, and publications against Christianity; it would render them insolent to their superiors; and in a few years the result would be that the legislature would find it necessary to direct the strong arm of power towards them, and to furnish the executive magistrate with much more vigorous laws than were now in force." [3]

In spite of these grave warnings, the nonconformists proceeded to found schools, and the Church, for fear of losing its hold on the young, was compelled to follow suit. In the nonconformist movement the Benthamites were active.

The reader may remember that Dr. Folliott, as quoted in the motto to this section, objected to sixpenny tracts on hydrostatics, the Steam Intellect Society, and the learned friend. Whether sixpenny tracts on hydrostatics existed, I doubt; but the learned friend was Brougham, and the Steam Intellect Society was the "Society for the Diffusion of Useful Knowledge," of which Brougham was chairman and Lord John Russell vice-chairman. Brougham, if not a complete Benthamite, was very closely allied with those who were; James Mill, according to his son, "was the good genius by the side of Brougham in most of what he did for the public, either on educa-

[3] Hammond, *Town Labourer* (1932 ed.), p. 57.

tion, law reform, or any other subject." Much useful knowledge was diffused by the society in question, in spite of the hostility of Dr. Folliott and the President of the Royal Society. Nevertheless, the prejudice against popular education died hard. When, in 1853, my grandfather established a school in the village of Petersham (where he lived), the gentry complained that "he had destroyed the hitherto aristocratic character of the neighborhood." Nor is the prejudice extinct even now.

There is one other point in Benthamite politics that is important, and that is hostility to imperialism. Bentham, even in his Tory days, saw no use in over-seas possessions. At the height of the French Revolution he wrote, and presented to Talleyrand, a work called: *Emancipate your Colonies! addressed to the National Convention of France, Anno 1793. Shewing the uselessness and mischievousness of distant dependencies to an European State.* This was not merely an opinion for the French; he held the same views as regards British colonies. He converted his friend Lord Lansdowne, who stated in the House of Lords in 1797: "A greater good could not be done to Spain, than to relieve them from the curse of these settlements [Spanish America], and make them an industrious people like their neighbours. A greater evil could not happen to England than to add them to our already overgrown possessions." Bentham's later disciples on the whole retained his view on this subject. As believers in free trade, they saw no economic benefit in sovereignty, and they were incapable of the sentiment of imperial pride. In the eighteenth century, the Whigs were more imperialistic than the Tories; in the nineteenth, under the influence of the Benthamites, the most typical Liberals were Little Englanders. In this respect, however, national pride proved too strong for philosophy. In the very hey-day of Benthamism, Palmerston was the idol of the Liberal party, partly because he cared more for British prestige than for any theories under the sun.

It must also be admitted that there was one respect in which even Bentham was seduced from his austere cosmopolitanism. After James Mill had come to be employed by the East India Company, both he and Bentham felt that a promising field had been opened to experimentation. Bentham hoped to inspire an Indian legal code: "I shall be the dead legislative of British India. Twenty years after

I am dead, I shall be a despot." After quoting this remark, Halévy adds: "Twenty-eight years after his death the Indian penal code came into force; it had been drawn up by Macaulay under the influence of Bentham's and James Mill's ideas, so that Bentham, who had failed to give a legal code to England, did actually become the posthumous legislator of the vastest of her possessions." [4]

The moral outlook of the Benthamites was somewhat singular. Intellectually, they were emancipated; in theory, they lived for pleasure; in economics, they held that a sane man will pursue his pecuniary self-interest. Politically, they advocated great changes, but without heat, without enthusiasm, without visible generosity of sentiment even when they went against their own interest and that of their class; some of them, and notably Bentham, showed a rare indifference to pecuniary self-interest, and a readiness to sacrifice large sums to friendship or a public object; as for pleasure, one feels that they had read of it in books, and supposed it must be a good thing, but that in their lives they knew nothing of it; and their intellectual emancipation never passed over into any action contrary to the received moral code—except, perhaps, in James Mill's rather timid advocacy of neo-Malthusianism, and Place's rather bolder propaganda in the same direction. With the exception of Place, they were all "bookish" men; the action in which their impulse to activity found its most natural outlet was that of writing. There was no rough-and-tumble in their lives; none of them would have known what to do with a horse-dealer or a card-sharper or even an ordinary drunkard.

The morals of James Mill as described by his son are typical of the sect:

In ethics, his moral feelings were energetic and rigid on all points which he deemed important to human well being, while he was supremely indifferent in opinion (though his indifference did not show itself in personal conduct) to all those doctrines of the common morality, which he thought had no foundation but in asceticism and priestcraft. He looked forward, for example, to a considerable increase of freedom in the relations between the sexes, though without pretending to define exactly what would be, or ought to be, the precise conditions of that freedom. This opinion was connected in him with no sensuality either of a theoretical or of a practical kind. He anticipated, on the contrary, as one of the beneficial effects of

[4] Halévy, *The Growth of Philosophic Radicalism*, p. 510.

increased freedom, that the imagination would no longer dwell upon the physical relation and its adjuncts, and swell this into one of the principal objects of life; a perversion of the imagination and feelings, which he regarded as one of the deepest seated and most pervading evils in the human mind.

In fact, he regarded sex much as I regard football. I have no wish to forbid people to watch football matches, but I cannot imagine why they do it, and I hope in time they will grow too sensible to wish to do so. If I lived in a country where football was thought wicked, and where the game was played in secret while every one pretended that it was unknown, I might be driven to champion the cause of the oppressed footballer, but without much enthusiasm. This represents the attitude of these highly refined hedonists on matters of sexual morality.

The virtue which, in practice, they prized above all others, was prudence. For this there were many reasons. One was Malthus: to marry young and have a large family was the cardinal crime, and only prudence could lead men to avoid it. Another was the fact that, for those who had even a little capital, profitable investment was easy, while for those who had none life was very hard. Another, which affected all shades of opinion, was fear of the French Revolution, and the feeling that such events could only be prevented by keeping a tight hold over the emotions and passions.

The Utilitarians had another virtue, closely allied to prudence, namely intellectual sobriety. They reasoned carefully on every subject of which they treated; they never imagined that they knew things by the light of nature; they were seldom misled by emotion; and although they were systematic, love of system hardly ever led them into errors which they would not have committed in any case. Much of this intellectual sobriety descends to them from Locke. There is in his *Essay on the Human Understanding* a chapter headed "Of enthusiasm," which deals with means of preventing it, and is directed against Cromwellian sectaries. Intellectually, though not politically, the Methodists occupied a similar position in the time of the Utilitarians. The Methodists knew all about the next world, which they regarded as more important than our life here on earth.

The Benthamites knew nothing of such matters: they were not atheists, but what came to be called agnostics. Where there was no evidence, they suspended judgment—a practice as admirable as it is rare.

The Utilitarians were, and still are, made fun of for the supposed habit of judging all things by their usefulness rather than by any quality they may possess on their own account. "A Utilitarian says, What is the use of a nightingale, unless roasted? What profit is there in the fragrance of a rose, unless you can distil from it an otto at ten shillings a drop? What can you mint out of the red flush of a morning cloud, save a shepherd's warning to take his waterproof with him when going out in the world?" [5] It must be admitted that the temperament of the early Utilitarians gave some color to this accusation, but I think it results much more from the suggestions of the word. Certainly there was nothing in the doctrine of the school to warrant this common criticism. The doctrine was that pleasure is the good. If you derived more pleasure from hearing the nightingale than from eating it, you would abstain from roasting it. If you and the nightingale, jointly, would enjoy a greater sum of pleasure if he were left to sing than if he were eaten, the legislator would arrange the laws so that you should not kill the bird. This was the doctrine; and what could any one ask more?

Even as regards temperament, while there is a measure of truth in the current view, it has very definite limitations. Bentham was fond of music; James Mill caused John to read more poetry than was read by any other boy then living. John himself, when he grew up, turned out to be poetic, slightly sentimental, with hankerings after emotional delights that his father had made difficult for him. The reason for the name "Utilitarian" was that Bentham and his disciples would not put up with things that had no use, merely because they were traditional. The procedure of the Court of Chancery, which Dickens attacked in *Bleak House*, had certainly none of the intrinsic merit of the nightingale's song. It was, therefore, to be judged by the test of utility, and by this it was condemned. Bentham applied this test to all the old lumber of English law, preserved only to provide incomes for lawyers. He thought this an insufficient

[5] *The Evangelical Revival*, by S. Baring-Gould, M.A., 1920, p. 7.

utility, and set to work to try to reform the law. In all such regions, the Utilitarian standard is admirable, and by this standard the Utilitarians were justified. They may not have possessed the charm of the nightingale, but they did possess the merit of usefulness.

CHAPTER XIII

DEMOCRACY IN ENGLAND

DEMOCRACY, in its triumphant and self-confident form, came to the world from the United States, in association with the doctrine of the Rights of Man. In England, the first thorough-going democratic movement, that of the Chartists, took its philosophy in the main from America, but it failed, and was succeeded, after an interval, by a new demand for popular representation, led first by Bright, the friend of Cobden, and later by Gladstone, who, during the Parliament of 1841–46, had become Cobden's disciple. The inspiration of this later successful movement was derived from the Philosophical Radicals, one of whose most important effects on British politics was the character which, except during the Chartist interlude, they gave to democratic theory.

Democratic sentiment, as it existed in England, was different, in various important respects, from the democratic sentiment of America and the Continent, which will be considered in later chapters. One very important difference was that, in England, advocates of democracy appealed to history and tradition. Representative institutions, which are an important element in modern democracy, had existed uninterruptedly since the thirteenth century; no doubt the House of Commons had not at any time represented the people, but it had represented classes other than the aristocracy, and, in the seventeenth century, these classes had used it in a vigorous and successful contest for their rights. Speaking of John Bright, who won the vote for working men in 1867, Lord Morley says: "A political leader does well to strive to keep our democracy historic. John Bright would have been a worthy comrade of John Hampden, John Selden, and John Pym. He had the very spirit of the Puritan leaders." John Bright himself, as a Quaker, with the tradition of persecution under the Stuarts, was thoroughly conscious of his continuity with the age of Cromwell.

The desire to represent reform as a return to the purer customs of our ancestors was very common among Radicals. At one of the first of the great Chartist open-air meetings, in 1838, Doubleday, the Chairman, in demanding manhood suffrage, said:

Universal suffrage was the usage of the country up to the middle of the reign of Henry the Sixth. Well, how was this lost? It was in the confusion of the civil wars. The people did not know its value, and under plausible pretences the law was altered. From that time to this Englishmen had been feeling the effects of this treacherous deed. The evil crept on gradually. The country was then rich, and the common people wealthy to an extent they [his hearers] had no idea of. There were hardly any taxes; and there could be none, because a parliament elected by the people took care of the people's earnings. But when this was lost all changed. The Aristocracy gradually found out that the people were too rich, and so they made laws to cure this evil.[1]

Doubleday's historical accuracy is open to question, but it is characteristic of England that an extreme Radical should defend his proposals as a revival of the distant past. In Wat Tyler's rebellion, which occurred during Doubleday's Golden Age, the aim was a return to the social system of Adam and Eve.

An important difference between England and America as regards democratic sentiment is that in America it was agricultural, whereas in England it was mainly urban and industrial. The old Poor Law kept the rural laborers submissive in spite of poverty (except for the brief outbreak of 1830), and the farmers usually sided with the landowners. In the industrial region, a different situation arose. The landowners, as a rule, did not live on the spot, and they made laws which hampered the manufacturers. From 1815 to 1846, owing to the tariff, the manufacturers were politically opposed to the aristocracy, and they enlisted the wage-earners on their side as far as seemed safe. Industry was rapidly increasing, and was technically progressive. Thus everything combined to drive the industrial population, both masters and men, into Radicalism, while the rural districts remained feudal and almost unchanging.

In America and on the Continent, democracy was intimately associated with nationalism, whereas in England the opposite was the case. The American War of Independence and the French revolu-

[1] Gammage, *History of the Chartist Movement*, p. 23.

tionary wars had associated democracy with the military power of the nation, whereas in England the military power was associated with reaction and the Duke of Wellington, and was used rather for oppression of subject nations than for self-defence. For this reason, in England, the democratic parties and statesmen were also the least warlike and imperialistic. This continued to be the case until the retirement of Gladstone in 1894.

English democratic feeling in the nineteenth century was largely generated by the period of aristocratic and regal misgovernment which began in 1760 and persisted throughout the reigns of George III and George IV. The House of Lords, through the system of rotten boroughs, controlled the House of Commons; the government was inefficient and inconceivably corrupt; the taxes were oppressive, especially to the poorest part of the population, since they were largely on necessaries. The whole legislative power of Parliament was used to enrich the landowners at the expense of all other sections of the community. Everything needed reforming—education, the law, the judicial system, the prisons, the insanitary condition of the towns, taxation, the Poor Law, and much else. Meanwhile the rulers of the country hunted foxes, shot pheasants, and made more stringent laws against poachers. The intelligence of the nation, as well as its humanity and common sense, rebelled against the continuation of such a system.

The revolt of intelligence took the form of Philosophical Radicalism, and it was fortunate that, when reform became possible, there were men with a capacity for detail who had thought out what should be done. Owing to Bentham and his school, there was little vague declamation about the Rights of Man, except among the Chartists. Sentiment, on the whole, was left to the reactionaries, and attention to utility was the characteristic of the reformers. Perhaps it is for this reason that the movement which sprang from them continued for over fifty years before it produced a reaction.

The most difficult battle in the movement towards democracy was the first, the battle for the Reform Bill, which was won in 1832. Reform of the House of Commons, both by abolishing rotten boroughs and by extending the franchise, was already advocated by influential politicians before the French Revolution, but was set aside, along with all other forms of legislative progress, for the period of the French wars. Nevertheless, it remained an aspiration of that section of the Whigs which followed Fox. When, therefore, the Whigs under Grey came into power in 1830, they set to work to carry a measure which in their view ought to have been introduced by the younger Pitt when he first came into power. Although their proposals were moderate, their language was that of democracy. Lord John Russell, in introducing the Reform Bill, said they were determined that the House of Commons should "not be the representatives of a small class or of a particular interest; but form a body . . . representing the people, springing from the people, and sympathizing with the people."

The aristocratic Whigs of 1832 were analogous in their outlook to the aristocratic reformers in France in 1789. Mirabeau, Lafayette, and the Feuillants would have liked to achieve a peaceful and moderate reform, which would have given to France a constitution very similar to that of England after 1832. Why did the party of constitutional reform succeed in England and fail in France? No doubt for a number of reasons, but chiefly, I think, because the revolution in France was agrarian as well as urban, which was not the case in England. The French aristocrats, in spite of voting away their feudal privileges, found themselves faced by a hostility which involved financial ruin. This chilled their reforming ardor, and led them to invite foreign aid against the Revolution. The English reformers, at the very beginning of the agitation for the Reform Bill, quenched agrarian revolt in blood, and therefore felt their incomes safe. The opposition of the Tories gave way to the threat of revolution, because the matter did not appear to be one of life and death for the aristocracy. And so ultimate political power passed peacefully into the hands of the middle class.

Although the Reform Bill was passed by strictly constitutional means, it could not have become law without an effective threat of revolution. To make such a threat effective, the middle class had to enlist the support of the working men, and this necessitated raising their hopes. The measure which was actually carried did nothing for working men, but actually deprived them of the vote in the few places, such as Westminster, where they had previously had it. The middle class, while they detested the aristocratic monopoly of political power, had no wish for a system in which their employees would have votes. The Reform Bill was, in fact, just such as the middle class desired. From 1832 until Disraeli's extension of the franchise in 1867, although most of the ministers continued to be aristocrats, the constituency to which they had to appeal was one of business men, manufacturers, and shopkeepers. The ultimate power was in new hands, and gradually the tone of British politics was changed.

To the working class, the Reform Bill and its consequences was a bitter disenchantment. One of the first measures of the reformed Parliament was the new Poor Law, which introduced the system represented in *Oliver Twist*. The old Poor Law needed to be changed, and in its ultimate effects the new Poor Law was no doubt less disastrous. But it involved intolerable cruelty and hardship, which its advocates justified on grounds derived from Malthus. The working men had helped the middle class to acquire power, and the new Poor Law was their reward. Working class political consciousness arose out of this betrayal. As Malthus had sprung from the old Poor Law, so Marx and Engels sprang from the new.

The first effect of disenchantment on the wage-earners was the growth of trade-unionism (described in a later chapter) which was led by Robert Owen, the founder of Socialism. When this collapsed, the belief in political rather than industrial methods revived, and led, for a while, to the Chartist movement. This movement grew out of the London Working Men's Association, founded in 1836, which advocated a "Charter" consisting of six points: Manhood Suffrage, Annual Parliaments, Vote by Ballot, no Property Qualification, Payment of Members, and Equal Electoral Districts.

Towards Chartism, as towards all movements of political reform, Owen was unsympathetic. "Were you to have," he said, "a Parliament chosen next year by universal suffrage and vote by ballot, it would be most probably the least efficient, most turbulent, and worst possible public assembly that has yet ruled this country."

Agitation against the new Poor Law came from two opposite quarters. As a measure of middle-class Radicalism, it was opposed by Tories and by Chartists. The Tories liked the subservience to rural landowners that had been generated by the old Poor Law, but were disgusted when meetings against the new Poor Law were converted into meetings for the Charter.

The Rev. G. S. Bull refused to take part in a great anti-Poor Law demonstration on Hartshead Moor because a resolution was to be proposed in favour of Universal Suffrage . . . and next year he complained that anti-Poor Law meetings were converted into Radical meetings and declared that he would never again act with Radicalism. . . . On the other side, the Chartists were not less critical of their allies. "In the hands of a red-hot Tory like Earl Stanhope, the nephew and admirer of that base and bloody tool of tyranny, Wm. Pitt," wrote the *Chartist*, "the anti-Poor Law agitation becomes nothing more than a trick of faction, a trick by which the Tories hope to get hold of the places and salaries of the Whigs with the intention of using their power when they get it in a much worse manner than the Whigs ever have or ever can use it." [2]

Although the measures advocated in the Charter were purely political, the ultimate aims of the Chartists were economic. As their historian Gammage (who was one of them) puts it:

The masses look on the enfranchised classes, whom they behold reposing on the couch of opulence, and contrast that opulence with the misery of their own condition. Reasoning from effect to cause there is no marvel that they arrive at the conclusion—that their exclusion from political power is the cause of our social anomalies.

But to avoid confusing the issue they never, as a body, went beyond the six points, or discussed the economic changes which they would introduce if they had the power.

The Chartist movement came to grief without having achieved any of its objects. It was hampered by the imprisonment of many of its leaders, and it suffered from internal dissensions on the question of the wisdom of appealing to physical force. But the chief cause of its collapse was the rise of the Anti-Corn Law League, which raised an issue as to which the interests of the middle and working classes were identical. The agitation for free trade, and the rapid improvement in the condition of the wage-earners after the repeal of the Corn Laws, put an end, for a time, to the bitterness of the working class against middle-class politicians.

It was John Bright, himself a middle-class cotton manufacturer, and Cobden's colleague in the Anti-Corn Law agitation, who was the leader in obtaining the vote for urban working men. He had no

2 J. L. and Barbara Hammond, *The Age of the Chartists*, p. 268.

personal interest in the extension of the franchise, and was chiefly actuated by dislike of war. He had opposed the Crimean War, and temporarily lost his seat in Parliament as a consequence. He hated Palmerston's swaggering bellicosity, which was popular with the bulk of the middle class, and he believed that the working class would favor a less warlike policy. So long as Palmerston lived, he was able to block all Bright's efforts for reform, but after his death in 1865 Liberals began to feel that they ought to be liberal, and Disraeli set to work to educate the Conservative party. The result was the enfranchisement of urban working men in 1867. Rural laborers, for some reason, were considered more dangerous, and had to wait till they were given the vote by Gladstone in 1885.

CHAPTER XIV

FREE TRADE

THE middle class in Great Britain, having acquired political power in 1832, naturally set to work to alter the laws so as to increase its own wealth. Two kinds of legislation were needed for the progress of the nation: one to improve conditions in the factories and mines, the other to sweep away the laws which hampered the growth of industrialism. The latter kind alone was in accordance with the interests of the manufacturers. But its most important item, the abolition of the duty on corn, was contrary to the interests of agricultural landowners, and was therefore strenuously opposed by the bulk of the aristocracy. When the industrialists spoke of the evils of dear bread, the landowners retorted with the evils of child labor and long hours in factories. In the end, each side was successful in reforming the evils by which the other side profited: Lord Shaftesbury carried his Factory Acts and Cobden carried free trade. The dispute between manufacturers and landowners was extraordinarily fortunate, since it obliged each to appeal to the tribunal of disinterested humane people.

The two sets of disputants were not, however, on a level, since the manufacturers were creating modern methods of production, while the landowners were merely receiving their rents. The British industrialists of that time were men full of ruthless energy, with the self-confidence that comes of success and new power. Many of them had risen by their own efforts. Following the Philosophical Radicals, they believed in competition as the motive force of progress, and they were impatient of everything that mitigated its intensity. They demanded the abolition of protective duties on the goods that they made as well as on the goods made by others: they felt that, given a free field and no favor, they were sure to win.

In the matter of free trade in corn, they were fighting not only for their own interests, but for the interests of their country and the world. Corn could be produced more cheaply in other countries than in England, while cotton goods could be produced more cheaply in England than in other countries. While England persisted in producing its own food, there was less wealth to be divided among the population than there would be if England produced less food and more manufactures. And of that smaller total, a larger proportion went to the landlords in the shape of rent than would go if the worst lands were allowed to go out of cultivation. All this followed from Ricardo's law of rent, according to which the rent of a piece of land is the difference between its produce and that of the worst land in cultivation. Consequently free trade in corn would doubly benefit the non-landowning classes: there would be more wealth in the country, and they would obtain a larger share of the increased total. Free trade, therefore, was in the interests of the industrious classes, both masters and men.

It was, moreover, in the interests of the world at large. The nations from whom Great Britain bought food would be enriched, and the mutual benefit of trade would appease international rivalries, thus tending to promote peace. So, at least, the advocates of free trade believed.

In this way there arose a situation in which a powerful class could advocate its own interests while furthering the general good. Such situations are apt to call forth as leaders men of broad and humane outlook, in whom the element of self-interest is concealed by public spirit. Cobden, the leader in the battle for free trade, was such a man. Himself a cotton manufacturer, he was intimately aware of the pecuniary advantages of free trade to his class, but he was at the same time an internationalist, to whom free trade was part of a larger cause, the cause of world peace. When he had won free trade for his fellow manufacturers, he found, to his chagrin, that they had no use for the rest of his programme. His public spirit was an asset to them while it accorded with their self-interest, but when it ceased to do so they turned against it.

Cobden had a general outlook on politics which, though it remained largely inoperative during his lifetime owing to the adverse influence of Palmerston, became subsequently very important, since it was adopted, in the main, by Gladstone and the less Whiggish section of the Liberal party. Moreover the prestige which he acquired through the success of the Anti-Corn-Law agitation caused Continental liberalism to be greatly influenced by his outlook, and gave him an importance which was by no means purely British.

Like many reformers, he was inspired by common sense. He considered that nations should pursue national wealth, without too much regard to such things as glory and territory. He advocated pacifism, not on any abstract *a priori* ground, but on the ground that wars and preparations for wars are wasteful considered as investments. His explicit argument for internationalism was that nationalism diminished the wealth of mankind. At the same time, behind his economic façade, he had a kind heart and a good deal of humanitarian sentiment. He suffered, it is true, from a blind spot as regards the bad conditions of industrial workers; but the policy of free trade undoubtedly improved their real wages enormously, as Cobden always contended that it would. He was no believer in Malthus or in the "iron law of wages"; throughout the Anti-Corn-Law agitation he maintained that free trade in food would improve the position of both employer and employed in industry, and experience showed that he was right. His economics were sensible and practical, not theoretical and rigid, like the economics of James Mill or McCulloch; he selected from the economists the arguments that favored free trade, and ignored the rest.

It was the custom in Cobden's day, and it is even more the custom in our own, to decry him as a man of base soul, who thought nothing so important to a nation as material wealth. When Cobden and Bright opposed the Crimean War (about which the nation went quite as mad as it did about the Great War), everybody declared that this showed them to be men who could not rise above considerations of pounds, shillings, and pence. Tennyson, in *Maud*, gave expression to this point of view in lines that deserve to be continually quoted as a warning to "idealists." Here is his description of Bright addressing a peace meeting:

> Last week came one to the county town,
> To preach our poor little army down,
> And play the game of the despot kings,
> Tho' the state has done it and thrice as well:
> This broad-brimmed hawker of holy things,
> Whose ear is stuffed with his cotton, and rings

> Even in dreams to the chink of his pence,
> This huckster put down war!

When Tennyson saw the Crimean War coming, his reflections were:

> —I thought that a war would arise in the defence of the right,
> That an iron tyranny now should bend or cease,
> The glory of manhood stand on its ancient height,
> Nor Britain's one sole God be the millionaire:
> No more shall commerce be all in all, and Peace
> Pipe on her pastoral hillock a languid note,
> And watch the harvest ripen, her herd increase,
> Nor the cannon-bullet rust on a slothful shore—

And the poem ends in a blaze of patriotic nobility:

>   —I wake to the higher aims
> Of a land that has lost for a little her lust of gold,
> And love of a peace that was full of wrongs and shames,
> Horrible, hateful, monstrous, not to be told;
> And hail once more to the banner of battle unrolled!
> Tho' many a light shall darken, and many shall weep
> For those that are crushed in the clash of jarring claims,
> Yet God's just wrath shall be wrecked on a giant liar;
> And many a darkness into the light shall leap,
> And shine in the sudden making of splendid names,
> And noble thought be freer under the sun,
> And the heart of a people beat with one desire;
> And now by the side of the Black and the Baltic deep
> And deathful-grinning mouths of the fortress, flames
> The blood-red blossom of war with a heart of fire.
> Let it flame or fade, and the war roll down like a wind,
> We have proved we have hearts in a cause, we are noble still
> And myself have awaked, as it seems, to the better mind;
> I have felt with my native land, I am one with my kind,
> I embrace the purpose of God, and the doom assigned.

Cobden's sentiments at the same time were less exalted:

Hitherto the effects of the war have been felt by the working class, not in the form of loss of employment, but through the high price of food, which has told with great severity on the unskilled labourer, receiving the lowest rate of wages. The most numerous of this class, the agricultural labourers—that mute and helpless multitude who have never made their voices heard in the din of politics—or their presence felt in any social movement—are the greatest sufferers. We have a school of sentimentalists who tell us that war is to elevate man in his native dignity, to depress the money power, put down mammon-worship, and the like. Let them take a rural walk (they require bracing) on the downs, or the weald, or the fens, in any part of this island south of the Trent, and they will find the wages of agricultural labourers averaging, at this moment, under twelve shillings a week; let them ask how a family of five persons, which is below *their* average, can live with bread at 2½d. a lb. Nobody can tell.

The opposition between economic common sense and "idealism," which reached a sharp point in the Crimean War, has gone on ever since, and, unfortunately for mankind, the "idealists" have, on the whole, won the day. I am not prepared to maintain, as an abstract proposition of ethics, that there is nothing better than material prosperity, but I do maintain, in common with Cobden, that of all political purposes which had had important social effects the pursuit of general material wealth is the best. Nay, more: when well-fed people tell the poor that they ought to have souls above the cravings of the belly, there is something nauseous and hypocritical about the whole performance. This convenient idealism has had many forms. In the worst days of the Napoleonic wars, the Methodist and Evangelicals told the poor to centre their hopes upon Heaven, and to leave the rich in undisturbed possession here on earth. They were followed by the mediaevalists of various kinds: Coleridge, Carlyle, Disraeli, the Tractarians, and so on, whose doctrines were, in essence, a reaction against machinery and the industrial plutocrat from an aesthetic point of view. More important still, there is the nationalist point of view, represented in Cobden's England by Palmerston, and destined to prove stronger than either Cobdenism or Socialism—at least up to the present time.

All these "noble" creeds are, in their various ways, outlets for concealed passions of cruelty or despotism or greed. Religion which teaches the worthlessness of earthly wealth may be respected when, as in the case of St. Francis, it leads to a vow of poverty; but in a man like Tennyson we can hardly help suspecting that, subconsciously, it is a dodge for keeping the poor quiet. The mediaevalists of the better sort—among whom I include Coleridge and the Tractarians—

are men who find the modern world so painful that they seek escape from present reality in opium, fairy tales, or the invention of a Golden Age in the past. They are not sinister, but only lacking in the robustness required in order to think useful thoughts. Disraeli, who dreamed the same dreams, was powerful enough to twist reality to his fancy: he saw our Indian Empire, not merely as a market for cotton goods, but as a revival of the splendors of Solomon or Augustus. But by lending a romantic glamour to imperialism he encouraged tyranny and plunder on the part of those whom he persuaded to share his self-deception. As for Carlyle, his idealism is of the old fashioned sort which affords an excuse for the punishment of sinners. The men he admires most are men of blood: his typical hero is Dr. Francia, dictator of Paraguay, in whose praise he can find nothing to say except that he hanged some forty scoundrels without trial. His stern morality is, in fact, only a cloak for his dyspeptic hatred of the human race. His ideals, such as they are, lead to Nietzsche, and through him, to the Nazis. As for nationalism, in so far as it is not undisguised greed, it may be defined as the association of a genuine ethical principle with a geographical or racial unit. It is argued—let us say—that the purity of family life is a matter of the highest moral import, and that it is best found between such and such parallels of latitude and such and such meridians of longitude. It follows that those who live in this virtuous area have a right, and almost a duty, to kill as many people as may be convenient in other areas, and to compel the survivors to pay tribute. Unfortunately, the superior virtue of the conquerors is apt to disappear in the process of conquest. But on the subject of nationalism I will say no more at present, since we shall be concerned with it at a later stage.

The rise of Jingoism in the middle classes was a great disappointment to Cobden. In 1835, when they had not yet grown accustomed to power, he could believe that they would support him in his love of peace. "The middle and industrious classes of England," he says, "can have no interest apart from the preservation of peace. The honours, the fame, the emoluments of war belong not to them, the battle-plain is the harvest-field of the aristocracy, watered with the blood of the people." "At some future election," he continues, "we may probably see the test of *no foreign politics* applied to those who

offer to become the representatives of free constituencies." Experience
was to prove that in this expectation he had been mistaken: Palmerston, the most reckless of interventionists, became the idol of the
middle class, and Cobden lost his seat for having opposed the
Crimean War. In like manner, Marx thought that the proletarians
would not willingly suffer imperialist wars. Neither Marx nor
Cobden realized the change of psychology produced by the possession of political power, or the means which could be used by the rich
to cajole the democracy. A disfranchised class may oppose wars made
by its rulers, but when it has gained the vote it feels that wars are
its wars, and becomes as bellicose as the former oligarchy.

Another of Cobden's illusions was that commerce tends to promote peace:

> Commerce is the grand panacea, which, like a beneficent medical dis-
> covery, will serve to inoculate with the healthy and saving taste for civili-
> zation all the nations of the world. Not a bale of merchandise leaves our
> shores, but it bears the seeds of intelligence and fruitful thought to the
> members of some less enlightened community; not a merchant visits our
> seats of manufacturing industry, but he returns to his own country the
> missionary of freedom, peace, and good government—whilst our steam
> boats, that now visit every port of Europe, and our miraculous railroads,
> that are the talk of all nations, are the advertisements and vouchers for
> the value of our enlightened institutions.

The reasons which have prevented commerce from promoting
peace are worth considering, since they are among the main reasons
for the failure of Cobdenism. When two countries are in no degree
competitors as regards the products interchanged, that is to say,
when each is incapable of producing what it buys, commerce is felt
to be beneficial to both, and the effects for which Cobden hoped do
really take place. In his day, most commerce was of this sort. We
sold our manufactures largely in countries which had no machine
production, and we bought from them natural products which do not
exist in the British Isles. Where commerce is of this sort, it encourages
friendship between nations. But as soon as one country sells to another goods which the other is capable of producing, the anger of
competitors becomes more intense than the gratification of customers,
and friendship is turned into enmity. In the years before the Great

War, when, under the Merchandise Marks Act, all foreign goods sold in the United Kingdom had to be marked with the country of origin, the constant sight of the legend "Made in Germany" caused people to think that England was losing her trade owing to German competition—a belief which had much to do with stimulating bellicose feeling. The free trade argument, that imports are paid for by exports, and do not therefore injure home production as a whole, was at no time effective with those who suffered from foreign competition. In all advanced countries outside Great Britain, emulation of British industry was beginning in Cobden's time, but manufacturers were at a disadvantage as compared with the English and Scottish industrialists, and therefore demanded protection, which they obtained wherever they had sufficient political influence. Great Britain was not loved on account of cheap goods in the countries that were trying to build up industries on the British model. Intensification of commerce brought intensification of national enmity, and the development of sentiment was the opposite of what Cobden had expected. This was one of his most important mistakes in political psychology.

Cobden was politically opposed to the aristocracy, and in his earlier years to the working class, though to a lesser degree: to the former, because they represented privilege without brains; to the latter, because they lacked education. He had a very great admiration for America, largely because in that country industrial enterprise is not hampered by aristocratic influence and tradition, and foreign policy is free from the habit of meddling in the affairs of other countries. He chose as the motto of his first pamphlet Washington's dictum: "The great rule of conduct for us in regard to foreign nations is, in extending our commercial relations, to have with them as little political connection as possible." Throughout his political career, he urged this maxim upon English statesmen, but in vain. When, in 1859, Palmerston offered him Cabinet office, he refused because he could not acquiesce in the foreign policy of that blustering old ruffian.

Unlike most of the politicians of his day, Cobden regarded industry rather than armaments as the source of national power, and accordingly considered America more important than Russia. He says:

It is to the industry, the economy, and peaceful policy of America, and not to the growth of Russia, that our statesmen and politicians, of whatever creed, ought to direct their anxious study; for it is by these, and not by the efforts of barbarian force, that the power and greatness of England are in danger of being superseded: yes, by the successful rivalry of America shall we, in all probability, be placed second in the rank of nations.

To have arrived at this conviction in 1835 showed more sagacity than most people would now realize. Even as late as 1898, the Kaiser still expected Spain to be victorious in the Spanish-American War. The British Government was perhaps less belated than William II, but certainly did not reach the opinion expressed by Cobden until after the American Civil War.

With regard to the freedom of industrialists from aristocratic interference in America, Cobden says:

Nothing more strongly illustrates the disadvantages under which an old country, like Great Britain, labours in competing with her younger rival, than to glance at the progress of railroads in the two empires.

At the same time that, in the United States, almost every day beheld a new railway company incorporated, by some one of the States' legislatures, at the cost only of a few dollars, and nearly by acclamation, the British Parliament intercepted by its votes some of the most important projects that followed in the train of the Liverpool railroad.

The London and Birmingham Company, after spending upwards of forty thousand pounds, in attempting to obtain for its undertaking the sanction of the legislature, was unsuccessful in the House of Lords. The following characteristic questions are extracted from the evidence taken before the committee:

Do you know the name of Lady Hastings' place?—How near to it does your line go?—Taking the look out of the principal rooms of the house, does it run in front of the principal rooms?—How far from the house is the point where it becomes visible?—That would be about a quarter of a mile?—Could the engines be heard in the house at that distance?—Is there any cutting or embankment there?—Is it in sight of the house?— Looking to the country, is it not possible that the line could be taken at a greater distance from the residence of Lady Hastings?

In this emphasis on the evils of control by ignorant landowners Cobden was wholly justified. There is, however, another side to the question of American railways. The capitalists, being uncontrolled except by corruptible legislatures, acquired enormous areas of public land for nothing, and invented ingenious devices for swindling ordinary shareholders in the interests of directors. A regular technique was developed for transferring wealth first from public ownership to the shareholders in a company, and from them to the directors. By this means economic power came to be concentrated in the hands of a few unprecedentedly rich men.

Of the corruption in American business and politics, Cobden seems to have been unaware, although it had existed ever since Washington's first Presidency. Like almost all the men of his time, he believed in competition, but it was to be competition according to certain rules, like cricket. He would not have liked competition in buying judges to sanction breaches of the law, or inducing railways to carry the goods of one competitor more cheaply than those of the others. It was also against the rules, as he conceived them, for the State to take a hand in the game by helping its nationals at the expense of foreigners. The State was merely to be umpire, and to see that the competitors stuck to the rules. William James tells of a young man who, having learnt that the purpose of football is to get the ball to the other side of the goal-posts, got up one dark night and put it there. People who grow rich by the help of government seemed, to Cobden and the "Manchester School," as unsportsmanlike as this young man. This analogy would, however, have seemed to them grossly unfair. They did not realize that competition, as they conceived it, was a game with rules; they thought of it as a law of nature. As they were honest and worthy citizens, the criminal law in the background imposed no *conscious* limitation upon their activities. When they heard of the doings of Vanderbilt and Gould, they were shocked: this was not what they had meant at all! Yet undeniably it was competition.

Cobden regarded imperialism as folly, and had very just views on India, even during the mutiny, when most English people lost their heads. At the height of the madness on the subject of the mutiny he writes:

Unfortunately for me I can't even co-operate with those who seek to "reform" India, for I have no faith in the power of England to govern that country at all permanently; and though I should like to see the company abolished—because that is a screen between the English nation and a full sight of its awful responsibilities—yet I do not believe in the possibility of the Crown governing India under the control of Parliament. If the

House of Commons were to renounce all responsibility for domestic legislation, and give itself exclusively to the task of governing one hundred millions of Asiatics, it would fail. Hindostan must be ruled by those who live on that side of the globe. Its people will prefer to be ruled badly— *according to our notions*—by its own colour, kith and kin, than to submit to the humiliation of being better governed by a succession of transient intruders from the Antipodes.

At the same period, writing to Bright, he says:

It will be a happy day when England has not an acre of territory in Continental Asia. But how such a state of things is to be brought about is more than I can tell. I bless my stars that I am not in a position to be obliged to give public utterance to my views on the all-absorbing topic of the day, for I could not do justice to my own convictions and possess the confidence of any constituency in the kingdom. For where do we find even an individual who is not imbued with the notion that England would sink to ruin if she were deprived of her Indian Empire? Leave me, then, to my pigs and sheep, which are not labouring under any such delusions.

He was not at this time in Parliament, and was not obliged to give public expression to his views on India, but he felt himself even more isolated than during the Crimean War. He found that the manufacturers of Lancashire and Yorkshire regarded India as a market to be preserved for them by British bayonets, and he complained that they did not understand free trade principles. It does not seem to have occurred to him that India, left to itself, might develop a cotton industry by the help of a tariff, and no longer have need of imports from Manchester. The reasons for not attempting to govern India by force are, to my mind, perfectly valid, but I do not think that, at that time, they could have been reconciled with the pecuniary self-interest of the British textile industry. Free trade was, for Cobden, much more than a measure of fiscal common sense; it was part of a deep moral conviction. He believed firmly that honesty was the best policy, and was therefore sometimes a little blind to the best policy when this was in fact dishonest. The development of industry from this day to our own has shown that on this point his heart was better than his head.

Cobden is criticized, in our day, from two opposite points of view: by nationalists, on account of the cosmopolitanism which inspired his enthusiasm for free trade, and by Socialists on account of his dislike of trade unionism and Factory Acts. I think that perhaps the criticism of him from the latter point of view has been somewhat more fierce than it should have been. He certainly desired to improve the condition of the working classes, and he certainly did improve their condition most remarkably. From the time when free trade was adopted, real wages rose with great rapidity, except during the Crimean War, when we were blockading the ports from which most imported grain had come. The opening of the Middle West by means of railways caused a further improvement in real wages, but could not have done so without free trade. Lord Shaftesbury, who tackled the problem of conditions of labor philanthropically, was successful in causing the adoption of various valuable Factory Acts; but I do not think a sober inquirer can attribute nearly as much of the increase in the happiness of wage-earners to him as to Cobden. Nevertheless, owing to sentimentalism, Lord Shaftesbury has received much more credit than Cobden in this respect.

It is, of course, impossible to judge with any accuracy the share of free trade in promoting British prosperity, but it is at any rate obvious that, if the Corn Laws had remained in force, much more agricultural labor would have been required to feed the increasing population, and less food would have been secured by a given amount of labor on British land than by exchanging manufactures for food produced abroad. The increase of real wages, however caused, was remarkable. According to Clapham, real wages rose sharply from 1850 to 1874, after which they fell somewhat until 1886, and then rose again, until in 1890 they had surpassed the level of 1874. The average of real wages in 1874 was between 50 and 60 per cent above that of 1850. As for the cotton trade, with which Cobden was specially connected, even at the worst moment, in 1886, average earnings were still 48 per cent above the level of 1850. As regards the period before the repeal of the Corn Laws, money wages were lower in 1850 than in 1810, and real wages had risen little, if at all, between 1810 and 1846, when Peel became converted to free trade. In view of these facts, the importance of Cobden in raising wages can hardly be denied.

At the same time, it is clear that Cobden was opposed to all restrictions upon free competition between wage-earners. His attitude towards child labor was less doctrinaire. He was in favor of limiting the hours of labor for children, and the age at which they could be employed, but he was opposed to the Ten Hours Bill, which would have made sure that children did not work more than ten hours in factories by forbidding the factories to be at work more than this period in each day. Interference with the hours of adult labor seemed to him objectionable in principle, although experience had shown that it was very difficult to limit effectually the labor of children alone. In a letter written in 1836, in connection with his candidature at Stockport, he makes the highly unrealistic suggestion that every working man should save £20 out of his wages, so as to be free to emigrate to America. He appears to have been quite unaware of the evils revealed by Royal Commissions. In his first pamphlet, on England, Ireland, and America, he argues with much force that we ought to set to work to cure the poverty of Irish peasants before we interfere philanthropically in Continental affairs, but it never occurs to him that the same argument applies to industrial conditions in England.

His attitude to trade unions is frankly expressed in a letter to his brother in 1842. "Depend upon it," he says, "nothing can be got by fraternising with Trade Unions. They are founded upon principles of brutal tyranny and monopoly. I would rather live under a Dey of Algiers than a Trades Committee." This view was, no doubt, that of the bulk of employers in his day; moreover, it was in accordance with his general belief in free competition. But it illustrates his incapacity to see labor questions except from the standpoint of the employer.

He was, of course, opposed to all industrial action by the State except when absolutely necessary. In the last year of his life, in an elaborate speech, he argued that "the Government should not be allowed to manufacture for itself any article which could be obtained from private producers in a competitive market."

The victory of free trade in 1846 was not quite complete. It was then decided that from 1849 onwards there should be a duty of 1s. a quarter on grain; some other remnants of protection also remained, and the last of them was not abolished until 1874. The general policy of the Government was in favor of free trade until 1914, in spite of a protectionist campaign in the '80's, and another, more formidable, inaugurated by Joseph Chamberlain in 1903. What defeated him with the electorate was largely the lingering memory of the "hungry forties." During the earlier part of the free trade period, especially, every class in England made extraordinarily rapid progress. Free trade alone, of course, did not account for this; the industrial supremacy of England and the trans-continental railways in America were essential factors. But without free trade, progress could not have been so rapid. From 1846 to 1914, the doctrines of the economists, with occasional modifications, proved, on the whole, sufficient to provide continually increasing well-being in all classes.

Elsewhere, there were more complications. Napoleon III, it is true, was induced by Cobden to introduce free trade with England by the Commercial Treaty of 1860, which abolished previous prohibitions of imports on a host of articles, and reduced French duties on almost all imports from England to 30 per cent or less. But this was only passed by Napoleon's fiat, and was never widely popular in France. The manufacturers, as was natural, felt it impossible to stand up against English competition without the help of a tariff. In spite of their lack of enthusiasm, however, Napoleon made a similar treaty two years later with the German Zollverein. The only class in France who were whole-heartedly in favor of free trade were the vine-growers, since they depended upon exports. But when their business was ruined by the phylloxera, they became persuaded that, in some inscrutable manner, a tariff would enable them to cope with this noxious micro-organism. From that moment there have been no free-traders in France, except a few isolated intellectuals. But owing to commercial treaties, concluded under the influence of Cobden, it was not till 1892 that France adopted a tariff involving general high protection.

In Germany, where the multitude of petty states with separate customs caused intolerable vexations to commerce, the most important step towards free trade, from the industrialist's standpoint, was the establishment of the Zollverein (Customs Union), which, chiefly through the action of Prussia, gradually came to include all Northern Germany, and, after 1871, the whole of the new Empire except Hamburg and Bremen. In the formation of this Union, especially before the political unification of Germany, free trade theory, which was first introduced to Germans by Stein, naturally played a part. Moreover political power was mainly in the hands of territorial magnates, with the result that industrialists felt as they did in England before 1846. Consequently Liberal and middle-class Germany was on the whole in favor of free trade until German unity substituted the sentiment of nationalism for that of liberalism. In 1879, Bismarck led Germany to abandon the policy of virtual free trade which had been dominant. From this moment, belief in free competition played no part in German policy.

In America, half of Cobden's creed was adopted in the North, and the other half in the South. The South was in favor of free trade, since it lived by exporting cotton, and the only effect of a tariff was to raise the prices of what it had to buy. But the South depended on slavery. The North had democracy and free labor, but was determined to build up its industries by means of a high tariff. It was during the Civil War, and by means of a war-time tariff, that Northern industry first became really important. From that time onwards, America has been protectionist even at times when the revenue due to the tariff was not needed and was an embarrassment to the Administration.

But although, outside England, his influence on legislation was superficial and transient, Cobden's prestige on the Continent was immense. In 1846, after his great victory in England, he made a triumphal progress round Europe.

His reception was everywhere that of a great discoverer in a science which interests the bulk of mankind much more keenly than any other, the science of wealth. He had persuaded the richest country in the world to revolutionize its commercial policy. People looked on him as a man who had found out a momentous secret. In nearly every important town that he visited in every great country in Europe, they celebrated his visit by a banquet, toasts, and congratulatory speeches. He had interviews with the Pope, with three or four kings, with ambassadors, and with all the prominent statesmen. He never lost an opportunity of speaking a word in season. Even from the Pope he entreated that His Holiness's influence might be used against bull fighting in Spain.[1]

His Holiness, who was at this time (1847) still Liberal, and who had not yet realized that commerce is productive of sin, was very gracious. He promised to look into the question of bull-fighting, "professed himself to be favourable to Free Trade, and said all he

[1] Morley, *Life of Cobden*, Vol. I, p. 464.

could do should be done to forward it, but modestly added that he could do but little."

Metternich, whom he saw a few months later, talked to him incessantly for a long time, but not about free trade. He did not therefore greatly impress Cobden, who thought that his appearance suggested "high polish rather than any native force of character" and that his conversation was "more subtle than profound." After the interview he wrote optimistically in his journal:

He is probably the last of those State physicians who, looking only to the symptoms of a nation, content themselves with superficial remedies from day to day, and never attempt to probe beneath the surface, to discover the source of the evils which afflict the social system. This order of statesmen will pass away with him, because too much light has been shed upon the laboratory of Governments, to allow them to impose upon mankind with the old formulas.[2]

Austria and Russia were polite though not enthusiastic, but in Spain, Italy, and Germany, his popularity was overwhelming. In Spain he was likened to Christopher Columbus, in Italy he was serenaded by musicians, while his German admirers presented him with a large sum of money. This annoyed Treitschke, who hated him as a "materialist" and said:

The transformation in England inspired the free traders of all lands with victorious self-confidence, and during the ensuing two decades their doctrines maintained the upper hand almost universally throughout the civilised world. Every new discovery which the century could boast had contributed to bind the nations together, so that it seemed almost irrational to sever them by hostile tariffs. A long period of the mutual concession of commercial facilities began, and this favoured general well-being. But in the end the old truth was realised, that the home market is of much more importance than world trade.

The immense vogue of free trade doctrine in the mid-nineteenth century was due to Cobden, but the doctrine itself was first promulgated, so long ago as 1776, by Adam Smith, and was later submerged in the Napoleonic wars. The abstract argument in favor of free trade, as set forth by Smith and accepted by most subsequent British economists, is derived from the principle of division of

[2] *Ibid.*, p. 474.

labor. If A is good at making motor cars and B is good at making wine, it is profitable to both that each should confine himself to his own specialty and should exchange his product with the other. If each spent half the day making cars and half making wine, each would have fewer cars and less wine than if each sticks to his own job. This argument remains valid if A lives in one country and B in another. But these abstract considerations had little effect on governments.

It was the German economist List who first (in 1841) provided a theoretical defence of protectionism. This was the famous "infant industries" argument. Take, say, steel. It may be that a country is well suited by nature to the development of a great steel industry, but that, owing to foreign competition, the initial expenses are prohibitive, unless government assistance is obtainable. This situation existed in Germany when List wrote and for some time after that. But experience has shown that protection, once granted, cannot be withdrawn even when the infant has grown into a giant.

Another argument, which is not purely economic, and which has had more influence on governments, is that a nation should, as far as possible, produce all that is needed in time of war. This contention is part of the doctrine of economic nationalism, to which the Manchester School, who were pacifists and anti-imperialists, were bitterly opposed. Economic nationalism proved, in the end, more powerful than the purely commercial outlook of Cobden; but this was only one aspect of the growth of nationalism in general.

The principle of free competition, as advocated by the Manchester School, was one which failed to take account of certain laws of social dynamics. In the first place, competition tends to issue in somebody's victory, with the result that it ceases and is replaced by monopoly. Of this the classic example is afforded by the career of Rockefeller. In the second place, there is a tendency for the competition between individuals to be replaced by competition between groups, since a number of individuals can increase their chances of victory by combination. Of this principle there are two important examples, trade unionism and economic nationalism. Cobden, as we have seen, objected to trade unions, and yet they were an inevitable result of competition between employers and employed as to the share of the total product which each should secure. Cobden objected also to economic nationalism, yet this arose among capitalists from motives very similar to those which produced trade unionism among employees. Both in America and in Germany, it was obvious to industrialists that they could increase their wealth by combining to extract favors from the State; they thus competed as a national group against national groups in other countries. Although this was contrary to the principles of the Manchester School, it was an economically inevitable development. In all these ways, Cobden failed to understand the laws of industrial evolution, with the result that his doctrines had a merely temporary validity.

Although the principle of free competition was increasingly limited in practice—by Factory Acts, trade unions, protective tariffs, and trusts—it remained an ideal to which business men appealed whenever there was any proposal to interfere with their activities. The men at the head of vast monopolies in America still profess to believe in competition—meaning, however, competition for jobs on the part of those who wish to be employed by them. They still believe, as Francis Place did, that competition is the only possible incentive to industry. This belief has become harmful, since it interferes with organization where this would be more efficient than unregulated competition. However, it has much less intensity than it had sixty years ago. At that time it seemed consecrated as a cosmic law by Darwin.

Darwin's *Origin of Species* was published in 1859. It may be regarded as the application of Benthamite economics to the animal world. As every one knows, it was through reading Malthus that Darwin was led to the principles of the Struggle for Existence and the Survival of the Fittest. In his theory, all animals are engaged in the economic struggle to procure a livelihood, and those that have most thoroughly acquired the maxims of Smiles's *Self-Help* survive and found families, while the others perish. Hence emerges a general tendency to progress: the cleverest animals gradually oust the stupid ones, until at last we arrive at man.

Darwinism, as it appears in the writings of its founder, and still more in those of Herbert Spencer, is the completion of Philosophical Radicalism. But it contained elements which would have shocked Helvetius and James Mill, more especially those elements connected with heredity. It has been one of the characteristic doctrines of Radicalism that the mental differences between men are due to differences of education, taking that word in its widest sense. But Darwin regards heredity combined with spontaneous variation as essential to evolution. There are many species of insects among which one generation dies before the next is born; obviously their adaptation to environment owes nothing to education. Every Darwinian must hold that, among human beings, there are congenital differences of mental powers. James Mill informed his son John that his (John's) attainments were due, not to native ability, but to his having a father willing to take so much trouble in teaching him. A Darwinian would have attributed some of John's progress to his heredity. This made a breach in the Radical doctrine that all men are born equal.

It was, of course, easy to adopt Darwinism to nationalism. The Jews, or the Nordics, or the Ecuadorians, are pronounced to be the best stock, and it is inferred that everything ought to be done to make them rich—although statistics prove that the rich have fewer descendants than the poor. In this way, also, Darwinism afforded a transition from the cosmopolitan outlook of the Philosophical Radicals to the racial bigotry of the Hitlerites.

It is amusing to observe how, as belief in free competition in the economic world decayed, the biologists began to be dissatisfied with the Struggle for Existence as the driving force of evolution. What they have substituted is far from definite, but at any rate it is something quite different. Perhaps when our politics have settled down our theory of evolution will again become clear.

There was one other respect in which Darwinism was fatal to the Cobdenite form of belief in competition. Competition, as conceived by the Manchester School, was not only between individuals rather than between groups, but was purely economic, and within a framework of law. Competition between animals is not thus limited, and it was obvious historically that the most important form of competition between human beings has been war. Thus Darwinism in its popular form tended to be bellicose and imperialistic, although Darwin himself had no such tendencies.

Darwinism, therefore, in spite of its origin, has been a force inimical both to Cobdenism and to Philosophical Radicalism. By emphasizing heredity, it has lessened men's belief in the omnipotence of education, and has substituted the conviction that some races are inherently superior to others. This, in turn, has led to an emphasis upon nationalism. And the recognition of war as a means of competition has dissolved the marriage of competition with pacifism, which was always an ill-assorted union, since the natural partner of pacifism is cooperation.

I am not suggesting that popular Darwinism, in drawing these inferences, has been scientifically justified. In a different environment, it might have retained the political outlook of Darwin and Spencer. Certainly biology, as it is at present, does not warrant nationalism or love of war. But just as the doctrines of Malthus caused an intellectual difficulty for the earlier forms of Radicalism, so the doctrines of Darwin caused an intellectual difficulty for the later forms. Just as the earlier difficulty was overcome by birth control, so the later difficulty will be overcome by eugenics. But it will have to be a more scientific and less biassed form of eugenics than any now in vogue.

CHAPTER XV

OWEN AND EARLY BRITISH SOCIALISM

THE doctrine of *laissez faire* was not left unchallenged, even in the days of its greatest influence. Most owners of factories thought of the State as the source of tariffs and Orders in Council, and sought to reduce its functions to the punishment of discontented workmen. Organization appeared to them an evil, and they wished every man (within the limits of the law) to be left to sink or swim as his own strength might decide.

The factory could, however, suggest a quite different order of ideas. On the one hand, any large factory is itself an organization, and derives its efficiency from being well organized. In the second place, the productive capacity of a well-equipped factory is so great that, if there is no organization of output, there may be a glut, by which employers will be ruined and men will be thrown out of work. Thus the factory viewed from within suggests the utility of organization, while viewed from without it shows the dangers of unfettered production. It was reflections such as these that caused Robert Owen, after many successful years as a manufacturer, to become the founder of Socialism.

In every important movement, the pioneers are not the intellectual equals of the men who come later. There were writers of Italian verse before Dante, Protestant Reformers before Luther, inventors of steam engines before James Watt. Such men deserved the credit of originality in conception, but not of success in execution. The same may be said of Robert Owen. He is not so comprehensive as Karl Marx: he is not so able a reasoner as his orthodox contemporaries who built upon the foundation laid by Adam Smith. But just be-

146

cause his ideas are not rigidly confined within a system, he is an initiator of various important lines of development. In some ways he is curiously modern. He considers industry from the standpoint of the wage-earner's interests, while retaining the dictatorial mentality of the large employer. In this he reminds one of Soviet Russia: it is easy to imagine him entering with zest into the preparation of Five Year Plans, and coming to grief through failure to understand agriculture. It would, however, be misleading to press the analogy. Owen was not quite a sage, but he was quite a saint; few men have been more wholly lovable. After the dry and dusty atmosphere of the Utilitarians, and amid the horrors of the factory system of his day, his warm and generous personality is as refreshing as summer rain.

Robert Owen was born in the small town of Newtown, Montgomeryshire, in the year 1771, and died in the same place in 1858.[1] During these eighty-seven years his incredibly active life passed through many phases, some important, some unimportant, but all interesting as illustrating a very remarkable character. His father was a saddler, and also postmaster, but the salary of this office certainly did not exceed £10 a year. Robert went to school at about four years old, but at the age of seven, having mastered the three R's, he became an usher, and during the next two years he learnt little in school except the art of teaching. He had, however, certain advantages outside school hours. "As I was known to and knew every family in the town, I had the libraries of the clergyman, physician, and lawyer—the learned men of the town—thrown open to me, with permission to take home any volume which I liked, and I made full use of the liberty given to me." Three maiden ladies, all Methodists, tried to convert him to their faith, but "as I read religious works of all parties, I became surprised, first at the opposition between the different sects of Christians; afterwards at the deadly hatred between the Jews, Christians, Mahomedans, Hindoos, Chinese, etc., etc., and between these and what they called Pagans and Infidels. The study of these contending faiths, and their deadly hatred to each other, began to create doubts in my mind respecting the truth of any one of these divisions . . . My reading religious works combined with my other

---

[1] The biographical material in what follows is mainly from Podmore's *Robert Owen, a Biography*, 1906; Cole's *Life of Owen* is also useful.

readings, compelled me to feel strongly at ten years of age that there must be something fundamentally wrong in all religions, as they had been taught up to that period."

According to his own recollection, he was only once punished by his parents:

I was always desirous to meet the wishes of both my parents, and never refused to do whatever they asked me to do. One day my mother indistinctly said something to me to which I supposed the proper answer was "no," and in my usual way I said "no"—supposing I was meeting her wishes. Not understanding me, and supposing that I refused her request, she immediately, and to me rather sharply—for her custom was to speak kindly to me—said "What! Won't you?" Having said "no," I thought if I said "yes, I will" I should be contradicting myself, and should be expressing a falsehood, and I said again "no," but without any idea of disobeying her. If she had then patiently and calmly enquired what my thoughts and feelings were, a proper understanding would have arisen, and everything would have proceeded as usual. But my mother, not comprehending my thoughts and feelings, spoke still more sharply and angrily—for I had never previously disobeyed her, and she was no doubt greatly surprised and annoyed when I repeated that I would not. My mother never chastised any of us—this was left for my father to do, and my brothers and sisters occasionally felt a whip which was kept to maintain order among the children; but I had never previously been touched with it. My father was called in and my refusal stated. I was again asked if I would do what my mother required, and I said firmly "no," and I then felt the whip every time after I refused when asked if I would yield and do what was required. I said "no" every time I was so asked, and at length said quietly but firmly—"You may kill me, but I will not do it"; and this decided the contest. There was no attempt ever afterwards to correct me. From my own feelings, which I well remember when a child, I am convinced that very often punishment is not only useless, but very pernicious, and injurious to the punisher and the punished.

At the age of ten, Owen persuaded his parents that he was old enough to seek his fortune in the world. His father gave him forty shillings and sent him to London, to stay with his elder brother, who had a saddler's business in High Holborn. After six weeks, this ten-year-old boy obtained a situation with a Mr. James McGuffog, a shopkeeper at Stamford in Lincolnshire. From that moment, he never cost his parents a penny. All went well: his employer liked him, and he liked his employer. Their only disagreements seem to have been about religion:

It was with the greatest reluctance, and after long contests in my mind, that I was compelled to abandon my first and deep-rooted impressions in favour of Christianity. But being obliged to give up my faith in this sect, I was at the same time compelled to reject all others, for I had discovered that all had been based on the same absurd imagination, "that each one formed his own qualities—determined his own thoughts, will, and action, —and was responsible for them to God and to his fellow-men." My own reflections compelled me to come to very different conclusions. My reason taught me that I could not have made one of my own qualities—that they were forced upon me by Nature; that my language, religion, and habits were forced upon me by Society; and that I was entirely the child of Nature and Society; that Nature gave the qualities, and Society directed them. Thus was I forced, through seeing the error of their foundation, to abandon all belief in every religion which had been taught to man. But my religious feelings were immediately replaced by the spirit of universal charity—not for a sect or a party, or for a country or a colour, but for the human race, and with a real and ardent desire to do them good.

However, it presently became necessary to obtain a new situation, and one was found in the shop of Messrs. Flint & Palmer, on London Bridge, where he thought himself rich on £25 a year. His duties here were onerous. He had to be in the shop by eight o'clock, ready dressed, "and dressing then was no slight affair. Boy as I was then, I had to wait my turn for the hairdresser to powder and pomatum and curl my hair, for I had two large curls on each side, and a stiff pigtail, and until all this was very nicely and systematically done, no one could think of appearing before a customer." The work was not finished when the shop closed, and often it was two o'clock in the morning before he could get to bed. He did not like having no leisure for self-education, and he feared the long hours might, in the end, injure his health, so he obtained a new situation with a Mr. Satterfield of Manchester. Here he remained until 1789, when, having reached the mature age of eighteen, he decided to start in business on his own account.

At this time, Crompton's mule was a very recent invention, but was not patented. Owen borrowed £100 from his brother, and, in partnership with a man named Jones, set to work to manufacture spinning-mules. But in the following year Jones found a partner with more capital, and Owen was bought out; he was to receive six mules in payment, but in fact received only three. With these three, he started a factory, and in the first year made a profit of £300.

At the end of this year, he heard that a Mr. Drinkwater, a rich fustian manufacturer, was in need of a new manager, and he applied for the job. Being asked what salary he wanted, he said: "Three hundred a year." Mr. Drinkwater, in horror, exclaimed that he had already that morning interviewed many applicants, and all their demands together did not amount to so much. Owen, however, refused to come down, and proved that he was earning as much by his own factory. In the proper style of the go-getter's manual, Owen managed to impress Mr. Drinkwater and to obtain the job. He was very successful, and was soon taken into partnership. (He was now twenty.) However, when an opportunity occurred of amalgamating with the important firm of Mr. Oldknow, who wished to marry Drinkwater's daughter, Owen was asked how much he would take to cancel the partnership; his feelings were hurt, he destroyed the deed of partnership, and resigned his position as manager. He suffered no loss by this rash action, being so favorably known that nothing interfered with his success, and he was soon in a new partnership, in which, as before, everything prospered with him.

His next step—which determined his subsequent business career—was to marry the daughter of a rich Scottish manufacturer, David Dale, and buy up his mills at New Lanark. This occurred when he was twenty-eight. David Dale, who was very devout, had for some time objected to Owen as a son-in-law, on account of his views on religion. But no one could long resist the charm of Owen's character. When it came to selling the mills, Mr. Dale—a very successful business man, and a Scotchman—left it to Owen to fix the price. Owen said he valued the mills at £60,000. "If you think so," replied Mr. Dale, "I will accept the proposal as you have stated it, if your friends also approve of it." Owen's friends (who were his partners) did approve, and the transaction was completed. Owen's marriage to Mr. Dale's daughter took place shortly afterwards, in September 1799. She remained devout, and was persuaded that her husband would go to hell. Nevertheless she loved him all her life, and he loved her when his projects left him leisure to remember her. For many years they lived at New Lanark, and he, as far as his partners would let him, conducted the place on model lines. It was invariably successful from a business point of view, and its success in other respects made it famous throughout the world.

Owen's years in Manchester had given him the opportunity of making friends with men of intellectual ability. In 1793 he became a member of the Manchester Literary and Philosophical Society, to which he in turn proposed Dalton, the man who introduced the atomic theory into chemistry. Dalton was an intimate friend of Owen. Dr. Perceval, the founder of the Manchester Literary and Philosophical Society, was a strong advocate of factory legislation, and probably influenced Owen on the subject. After this time, there is little evidence of Owen learning from others.

The life of Robert Owen may be divided into four periods. In the first, he is the typical hero of Smiles's *Self-Help*, rising rapidly by his own efforts to a position of wealth and influence. This period ends with his acquisition of New Lanark. In the second period he appears as the benevolent yet shrewd employer, who could make his factory pay in spite of philanthropic methods which other employers thought sure to lead to ruin. In this period he was still amazingly successful, but what made his success amazing was the combination of business and virtue. This phase of his life begins, in 1815, to give way to the phase of social reform, though he remained associated with New Lanark, more or less loosely, until 1828 or 1829. In his social reform period he was not successful in any immediate sense, though he inaugurated Socialism, the co-operative movement, and working-class free thought. Gradually he passed from being a revered leader of the working-class movement to being the High Priest of a small sect; after about 1835, he ceased to have public importance and became a mere visionary, ending in spiritualism. His early successes and his subsequent failures have the same source: self-confidence. So long as he was attempting things essentially feasible, his self-confidence was an asset; when, later, he tried to achieve in a few years changes requiring at least a century, his failure and his self-confidence came into conflict, driving him away from the real world—further and further away, till he was left with voices out of his own past, where alone his unconscious will had the omnipotence that he unconsciously expected of it in every sphere. Perhaps no man can be a great innovator without more belief in himself than reason can warrant. The greatest innovators have thought themselves divine, or nearly so; in Owen this same disease existed, but in a mild and not unamiable form. Where other prophets have declared the word of God, Owen declared the word of Reason, and it amazed him that men's intellects could be so blind; but of their hearts he always thought well.

At New Lanark, Owen's aims were still modest, and his success was great. He first installed up-to-date machinery and an efficient manager. He then extirpated theft, which had been rampant, without any legal punishment. He next tackled drunkenness: he appointed men to patrol the streets of New Lanark at night, and report any cases of drunkenness, for which a fine was inflicted. Within a few years, partly by this method and partly by personal influence, he succeeded in almost entirely stopping drunkenness except on New Year's Day. He insisted on cleanliness in the streets. To encourage industrious habits in the mills, he invented a curious scheme. He had bits of wood, with the four sides painted black, blue, yellow and white respectively: black for bad, blue for indifferent, yellow for good, and white for excellent. One of these was prominently displayed near each workman, showing whichever color his work and conduct deserved. Oddly enough, this method was found very effective; in the end, almost everybody deserved yellow or white.[2]

So far, we have been considering what Owen did to make the mills productive. In this he was so successful that, during the first ten years of his management, the business earned a profit of £60,000 in addition to interest at 5 per cent on the capital. His partners, therefore, had every reason to be satisfied with him. Having secured their approbation, he was free to attempt more philanthropic measures.

When Owen took over New Lanark, the number of employees was between 1,800 and 2,000, of whom 500 were apprenticed children from the workhouses. He resolved at once to take no more pauper children. He took only children over ten, and these he obtained from the neighboring town of Lanark, by the consent of their parents. His partners insisted on a working day of fourteen

[2] An analogous custom exists in the U.S.S.R. at the present time. Collective farms are awarded badges symbolizing their degrees of merit: for example, an aeroplane for the best and a crawling crab for the worst.

hours, less two hours' interval for meals; but in 1816 he succeeded in getting these hours somewhat reduced. As for wages: in 1819, the average wages were, for men, 9s. 11d. a week; for women, 6s.; for boys, 4s. 3d.; for girls, 3s. 5d. It must be admitted that there is nothing Utopian about these figures. In such matters, Owen was not free, since he had to earn dividends. As it was, his partners were always complaining of his philanthropy. In 1809, and again in 1813, he bought out the existing partners by the help of new ones, who, he hoped, would give him a freer hand. On the second occasion, the bulk of the new money was supplied by Jeremy Bentham and a Quaker, William Allen. With the latter he still had difficulties, but they were of a different sort from those that he had had with his former partners, and on the whole less serious.

At first, he had some trouble with his workpeople, owing to his being a southerner and a stranger. But he gradually won them over, partly by his personality, but still more by his action in 1806, when the United States placed an embargo on all exports to Great Britain, thereby cutting off the supplies of raw cotton. For four months the mills had to be closed, but he kept on all his employees at full wages. After this, all had confidence in him.

One of the most interesting parts of Owen's management was the establishment of a school in connection with the factory. Like all other reformers of that period, he attributed enormous importance to education, and held that character is wholly, or almost wholly, the product of circumstances. But unlike the others, who acknowledged the authority of Helvetius, he discovered this great truth himself (or so he says) through the effect upon his digestion of very hot "flummery," a kind of porridge. He certainly had one advantage over James Mill: he loved and understood children. Everything that he says about education is good, and he understands the emotions and the bodies of children as well as their intellects. There was a nursery school on thoroughly modern lines. Dancing, in suitable costume, was an important part of the curriculum, which pained Mr. Allen, especially as the boys wore kilts instead of trousers. He made Owen promise that this sort of thing should cease, but apparently it continued none the less.

New Lanark was famous throughout the world, and in ten years nearly 20,000 persons visited it. Among others came the Grand Duke

Nicholas (afterwards Tsar), who stayed the night at Owen's house and listened to Owen expounding his views for two hours or more. He offered to take one of Owen's sons into his service, and even suggested that Owen himself should come to Russia with two millions of the surplus population and their families. In view of Nicholas's later career, this incident is curious.

When Owen, in 1813, visited London with a view to getting new partners, he made the acquaintance of almost everybody of note—not only all the Philosophical Radicals, but also the Prime Minister, the Archbishop of Canterbury, and many other prominent men. Everybody liked him, and he had not yet advocated any obviously subversive doctrines. In 1814 he published *A new view of Society,* in which he set forth his favorite doctrine of the power of circumstances in molding character, and deduced that enormous improvements could easily be effected. This work was sent to almost everybody who had influence, and even to Napoleon in Elba. Strange to say, Napoleon read it, and returned it with favorable comments. When he returned from Elba, Owen held that he should be allowed a chance to put its precepts into practice. Owen's friend the Prime Minister, however, thought otherwise.

It was in 1815 that Owen first came into contact with practical politics, through an attempt to carry a Bill regulating the labor of children in factories. He wished to forbid completely the employment of children under ten in textile factories, and to allow not more than ten and a half hours a day of work for any one under the age of eighteen. At first all went well. Owen secured the good will of the Government, provided he could obtain the support of Parliament. In Parliament he won many supporters. The Bill was put in charge of the elder Sir Robert Peel, who had carried in 1802 the only Factory Act then in force, that regulating the employment of pauper apprentices in cotton factories. But Sir Robert Peel was himself a manufacturer; he insisted upon consulting the others; the others began to organize opposition, and it became clear that the Bill could only be carried after a long fight, and then with many concessions.

Peel, after introducing a Bill on Owen's lines in 1815, allowed it to be postponed, and in 1816 contented himself with a committee of inquiry. Before this committee employers gave evidence of the beneficial effect of long hours on children's moral character. Fourteen hours

a day spent in the mill made them obedient, industrious, and punc-
tual; for their own sakes, nothing should be done to shorten their
hours. Besides, it would be impossible to face foreign competition if
the legislature interfered; the manufacturers would be ruined, and
everybody would be out of work. As against these witnesses, various
medical men maintained that the long hours were injurious to health.
Owen and Peel, alone among employers who gave evidence, were in
favor of the Bill.

Nothing was done in 1817, because Peel was ill. In 1818, however,
he re-introduced his Bill, somewhat modified in the hope of diminishing the employers' opposition; it passed the Commons, but was defeated in the Lords. Their Lordships succeeded in finding a number
of medical men willing to swear that nothing is so good for the health
of children as fifteen hours a day in factories. "One well-known doctor even refused to commit himself to the statement that a child's
health would be injured by standing for twenty-three out of the
twenty-four hours." [3]

At last, in 1819, a Bill passed through both Houses. It was in
many respects less satisfactory than that of 1815. It applied only to
cotton, not to all textiles; it put the age limit at nine instead of ten;
it allowed twelve hours of actual work, and thirteen and a half in the
factory, including meal-times; instead of appointing inspectors, it left
the business of inspection to magistrates and clergymen. Experience
of the Act of 1802 had shown that magistrates and clergymen could
be relied upon to neglect their duty, and the new Act, as was hoped,
proved totally ineffective in consequence.

Owen, meanwhile, had embarked upon his first great scheme for
regenerating the world. Considering that Socialism sprang from this
scheme, it is amazing to find the extent to which, at first, Owen was
favored by the great. The Duke of Kent, Queen Victoria's father,
remained his friend so long as he lived (he died in 1820). The Duke
of York, the Archbishop of Canterbury, various Bishops and many
Peers, listened to him with respect, both on account of his persuasive
and conciliatory manner, and on account of his practical success at
New Lanark. Bit by bit, as his honesty got the better of his tact,
his fine friends fell away from him, but at first all the world was
predisposed in his favor.

[3] Hammond, *Town Labourer*, p. 167.

Owen's original proposals were made to a Select Committee in 1817, which was inquiring into the Poor Law. The Peace had brought wide-spread unemployment; as Owen said, "on the day on which peace was signed the great customer of the producers died." But apart from this temporary cause, machinery was more and more displacing human labor. There was an optimistic doctrine that the cheapness of machine-made goods so stimulated demand that as much labor could be employed as in the days of handicrafts. In so far as there was truth in this belief, it depended upon a continually expanding foreign market. In 1816 and 1817, however, the foreign market was not expanding: tariffs were being imposed on the Continent, and the South American market was as yet only very partially opened. In any case, as every one knows now, foreign markets cannot expand indefinitely. Owen was the first man who fully realized the problems raised by the productive power of machines. Peace, he says,

found Great Britain in possession of a new power in constant action, which, it may be safely stated, far exceeded the labour of one hundred millions of the most industrious human beings in the full strength of manhood. To give an instance of this power, there is machinery at work in one establishment in this country, aided by a population not exceeding 2,500 souls, which produces as much as the existing population of Scotland could manufacture after the mode in common practice fifty years ago! And Great Britain contains several such establishments! . . . Thus our country possessed, at the conclusion of the war, a productive power which operated to the same extent as if her population had been actually increased fifteen or twenty fold; and this had been chiefly created within the preceding twenty-five years.[4]

He continues:

The war demand for the productions of labour having ceased, markets could no longer be found for them; and the revenues of the world were inadequate to purchase that which a power so enormous in its effects did produce: a diminished demand, consequently, followed. When, therefore, it became necessary to contract the sources of supply, it soon proved that mechanical power was much cheaper than human labour. The former, in consequence, was continued at work, whilst the latter was superseded; and human labour may now be obtained at a price far less than is absolutely necessary for the subsistence of the individual in ordinary comfort.[5]

[4] Cole, *Owen*, p. 177.   [5] *Ibid.*, p. 179.

"The working classes," he concludes, "have now no adequate means of contending with mechanical power." Since machinery cannot be discontinued, either millions must starve or "advantageous occupation must be found for the poor and unemployed working classes, to whose labour mechanism must be rendered subservient, instead of being applied, as at present, to supersede it."

This was, I think, the first time that any one had perceived our modern problem. To rail at machinery is useless, and yet, if the matter is left to the free play of the old economic forces, a mechanized world is one in which labor is impoverished and enslaved. This evil can only be prevented by deliberate planning, not by a policy of *laissez faire*. So Owen contended, in an economic situation which was like our own in miniature. The growth of foreign trade first, and then of economic imperialism, concealed the truth of his doctrine for a hundred years. At last time has proved that he perceived important laws of industrial development which were entirely overlooked by the orthodox economists of his day. Among the Radicals, Place defeated him in argument by means of the principle of population, and had in fact, on what was then known, a better case; but in the long run Owen's diagnosis has proved its validity.

Owen's cure was not so perspicacious as his analysis of the evil. At first, since he was presenting his Plan to a body which was inquiring into the Poor Law, he presented it mainly as a method of dealing with pauperism. His scheme was to collect the unemployed into villages, where they should co-operate in cultivating the soil, and also in manufacturing, though the bulk of their work should usually be agricultural. They were all to live in one large group of buildings, containing public reading rooms and a common kitchen, all meals being taken in common. All children over three years old were to live in a separate boarding house, and there was to be adequate provision for their education from the earliest age. All were to live in harmony and produce in common. The latest results of chemistry were to be utilized in making the agriculture scientific, but, like Kropotkin at a later date, Owen believed in intensive cultivation. On quite inadequate grounds he preferred the spade to the plough. While his factories were to be up-to-date and his manuring scientific, the actual tilling of the soil was to remain primitive.

Owen's Plan astonished and amused his contemporaries. Peacock introduces him as "Mr. Toogood, the co-operationist, who will have neither fighting nor praying; but wants to parcel out the world into squares like a chess-board, with a community on each, raising everything for one another, with a great steam-engine to serve them in common for tailor and hosier, kitchen and cook. When everybody is advancing a scheme to regenerate the world, Mr. Toogood says: 'Build a grand co-operative parallelogram, with a steam-engine in the middle for a maid of all work.' " Owen's "parallelograms" were a general subject for laughter, and were not taken seriously except by a very few people. As a matter of fact, apart from all other difficulties, the financial obstacles were insuperable. He himself estimated the cost of starting an establishment for 1,200 men, women, and children at £96,000. True, once started it was to be self-supporting and to pay interest on the capital invested. But who was going to regenerate mankind at a cost of £80 per head? The thing might be tried experimentally on a small scale, but as a cure for the ills of the nation it was clearly out of the question.

Owen did not fail for lack of skill in securing the right kind of publicity. He formed a committee containing most of the important personages; he received encouragement from the Government; and he induced *The Times* and other leading newspapers to write in his praise and to insert articles by him. Whenever they did so, he purchased 30,000 copies for distribution—which may possibly have influenced them in his favor.

He did not claim originality for his Plan. He himself maintained that priority belonged to a writer named John Bellers, who published, in 1696, a pamphlet called *Proposals for raising A College of Industry of all useful Trades and Husbandry, etc.* It is probable that he also owed something to a community of Rappites in Pennsylvania. His enemies said that his ideas were much the same as those of Thomas Spence, who held that the land belonged to the people, and ought not to be left in private ownership. Thomas Spence, whether or not his ideas contributed to Owen's, is a man who deserves to be remembered. He was born in 1750, and died in 1814; from the year 1775 onwards, and throughout the worst period of the anti-Jacobin reaction, he continued to advocate the nationalization of the land, first in Newcastle, and then as a bookseller in Chancery Lane. He was led to his opinions by an incident which occurred in Newcastle in 1775. The Corporation enclosed and let part of the Town Moor, but the freemen brought an action claiming the rent, and won. He published a book with the attractive title *Pig's Meat, or Lessons for the Swinish Multitude*. His first paper, which he read to the Newcastle Philosophical Society, was called "On the mode of administering the landed estates of the Nation as a Joint Stock property in Parochial Partnership by dividing the rent." He was frequently in prison, and so were his followers, who called themselves "Spencean philanthropists." The Government accused them of plots, and suspended *Habeas Corpus* on account of them. Such an ancestry for Owen's ideas was not calculated to conciliate Archbishops. But it was not the bugbear of Spence that finally lost Owen his support in high places.

He had expounded his Plan at a public meeting on August 14, 1817, with complete confidence that it would soon be adopted throughout the whole world. He had much support, but there were some who rejected his scheme from the first. There were Radicals, including Cobbett, who regarded it as "nothing short of a species of monkery." Malthus objected to his scheme on grounds of population, though Ricardo was on the whole favorable. The poet Southey nosed out the insufficiency of religion in Owen's method of regenerating the world. As regards this last accusation, Owen decided that it would not be honest to keep silent. At a second meeting, on August 21st, he delivered a carefully prepared address, in the course of which he stated, with all possible emphasis, not only that he himself was not a Christian, but further that he regarded religion as the chief source of all human ills:

My friends, I tell you, that hitherto you have been prevented from even knowing what happiness really is, solely in consequence of the errors— gross errors—that have been combined with the fundamental notions of every religion that has hitherto been taught to men. And, in consequence, they have made man the most inconsistent, and the most miserable being in existence. By the errors of these systems he has been made a weak, imbecile animal; a furious bigot and fanatic; or a miserable hypocrite; and should these qualities be carried, not only into the projected villages, but *into Paradise itself, a Paradise would be no longer found!* . . .

After this, naturally, Owen was dropped by the Archbishop and

Bishops, the Dukes and Cabinet Ministers, *The Times* and the *Morning Post*. Among the great, only the Duke of Kent, and to a lesser extent the Duke of Sussex, continued to stand up for him. The opponents of factory legislation in Parliament found their most telling argument against mercy to children in the fact that the champion of mercy was an infidel. Nothing daunted, Owen went on his way as if everything were succeeding perfectly, and set to work to try to obtain the capital required for starting at least one co-operative village. For the moment, however, nothing came of his efforts.

In the following year, being on the Continent, he presented a memorial to the Congress at Aix-la-Chapelle. Here he had his one (not very fortunate) meeting with the Emperor Alexander:

He introduced himself to the Czar (Alexander I., elder brother of Owen's guest, the Grand Duke Nicholas) as the latter was leaving his hotel, and offered him a copy of the two Memorials. The Czar had no pocket big enough to hold the papers and refused to accept them at the moment, asking Owen to call on him that evening. The brusqueness of his tone offended Owen, and he refrained from accepting the invitation. Owen entrusted copies of his Memorial, however, to Lord Castlereagh, one of the British representatives at Aix-la-Chapelle, to present to the Congress, and he learnt afterwards from various sources that they were considered to be amongst the most important documents laid before the assembly.

He should have remembered that a well-dressed man, however devout he may become, does not care to spoil his clothes by filling the pockets with papers.

Owen gradually became aware that the Government would not take up his Plan, but he still had hopes of the local authorities. In 1820, he presented a long Report to the County of Lanark, explaining his ideas in considerable detail. The most important novelty in this Report is his proposal that Labor Notes should take the place of money. The Government was about to resume gold payments, which had been suspended in 1797 on account of the war; currency questions were therefore to the fore. According to Owen's proposal, all prices would be fixed in proportion to the labor involved in production, and all payments would be in labor units. "The natural unit of value," he says, "is, in principle, human labour, or the combined manual and mental powers of men called into action." To the adoption of this system he attributed almost magical powers. As always after 1817, his hopes were excessive, and his consciousness of obstacles almost non-existent. As he grew older, his sense of reality grew less, and the apocalyptic strain in his character became more and more prominent.

There is, however, a great deal that is true and important in the Report to the County of Lanark. It begins by stating that labor is the source of all wealth,[6] and it argues that there is no difficulty in producing enough, but only in finding a market. The markets are created by working-class demand, which depends upon wages; therefore to improve markets it is only necessary to raise wages. "But the existing arrangements of Society will not permit the labourer to be remunerated for his industry, and in consequence all markets fail." After expounding his labor-currency and his villages, he goes on to argue against excessive division of labor. Children are to have an all-round training, and adults are to combine agriculture with industrial work. Education, as always with Owen, is treated as the basis of all the rest. But the consequences aimed at are far-reaching. All will have enough, and therefore there will be no more wars, no more crimes, no more prisons; instead, there will be universal happiness.

The four years 1824 to 1828 were largely occupied in an experimental community on the lines of the co-operative parallelograms. George Rapp, a German religious reformer, had conducted to America a number of earnest Rappites, who founded a colony called Harmony, first in Pennsylvania, and later in Indiana. They renounced marriage and tobacco, with the result that they became prosperous. In 1824 they decided to move again, and early in 1825 they sold all that they owned in Indiana to Owen, who called the place New Harmony, and proceeded, after addressing the President and Congress in Washington, to organize such a community as he had dreamed of. Everything went wrong, as it generally does in such experiments. Owen lost £40,000, and emerged a poor man. His sons, however, who came to New Harmony with him, retained some of the land, and in the end became successful American citizens.

Oddly enough, there was just one respect in which New Harmony

[6] This, of course, is only partially true, as we have seen in connection with Ricardo.

achieved success, and that an entirely surprising one. Owen imported from Europe a number of men of science, many of whom did valuable work. His own sons were in charge of the United States Geological Survey, the headquarters of which was at New Harmony till 1856. Podmore, writing in 1906, says:

Thus, though Owen's great experiment failed, a quite unlooked-for success in another direction rewarded his efforts. New Harmony remained for more than a generation the chief scientific and educational centre in the West; and the influences which radiated from it have made themselves felt in many directions in the social and political structure of the country. Even to this day the impress of Robert Owen is clearly marked upon the town which he founded. New Harmony is not as other towns of the Western States. It is a town with a history. The dust of those broken hopes and ideals forms the soil in which the life of the present is rooted. The name of Owen is still borne in the town by several prominent citizens, descendants of the great Socialist. The town is proud in the possession of a public library—the librarian himself a grandson of one of the original colonists—of some fifteen thousand volumes, many of them scarce and valuable works.

After a meteoric career in the trade union movement (which will be considered in the next chapter, and which ended in 1834), Owen no longer had any intimate connection with working-class Radicalism. He became the leader of a small sect of free-thinkers, and was no longer, in the eyes of respectable people, "the benevolent Mr. Owen"; he was a dangerous character, inciting the populace to atheism and revolutionary activity. In 1835, he added to his unpopularity by proclaiming unorthodox views of marriage in a series of lectures published under the title: *Lectures on the Marriages of the Priesthood of the Old Immoral World*. The title is misleading; he means marriages celebrated by the priesthood. Owen was by this time a complete Communist, and he objected to marriage as an institution connected with private property, and involving something like property in persons. He denounced not only marriage but the family environment for children, and that in very violent language. But he seems to have hoped that, in spite of liberty, there would still be many life-long unions.

Whether these views were a theoretical outcome of Communism, as in Plato, or were suggested by some circumstance in his private life, I do not know. Mrs. Owen died in 1831, and although he was frequently away from her for long periods, there is no evidence that he ceased to feel affection for her. In the last year of her life she wrote to him:

Oh my dear husband, how much I feel the want of you to advise with in a time of so much anxiety. . . . I hope you will remember next Thursday, the day when we became *one*—thirty-one years ago, and I think from what I feel myself that we love one another as sincerely and understand one another much better than we did thirty-one years ago. My sincere wish is that nothing may ever happen to diminish this affection.

His enemies, though they denounced his doctrines, found nothing to say against his private life. Parallelograms, nursery schools, abolition of private property, and abolition of marriage form a logically consistent body of doctrine, and there is no reason to look for any other source of his views of morals.

In these gloomy days, there were only two people who were not shocked by Owen's wickedness; one was Lord Melbourne, and the other was—Queen Victoria. In spite of the business of the Dorchester Laborers,[7] Owen had remained on friendly terms with Melbourne, who presented him to the Queen in 1839. Owen never met anybody without presenting a document, so he gave his Sovereign "an address from the Congress of the Delegates of the Universal Community Society of Rational Religionists, soliciting the Government to appoint parties to investigate measures which the Congress proposes to ameliorate the condition of Society." History does not relate whether, in view of this alluring title, Her Majesty was graciously pleased to peruse the work.

No one ever found fault with Melbourne for his crimes, but for presenting to the Queen a notorious unbeliever he was severely hauled over the coals.[8] The Bishop of Exeter, in presenting a petition against Socialism from the personages of Birmingham, pointed out that Owen's organization was illegal, and that he could and should be put in prison.

There were other horrid blasphemies and immoralities, he added, with

---

[7] See next chapter.

[8] Melbourne himself was, apparently, a dogmatic unbeliever. See Greville, December 16, 1835.

the recital of which he would not pain their Lordships' ears. There was a book by Owen which had been put into the Bishop's hands—the reference is no doubt to the *Marriages of the Priesthood*—and one passage in that book had been placed before the episcopal eyes, but he had never since permitted his mind to be polluted by looking at it again. Some of the worst blasphemies and obscenities he could not bring himself to quote, not even to convince the noble Marquis (Normanby) of the necessity for prompt action—he could not and would not do it.

This, however, was not the worst. It appeared that at Queenwood (an Owenite community) music, dancing, and singing actually took place on the Sabbath! And this was the man whom the Prime Minister saw fit to present to his young and innocent Sovereign!

The episcopal oratory was vigorously followed up by lesser men throughout the country, with the result that Owenites were mobbed in the name of Christian charity. But nothing very drastic occurred, and the sect gradually sank into obscurity. How firmly the association of Socialism with free love became established in the minds of the well-to-do is shown in the answers of a clerical witness in 1846 before a Parliamentary Committee on railway construction. In connection with the morals of the navvies employed on the work, this clergyman was asked:

"You speak of infidel opinions. Do you believe that many of them are Socialists?"

"Most of them in practice," he replied. "Though they appear to have wives, very few of them are married." [9]

The Victorian delicacy of this answer is to be applauded, but there is no likelihood that the navvies were Socialists in any other sense. The Socialists of that period were few, earnest, and intellectual; the navvies were none of these.

To form a correct judgment of Owen's work and influence is far from easy. Down to 1815, he appears as a thoroughly practical man, successful in all that he undertakes, and not led by the impulses of a reformer into impossible undertakings. After this time, his vision is enlarged, but his every-day sagacity is diminished. In his attempts to transform the world he failed through impatience, through failure to pay due attention to finance, and through the belief that every-

---

[9] Clapham, *Economic History of Modern Britain*, Vol. I, p. 412.

body could easily and quickly be persuaded to see what appeared to him self-evident truth. His success at New Lanark misled him, as, at first, it misled others. He understood machines, and he knew how to make himself liked; these qualities sufficed at New Lanark, but not in his later ventures. He had not the qualities that make either a successful leader or a successful organizer.

As a man of ideas, however, he deserves a high place. He emphasized problems concerned with industrial production which time has shown to be important, though in the period immediately following that of his activity their importance was temporarily masked by the development of railways. He saw that the increased output due to machines must lead to over-production or under-employment, unless the market could be increased by a great increase of wages. He saw also that such an increase of wages was not likely to be brought about by economic forces under a reign of free competition. He deduced that some more socialized method of production and distribution was necessary if industrialism was to bring general prosperity. The nineteenth century, by continually finding new markets and new countries to exploit, succeeded in evading the logic of over-production, but in our day the truth of Owen's analysis is beginning to be obvious.

In his own day the most serious objections to his schemes were: the principle of population, and the necessity of competition as an incentive to industry. Malthus, who speaks to him as "a man of real benevolence" and approves of his proposed Factory Act as well as of his methods of education, nevertheless advances both of these arguments. All systems of equality, he says, involve absence of "those stimulants to exertion which can alone overcome the natural indolence of man," while the prudential checks to population, which all depend upon private property, would be removed. "As all would be equal, and in similar circumstances, there would be no reason whatever why one individual should think himself obliged to practice the duty of restraint more than another.—His [Owen's] absolute inability to suggest any mode of accomplishing this object [limiting population] that is not unnatural, immoral, or cruel in a high degree, together with the same want of success in every other person, ancient or modern, who has made a similar attempt, seem to show that the argument against systems of equality founded on the principle of population does not admit of a plausible answer, even in theory."

As for the validity of these two objections, the population argument has been answered by a fall in the birth-rate. By a curious irony it was mainly from some of the middle-class Radicals that the working classes ultimately learnt birth-control, which is essential to the possibility of successful Socialism, while Socialists have been mostly hostile or indifferent. The other argument has grown less serious owing to the increased productivity of labor. When the ordinary working day was from 12 to 15 hours, no doubt dread of destitution was a necessary incentive. But with modern methods, given proper organization, very few hours a day would suffice, and these could be secured by a discipline which would not be difficult to enforce.

Owen's villages, considered as a solution, were of course a trifle absurd. A communistic system cannot be adequately tried on a small scale; it must be extended at least over a whole nation, if not over the whole world. The villages were to combine agriculture and industry; each was to be as nearly as possible self-supporting in the matter of food. Such a scheme seemed natural in the industrial North in 1815, where isolated factories, worked by water-power, were established in rural districts; but in the modern world it is impossible for industrial districts to produce their own food. No small community, now-a-days, can aim at being economically self-contained, unless it is prepared to accept a very low standard of life.

In other respects, however, there is still a very great deal to be said for Owen's parallelograms. Unlike his contemporaries, he did not think of life in terms of profit and loss; he remembered beauty, the cultivation of the senses and the intellect, and, above all, children. In a communal life such as he planned, it is possible to have all the beauty of the Oxford and Cambridge Colleges; it is possible to have space, fine public rooms, freedom for children's work and play. All these things the family individualism to which we are accustomed makes impossible. It is only by combination that men who are not richer than any one should be can escape from squalor and enjoy the aesthetic delights belonging to spacious architecture and an abundance of air and sunshine. For children the modern urban world is a prison, unless they are poor enough to be allowed to play in the streets, and even then it is unhealthy and dangerous. Owen would have provided for important needs which are overlooked in an individualistic and competitive world.

He thought the transformation to the new society an easier and swifter matter than was possible, but the things he desired were good, they were neglected by almost all other reformers, and, with some technical adjustments, they were such as the growth of machine production has made more practicable, not less. For these reasons, in spite of his limitations, he is important, and his ideas are still capable of bearing fruit.

CHAPTER XVI

EARLY TRADE UNIONISM

WHOEVER has a commodity to sell is likely to obtain a better price if he possesses a monopoly than if he is subject to competition. If he has competitors, it is usually to his interest to combine with them, so that he and they may jointly secure the advantages of monopoly. It is, however, often very difficult to secure such combinations, since those who have been competitors are apt to be suspicious of each other, and any one among them, after combination has been agreed upon, can obtain a temporary gain by breaking away and negotiating independently with purchasers. Moreover purchasers, being aware of the loss that they are likely to suffer from agreement among sellers, put every possible obstacle of law and public opinion in the way of such agreement. Accordingly the benefits of competition are urged by consumers, and the benefits of combination by producers. The conflict between these two opposed points of view, and the general doctrines as to the public good to which they give rise, runs through the economic history of the nineteenth century.

Labor, considered as a commodity, is sold by wage-earners and bought by capitalists. Given an increasing population and free competition among wage-earners, wages must tend to fall to subsistence level. Trade unions are, at least in their origin, an attempt to prevent this result by combination among the sellers of labor—at first only in particular crafts, but gradually over a widening area, embracing at last, in Great Britain, an overwhelming majority of industrial wage-earners. There can be no question that the economic bargaining power of wage-earners, and the general status of labor, have been immensely enhanced by trade unionism, but the early steps were difficult, and early excessive hopes were repeatedly disappointed.

The earliest trade unions, according to Mr. and Mrs. Sidney Webb, date from the late seventeenth century, and thus began a hundred years before the era of machine production, but it was only at the time of the Industrial Revolution that trade unionism began to be important. "In all cases in which Trade Unions arose, the great bulk of the workers had ceased to be independent producers, themselves controlling the processes, and owning the materials and the products of their labour, and had passed into the condition of lifelong wage-earners, possessing neither the instruments of production nor the commodity in its finished state." [1] In some trades, for instance tailoring, this reduction of the worker to the condition of proletarian was prior to the machine age, but it was only through machinery and the factory system that the conditions for the existence of trade unionism began to exist on a large scale. For this reason, they were important in Great Britain at a much earlier date than elsewhere.

In the eighteenth century trade unions were not sufficiently important to attract much hostile notice from the law, but from 1799 to 1913 they were subjected to legal persecution, first by the legislature and the law-courts in combination, and afterwards by the law-courts in defiance of the intentions of the legislature. An Act proposed by Pitt and hurried through Parliament in 1799 made all combinations of workmen illegal. In theory, combinations of employers were also illegal; but this part of the law remained a dead letter. Other statutes, as well as the common law, were invoked when more convenient. In 1812, in a cotton-weavers' strike, the committee were arrested for the common-law crime of combination, and sentenced to terms of imprisonment varying from four to eighteen months. In 1818, the leaders in a cotton-spinners' strike were sentenced to two years under a statute of 1305 entitled "Who be Conspirators and who be Champertors." Prosecutions were frequent, even when no strike was in progress. "The first twenty years of the nineteenth century," say the Webbs, "witnessed a legal persecution of Trade Unionists as rebels and revolutionaries—thwarting the healthy growth of the Unions, and driving their members into violence and sedition."

A new phase of trade unionism begins in 1824, owing to the intervention of middle-class Radicals. Until this time, the movement had been a spontaneous growth, ignored or disliked by all outside the ranks of wage-earners. A prosecution of the compositors of *The Times* in 1810 drew the attention of Francis Place, the Radical tailor, to the iniquity of the Combination Acts, and when, in the early

[1] *The History of Trade Unionism*, by Sidney and Beatrice Webb, Revised Edition, 1920, pp. 25–6.

twenties, the tone of British politics began to be less virulently re-actionary, he secured in favor of their repeal the support of two Philosophical Radicals, McCulloch and Joseph Hume. In the year 1824, Hume succeeded in getting through Parliament a measure securing complete freedom of combination. In those days not even the Government paid much attention to business, and Hume, by keeping quiet, succeeded in preventing not only Members of Parliament, but also Ministers, from noticing what was happening.[2] There was a great outbreak of strikes, and people were surprised to find that the old laws were no longer in force. In the next year, 1825, Parliament re-enacted some of the provisions which it had unintentionally repealed, but it did not go so far as to make strikes and trade unions illegal. From this time onwards, trade unionism, though with many ups and downs, was important both in industry and in politics.

So long as the trade unions were free from middle-class influences, they had no large aims, either political or economic, nor had they much sense of working-class solidarity. They consisted of local combinations, mostly of skilled craftsmen in some particular craft, sometimes co-operating with similar combinations elsewhere, but seldom concerned with anything beyond the maintenance of their own rate of wages. Some of their leaders, however, after having come into contact with Philosophical Radicalism in connection with the repeal of the Combination Laws, became aware of the existence of another doctrine, which offered more to wage-earners than the cold comfort of Malthusian self-restraint and economy with a view to emigration. Socialism was being preached, not only by Owen, but by several economists, of whom the most important was Thomas Hodgskin, a man who enjoys the rare distinction of being quoted with respect by Marx. Hodgskin taught, following Ricardo, that labor is the source of value, and, not following Ricardo, that labor should receive the whole produce of industry. The result of his activities terrified James Mill, who on October 25, 1831, wrote in great anxiety to Place about a deputation "from the working classes" who had been preaching Communism to Mr. Black, the editor of the *Morning Chronicle*.

---

[2] See Wallas's *Life of Francis Place*, Chap. VIII.

Their notions about property look ugly; they not only desire that it should have nothing to do with representation, which is true, though not a truth for the present time, as they ought to see, but they seem to think that it should not exist, and that the existence of it is an evil to them. Rascals, I have no doubt, are at work among them. Black, it is true, is easily imposed upon. But the thing needs looking into. Nobody has such means of probing the ulcer as you, and nobody has so much the means of cure. The fools, not to see that what they madly desire would be such a calamity to them as no hands but their own could bring upon them.

Place answered:—

My dear Mill,—As you sometimes take pains to serve the common people, and as you are an influential man, I send you an essay in reply to your note. The men who called on Black were not a deputation from the working people, but two out of half-a-dozen who manage, or mismanage, the meetings of the Rotunda in Blackfriars Road, and at the Philadelphian Chapel in Finsbury. The doctrine they are now preaching is that promulgated by Hodgskin in a tract in 1825, entitled *Labour defended against the Claims of Capital*, . . .

and so on through a long letter.[3]

A year later Mill passed on Place's information to Brougham:

The nonsense to which your Lordship alludes about the rights of the labourer to the whole produce of the country, wages, profits, and rent, all included, is the mad nonsense of our friend Hodgskin [*sic*] which he has published as a system, and propagates with the zeal of perfect fanaticism. Whatever of it appears in the *Chronicle* steals in through his means, he being a sort of sub-editor, and Black (the editor) not very sharp in detecting; but all Black's opinions on the subject of Property are sound. These opinions, if they were to spread, would be the subversion of civilized society; worse than the overwhelming deluge of Huns and Tartars.[4]

The result of Socialist teaching was a revolt against middle-class Radicalism, and the rapid growth of a purely working-class movement, partly trade unionist and partly co-operative, which, to a great extent, looked upon Owen as its prophet. While he was busy with New Harmony, the co-operative movement began, in close connection with Owen's doctrines. The first known use of the word

[3] Wallas, *Place*, p. 274.
[4] Mill to Brougham, in Bain's *James Mill*, p. 364.

"Socialist," as applied to Owen's followers, occurs at this time, in *The Co-operative Magazine* for 1827, in which the advocates of Owen's villages are spoken of as "the Communionists and Social-ists." [5] As the capital required for founding villages was not forth-coming, the co-operative movement was led to develop in more practical ways. The present immense growth of co-operative stores is the outcome of a development which starts from Owen; but before reaching its ultimate highly practical form it went through various vicissitudes and tried a number of unsuccessful experiments.

In September, 1832, Owen opened the "National Equitable Labor Exchange" in rather magnificent premises in Gray's Inn Road, which had been used by a disciple of his, named Bromley, as an "Institution for Removing Ignorance and Poverty." Here goods were to be bought and sold, not for money, but for labor notes, which more or less purported to represent their cost in labor. An immense busi-ness was done, but no one quite knew whether it was done at a profit or at a loss. Bromley began to demand that Owen should pay a large rent (not in labor notes); the result was that Owen moved to new premises, and in July, 1833, he ceased to be connected with the enter-prise. There were other Labor Exchanges, conducted on similar principles, mostly in London. And in connection with them there was formed a "United Trades Association," where work was given to the unemployed, who were paid in labor notes, and whose produce was sent to the Labor Exchange. The whole movement, however, quickly came to grief. William Lovett, later a Chartist leader, an Owenite closely connected with the United Trades Association, attributed the failure to "religious differences, the want of legal security, and the dislike which the women had to confine their dealings to one shop." Owen's inability to keep religious questions in the background is constantly surprising.

The trade union movement was, for a short time, intimately con-nected with these early abortive attempts at co-operation. Although some trade unions held aloof, most, in 1833, accepted Owen's gospel, and under his leadership there was a large sudden growth of mem-bership and an attempt to realize wide socialistic aims.

As always, he expected quick results. He thought that the trade union movement could transform the whole economic system within

[5] Clapham, *Economic History of Modern Britain*, Vol. I, p. 315.

a few years. To the Operative Builders' Union, which had written to him, he replied: "You may accomplish this change (to the new age of co-operation) for the whole population of the British Empire in less than five years, and essentially ameliorate the condition of the producing classes throughout Great Britain and Ireland in less than five months." [6] The builders formed a "National Building Guild of Brothers." They were prepared to undertake building contracts themselves; employers were informed that their power was ending, but that they could be admitted to the Guild as managers on proof of competence; meanwhile, the operative builders demanded higher wages. The employers showed no enthusiasm for the Owenite millennium, and refused to employ members of the union. There was a strike, and the strikers set out to build a Guildhall for themselves at Birmingham. However, funds gave out before the building was finished, and the whole enterprise collapsed. But meanwhile it had become absorbed in a still wider movement.

In October, 1833, delegates from trade unions all over the country met at the National Equitable Labor Exchange, and recommended the formation of a "Grand National Moral Union of the Productive and Useful Classes." Within a few weeks it had half a million members, and the total number of trade unionists was estimated at a million. While some unions had their doubts about Owen, the Grand National Consolidated Trades Union was completely devoted to his doctrine. His optimism and the rapid increase of membership seem to have made the unionists rash; everywhere there were strikes, employers became alarmed, unionists were refused employment, with the result that there were no funds.

At this moment came the case of the Dorchester Laborers. These were six men who had been engaged in forming a lodge of the Friendly Society of Agricultural Laborers, which was not in itself illegal; but they had administered oaths, and on this ground were sentenced to seven years' transportation. Owen and the other leaders had to devote their energies to agitation on behalf of these unfortunate men. Everything possible was done, but Melbourne, the Home Secretary, was adamant.

The affairs of the Consolidated Union were now in a bad way, and Owen's quarrels with his lieutenants, primarily about religion,

[6] Cole, *Owen*, p. 271.

completed the collapse. His chief coadjutor, J. E. Smith, got tired of Socialism, and founded the Universalist religion, after which episode he lived a quiet and prosperous life as editor of the *Family Herald*. Amid personal and financial troubles, the Grand National Consolidated Trades Union came to a painful end. Owen, abandoning his hopes of it, persuaded such of his followers as remained faithful to follow him into a new organization, The British and Foreign Consolidated Association of Industry, Humanity, and Knowledge, and trade unionism, for a time, passed into obscurity. Working-class fervor was diverted first into purely political channels by the Chartists, and then, after the foundation of the Rochdale Pioneers in 1844, into the second co-operative movement, which still looked to Owen as a prophet, but pursued more practicable means towards a less revolutionary end. By 1848, say the Webbs,

The danger of revolution had passed away. A new generation of workmen was growing up, to whom the worst of the old oppression was unknown, and who had imbibed the economic and political philosophy of the middle-class reformers. Bentham, Ricardo, and Grote were read only by a few; but the activity of such educationalists as Lord Brougham and Charles Knight propagated "useful knowledge" to all the members of the Mechanics' Institutes and the readers of the *Penny Magazine*. The middle-class ideas of "free enterprise" and "unrestricted competition" which were thus diffused received a great impetus from the extraordinary propaganda of the Anti-Corn-Law League, and the general progress of Free Trade.

The fiasco of Owenite trade unionism, combined with the universal increase of prosperity from the forties to the eighties, when the Manchester School controlled British economic policy, turned even working-class leaders into individualist Radicals. Nevertheless trade unionism, after a great collapse (the Webbs estimate that in 1840 there were not 100,000 trade unionists in the kingdom), grew steadily, and spread to all industrial countries. In Great Britain it succeeded in meeting the periodical hostility of the judges by periodical fresh legislation. When, in the eighties, bad times came again, and wages began to fall, the trade unions remembered Owen and renewed their Socialist faith. Hyndman, in 1885, praised "noble Robert Owen" for perceiving the uselessness of half-measures. "But the revolution which in his day was unprepared is now ripe and ready . . . The great social revolution of the nineteenth century is at hand." [7] The revolution did not come in 1885, any more than in 1834. But the later Socialists found useful work to do. Owen, for a moment, had enlisted unskilled workers in his unions, but had led them only to starvation, prison, and exile. In the late '80's, when trade unionism once again reached the unskilled, it led to a series of dramatically successful strikes. And while national Socialism proved impracticable, much useful work was achieved in the way of municipal Socialism.

Trade revived, and Socialism decayed. Now trade has again decayed and Socialism has again revived. Perhaps this is not the last turn of the cycle, but the last turn must come.

[7] Webb, *op. cit.*, p. 411.

CHAPTER XVII

MARX AND ENGELS

SOCIALISM, unlike the creed of the Philosophical Radicals, did not quickly become a powerful force in practical politics, but remained, broadly speaking, the ineffective creed of a minority until 1917. As a system of thought, however, it belongs to the same period as Ricardo and James Mill. After the failure of Robert Owen, the Socialist movement, for a time, became mainly French, and was adapted to pre-industrial conditions. The doctrines of Saint Simon and Fourier had considerable influence, and the Socialists were sufficiently powerful to dominate the beginnings of the Revolution of 1848. French Socialism of that period, however, had still some of the defects of Owenism, as well as others peculiar to itself. It had not a consistent body of doctrine, or a practicable scheme for the transition from capitalistic to socialized production.

It was only with Marx and Engels that Socialism reached intellectual maturity, and became capable of inspiring a serious political party. The Communist Manifesto, which already contained all the essentials of their doctrine, was published just before the outbreak of the French Revolution of 1848. Mentally, it is to this period that Marx's system belongs.

To understand Marx, it is necessary to take account of the extremely complex influences by which he was molded. The first influence was that of Hegel, which Marx encountered during his university career and never shook off, and of which elements remain in Communism to the present day. From Hegel came the love of an all-embracing system, and the belief that history is the orderly working out of an intellectual scheme, with the same inevitability and the same sharpness of logical opposition as in the Hegelian dialectic. Marx's next experience was as a German Radical journalist subject to all the difficulties of the censorship as it then existed. After this, his desire for knowledge brought him into contact with French Socialism, and from the French he learnt to regard revolution as the normal method of political advance. But it was Engels who first contributed to their joint work the all-important element of first-hand knowledge concerning British industrialism. Engels published in 1845 his book on *The Condition of the English working class in 1844,* and the impress of this gloomy period is stamped on everything that Marx and Engels subsequently wrote. But for contact with England, Marx might have remained unduly abstract and metaphysical, and lacking in that intimate knowledge of industrial facts from which so much of his persuasive power is derived. By the time his doctrine was completed, it combined elements of value from three countries. Germany made him a system-builder, France made him a revolutionary, and England made him learned.

Marx was born in 1818, at Treves in the Rhineland, where French influence had penetrated more deeply than in most parts of Germany.[1] His ancestors, for generations, had been rabbis, but his father was a lawyer. On the death of the father's mother, which occurred when Marx was six years old, the family became Christian, and Marx was educated as a Protestant. When he was only seventeen, he fell in love with a beautiful and aristocratic girl, and persuaded both his parents and hers to permit an engagement. It was, however, seven years before he was able to marry her, and by that time her parents had become strongly opposed to the match.

As a university student he showed already that titanic but somewhat ill-directed energy which characterized him through life. In a long letter to his father, written at the age of nineteen, he tells how he had written three volumes of poems to his Jenny, translated large parts of Tacitus and Ovid, and two books of the *Pandects,* written a work of three hundred pages on the philosophy of law, perceived that it was worthless, written a play, and "while out of sorts, got to know Hegel from beginning to end," besides reading innumerable books on the most diverse subjects.

Hegel had died in 1831, and his influence in Germany was still very great. But his school had broken into two sects, the Old and Young Hegelians, and in 1839 his system was destructively criticized by Feuerbach, who reverted from Hegel's Absolute Idealism to a form of materialism, and carried with him many of the Young

---

[1] In relation to Marx's life I have relied in the main upon *Karl Marx: His Life and Work,* by Otto Rühle.

Hegelians, who were distinguished from the Old by their Radicalism. In academic Germany, especially among the young, it was a time of very intense intellectual activity. While Germany, from the standpoint of learning, was ahead of the rest of the world, it was politically and economically far behind both France and England. The censorship was preposterous, and the middle classes had no political power. It resulted inevitably that the intelligent young were radical if not revolutionary, and that they were very open to political ideas coming from abroad, especially from France. Marx in his youth was not isolated, but was one of a group of eager young men, all persuaded that philosophy is the key to everything, but all choosing the philosophy that best lent itself to Radical politics.

Marx first sought a career in journalism. In 1842 he became a contributor, and soon afterwards the editor, of the *Rheinische Zeitung*, and now he first became aware of problems for which nothing in academic philosophy offered any solution. The first of such problems that came to his attention was the question of a law for the imprisonment of the poor for stealing wood from the forest. He realized that economic questions had been unduly neglected, and was confirmed in this by reading a book on French Socialism. When the *Rheinische Zeitung* was suppressed by the censorship in January, 1843, Marx had leisure for study, and decided to become acquainted with Socialism.

With this end in view, he went to Paris, as Socialism at that time was predominantly French. English Socialism, under the leadership of Robert Owen, had become mainly secularist and anti-Christian. Owen, as we have seen, had always been opposed to political methods, and Radical politics in England was left to the Chartists, whose programme did not directly concern itself with economic questions. In France, on the contrary, the movement inaugurated by Saint Simon and Fourier had continued and was full of vigor. Marx made the acquaintance of the leaders, of whom the most important were Proudhon and Louis Blanc. He learnt what there was to know about Socialism, but did not make friends with any of the French Socialists. It must be said that Socialism before Marx was not worthy of any great degree of intellectual respect. Saint Simon was essentially a mediaevalist who disliked industrialism and the modern world, and sought renovation in a purified Christianity. Fourier, though he had merit as a critic of the existing economic system, became completely fantastic when he advanced schemes for a better organization of production. Their importance lay in the fact that they caused a certain number of intellectuals to feel dissatisfaction with capitalism, and to look out for ways of ending it or at least greatly mitigating its evils. In France, such men had succeeded in creating a labor movement neither purely political, like the Chartists, nor purely economic, like the trade unions, but both at once. It was realized that political means, such as manhood suffrage, were necessary, but they were to be used for the achievement of economic objects of importance to the proletariat. This conception of the relation of politics to economics Marx learnt in France and retained through life.

The belief in an intimate relation between philosophy and politics, which Marx, in common with all his circle, accepted as axiomatic in his student years, remained part of his creed. "Philosophy," he says at this time, "cannot be realized without the uprising of the proletariat; and the proletariat cannot rise without the realization of philosophy." To English-speaking people, who do not take philosophy seriously, this must seem an odd sentiment, unless they have learnt to accept the Communist creed. To Marx at that rate, it would seem, the realization of philosophy was as important as the rising of the proletariat. He was, in fact, well on the way towards the theory that all philosophy is an expression of economic circumstances.

His friendship with Engels began at this time, in Paris, in the year 1844. Engels was two years younger than Marx, and had been subjected to the same intellectual influences in his university years. But his father was a cotton spinner with factories both in Germany and in Manchester, and Engels had been sent to Manchester to work in the family business. This had given him first hand knowledge of up-to-date industrialism, and of English factory conditions at a very bad period. He was at this time writing his book on the condition of the English working class. This book uses powerfully the same kind of material that Marx afterwards used in the first volume of *Capital*. It is concrete, full of facts from official sources, gloomy as to the present but hopeful of a proletarian revolution in the near future. It makes it possible to judge of the importance to be attached to Engels in the joint work of the two men. Marx had been, until he met Engels, too academic. There were evils on the

Continent, perhaps as great as those in England, but they were less modern, and less appropriate in an indictment of capitalism. Engels invariably minimized his share in all that the two men did together, but undoubtedly it was very great. And above all he first directed the attention of Marx to the kind of facts best calculated to win assent to his economic theory. The materialistic conception of history appears to have been, at least in its main outlines, discovered independently by the two men before their collaboration began.

Engels was already a Communist when he first met Marx, having been converted by a man named Moses Hess, who was prominent among the German radicals. Hess, writing in 1843, said:

"Last year, when I was about to start for Paris, Engels came to see me on his way from Berlin. We discussed the questions of the day, and he, a revolutionist of the Year One, parted from me a convinced Communist. Thus did I spread devastation."

It is interesting to note that at this time Marx made friends with Heine, who much admired him and became a Communist.

The Continental intellectuals of that day were far more advanced politically than those in England, no doubt because the middle classes had less power, and because revolution was the obvious first step in progress. The views held by Marx and his friends before 1848, while Metternich still ruled, would bring down worse persecution upon their holders now than they did then.

In January, 1845, at the request of the Prussian Government, Marx was expelled from Paris, and therefore went to Brussels. It was at this time that he first profited by the pecuniary generosity of Engels, which remained his chief financial resource down to the day of his death. From Brussels, with the help of Engels, Marx conducted Communist propaganda, and came in touch with various bodies such as The Workers' Educational Society, The Federation of the Just, The Democratic League, and The Fraternal Democrats. The Federation of the Just, which met in Great Windmill Street in London, developed into the Communist League, which included in its programme "the overthrow of the bourgeoisie, the dominion of the proletariat, the abolition of a class society, and the introduction of an economic and social order without private property and without classes." In December, 1847, this body decided that Marx and Engels should draw up a statement of its aims. The whole importance of the Communist League in history is due to this decision, since its outcome was the Communist Manifesto.

The Communist Manifesto, as regards style, vividness, compression, and propagandist force, is the best thing that Marx ever did. It has the buoyancy and swiftness characteristic of the eve of a revolution; it has the clarity due to a newly-won theoretical insight. It opens with the words:

"A spectre is haunting Europe—the spectre of Communism. All the powers of old Europe have entered into a holy alliance to exorcise this spectre: Pope and Czar, Metternich and Guizot, French radicals and German police spies."

It ends:

"The Communists disdain to conceal their views and their aims. They openly declare that their ends can be attained only by the forcible overthrow of all existing social conditions. Let the ruling classes tremble at a Communist revolution. The proletarians have nothing to lose but their chains. They have a world to win.

"Working men of all countries, unite!"

The remainder consists of a history of the world, beginning "The history of all hitherto existing society is the history of class struggles," showing what a fierce revolution has been effected by modern capitalism, and leading on, apparently with the inevitability of a syllogism, to the next stage in world history, the proletarian revolution.

I do not know of any other document of equal propagandist force. And this force is derived from intense passion intellectually clothed as inexorable exposition.

It was the Communist Manifesto that gave Marx his position in the Socialist movement, and he would have deserved it even if he had never written *Das Kapital*.

Scarcely was the Manifesto finished when the Revolution broke out in Paris. The Provisional Government, which was largely Socialist, invited Marx to Paris, and he went. But he stayed there only a month: at the end of that time, the Revolution having spread to Germany, he naturally wished to be active in his own country.

Few movements in history have disappointed all participants more completely than the revolutions of 1848. For milder revolution-aries, the disappointment was only temporary, but for Marx it was life-long.

He was expelled from Prussia in May, 1849, and never received permission to return, though in fact he returned a few times sur-reptitiously for brief periods. His activities in Germany had been purely journalistic, and milder than might have been expected; they were, however, such as the reaction could not tolerate. From Germany he went to Paris, from which he was expelled after a month. The only remaining refuge was England, the "Mother of the Exiles," as it was then called. In England, with brief intervals, he lived for the rest of his life, no longer attempting to stir up revolution in his own day, but providing the mental stimulus to revolution at some indefinite future date.

Marx's life is sharply divided into two periods by the failure of the 1848 revolutions, which deprived him of immediate hopefulness and turned him into an impoverished exile. If his belief in the ultimate victory of Communism had had a less firm intellectual foundation, he could hardly have persisted, as he did, in the laborious preparation of a monumental work, with little encouragement except from a few friends and disciples. His tenacity and industry through-out his later life are truly astonishing.

So far as private circumstances went, his life was like Mr. Micaw-ber's, an affair of duns, pawnbrokers, disputes about dishonored bills, and so on. The whole family lived in two small rooms in Dean Street, Soho. When, in 1852, one child died in infancy, Mrs. Marx wrote:

"Our poor little Francisca fell ill with severe bronchitis. For three days the poor child struggled with death. She suffered so terribly. When it was over, her little body rested in the small back room, and we all came into the front room. At night, we lay down on the floor. The three other children were with us, and we wept at the loss of the little angel. . . . The dear child's death happened at a time when we were in the direst need. Our German friends were unable to help us. . . . Ernest Jones, who paid us a visit at this time, and had promised to help, was unable to do anything. . . . In my overwhelm-ing need, I hastened to a French refugee who lived in the neighbour-hood, and had visited us not long before. At once, in the most friendly way possible, he gave me two pounds. With this sum I was able to buy the coffin in which my poor child now lies at peace. She had no cradle when she came into the world, and for a long time it was difficult to find a box for her last resting place."

Engels, who continued to work in the family business at Manchester, devoted every penny that he could spare to the support of Marx. But Engels, naturally, was not on good terms with his father, who was a pious Calvinist; the sums available were therefore not very large. They were augmented by journalism, chiefly in America, but the income obtained in this way was small and precarious. Marx's only son died at the age of nine; "the house is desolate and orphaned since the death of the poor child, who was its living soul," he wrote to Engels. He was always lovable in his dealings with children: those of the neighborhood called him "Daddy Marx," and looked to him for sweets, not in vain. With children he was free from rivalry and fear of inferiority, which made him irritable and quarrelsome with adults. On October 28, 1933, the *New Statesman and Nation* published the following letter:

Maiden Towers.
3. 7. 1865.

Dear Miss Lilliput,

You must excuse the belated character of my answer. I belong to that sort of people who always look twice at things before they decide one way or the other. Thus, I was rather startled at receiving an invitation on the part of a female minx quite unknown to me. However, having ascertained your respectability and the high tone of your transactions with your tradespeople, I shall feel happy to seize this rather strange opportunity of getting at your eatables and drinkables. Suffering somewhat from an attack of rheumatism, I hope you keep your reception room clear of anything like draft. As to the ventilation required, I shall provide it for myself. Being somewhat deaf in the right ear, please put a dull fellow, of whom I dare say your company will not be in want of, at my right side. For the left I hope you will reserve your female beauty, I mean the best looking female among your guests.

I am somewhat given to tobacco chewing, so have the stuff ready. Having former intercourse with Yankees taken to the habitude of spitting, I hope spittoons will not be missing. Being rather easy in my manners and disgusted at the hot and close English atmosphere, you must prepare for seeing me in a dress rather adamatic. I hope your female guests are some-what in the same line.

Addio, my dear unknown little minx,

Yours for ever,
Dr. Crankley.

Readers were challenged to guess the authorship, but nobody guessed correctly; it was in fact written by Marx to his daughter.

His letters to Engels are a monotonous list of lamentations. He was ill, his wife was ill, his children were ill; the butcher and baker wished to be paid; his mother would do nothing further for him. He came to take Engels's help as a matter of course, and to pour out the catalogue of his troubles even at the most inappropriate moments. Engels lived in a free union with an Irish girl who was devoted to him, and whose sudden death was a great blow to him. In reply to the letter announcing his loss, Marx writes:

"Dear Engels: The news of Mary's death has both astonished and dismayed me. She was extremely good-natured, witty, and much attached to you. The devil knows that there is nothing but trouble now in our circles. I myself can no longer tell whether I am on my head or my heels. My attempts to raise some money in France and Germany have failed, and it is only to be expected that £15 would not hold off the avalanche more than a week or two. Apart from the fact that no one will give us credit any more, except the butcher and the baker (and they only to the end of this week), I am harried for school expenses, for rent, and by the whole pack. The few of them to whom I have paid a little on account, have pouched it in a twinkling, to fall upon me with redoubled violence. Further-more, the children have no clothes or shoes in which to go out. In a word, there is hell to pay. . . . We shall hardly be able to keep going for another fortnight. It is abominably selfish of me to retail all these horrors to you at such a moment. But the remedy is homoeopathic. One evil will help to cancel the other." [2]

Financial troubles continued to beset Marx until 1869, when Engels (whose father was now dead) sold out his interest in the business, paid Marx's debts (£210), gave him a settled income of £350 a year, and himself came to live in London, with freedom at last to give all his time to Socialist work.

[2] Otto Rühle, *op. cit.*, p. 225.

Throughout, Marx worked in the British Museum. In 1859 he published his *Critique of Political Economy*, in 1867 the first volume of *Capital*. The second and third were published by Engels after his death. Pawnbrokers, family troubles, illnesses, and deaths failed to distract him from the composition of his *magnum opus*.

Apart from his writing, Marx's only important work after 1849 was in connection with the International Working Men's Association, the "First International." This organization, in which Marx was the leading spirit, was founded in London in 1864, and was the basis for the subsequent international Socialist movement. But although it contained the germ of great things, it did not itself achieve any great measure of success. In England, the trade unions, after some hesitation, held aloof with few exceptions. In Germany, the General Union of German Workers, the organization founded by Lassalle, was antagonized by Marx's jealousy both of Lassalle and of his successor, Schweitzer, whom he falsely accused of working with Bismarck. In Switzerland and the Latin countries, the influence of Bakunin led to the spread of Anarchist Communism, which differed from Marxism as to the use of political action and the function of the State. Bakunin and his followers, it is true, ultimately joined the International and tried to dominate it, but their quarrel with Marx brought about its disruption in 1872.

Marx was at no time tolerant of rivals. Speaking of the time just before 1848, Rühle says:

"The intolerant way in which the purging of the communist ranks was effected and in which the cleavage in the communist camp was brought about, was not the outcome of unavoidable necessity, not dependent upon the progress of economic evolution. Its primary cause was Marx's craving for exclusive personal predominance, which he rationalized into a fanatical confidence in the conquering power of his own idea."

In this respect, he did not improve with age. Of all his enmities, the attack on Bakunin was the most envenomed and the most unscrupulous. Bakunin was a Russian aristocrat who threw in his lot with the German Revolution of 1848, with the result that he was condemned to death in Saxony in 1849, handed over to the Austrians, who again condemned him to death, passed on by them to Tsar Nicholas, who shut him up in Peter and Paul and afterwards sent him to Siberia, whence he escaped in 1861, finally reaching London by way of Japan and America. Marx, as early as 1848, accused him in print of being a spy, and, although the accusation was then proved to be baseless, repeated it in subsequent years on appropriate occasions. When Bakunin, after twelve years of prison and penal settlement, endeavored to resume his connection with former revolutionary comrades, he found himself treated with suspicion, and at last discovered that Marx was the source of the trouble. Instead of showing resentment, he wrote a friendly letter to Marx, which led to an interview in which he persuaded him of his revolutionary integrity. For a moment, Marx was mollified. He wrote to Engels: "I saw him yesterady evening once more, for the first time after sixteen years. I must say that I liked him very much, much better than before. . . . On the whole he is one of the very few persons whom I find not to have retrogressed after sixteen years, but to have developed further."

Friendship between these two men could not, however, be of long duration. Bakunin was the apostle of Anarchist Communism, as Marx was of political Communism; Marx hated Slavs, Bakunin hated Jews. There were both personal and impersonal reasons which made cooperation impossible. So far as Bakunin is concerned, the personal reasons would not have sufficed to produce an estrangement. After reading *Capital* he wrote: "For five and twenty years Marx has served the cause of socialism ably, energetically, and loyally, taking the lead of everyone in this matter. I should never forgive myself if, out of personal motives, I were to destroy or diminish Marx's beneficial influence. Still, I may be involved in a struggle against him, not because he has wounded me personally, but because of the State socialism he advocates."

Bakunin joined the International in 1868, and set to work to bring it over to his views. He and Marx fought a fierce fight, in which Marx and his followers proved themselves far from scrupulous. The spy accusation was revived; Bakunin was said to have embezzled 25,000 francs. At the Congress at The Hague, in 1872, where Marx had a majority, it was decided to expel Bakunin on the ground that he had "resorted to fraudulent manoeuvres in order to possess himself of other people's property." But it was a barren victory. By the next year, the International was dead.

Both sections, Socialists and Anarchists, survived the end of the International, but while the Socialist movement prospered, the Anarchists remained always politically insignificant. In Russia, Bakunin had a successor in many ways superior to himself, namely Kropotkin, who lived to see the Marxists gain control of the Russian State. Elsewhere, except in Spain, Bakunin's following died out. Whatever may be thought of Marx's methods, there can be no doubt that his programme was more practicable than his rival's, and based upon a sounder estimate of human nature.

With the end of the First International in 1873, Marx's part in public affairs came to an end.

Marx was the first intellectually eminent economist to consider the facts of economics from the standpoint of the proletariat. The orthodox economists believed that they were creating an impersonal science, as free from bias as mathematics; Marx, however, had no difficulty in proving that their capitalist bias led them into frequent errors and inconsistencies. The whole of economics, he maintained, took on a completely different aspect when viewed from the wage-earner's point of view. His devotion to the interests of the proletariat is perhaps somewhat surprising, in view of his bourgeois origin and his academic education. He had all his life a love of domination associated with a feeling of inferiority, which made him prickly with social superiors, ruthless with rivals, and kind to children. It was probably this trait in his character that first led him to become the champion of the oppressed. It is difficult to say what caused his feeling of inferiority, but perhaps it was connected with his being a Jew by race and a Christian by education. He may, on this account, have had to endure the contempt of school-fellows in his early years, without being able to fall back upon the inner self-assurance that would be possible to a Jew by religion. Anti-Semitism is an abomination, but it has had one incidental good effect: that it has raised up, among Jews, tribunes of the people who might otherwise have been supporters of the *status quo*. If this view is just, Marxism is a suitable punishment for the illiberality of well-to-do anti-Semites.

CHAPTER XVIII

DIALECTICAL MATERIALISM

THE contributions of Marx and Engels to theory were twofold: there was Marx's theory of surplus value, and there was their joint theory of historical development, called "dialectical materialism." We will consider first the latter, which seems to me both more true and more important than the former.

Let us, in the first place, endeavor to be clear as to what the theory of dialectical materialism is. It is a theory which has various elements. Metaphysically it is materialistic: in method it adopts a form of dialectic suggested by Hegel, but differing from his in many important respects. It takes over from Hegel an outlook which is evolutionary, and in which the stages of evolution can be characterized in clear logical terms. These changes are of the nature of development, not so much in an ethical as in a logical sense—that is to say, they proceed according to a plan which a man of sufficient intellect could, theoretically, foretell, and which Marx himself professes to have foretold, in its main outlines, up to the moment of the universal establishment of Communism. The materialism of its metaphysics is translated, where human affairs are concerned, into the doctrine that the prime cause of all social phenomena is the method of production and exchange prevailing at any given period. The clearest statements of the theory are to be found in Engels, in his *Anti-Dühring*, of which the relevant parts have appeared in England under the title: *Socialism, Utopian and Scientific*. A few extracts will help to provide us with our text:

"It was seen that *all* past history, with the exception of its primitive stages, was the history of class struggles: that these warring classes of society are always the products of the modes of production and of exchange—in a word, of the economic conditions of their time; that the *economic* structure of society always furnishes the real basis, starting from which we can alone work out the ultimate explanation of the whole superstructure of juridical and political institutions as well as of the religious, philosophical, and other ideas of a given historical period."

The discovery of this principle, according to Marx and Engels, showed that the coming of Socialism was inevitable.

"From that time forward Socialism was no longer an accidental discovery of this or that ingenious brain, but the necessary outcome of the struggle between two historically developed classes—the proletariat and the bourgeoisie. Its task was no longer to manufacture a system of society as perfect as possible, but to examine the historico-economic succession of events from which these classes and their antagonism had of necessity sprung, and to discover in the economic conditions thus created the means of ending the conflict. But the Socialism of earlier days was as incompatible with this materialistic conception as the conception of Nature of the French materialists was with dialectics and modern natural science. The Socialism of earlier days certainly criticized the existing capitalistic mode of production and its consequences. But it could not explain them, and, therefore, could not get the mastery of them. It could only simply reject them as bad. The more strongly this earlier Socialism denounced the exploitation of the working-class, inevitable under Capitalism, the less able was it clearly to show in what the exploitation consisted and how it arose."

The same theory which is called Dialectical Materialism, is also called the Materialist Conception of History. Engels says: "The materialist conception of history starts from the proposition that the production of the means to support human life and, next to production, the exchange of things produced, is the basis of all social structure; that in every society that has appeared in history, the manner in which wealth is distributed and society divided into classes or orders, is dependent upon what is produced, how it is produced, and how the products are exchanged. From this point of view the final causes of all social changes and political revolutions are to be sought, not in men's brains, not in man's better insight into eternal truth and justice, but in changes in the modes of production and exchange. They are to be sought, not in the *philosophy*, but in the *economics* of each particular epoch. The growing perception that existing social institutions are unreasonable and unjust, that reason has become unreason, and right wrong, is only proof that in the modes of production and exchange changes have silently taken place, with which the social order, adapted to earlier economic conditions, is no longer in keeping. From this it also follows that the means of getting rid of the incongruities that have been brought to light, must also be present, in a more or less developed condition, within the changed modes of production themselves. These means are not to be invented by deduction from fundamental principles, but are to be discovered in the stubborn facts of the existing system of production."

The conflicts which lead to political upheavals are not primarily mental conflicts in the opinions and passions of human beings.

"This conflict between productive forces and modes of production is not a conflict engendered in the mind of man, like that between original sin and divine justice. It exists, in fact, objectively outside us, independently of the will and actions even of the men that have brought it on. Modern Socialism is nothing but the reflex, in thought, of this conflict in fact; its ideal reflection in the minds, first, of the class directly suffering under it, the working-class."

There is a good statement of the materialist theory of history in an early joint work of Marx and Engels (1845–6), called *German Ideology*. It is there said that the materialist theory starts with the actual process of production of an epoch, and regards as the basis of history the form of economic life connected with this form of production and generated by it. This, they say, shows civil society in its various stages and in its action as the State. Moreover, from the economic basis the materialist theory explains such matters as religion, philosophy, and morals, and the reason for the course of their development.

These quotations perhaps suffice to show what the theory is. A number of questions arise as soon as it is examined critically. Before going on to economics one is inclined to ask, first, whether materialism is true in philosophy, and second, whether the elements of Hegelian dialectic which are embedded in the Marxist theory of development can be justified apart from a full-fledged Hegelianism. Then comes the further question whether these metaphysical doctrines have any relevance to the historical thesis as regards economic development, and last of all comes the examination of this historical thesis itself. To state in advance what I shall be trying to prove, I hold (1) that materialism, in some sense, may be true, though it cannot be known to be so; (2) that the elements of dialectic which Marx took over from Hegel made him regard history as a more rational process than it has in fact been, convincing him that all changes must be in some sense progressive, and giving him a feeling of certainty in regard to the future, for which there is no scientific warrant; (3) that the whole of his theory of economic development may perfectly well be true if his metaphysic is false, and false if his metaphysic is true, and that but for the influence of Hegel it would never have occurred to him that a matter so purely empirical could depend upon abstract metaphysics; (4) with regard to the economic interpretation of history, it seems to me very largely true, and a most important contribution to sociology; I cannot, however, regard it as *wholly* true, or feel any confidence that all great historical changes can be viewed as developments. Let us take these points one by one.

(1) *Materialism.* Marx's materialism was of a peculiar kind, by no means identical with that of the eighteenth century. When he speaks of the "materialist conception of history," he never emphasizes philosophical materialism, but only the economic causation of social phenomena. His philosophical position is best set forth (though very briefly) in his *Eleven theses on Feuerbach* (1845). In these he says:

"The chief defect of all previous materialism—including that of Feuerbach—is that the object (Gegenstand), the reality, sensibility, is only apprehended under the form of the object (Objekt) or of contemplation (Anschauung), but not as human sensible activity or practice, not subjectively. Hence it came about that the active side was developed by idealism in opposition to materialism. . . .

"The question whether objective truth belongs to human thinking is not a question of theory, but a practical question. The truth, i.e. the reality and power, of thought must be demonstrated in practice. The contest as to the reality or nonreality of a thought which is isolated from practice, is a purely scholastic question. . . .

"The highest point that can be reached by contemplative materialism, i.e. by materialism which does not regard sensibility as a practical activity, is the contemplation of isolated individuals in 'bourgeois society.'

"The standpoint of the old materialism is 'bourgeois' society; the standpoint of the new is *human* society or socialized (vergesellschaftete) humanity.

"Philosophers have only *interpreted* the world in various ways, but the real task is to *alter* it."

The philosophy advocated in the earlier part of these theses is that which has since become familiar to the philosophical world through the writings of Dr. Dewey, under the name of pragmatism or instrumentalism. Whether Dr. Dewey is aware of having been anticipated by Marx, I do not know, but undoubtedly their opinions as to the metaphysical status of matter are virtually identical. In view of the importance attached by Marx to his theory of matter, it may be worth while to set forth his view rather more fully.

The conception of "matter," in old-fashioned materialism, was bound up with the conception of "sensation." Matter was regarded as the cause of sensation, and originally also as its object, at least in the case of sight and touch. Sensation was regarded as something in which a man is passive, and merely receives impressions from the outer world. This conception of sensation as passive is, however, —so the instrumentalists contend—an unreal abstraction, to which nothing actual corresponds. Watch an animal receiving impressions connected with another animal: its nostrils dilate, its ears twitch, its eyes are directed to the right point, its muscles become taut in preparation for appropriate movements. All this is action, mainly of a sort to improve the informative quality of impressions, partly such as to lead to fresh action in relation to the object. A cat seeing a mouse is by no means a passive recipient of purely contemplative impressions. And as a cat with a mouse, so is a textile manufacturer with a bale of cotton. The bale of cotton is an opportunity for action, it is something to be transformed. The machinery by which it is to be transformed is explicitly and obviously a product of human activity. Roughly speaking, all matter, according to Marx, is to be thought of as we naturally think of machinery: it has a raw material giving opportunity for action, but in its completed form it is a human product.

Philosophy has taken over from the Greeks a conception of passive contemplation, and has supposed that knowledge is obtained by means of contemplation. Marx maintains that we are always active, even when we come nearest to pure "sensation": we are never merely apprehending our environment, but always at the same time altering it. This necessarily makes the older conception of knowledge inapplicable to our actual relations with the outer world. In place of knowing an object in the sense of passively receiving an impression of it, we can only know it in the sense of being able to act upon it successfully. That is why the test of all truth is practical. And since we change the object when we act upon it, truth ceases to be static, and becomes something which is continually changing and developing. That is why Marx calls his materialism "dialectical," because it contains within itself, like Hegel's dialectic, an essential principle of progressive change.

I think it may be doubted whether Engels quite understood Marx's views on the nature of matter and on the pragmatic character of truth; no doubt he thought he agreed with Marx, but in fact he came nearer to orthodox materialism.[1] Engels explains "historical materialism," as he understands it, in an Introduction, written in 1892, to his *Socialism, Utopian and Scientific*. Here, the part assigned to action seems to be reduced to the conventional task of scientific verification. He says: "The proof of the pudding is in the eating. From the moment we turn to our own use these objects, according to the qualities we perceive in them, we put to an infallible test the correctness or otherwise of our sense-perceptions. . . . Not in one single instance, so far, have we been led to the conclusion that our sense-perceptions, scientifically controlled, induce in our minds ideas respecting the outer world that are, by their very nature, at variance with reality, or that there is an inherent incompatibility between the outer world and our sense-perceptions of it."

There is no trace, here, of Marx's pragmatism, or of the doctrine that sensible objects are largely the products of our own activity. But there is also no sign of any consciousness of disagreement with Marx. It may be that Marx modified his views in later life, but it seems more probable that, on this subject as on some others, he held two different views simultaneously, and applied the one or the other as suited the purpose of his argument. He certainly held that some propositions were "true" in a more than pragmatic sense. When, in *Capital*, he sets forth the cruelties of the industrial system as reported by Royal Commissions, he certainly holds that these cruelties really

[1] Cf. Sidney Hook, *Towards the Understanding of Karl Marx*, p. 32.

took place, and not only that successful action will result from supposing that they took place. Similarly, when he prophesies the Communist revolution, he believes that there will be such an event, not
merely that it is convenient to think so. His pragmatism must, therefore, have been only occasional—in fact when, on pragmatic grounds,
it was justified by being convenient.

It is worth noting that Lenin, who does not admit any divergence
between Marx and Engels, adopts in his *Materialism and Empirio-
Criticism* a view which is more nearly that of Engels than that of
Marx.

For my part, while I do not think that materialism can be *proved*,
I think Lenin is right in saying that it is not *dis*proved by modern
physics. Since his time, and largely as a reaction against his success,
respectable physicists have moved further and further from materialism, and it is naturally supposed, by themselves and by the general
public, that it is physics which has caused this movement. I agree
with Lenin that no substantially new argument has emerged since
the time of Berkeley, with one exception. This one exception, oddly
enough, is the argument set forth by Marx in his theses on Feuerbach, and completely ignored by Lenin. If there is no such thing as
sensation, if matter as something which we passively apprehend is
a delusion, and if "truth" is a practical rather than a theoretical conception, then old-fashioned materialism, such as Lenin's, becomes
untenable. And Berkeley's view becomes equally untenable, since it
removes the object in relation to which we are active. Marx's in-
strumentalist theory, though he calls it materialistic, is really not so.
As against materialism, its arguments have indubitably much force.
Whether it is ultimately valid is a difficult question, as to which I
have deliberately refrained from expressing an opinion, since I could
not do so without writing a complete philosophical treatise.

(2) *Dialectic in history*. The Hegelian dialectic was a full-blooded
affair. If you started with any partial concept and meditated on it,
it would presently turn into its opposite; it and its opposite would
combine into a synthesis, which would, in turn, become the starting
point of a similar movement, and so on until you reached the Absolute Idea, on which you could reflect as long as you liked without
discovering any new contradictions. The historical development of
the world in time was merely an objectification of this process of

thought. This view appeared possible to Hegel, because for him mind was the ultimate reality; for Marx, on the contrary, matter is the ultimate reality. Nevertheless he continues to think that the world develops according to a logical formula. To Hegel, the development of history is as logical as a game of chess. Marx and Engels keep the rules of chess, while supposing that the chessmen move themselves in accordance with the laws of physics, without the intervention of a player. In one of the quotations from Engels which I gave earlier, he says: "The means of getting rid of the incongruities that have been brought to light, *must* also be present, in a more or less developed condition, within the changed modes of production themselves." This "must" betrays a relic of the Hegelian belief that logic rules the world. Why should the outcome of a conflict in politics always be the establishment of some more developed system? This has not, in fact, been the case in innumerable instances. The barbarian invasion of Rome did not give rise to more developed economic forms, nor did the expulsion of the Moors from Spain, or the destruction of the Albigenses in the South of France. Before the time of Homer the Mycenaean civilization had been destroyed, and it was many centuries before a developed civilization again emerged in Greece. The examples of decay and retrogression are at least as numerous and as important in history as the examples of development. The opposite view, which appears in the works of Marx and Engels, is nothing but nineteenth-century optimism.

This is a matter of practical as well as theoretical importance. Communists always assume that conflicts between Communism and capitalism, while they may for a time result in partial victories for capitalism, must in the end lead to the establishment of Communism. They do not envisage another possible result, quite as probable, namely, a return to barbarism. We all know that modern war is a somewhat serious matter, and that in the next world war it is likely that large populations will be virtually exterminated by poison gases and bacteria. Can it be seriously supposed that after a war in which the great centres of population and most important industrial plants had been wiped out, the remaining population would be in a mood to establish scientific Communism? Is it not practically certain that the survivors would be in a mood of gibbering and superstitious brutality, fighting all against all for the last turnip or the last mangel-wurzel? Marx used to do his work in the British Museum, but after the Great War the British Government placed a tank just outside the museum, presumably to teach the intellectuals their place. Communism is a highly intellectual, highly civilized doctrine, which can, it is true, be established, as it was in Russia, after a slight preliminary skirmish, such as that of 1914–18, but hardly after a really serious war. I am afraid the dogmatic optimism of the Communist doctrine must be regarded as a relic of Victorianism.

There is another curious point about the Communist interpretation of the dialectic. Hegel, as everyone knows, concluded his dialectical account of history with the Prussian State, which, according to him, was the perfect embodiment of the Absolute Idea. Marx, who had no affection for the Prussian State, regarded this as a lame and impotent conclusion. He said that the dialectic should be essentially revolutionary, and seemed to suggest that it could not reach any final static resting-place. Nevertheless we hear nothing about the further revolutions that are to happen after the establishment of Communism. In the last paragraph of *La Misère de la Philosophie* he says:

It is only in an order of things in which there will no longer be classes or class-antagonism that *social evolutions* will cease to be *political revolutions*.

What these social evolutions are to be, or how they are to be brought about without the motive power of class conflict, Marx does not say. Indeed, it is hard to see how, on his theory, any further evolution would be possible. Except from the point of view of present-day politics, Marx's dialectic is no more revolutionary than that of Hegel. Moreover, since all human development has, according to Marx, been governed by conflicts of classes, and since under Communism there is to be only one class, it follows that there can be no further development, and that mankind must go on for ever and ever in a state of Byzantine immobility. This does not seem plausible, and it suggests that there must be other possible causes of political events besides those of which Marx has taken account.

(3) *Irrelevance of Metaphysics.* The belief that metaphysics has any bearing upon practical affairs is, to my mind, a proof of logical incapacity. One finds physicists with all kinds of opinions: some follow

Hume, some Berkeley, some are conventional Christians, some are materialists, some are sensationalists, some even are solipsists. This makes no difference whatever to their physics. They do not take different views as to when eclipses will occur, or what are the conditions of the stability of a bridge. That is because, in physics, there is some genuine knowledge, and whatever metaphysical beliefs a physicist may hold must adapt themselves to this knowledge. In so far as there is any genuine knowledge in the social sciences, the same thing is true. Whenever metaphysics is really useful in reaching a conclusion, that is because the conclusion cannot be reached by scientific means, i.e. because there is no good reason to suppose it true. What can be known, can be known without metaphysics, and whatever needs metaphysics for its proof cannot be proved. In actual fact Marx advances in his books much detailed historical argument, in the main perfectly sound, but none of this in any way depends upon materialism. Take, for example, the fact that free competition tends to end in monopoly. This is an empirical fact, the evidence for which is equally patent whatever one's metaphysic may happen to be. Marx's metaphysic comes in in two ways: on the one hand, by making things more cut and dried and precise than they are in real life; on the other hand, in giving him a certainty about the future which goes beyond what a scientific attitude would warrant. But in so far as his doctrines of historical development can be shown to be true, his metaphysic is irrelevant. The question whether Communism is going to become universal, is quite independent of metaphysics. It may be that a metaphysic is helpful in the fight: early Mohammedan conquests were much facilitated by the belief that the faithful who died in battle went straight to Paradise, and similarly the efforts of Communists may be stimulated by the belief that there is a God called Dialectical Materialism Who is fighting on their side, and will, in His own good time, give them the victory. On the other hand, there are many people to whom it is repugnant to have to profess belief in propositions for which they see no evidence, and the loss of such people must be reckoned as a disadvantage resulting from the Communist metaphysic.

(4) *Economic Causation in History*. In the main I agree with Marx, that economic causes are at the bottom of most of the great movements in history, not only political movements, but also those

in such departments as religion, art, and morals. There are, however, important qualifications to be made. In the first place, Marx does not allow nearly enough for the time-lag. Christianity, for example, arose in the Roman Empire, and in many respects bears the stamp of the social system of that time, but Christianity has survived through many changes. Marx treats it as moribund. "When the ancient world was in its last throes, the ancient religions were overcome by Christianity. When Christian ideas succumbed in the eighteenth century to rationalist ideas, feudal society fought its death-battle with the then revolutionary bourgeoisie." (*Manifesto of the Communist Party* by Karl Marx and F. Engels.) Nevertheless, in his own country it remained the most powerful obstacle to the realization of his own ideas,[2] and throughout the Western world its political influence is still enormous. I think it may be conceded that *new* doctrines that have any success must bear some relation to the economic circumstances of their age, but old doctrines can persist for many centuries without any such relation of any vital kind.

Another point where I think Marx's theory of history is too definite is that he does not allow for the fact that a small force may tip the balance when two great forces are in approximate equilibrium. Admitting that the great forces are generated by economic causes, it often depends upon quite trivial and fortuitous events which of the great forces gets the victory. In reading Trotsky's account of the Russian Revolution, it is difficult to believe that Lenin made no difference, but it was touch and go whether the German Government allowed him to get to Russia. If the Minister concerned had happened to be suffering from dyspepsia on a certain morning, he might have said "No" when in fact he said "Yes," and I do not think it can be rationally maintained that without Lenin the Russian Revolution would have achieved what it did. To take another instance: if the Prussians had happened to have a good General at the battle of Valmy, they might have wiped out the French Revolution. To take an even more fantastic example, it may be maintained quite plausibly that if Henry VIII had not fallen in love with Anne Boleyn, the United States would not now exist. For it was owing to this event that England broke with the Papacy, and therefore did not acknowl-

[2] "For Germany," wrote Marx in 1844, "the critique of religion is essentially completed."

edge the Pope's gift of the Americas to Spain and Portugal. If England had remained Catholic, it is probable that what is now the United States would have been part of Spanish America.

This brings me to another point in which Marx's philosophy of history was faulty. He regards economic conflicts as always conflicts between classes, whereas the majority of them have been between races or nations. English industrialism of the early nineteenth century was internationalist, because it expected to retain its monopoly of industry. It seemed to Marx, as it did to Cobden, that the world was going to be increasingly cosmopolitan. Bismarck, however, gave a different turn to events, and industrialism ever since has grown more and more nationalistic. Even the conflict between capitalism and Communism takes increasingly the form of a conflict between nations. It is true, of course, that the conflicts between nations are very largely economic, but the grouping of the world by nations is itself determined by causes which are in the main not economic.

Another set of causes which have had considerable importance in history are those which may be called medical. The Black Death, for example, was an event of whose importance Marx was well aware, but the causes of the Black Death were only in part economic. Undoubtedly it would not have occurred among populations at a higher economic level, but Europe had been quite as poor for many centuries as it was in 1348, so that the proximate cause of the epidemic cannot have been poverty. Take again such a matter as the prevalence of malaria and yellow fever in the tropics, and the fact that these diseases have now become preventable. This is a matter which has very important economic effects, though not itself of an economic nature.

Much the most necessary correction in Marx's theory is as to the causes of changes in methods of production. Methods of production appear in Marx as prime causes, and the reasons for which they change from time to time are left completely unexplained. As a matter of fact, methods of production change, in the main, owing to intellectual causes, owing, that is to say, to scientific discoveries and inventions. Marx thinks that discoveries and inventions are made when the economic situation calls for them. This, however, is a quite unhistorical view. Why was there practically no experimental science from the time of Archimedes to the time of Leonardo? For six centuries after Archimedes the economic conditions were such as should have made scientific work easy. It was the growth of science after the Renaissance that led to modern industry. This intellectual causation of economic processes is not adequately recognized by Marx.

History can be viewed in many ways, and many general formulae can be invented which cover enough of the ground to seem adequate if the facts are carefully selected. I suggest, without undue solemnity, the following alternative theory of the causation of the Industrial Revolution: industrialism is due to modern science, modern science is due to Galileo, Galileo is due to Copernicus, Copernicus is due to the Renaissance, the Renaissance is due to the fall of Constantinople, the fall of Constantinople is due to the migration of the Turks, the migration of the Turks is due to the desiccation of Central Asia. Therefore the fundamental study in searching for historical causes is hydrography.

CHAPTER XIX

THE THEORY OF SURPLUS VALUE

MARX'S theory of surplus value is simple in its main outline, though complicated in its details. He argues that a wage-earner produces goods equal in value to his wages in a portion of the working day, often assumed to be about half, and in the remainder of his working day produces goods which become the property of the capitalist although he has not had to make any payment for them. Thus the wage-earner produces more than he is paid for; the value of this additional product is what Marx calls "surplus value." Out of surplus value come profits, rent, tithes, taxes—in a word, everything except wages.

This view is based upon an economic argument which is not altogether easy to follow, the more so as it is partly valid, partly fallacious. It is, however, very necessary to analyze Marx's argument, since it has had a profound effect upon the development of Socialism and Communism.

Marx starts from the orthodox economic doctrine that the exchange value of a commodity is proportional to the amount of labor required for its production. We have already considered this doctrine in connection with Ricardo, and have seen that it is true only partially and in certain circumstances. It is true in so far as the cost of production is represented by wages, and there is competition among capitalists which keeps the price as low as possible. If the capitalists have formed themselves into a Trust or Cartel, or if the cost of raw material is a large part of the total cost of production, the theory is no longer true. Marx, however, accepted the theory from the economists of his day, although he despised them, apparently without any examination of the grounds in its favor.

The next step in the argument is derived (without adequate acknowledgment) from Malthus. It followed from Malthus's theory of population that there would always be competition among wage-earners, which would ensure that the value of labor, like that of other commodities, should be measured by its cost of production (and reproduction). That is to say, wages would suffice for the bare necessaries of the laborer and his family, and under a competitive system they could not rise above this level.

Malthus's theory of population, like Ricardo's theory of value, is subject to limitations which we have already considered. Marx always rejects it contemptuously, and is bound to do so, since, as Malthus was careful to point out, it would, if valid, make all communistic Utopias impossible. But Marx does not advance any reasoned argument against Malthus, and, what is still more remarkable, he accepts without question the law that wages must always (under a competitive system) be at subsistence level, which depends upon the acceptance of the very theory that he at other times rejects.

From these premises, the labor theory of value and the iron law of wages, the theory of surplus value seems to follow. The wage-earner, let us say, works twelve hours a day, and in six hours produces the value of his labor. What he produces in the remaining six hours represents the capitalist's exploitation, his surplus value. Although the capitalist does not have to pay for the last six hours, yet, for some unexplained reason, he is able to make the price of his product proportional to labor-time required for production. Marx forgets that this whole theory depended upon the assumption that all labor had to be paid for, and the further assumption that the capitalists competed with each other.[1] In the absence of these assumptions, there is no reason why value should be proportional to the labor-time of production.

If we assume that there are many competing capitalists in the business in question, then, supposing the state of affairs to have been initially as Marx supposes, it will be possible to lower the price and still make a profit, which will therefore be done as a result of competition. The capitalist, it is true, will have to pay rent, and probably interest on borrowed money; but so far as he is concerned, he will be forced down to the lowest profit at which he thinks it worth while to carry on the business. If, on the other hand, there is no competition, the price will be fixed, as with all monopolies, by the principle of "what the traffic will bear," which has nothing to do with the amount of labor involved.

[1] Though this is stated by Engels in his introduction to *La Misère de la Philosophie.*

While, therefore, it is undeniable that men make fortunes by exploiting labor, Marx's analysis of the economic process by which this is done appears to be faulty. And the main reason why it is not correct is the acceptance of Ricardo's theory of value.

I have written above as though (apart from currency fluctuations) value could be measured by price. This, indeed, follows from the definition of value, which is the amount of other commodities for which a given commodity will exchange. Price is merely a means of expressing the exchange values of different commodities in commensurable terms: if we wish to compare the values of a number of different commodities, we do so most easily by means of their price, i.e. (under a gold currency) by their exchange value in relation to gold. In so far as value means "exchange value," the fact that (at any given moment) value is measured by price is a mere logical consequence of the definition.

But Marx has another conception of value which obscurely conflicts with the definition of value as exchange value. This other conception, which never emerges clearly, is ethical or metaphysical; it seems to mean "what a commodity *ought* to exchange for." A few quotations will illustrate the difficulty of arriving at Marx's meaning on this point.

"Price," he says, "is the money-name of the labour realised in a commodity. Hence the expression of the equivalence of a commodity with the sum of money constituting its price, is a tautology, just as in general the expression of the relative value of a commodity is a statement of the equivalence of two commodities. But although price, being the exponent of the magnitude of a commodity's value, is the exponent of its exchange-ratio with money, it does not follow that the exponent of this exchange ratio is necessarily the exponent of the magnitude of the commodity's value. . . . Magnitude of value expresses a relation of social production, it expresses the connection that necessarily exists between a certain article and the portion of the total labour-time of society required to produce it. As soon as the magnitude of value is converted into price, the above necessary relation takes the shape of a more or less accidental exchange-ratio between a single commodity and another, the money-commodity. But this exchange ratio may express either the real magnitude of that commodity's value, or the quantity of gold deviating from that value, for which, according to circumstances, it may be parted with. The possibility, therefore, of quantitative incongruity between price and magnitude of value, or the deviation of the former from the latter, is inherent in the price-form itself."

So far it might be supposed that Marx is thinking only of accidental fluctuations, such as might be due to the relative shrewdness or impecuniosity of buyer and seller. He goes on, however, to a more serious distinction between price and value, which, if he had followed it up, would have raised difficulties for him of which he apparently remained unaware. He says:

"The price-form, however, is not only compatible with the possibility of a quantitative incongruity between magnitude of value and price, *i.e.*, between the former and its expression in money, but it may also conceal a qualitative inconsistency, so much so, that, although money is nothing but the value-form of commodities, price ceases altogether to express value. Objects that in themselves are no commodities, such as conscience, honour, &c., are capable of being offered for sale by their holders, and of thus acquiring, through their price, the form of commodities. Hence an object may have a price without having value. The price in that case is imaginary, like certain quantities in mathematics. On the other hand, the imaginary price-form may sometimes conceal either a direct or indirect real value-relation; for instance, the price of uncultivated land, which is without value, because no human labour has been incorporated in it."

It is of course necessary for Marx, with his labor theory of value, to maintain that virgin land has no value. Since it often has a price, the distinction between price and value is essential to him at this point. Exchange-value, it now appears, is not the actual amount of other goods for which a given commodity can, in fact, be exchanged; it is the amount of goods for which the commodity could be exchanged *if* people valued commodities in proportion to the amount of labor required for their production. Marx concedes that people do not so value commodities when they are buying and selling, for, if they did, it would be impossible to exchange virgin land, upon which no labor has been expended, for gold, which has had to be mined. Accordingly when Marx says that the value of a commodity is measured by the amount of labor required for its production, he does not mean to say anything about what the commodity is likely to fetch in the market. What, then, does he mean?

He may mean either of two things. He may be giving a mere verbal definition of the word "value": when I speak of the "value" of a commodity (he may be saying), I mean the amount of labor required to produce it, or rather, such quantity of other commodities as an equivalent amount of labor would produce. Or, again, he may be using "value" in an ethical sense: he may mean that goods *ought* to exchange in proportion to the labor involved, and would do so in a world ruled by economic justice. If he adopts the first of these alternatives, most of the propositions in his theory of value become trivial, while those which assert a connection between value and price become arbitrary and remain partly false. If he adopts the second alternative, he is no longer analyzing economic facts, but setting up an economic ideal. Moreover, this ideal would be an impossible one, for the reasons emphasized in Ricardo's theory of rent: a bushel of wheat grown on bad land embodies more labor than one grown on good land, but could not in any imaginable economic system be sold at a higher price. Either the verbal or the ethical alternative as to the meaning of "value," therefore, reduces Marx's economic theory to a state of confusion.

The ethical interpretation of "value," nevertheless, seems to have had some influence, not only on Marx, but on all those who upheld the labor theory of value. In the case of Marx, this is borne out by the fact that, in connection with the price of virgin land, he mentions such things as the price of a man's honor, where we feel that there is something ethically reprehensible in the existence of a price. In the case of other economists, it is interesting to observe that Hodgskin, from whom Marx learned much, and who first among theorists applied the labor-theory of value in the interests of the proletariat, finds the source of this theory in Locke's doctrine that the justification of private property is a man's right to the produce of his own labor.[2] If he exchanges the produce of his own labor for the produce of an equal amount of some one else's labor, justice is preserved; the labor-theory is therefore in conformity with ethics.

[2] Halévy, *Thomas Hodgskin*, pp. 208–9, Société Nouvelle de Librairie et d'édition, Paris, 1903.

This point of view, perhaps unconsciously, seems to have influenced Marx: where price and value diverged, he felt that price represented the wickedness of capitalism.

Much of the efficacy of Marx's writing depends upon tacit assumptions in his arithmetical illustrations. Let us take one of these as typical of many.

"One more example. Jacob gives the following calculation for the year 1815. Owing to the previous adjustment of several items it is very imperfect; nevertheless for our purpose it is sufficient. In it he assumes the price of wheat to be 8s. a quarter, and the average yield per acre to be 22 bushels.

Value Produced Per Acre

	£	s.	d.			£	s.	d.
Seed	1	9	0	Tithes, Rates, and Taxes		1	1	0
Manure	2	10	0	Rent		1	8	0
Wages	3	10	0	Farmer's Profit and Interest		1	2	0
Total	7	9	0	Total		3	11	0

"Assuming that the price of the product is the same as its value, we here find the surplus-value distributed under the various heads of profit, interest, rent, &c. We have nothing to do with these in detail; we simply add them together, and the sum is a surplus-value of £3 11s. 0d. The sum of £3 19s. 0d., paid for seed and manure, is constant capital, and we put it equal to zero. There is left the sum of £3 10s. 0d., which is the variable capital advanced: and we see that a new value of £3 10s. 0d. + £3 11s 0d. has been produced in its place. Therefore $\frac{s}{v} = \frac{£3\ 11s.\ 0d.}{£3\ 10s.\ 0d.}$, giving a rate of surplus-value of more than 100%. The labourer employs more than one-half of his working day in producing the surplus-value, which different persons, under different pretexts, share amongst themselves."

In this illustration, *s* means surplus-value, and *v* means variable capital, i.e. wages. It will be seen that Marx includes in surplus-value the whole of what the farmer makes, and the whole of the rates and taxes. It is therefore implied in the calculation (*a*) that the farmer does no work, (*b*) that the rates and taxes are wholly handed over to the idle rich. Marx would not, of course, make either of these assumptions in explicit terms, but they are implicit in his figures, both in this case and in every analogous illustration. In 1815, the year to which the above example applies, the rates were mainly expended in wages, under the old Poor Law. The taxes, it is true, went chiefly to the fund-holders, but of the remainder some part was certainly spent in useful ways—for example, in keeping up the British Museum, without which Marx could not have written his *magnum opus*.

More important than the question of rates and taxes is the question of the capitalist's work. In the case of a small capitalist, such as a farmer, it is ridiculous to treat him as one of the idle rich. If a farm were run by the State, it would need an overseer, and a competent overseer could probably obtain a salary about equal to the farmer's profit, taking one year with another. The cotton manufacturers of the years before 1846, who formed Engels's conception of the capitalist, and thence Marx's, were largely men in a rather small way, who worked almost entirely on borrowed capital. Their income depended upon their skill in using the money that had been lent to them. It is true that they were brutal, but it is not true that they were idle. Somebody has to organize a factory, somebody has to buy the machinery and sell the product, somebody has to do the day-to-day supervision. In the early days of capitalism, all this was done by the employer; yet Marx regards the whole of his earnings as entirely due to appropriation of the surplus value created by the employees. I know there are passages where the opposite is admitted, but they are isolated, whereas the assumption that the employer does no work is pervasive.

In the modern large-scale developments of capitalistic enterprise, it is true, the capitalist is often idle. The shareholders of railways do nothing, and the directors do not do much, in the way of managing the business. The work of management, in all large concerns, tends to fall more and more into the hands of salaried experts, leaving the capitalists as mere recipients of interest. In so far as Socialism represents a more scientific organization of industry, less chaotic and less lacking in forethought, salaried experts might be expected to sympathize with it. They seldom do so, however, because, as a result of the bias given by Marx, Socialism has tended to stand, not only for the workers as against the idle rich, but for the manual workers as against both the rich and the brain workers. Marx, by ignoring the functions of the small-scale capitalist in managing his business, produced a theory which could not do justice to the salaried experts who do the work of management in large-scale capitalism. The glorification of manual work as against brain work was a theoretical error, and its political effects have been disastrous.

It may be said that it is of no importance whether Marx was right in the niceties of his economic analysis. He was right in maintaining that the proletariat were brutally exploited, and that their exploitation was due to the power of the rich. To distinguish one class of rich men from another was, from this point of view, unprofitable; the important thing was to end exploitation, and this could only be done by conquering power in a fight against the rich collectively.

To this there are two objections. The first is, that the abolition of exploitation, if unwisely carried out, might leave the proletariat even more destitute than before; the second, that Marx has not rightly analyzed where the power of money resides, and has therefore given himself an unnecessary number of enemies.

The first of these objections applies to the destruction of any system in which power is unequally distributed. The holders of power will always use their position to obtain special advantages for themselves; at the same time, they will in general wish to prevent chaos, and to insure a certain efficiency in the system by which they profit. They will tend to have a monopoly of experience in government and management. It may well happen that, if they are suddenly dispossessed, lack of knowledge and experience on the part of those previously oppressed will cause them to fall into even greater sufferings than those from which they have escaped. If this is not to happen, there must be, on the side of the newly emancipated, a sufficient amount of governmental and technical intelligence to carry on the political and economic life of the community. Successful revolutions, such as the French Revolution, have had more knowledge and intelligence on the side of the rebels than among the defenders of the old system. Where this condition is not fulfilled, the transition is bound to be arduous, and may never succeed in producing any improvement. It is doubtful whether the population of Haiti has been happier since it threw off the power of the French.

As regards the analysis of the power of money, I think that Henry George was more nearly right than Marx. Henry George, following Spence and the French physiocrats, found the source of economic power in land, and held that the only necessary reform was the payment of rent to the State rather than to private landowners. This was also the view of Herbert Spencer until he became old and respected. In its older forms, it is scarcely applicable to the modern world, but it contains an important element of truth, which Marx unfortunately missed. Let us try to restate the matter in modern terms.

All power to exploit others depends upon the possession of some complete or partial, permanent or temporary monopoly, but this monopoly may be of the most diverse kinds. Land is the most obvious. If I own land in London or New York, I can, owing to the law of trespass, invoke the whole of the forces of the State to prevent others from making use of my land without my consent. Those who wish to live or work on my land must therefore pay me rent, and if my land is very advantageous they must pay me much rent. I do not have to do anything at all in return for the rent. The capitalist has to organize a business, the professional man has to exercise his skill, but the landowner can levy toll on their industry without doing anything at all. Similarly if I own coal or iron or any other mineral, I can make my own terms with those who wish to mine it, so long as I leave them an average rate of profit. Every improvement in industry, every increase in the population of cities, automatically augments what the landowner can exact in the form of rent. While others work, he remains idle; but their work enables him to grow richer and richer.

Land, however, is by no means the only form of monopoly. The owners of capital, collectively, are monopolists as against borrowers; that is why they are able to charge interest. The control of credit is a form of monopoly quite as important as land. Those who control credit can encourage or ruin a business as their judgment may direct; they can even, within limits, decide whether industry in general is to be prosperous or depressed. This power they owe to monopoly.

The men who have most economic power in the modern world derive it from land, minerals, and credit, in combination. Great bankers control iron ore, coalfields, and railways; smaller capitalists are at their mercy, almost as completely as proletarians. The conquest of economic power demands as its first step the ousting of the monopolists. It will then remain to be seen whether, in a world in which there is no private monopoly, much harm is done by men who have achieved success by skill without the aid of ultimate economic power. It is questionable whether, on the balance, the world would now be the better if Mr. Henry Ford had been prevented from making cheap cars. The harm that is done by great industrialists is usually dependent upon their access to some source of monopoly power. In labor disputes, the employer is the immediate enemy, but is often no more than a private in the opposing army. The real enemy is the monopolist.

CHAPTER XX

THE POLITICS OF MARXISM

MARX'S political doctrines were an outcome of his economic theory and of his dialectical materialism. Previous Socialists had appealed to men's benevolence and sense of justice. Owen remained, to the end of his days, essentially the kindly patriarch of New Lanark. Saint Simon's appeal was religious: he aimed at creating a new type of Christianity. Fourier, like Owen, aimed at founding colonies whose success should show the excellence of his principles. Marx realized the futility of such methods. He saw that benevolence will never be sufficiently powerful to transform the whole economic system; also that Socialism cannot be introduced in isolated little communities piecemeal, but must be inaugurated on a large scale as a result of a political upheaval. He and Engels condemned their Socialist predecessors as Utopians. The problem for them was: theoretically, to foresee the inevitable dialectical development of industrialism; practically, to insure the conquest of power by the proletariat, whose class interest was to bring about the transition from capitalism to Socialism.

Marx and Engels perceived, as early as 1848, that competition must issue in monopoly. They saw that businesses tend to increase in size, and that every advance in technique promotes this increase. Before Engels died, the growth of Trusts in America had made this obvious; but to have perceived it in 1848 showed a perspicacity which no one else at that period possessed. Marx argued that the concentration of capital would diminish the number of capitalists, and that those who had been defeated in the competitive struggle would sink into the proletariat. In the end, there would be left only a few capitalists, and almost all the rest of the population would be proletarians. The proletarians would have learnt, in the course of their conflicts with capital, to organize, first nationally, then internationally. At last, when the capitalists had grown sufficiently few and the proletariat sufficiently organized, they would conquer power and put an end to the capitalist era:

"Along with the constantly diminishing number of the magnates of capital, who usurp and monopolize all advantages of this process of transformation, grows the mass of misery, oppression, slavery, degradation, exploitation; but with this too grows the revolt of the working class, a class always increasing in numbers, and disciplined, united, organized by the very mechanism of the process of capitalist production itself. The monopoly of capital becomes a fetter upon the mode of production, which has sprung up and flourished along with and under it. Centralization of the means of production and socialization of labour at last reach a point where they become incompatible with their capitalist integument. The integument is burst asunder. The knell of capitalist private property sounds. The expropriators are expropriated." [1]

All politics, for Marx, consists in the conflict of classes, brought about by changing methods of economic technique. The bourgeoisie conquered the feudal nobility in the great French Revolution, and again, so far as was necessary, in the Revolution of 1830. In England, the same conquest was partially achieved by the Civil War, but was completed by the Reform Act of 1832 and the repeal of the Corn Laws. In Germany, the same thing was attempted, but without complete success, in the Revolution of 1848. In France, the same year saw a beginning of a new revolution, that of the proletariat against the bourgeoisie. In the early months of the French Revolution of 1848, the Socialists had considerable power, and were able to establish the national workshops, where in theory every man could obtain paid employment. The Socialists were, however, put down with great slaughter during the month of June, after which, for a long time, they played no ostensible part in politics. Marx looked forward to a series of such conflicts, in which the defeat of the Socialists would become progressively more difficult, and finally impossible. As the bourgeoisie had defeated the feudal nobility, so, in the end, the proletariat were certain to defeat the bourgeoisie.

No prophet is altogether right in his anticipations, but Marx was right in many respects. Competition has been largely succeeded by monopoly; the proletariat has become more and more Socialistic; in one great State, the government is attempting to establish Com-

[1] *Capital*, Vol. I, pp. 836-7.

munism. There are, however, a number of respects in which he was mistaken, and some of these are of very great importance.

His most serious mistake was that he underrated the strength of nationalism. "Proletarians of all nations, unite!" says the Communist Manifesto. But experience has shown that, as yet, most proletarians hate foreigners more than they hate employers; in 1914, even Marxists, with few exceptions, obeyed the orders of the capitalist State to which they happened to belong. Even if proletarians of white races could, in time, be induced to ignore national boundaries, it will require a much longer time before they feel any real solidarity with competitors of yellow, brown or black race. Yet, until they do so, and the yellow, brown and black proletarians reciprocate the feeling, they can hardly achieve any stable victory over the capitalists.

It is not only on the side of the proletariat that nationalism proved stronger than purely economic forces. On the side of the capitalists, also, the boundaries of States have proved to be usually the boundaries of combination. Most capitalist monopolies are national, not world-wide. In the steel industry, for example, there is monopoly, actual or virtual, in America, in France, in Germany, but these several monopolies are independent of each other. Almost the only industry which is truly international is the armament industry,[2] because to it the important thing is that wars should be long and frequent, not that either side should be victorious. With this exception, the monopolists of different countries compete against each other, and cause their respective governments to help them in the competition. The rivalry between nations is just as much an economic conflict as the class war, and at least as important in modern politics, yet according to Marx all politics are controlled by the conflict of classes.

Marx had the less excuse for his failure to give due weight to nationalism as he himself had taken part in the German Revolution of 1848, and had carefully noted the part played by nationalism in its suppression. In his book, *Revolution and Counter Revolution, or Germany in 1848*, which he wrote in 1851–2, he tells how the Slavs of the Austro-Hungarian Empire, whose nationalism afterwards became the proximate cause of the Great War, and who now form

[2] See *The Secret International* and *Patriotism Ltd.*, published by the Union of Democratic Control.

Czecho-Slovakia and part of Yugoslavia, endeavored to free themselves from the German yoke and were finally defeated. He has no sympathy with them whatsoever, but views the whole matter from the standpoint of an orthodox German nationalist. He says:

"Thus ended for the present, and most likely for ever, the attempts of the Slavonians of Germany to recover an independent national existence. Scattered remnants of numerous nations, whose nationality and political vitality had long been extinguished, and who in consequence had been obliged, for almost a thousand years, to follow in the wake of a mightier nation, their conqueror, the same as the Welsh in England, the Basques in Spain, the Bas-Bretons in France, and at a more recent period the Spanish and French Creoles in those portions of North America occupied of late by the Anglo-American race—these dying nationalities, the Bohemians, Carinthians, Dalmatians, etc., had tried to profit by the universal confusion of 1848, in order to restore their political *status quo* of A.D. 800. The history of a thousand years ought to have shown them that such a retrogression was impossible; that if all the territory east of the Elbe and Saale had at one time been occupied by kindred Slavonians, this fact merely proved the historical tendency, and at the same time physical and intellectual power of the German nation to subdue, absorb, and assimilate its ancient eastern neighbours: that this tendency of absorption on the part of the Germans had always been, and still was, one of the mightiest means by which the civilization of Western Europe had been spread in the east of that continent; that it could only cease whenever the process of Germanization had reached the frontier of large, compact, unbroken nations, capable of an independent national life, such as the Hungarians, and in some degree the Poles; and that, therefore, the natural and inevitable fate of these dying nations was to allow this process of dissolution and absorption by their stronger neighbours to complete itself. Certainly this is no very flattering prospect for the national ambition of the Panslavistic dreamers who succeeded in agitating a portion of the Bohemian and South Slavonian people: but can they expect that history would retrograde a thousand years in order to please a few phthisical bodies of men, who in every part of the territory they occupy are interspersed with and surrounded by Germans, who from time almost immemorial have had for all purposes of civilization no other language but the German, and who lack the very first conditions of national existence, numbers and compactness of territory? Thus, the Panslavistic rising, which everywhere in the German and Hungarian Slavonic territories was the cloak for the restoration to independence of all these numberless petty nations, everywhere clashed with the European revolutionary movements, and the Slavonians, although pretending to fight for liberty, were invariably (the Democratic portion of the Poles excepted) found on the side of despotism and reaction. Thus it was in Germany, thus in Hungary, thus even here and there in Turkey. Traitors to the popular cause, supporters and chief props to the Austrian Government's cabal, they placed themselves in the position of outlaws in the eyes of all revolutionary nations. And although nowhere the mass of the people had a part in the petty squabbles about nationality raised by the Panslavistic leaders, for the very reason that they were too ignorant, yet it will never be forgotten that in Prague, in a half-German town, crowds of Slavonian fanatics cheered and repeated the cry: 'Rather the Russian knout than German Liberty!' After their first evaporated effort in 1848, and after the lesson the Austrian Government gave them, it is not likely that another attempt at a later opportunity will be made. But if they should try again under similar pretexts to ally themselves to the counter-revolutionary force, the duty of Germany is clear. No country in a state of revolution and involved in external war can tolerate a Vendée in its very heart."

If Marx had had any power of self-criticism, the fact that he could write this passage should have shown him that even Marxists are not exempt from nationalist bias.

Marx sometimes took the view that nationalism is unavoidable under capitalism, and can only be superseded by the rule of the proletariat. Thus he wrote in 1846:

"The phantasms of a European Republic, of perpetual peace under political organization, have become just as laughable as the phrases concerning the union of the peoples under the aegis of free trade. . . . The bourgeoisie has in every country its special interests, and, as for it there is nothing superior to interests, it can never rise above nationality. . . . But the proletarians have in all countries one and the same interest, one and the same enemy, one and the same fight in prospect; the proletarians, as regards the great mass, are by nature without national prejudices, and their whole culture and movement is essentially humanitarian, anti-national. Only the proletarians can destroy nationality, the proletariat alone can allow the different nations to fraternize."

As yet, this remains an unfulfilled dream.

While Marx was right in prophesying the concentration of capitalist industry, so far at least as its more important branches are concerned, into monopolistic or nearly monopolistic forms, he was wrong in supposing that this implied a great diminution in the number of individual capitalists. In such countries as England, France, or Holland, there are innumerable old ladies, retired colonels, and *rentiers* of various kinds, who live on the interest of their investments. Such people are the backbone of the parties of extreme reaction, since they have nothing to occupy their minds except the stability of their shares. Even working men become interested in the maintenance of the capitalist system if they belong to a friendly society which has invested funds. There is, in fact, no such clear-cut division between capitalist and proletarian as Marx assumed. Following Hegel, he looked for the embodiment of logical categories in the actual world, and expected facts to have the sharp boundaries belonging to A and not-A in the text-books. In any country of old-established wealth, this is by no means the case; on the contrary, capitalistic interests penetrate far down into the proletariat, and are a means of welding together classes which Marx thought would increasingly diverge. For example, the following persons, as shareholders in Handley Page Ltd., manufacturers of aeroplanes, had on June 5, 1931, a common interest, not only in capitalism, but in war:

Sir Basil Mayhew, K.B.E., Sir Henry Grayson, K.B.E., many banks and investment companies, Wing Commander Louis Greig, C.V.O., Mr. C. R. Fairey, the Right Hon. J. Downe, C.M.G., D.S.O., the Duchess of Grafton, Lord Arthur Browne, Mr. F. Handley Page, Mr. Arthur J. Page, . . . taxi-drivers, municipal officers, printers, stationmasters, brass founders, boot repairers, woolsorters, carpenters, chemists, farmers, police constables, schoolmasters, fish merchants, naval officers, an Air Vice-Marshal, an occasional clergyman, a Brigadier-General, a civil servant in the Foreign Office, a professor of music, doctors, and the trustees for the Wesleyan Chapel Purposes (Ltd.), Manchester.[3]

[3] *The Secret International*, published by the Union of Democratic Control, p. 19.

This harmony of interest between different classes arises not only from concern for investments, but from causes connected with the nature of a man's work. Take, say a policeman. In so far as he is the guardian of capitalist law and order, he counts as an ally of the capitalist. When he wishes to improve his condition by promotion, he must please the authorities; but when he wishes to improve his condition by improving the condition of policemen in general, he becomes a proletarian, and resorts to the mechanism of unions and strikes. The same considerations apply to soldiers and sailors. But a capitalist State which has any wisdom and avoids defeat in war can always keep these classes on its side. Marx realized the existence of such classes but did not realize how large and important they would become.

There is another respect in which Marx's division of industrial mankind into capitalist and proletarian went wrong. This is as regards the salaried employees in large capitalistic undertakings. The work of management, which was done by the employer himself a hundred years ago, is now usually left to paid officials. And apart from management, there is often need of technical and scientific experts; this is true especially in chemical industries. There is thus a new middle class between the capitalist and the proletarian. This new middle class has taken on all or most of the functions formerly performed by the employer. In America, where capital is less hereditary than in Europe, the very rich still actually control industry in certain broad aspects, particularly as regards finance and general policy; but this state of affairs is likely to pass as American capitalism becomes more old-established. In England, the capitalist is becoming a *roi fainéant*, and the salaried employee is his *maire du palais*. This tendency will, in all likelihood, become universal.

The salaried worker has no reason to love the capitalist, who gets the lion's share of the booty without doing the work. But the salaried worker has a privileged position as compared to the wage-earner, and hesitates to throw in his lot with the wage-earner by becoming a Socialist. This is no doubt partly from snobbery, but by no means wholly. Marx minimized all work except manual work, and did not attempt to appeal to any class except the proletariat. Scientific experts are aware of their importance in the modern world, and are not prepared to subordinate themselves to manual workers. Under the capitalists their importance is at least recognized by their being employed and treated with a certain respect; they do not feel any security that their status would be as good after a proletarian revolution. Accordingly they remain, for the most part, the more or less reluctant allies of the capitalists.

Marx, by his teaching, created the class war which he prophesied, but by his excessive glorification of manual labor he caused the division of classes to come at a lower point in the social scale than was necessary, and thereby made enemies of the most important class in the modern economic world, the men who do the skilled work of industrialism. These men could have been won over to Socialism—or at any rate many of them could—if it had been presented, not as a doctrine of vengeance on the more fortunate classes, but as a more scientific and intelligent way of organizing the world's production and distribution. Private capitalism has proved itself impossibly chaotic, and unable to produce that prosperity which ought to result from the increased productivity of labor. It is clear that the incentive of profit is no longer the right one over a large field of production, and that some method of organization such as Socialists advocate has become necessary to the economic well-being of mankind.

It is possible, at the present day, to advocate international Socialism from the standpoint of efficiency rather than from that of the class-war. But in the England of the '40's, from which Marx's outlook was in the main derived, such a point of view was scarcely possible. Any man not utterly blinded by class bias was bound, unless he were a callous brute, to feel a fierce indignation against the industrial employers. At that time, the proletariat was growing rapidly, and the opposition of class against class in all industrial regions was fierce and sharp. Most of the middle-class economists made themselves apologists for the employers, and defended abominations by means of fallacies which Marx exposes with well-deserved scorn.

There is nothing astonishing in the fact that Marx's appeal was mainly to class antagonism, when one considers what British capitalism was in the first half of the nineteenth century. And although, in Great Britain, capitalism became less brutal after 1846, its cruelties continued in full force wherever it was conquering new territory; indeed, in the Belgian Congo it reached a pitch of atrocity far surpassing the worst evils of the mills and mines in the North of England. There is no limit to the cruelties men will inflict for the sake of gain. This is not a new fact produced by capitalism: Coeur de Lion's treatment of the Jews, Pizarro's treatment of the Incas, show the same cold-blooded cupidity as was shown by the employers who filled Marx with detestation. But when we consider him as a prophet for the present day, the matter is somewhat different. Marx's hatred, natural as it was, and hateful as were its objects, was not a good basis for a scientific study of economics, or for a constructive theory of the system by which capitalism was to be superseded. It has perhaps been a misfortune that Marxist doctrine became crystallized as a result of the study of industrial England in the '40's; at a later period, it might have taken a form less fierce and capable of winning adherents over a wider field.

Marxism, by appealing to proletarian hatred, has lost many important possible allies. At the same time, hatred being the most dynamic of human passions, it has generated a movement more energetic and determined than it could have been if it had had a less degree of fierceness. This fierceness was from the first quite deliberate. In an open letter against H. Kriege, written in 1846, Marx points out that love has not succeeded, in 1800 years, in bettering social conditions, and does not give the necessary energetic power of action. The actual circumstances of the present-day world, he says, with their sharp opposition of capital and labor, are a more powerful source of Socialist opinions than love of mankind. "These circumstances," he says, "call out to us: 'This cannot remain so, this must become different, and we ourselves, we human beings, must make it different.' This iron necessity gives to socialist efforts expansion and actively powerful supporters, and will open the way to socialist reforms by transformation of existing economic relations sooner than all the love that glows in all the feeling hearts of the world."

To appeal to hatred may be the right psychology for winning victory in a war; so all the belligerents thought from 1914 to 1918. But it is not the right psychology for subsequent construction; to us, who suffer the aftermath of the Treaty of Versailles, this should be obvious. Marx was not a wholly pleasant character: envy and malice abound in his pages. Unfortunately, much of what was least admirable in his disposition has been copied by his followers. One cannot but feel that any war waged in such a spirit must, if successful, lead to a peace as disastrous as that of Versailles. Hatred, indulged beyond a point, becomes a habit, and must seek perpetually new victims.

But, further, it is very doubtful whether, in an efficient modern State, the proletariat alone can hope to win the victory over capitalism. The capitalists, together with those who feel their interests at one with them, are not, as Marx supposed they would become, a small proportion of the population. Moreover, as things are now, they embrace the bulk of technical experts upon whom modern war depends. Is it likely that the air force would be on the side of the proletariat? Could the proletariat win without it? This is only one of many questions confronting the modern Marxist.

Marx's doctrine of the class war was one of the forces that killed nineteenth-century liberalism in Europe, by frightening the middle classes into reaction, and by teaching that political opinions are, and always must be, based upon economic bias rather than upon any consideration of the general good. In America, where Marx has had little political influence, old-fashioned liberalism still survives, and is at present engaged in a quite un-Marxian attempt at reconstruction. Perhaps it is too late for such gentle methods; perhaps the world cannot now escape the purgatory of violent class-war. But if this is inevitable, Marx's writing has helped to make it so.

Marx's doctrines, like those of other men, are partly true and partly false. There is much that can be controverted, but there are four points in his theory that are of such importance as to prove him a man of supreme intelligence.

The first is the concentration of capital, passing gradually from free competition to monopoly.

The second is economic motivation in politics, which now is taken almost for granted, but was, when he propounded it, a daring innovation.

The third is the necessity for the conquest of power by those who are not possessed of capital. This follows from economic motivation, and is to be contrasted with Owen's appeal to benevolence.

The fourth is the necessity of acquisition by the State of all the means of production, with the consequence that Socialism must, from its inception, embrace a whole nation, if not the whole world. Marx's predecessors aimed at small communities in which, as they supposed,

Socialism could be tried experimentally on a small scale, but he perceived the futility of all such attempts.

It is on these four grounds that Marx deserves to be considered
the founder of scientific Socialism. Like other founders of doctrines
he needs emendation in various respects, and misfortune is likely to
result if he is treated with religious awe. But if he is treated as fal-
lible, he will still be found to contain much of the most important
truth.

PART THREE

DEMOCRACY AND PLUTOCRACY
IN AMERICA

From the West swift Freedom came,
Against the course of Heaven and doom,
A second sun arrayed in flame,
To burn, to kindle, to illume.
From far Atlantis its young beams
Chased the shadows and the dreams.
France, with all her sanguine steams,
Hid, but quenched it not; again
Through clouds its shafts of glory rain
From utmost Germany to Spain.

   .   .   .   .   .

     Alas! for Liberty!
If numbers, wealth, or unfulfilling years,
Or fate, can quell the free!

SHELLEY.

IN connection with industrialism, as we have seen, there grew up two fairly complete systems of philosophy, each associated with a type of progressive politics. These were: the doctrine of the Philosophical Radicals, and the materialistic Socialism of Karl Marx. In the conquest of public opinion, each of these schools, but especially the former, allied itself with the pre-industrial liberalism connected with the American and French Revolutions. All progressive opinion, in such matters as democracy, opposition to feudalism, and enthusiasm for education, followed the lead of Jefferson. Most progressive opinion also accepted the nationalist principle of self-determination, of which the first clear statement, in the Declaration of Independence, is equally due to Jefferson.

The pattern of nineteenth-century progressive politics is largely formed by the co-operation and interaction of industrial Radicalism with eighteenth-century ideals of democracy, individual liberty, and intellectual enlightenment. Gradually, as the time goes on, industrialism becomes more aggressive and self-confident, and the eighteenth-century type of progress sinks into the background. Capitalists, having won emancipation from feudalism, reduce the ideal of "freedom" to that of "free competition." But free competition, after a period of lawless excess, issues in nation-wide monopoly, with the result that the State becomes a partner in competition, and the rivalry between private firms is replaced by economic nationalism.

Eighteenth-century liberalism, with which industrial Radicalism at first coalesced, thus sinks into the background. Industrial capital becomes conservative, and the impulse to progress becomes more and more confined to the proletariat. For the proletariat, the "individual liberty" of the Jeffersonian is useless, owing to the economic power of the employer. It follows that, as progressive politics becomes proletarian, it loses its eighteenth-century elements: organization and equality take the place of individual liberty.

CHAPTER XXI

JEFFERSONIAN DEMOCRACY

THROUGHOUT the first seventy-two years of its existence as an independent nation, the United States was interesting to Europeans chiefly as the most complete and important example of democracy then in existence. Opinion was divided as it now is about Russia: it was treason among Radicals to admit defects in America, and among conservatives to admit merits. Nor was this view confined to Europe. With the exception of the Federalists in early days, Americans felt themselves the bearers of progress. Jefferson, retiring from office in 1809, says: "Sole depositories of the remains of human liberty, our duty to ourselves, to posterity, and to mankind, call upon us by every motive which is sacred or honourable, to watch over the safety of our beloved country during the troubles which agitate and convulse the residue of the world." The same sentiment, fifty-four years later, animates Lincoln's Gettysburg speech. The common feeling of Americans was expressed by Walt Whitman:

Have the elder races halted?
Do they droop and end their lesson, wearied over there beyond the seas?
We take up the task eternal, and the burden and the lesson,
  Pioneers, O Pioneers!

As a theory, democracy, unlike the doctrines of the economists and Socialists, was by no means new. It had, in the modern world, two sources, one classical, the other Protestant. In the founders of American democracy, these two sources mingled: in their successors, only the Protestant source remained.

Herodotus, in a well-known passage, represents the Persian conspirators before the accession of Darius as debating the relative merits of monarchy, aristocracy, and democracy. Herodotus is, of course, attributing to Persians the sentiments of Greeks: in the Greece of his day, democracy was familiar as a form of government. The Romans, likewise, hated kings, and established a republic which gradually became more democratic until it was succeeded by the Empire. Such men as the Gracchi became models for rhetorical declamation, and Roman writers, especially under the Empire, produced noteworthy praises of popular liberty. Brutus and Cassius became symbols: Dante, admiring the Holy Roman Empire, regarded them as supreme sinners, and placed them, along with Judas Iscariot, in the threefold mouths of Satan. But those who hated tyrants made Brutus the prototype of republican virtue, even in Rome, and even in the middle ages.

With the revival of classical studies, the influence of Greece and Rome on political thought increased. In the eighteenth century, when all intelligent aristocrats were familiar with Latin, and many with Greek, a more or less literary republicanism was quite compatible with *le bon ton*. Horace Walpole hung on his walls a copy of Charles I's death sentence, with the inscription "Major Charta" to show its superiority to Magna Charta. In France, intellectual Radicalism was largely associated with admiration of the ancients, with the result that Napoleon hated Tacitus, and would not tolerate any professor who praised that author. In America also, in its early days, this influence made itself felt, although it was always less important than the influence derived from Protestantism. Jefferson, in 1809, was praised by the Legislature of Virginia for his "Roman" love of his country. On being consulted about Washington's statue, he advised that it should represent him in a toga. The early leaders of public opinion in America, especially those who were Virginians, were largely dominated by classical models, in thought as well as in style.

In France before the Revolution, the influence of Greece and Rome was, perhaps, the main cause of democratic opinions among those who, like the liberal aristocrats, had nothing to gain by change. There were, however, three other influences of great importance: Rousseau, the philosophy derived from Locke, and the experiences of Lafayette and his brother officers in America. All these three influences are ultimately derived from Protestantism.

In Germany, England, and America, theological revolt against the Papacy led, by a very easy transition, to revolt against the civil power. Luther had asserted the principle of private judgment, and in so doing had implied that there are matters as to which the authorities have no right to coerce the individual. Having been befriended by certain Princes, Luther confined his doctrine to the right of resistance to *ecclesiastical* authority, but in the resulting ferment many men refused to accept this limitation. The leaders of the Peasants' Revolt, in 1525, urged that serfdom should be abolished, "since Christ redeemed us all with His precious blood, the shepherd as well as the noble, the lowest as well as the highest, none being excepted." The Peasants' Revolt was suppressed, Luther joining in the suppression with unbelievable ferocity. But the movement was continued and developed by the Anabaptists, who carried it on to its logical conclusion in anarchist Communism—the same doctrine which Bakunin and Kropotkin opposed to that of Marx. After the suppression of the Anabaptists on the Continent, their doctrine passed to England, and became the origin of Quakerism. Winstanley, the leader of the Diggers, explained that they had no need of government, since they held all their goods in common.[1] Although such doctrines were as unacceptable to Cromwell as they had been to Charles I, his victorious Army of Saints was in theory democratic. And it had added to democracy as understood by the ancients a new principle, that of personal liberty. While equality followed from the fact that Christ died for all, liberty followed from the right of private judgment. Since liberty, if pushed to its logical conclusion, involved anarchy, Protestant statesmen had to find some way of making it compatible with the existence of government. The best way seemed a combination of democracy with a doctrine of the Rights of Man, laying down limits beyond which the interference of government with a man's private concerns should not go. Thus Protestant democracy was at once a theory of government, and a theory of the limits of governmental power.

Cromwell's army carried its doctrines, by means of emigration, to New England, where, if they did not actually control local government, at least they acted as a leaven which gradually worked towards a democratic régime. In England, the opponents of the restored Stuarts continued to teach natural liberty. These men, notably Algernon Sydney, seem to have had a considerable influence on Jefferson.[2] So, of course, had Locke, whose influence represents the common-sense residuum of the era of revolution when England settled down after

---

[1] *The Digger Movement in the Days of the Commonwealth*, by Lewis H. Berens, 1906.

[2] See F. W. Hirst, *Life and Letters of Thomas Jefferson*, pp. 508–9.

1688. It does not appear that Rousseau had any appreciable influence upon the leaders of the American Revolution.

The doctrine of Jeffersonian democracy was thus two-fold. On the one hand, government should be democratic; on the other hand, there should be as little government as possible. Where joint action is necessary, the will of the majority should prevail; but each individual has certain inalienable natural rights, with which no government ought to interfere.

Jefferson deserves to be regarded as the founder of American democracy for three reasons: first, he wrote the Declaration of Independence; second, he led and largely created the Republican party,[3] by which the Federalists, who were anti-democratic, were overthrown; third, he was the first President who believed in democracy and sought to establish it.

Jefferson was a democrat for the people, not of the people. His father rose by his own exertions, but his mother, a Randolph, belonged to one of the leading families of Virginia. He himself, from early youth, associated with the sons of rich planters, and enjoyed the comfortable independence of a landowner. He belonged, as a matter of course, to the governing class in Virginia, becoming a Justice of the Peace at the age of 21 and a member of the House of Burgesses at the age of 26, in 1769. When he was about to be married, he ordered from England a "forte-piano," a number of pairs of stockings, and various articles of finery. Although he was a fine gentleman, his contempt for social distinctions was genuine and deep-seated, and enabled him, throughout the French Revolution, to avoid the false sentimentalism inculcated by Burke. In 1794, he hopes the French will "bring, at length, kings, nobles, and priests, to the scaffolds which they have been so long deluging with human blood." During the War of Independence, in 1777, he induced the General Assembly of Virginia to abolish entail and primogeniture, which had, until then, kept in existence a land-owning aristocracy as prominent as that of England. His biographer Tucker, writing in 1837, remarks, as showing the effect of Jefferson's measures, that "there were probably twice or thrice as many four-horse carriages [in Virginia] before the revolution as there are at present; but the number of two-horse carriages may now be ten, or even twenty times as great as at the former

[3] Not the ancestor of the present Republican party.

period." If this shows the progress of democracy, it is democracy of a not very Jacobinical variety.

Before the War of Independence, Jefferson was deeply engaged in the disputes with England. During the War, he was first a member of Congress, then of the Assembly of Virginia, where he caused a complete revision of the laws, passing at one bound from mediaevalism to the modern conceptions of Beccaria, abolishing the death penalty except for murder and high treason, disestablishing the Church, and introducing complete religious freedom. (Until then, all religions except the Episcopalian had been subject to persecution in Virginia.) He endeavored unsuccessfully to bring about the gradual extinction of slavery, by bringing in a bill decreeing that all slaves born after its passage should be free. In 1779 he was elected Governor of Virginia. From 1784 to 1789 he was Minister to France. On his return he became Secretary of State, and held the office until the last day of 1794. In 1797 he became Vice-President, and was President from 1801 to 1809, when he had almost reached the age of sixty-six.

From this bare outline of his official career, it might have been supposed that he would not have time for many interests outside politics. In fact, however, his love for his home at Monticello, his interest in architecture, his omnivorous scientific curiosity, were all at least as strong as his political ambition, and caused him to be genuinely glad of his periods of leisure and retirement. His *Notes on Virginia,* written in 1782, when he had just narrowly escaped capture by the English in his own house and impeachment by his compatriots in his own legislature, illustrate the universality of his interests. This book was written in answer to queries by a Frenchman, M. de Marbois, who must have been astonished by the cataract of information that was poured out upon him. He had asked, for instance, about rivers; Jefferson gives him all the main facts about thirty-five of them, breaking out into occasional enthusiasm, such as: "The *Ohio* is the most beautiful river on earth. Its current gentle, waters clear, and bosom smooth and unbroken by rocks and rapids, a single instance only excepted." Mountains, cascades, and caverns, wild plants and animals, are enumerated with the minuteness of a careful observer who had traversed the State on horseback from North to South and from East to West.

He does not write only as a disinterested man of science; he writes also as a patriot. Buffon, the eminent naturalist, had dared to say that the animals of the New World are smaller than those of the Old, and that in America "*la nature vivante est beaucoup moins agissante, beaucoup moins forte.*" This was not to be endured. Three pages of small print give comparative weights of similar animals in Europe and America, beginning with the buffalo, which is many times heavier than any of the animals of M. Buffon's effete continent. But this is not all: if M. Buffon can sustain the weight of the buffalo, he must succumb beneath that of the mammoth, whose bones are found in Ohio. Nay more, some Indians who visited Jefferson on business when he was Governor assured him that the mammoth still lived in the Northwest. And apart from their testimony, "such is the economy of nature, that no instance can be produced, of her having permitted any one race of her animals to become extinct." The continued existence of mammoths on American soil remained an article of faith with Jefferson throughout his life, and even became an issue in political campaigns. There was nothing absurd in his opinion; it happened to be false, but might quite well have been true. And he was certainly less unscientific than the celebrated M. Buffon.

Jefferson as an architect was both original and successful. He was a pioneer in the adaptation of the classical style to American conditions. Monticello and the University of Virginia are exquisite, and both of his designing.

Everything that was admirable in eighteenth-century culture was to be found in Jefferson, without the somewhat limited and static quality that made that age unsatisfactory. American civilization, in the North, passed somewhat abruptly from the tone of the seventeenth century to that of the nineteenth, thereby missing a mellowing ingredient. Unfortunately Jefferson's influence, great as it was politically, was negligible in matters of culture; and such as it was, it existed only in the South, where it was destroyed by the Civil War. America has been the poorer for this lack of the eighteenth-century tradition.

Jefferson's political philosophy is expressed, tersely and forcibly, in the Declaration of Independence. The words are familiar, at least to Americans—so familiar that they have almost ceased to convey any meaning. Nevertheless I must ask the reader to tolerate some analysis of the crucial passage:

"We hold these truths to be self-evident: that all men are created equal; that they are endowed by their Creator with certain inalienable rights; that among these are life, liberty, and the pursuit of happiness; that to secure these rights, governments are instituted among men, deriving their just powers from the consent of the governed; that whenever any form of government becomes destructive of these ends, it is the right of the people to alter or abolish it."

When he says that these truths are "self-evident," he means exactly what he says: he means that they are known by the light of nature, which was much brighter in the eighteenth century than it is now. He relied equally upon the light of nature in regard to private ethics. At the end of his life, in a letter to Judge Johnson of South Carolina, explaining his early political actions, he says his party believed "that man was a rational animal, endowed by nature with rights, and with an innate sense of justice." Writing to Adams in 1815, he says: "The moral sense is as much a part of our constitution as that of feeling, seeing, or hearing, as a wise creator must have seen to be necessary in an animal destined to live in society." He adds that "every mind feels pleasure in doing good to another," and that "the essence of virtue is in doing good to others."

It is his belief in the moral sense and the innate goodness of man that gives the basis for his liberalism. If every man knows, by means of his conscience, what it is right to do, and if what it is right to do is what does good to others, then it is only necessary for the general happiness that each individual should follow the dictates of his conscience. Furthermore, in the absence of corrupting institutions and the degrading influences of tyranny, Jefferson believes that most men, on the whole, will follow their consciences. For the few exceptions, laws may be necessary; but in the main, liberty is all that is needful for the promotion of human happiness.

To refute the optimism of this philosophy is scarcely necessary for a generation which has lived through the Great War, the Treaty of Versailles, and the persecution of kulaks and Jews, all in the name of the loftiest morality. It is more fruitful to consider Jefferson's doctrines pragmatically, in regard to the effect that they were intended and likely to produce. Granting that interferences with liberty are *sometimes* unavoidable, it does not follow that they are *always* laudable. It has happened frequently, and it happened in Europe in Jefferson's time, that governments forbade many acts that were beneficial and enjoined many that were harmful. Trade was impeded, war was promoted; free thought was hampered, bigotry was encouraged. The punishment of acts which on any view were undesirable, such as theft, was so excessive as to amount to a greater evil than that which it sought to correct. The first necessity in such a world was to get rid of the misdirected activities of governments, and for this purpose a somewhat extreme philosophy of freedom was a useful instrument. *Laissez faire* may be indefensible as a theory, but as a political force it was undoubtedly beneficial in Jefferson's day.

In America, freedom was facilitated by the fact that there was room for expansion. Those who disliked the restraints of crowded cities could move westward; those who had criminal impulses could fight the Indians or the Mexicans. Jefferson's conception of democracy was agricultural; he feared the growth of great cities, and partly on that ground was opposed to tariffs on manufactures.[4] The bulk of his political party were small freeholders, who disliked urban capitalism. From his day to our own, progressive politics in America has been mainly agricultural, largely because there is nothing in his type of liberalism that is of any use to the industrial wage-earner. In a developed country, even the smallest freeholder is socially and economically superior to the bulk of the population: he may, and probably does, dislike capital in the guise of the banks, but he is on the side of capital as against the wage-earner. This made it difficult for America to develop any modern type of progressive political party, and made nominal progressives half-hearted: one hardly knows whether a man such as W. J. Bryan is to be classed as a Radical, or to be regarded as the last forlorn defender of antiquated forms of thought and action. But in Jefferson's day the small freeholders still had the future before them.

Another difficulty in the Jeffersonian philosophy, which was in time to become acute, concerned the right of self-determination. The Declaration of Independence states that when any government becomes destructive of "life, liberty, and the pursuit of happiness," it is the right of the people to alter or abolish it. The circumstances implied that the people concerned were to be themselves the judges on the matter, and there is no way of defining what group of persons

[4] Cf. Charles A. Beard, *Economic Origins of Jeffersonian Democracy*, *passim*.

constitutes a "people." The South could, not without plausibility, appeal to the principles of the Declaration of Independence to justify secession. It is, of course, obvious that there are cases where self-determination must yield before the superior interests of mankind. It would be absurd to leave the Suez Canal and the Panama Canal to the unfettered control of the populations through whose territory they pass. Self-determination must be subjected to the paramount test of general utility, and cannot be stated absolutely as a "natural right." As the world, through technical progress, has become more unified, it has become increasingly an obstacle to progress to allow absolute independence to separate nations: nations, like individuals, will have to learn to submit to government. In this matter, as in various others, the philosophy of liberalism is too anarchic for the needs of the modern world.

The Constitution of the United States, unlike the Declaration of Independence, was not due to Jefferson, being drawn up and adopted while he was in France. It was, of course, necessary that a constitution should be agreed upon, but the most active forces in promoting it were those to which Jefferson afterwards became politically opposed. Charles A. Beard, in an admirable book,[5] has analyzed the economic motives which animated those who framed the Constitution and caused its adoption. The impulse came mainly from the owners of personal property, especially the Federal and States Debts. There was a conscious desire to defeat democracy, for example in the powers conferred on the Supreme Court and in the clause ensuring the sanctity of contracts. Some of Beard's conclusions are worth quoting:

"The movement for the Constitution of the United States was originated and carried through principally by four groups of personalty interests which had been adversely affected under the Articles of Confederation: money, public securities, manufactures, and trade and shipping."

"The members of the Philadelphia Convention which drafted the Constitution were, with a few exceptions, immediately, directly, and personally interested in, and derived economic advantages from, the establishment of the new system."

"The Constitution was essentially an economic document based

[5] *An Economic Interpretation of the Constitution of the United States*, 1925.

upon the concept that the fundamental private rights of property are anterior to government and morally beyond the reach of popular majorities."

It will be seen that, while the groups that promoted the Constitution were not those in which Jefferson was specially interested, there was nothing in its philosophy to which he could legitimately object. He also believed in personal rights anterior to government, and was certainly not hostile to property as such. Nor did he object to the Constitution, except for the omission of a declaration of rights, as to which his wishes subsequently prevailed. None the less, the adoption of the Constitution was the first step in building up the political power of the plutocracy, by which Jeffersonian democracy has been rendered obsolete.

In the first Congress elected under the new Constitution, the business of using democratic machinery to make the rich richer was brilliantly inaugurated. During the War of Independence, the Government of the United States and the Governments of the several States had borrowed money, and had often given promises to pay to soldiers in place of cash. These debts had sunk to a small part of their nominal value, as there was great doubt whether they would ever be redeemed. Congress decided to redeem them at par. No pains were taken to prevent interested persons from obtaining knowledge in advance of this intention, with the consequence that rich speculators bought up the debts, very cheaply, from retired veterans in country places, who had not yet heard what was going on in Congress. There was an orgy of corruption, in which shrewd business men, most of whom had taken no part in the war, profited at the expense of old soldiers and other simple folk. There was much indignation, but it was powerless to influence the course of events.

The prime mover in these transactions was the Secretary of the Treasury, Alexander Hamilton, one of the ablest and most important men in history. There is no evidence that he was personally corrupt, indeed he left office a poor man. But he deliberately promoted corruption, which he considered desirable as giving due influence to the rich. What others defended only from self-interest, he defended disinterestedly; for instance, he advocated the growth of manufactures, partly because he thought child labor a good thing. "Women and children," he says, "are rendered more useful, and the latter more early useful, by manufacturing establishments, than they would otherwise be. Of the number of persons employed in the cotton manufactories of Great Britain, it is computed that four-sevenths, nearly, are women and children; of whom the greatest proportion are children, many of them of a tender age." He disliked democracy, and admired England. Throughout his career, he aimed at making America resemble England. He hoped that plutocracy would develop into aristocracy, and he rightly regarded corruption as the best method for causing plutocracy to prevail over democracy.

Hamilton, unlike Jefferson, was neither American nor aristocratic: he was the illegitimate son of a Scotch trader and a French West Indian. In the island of St. Kitt's, where his early youth was spent, he read Plutarch and dreamed of fame. As a boy in his early teens, he wrote a description of a hurricane which was widely praised. "The description of the hurricane made his fortune. Dreaming of rising by the sword, it was his pen that rallied friends who raised money to send him to America for an education. Through all his days he was to aspire to glory through the sword, little knowing that he was winning immortality with his pen." [6] He was nineteen years old at the beginning of the War of Independence, and eagerly sought the opportunity of military distinction, but his career as a soldier, though creditable, was not brilliant; it was as a politician, a financier, and a journalist that he showed his genius.

In the constitutional Convention, he argued that the President and Senators should be chosen for life, and that the President should appoint the State Governors, who should have the power of veto over State legislation. He would have preferred an undisguised monarchy, and continued for a long time to hope for it. But although the Constitution was not such as he desired, he saw its possibilities, and set to work to make the most of them. He became the leader of the Federalists, and accomplished a great deal in the way of a wide interpretation of the powers of the Federal Government. He used the tariff to encourage manufactures. He consolidated financial, commercial, and industrial capital, and so built up a party which controlled America, except to some extent in foreign policy, from 1789 till Jefferson's accession to the Presidency in 1801.

From 1790 and 1794, both Hamilton and Jefferson were members

[6] Claude G. Bowers, *Jefferson and Hamilton*, 1929, p. 24.

of Washington's Cabinet. At first, on his return from France, Jefferson failed to apprehend the drift of Hamilton's policy, and helped him to secure the assumption of the States Debts at par by the Federal Government—an action which he subsequently regretted. Before long, a bitter hostility developed between Jefferson and Hamilton, and they became the respective leaders of two violently hostile parties. No two men could have been more antithetical. Jefferson stood for democracy and agriculture, Hamilton for aristocracy and urban wealth. Jefferson, who had always been rich and prominent, believed men to be naturally virtuous; Hamilton, who had had to struggle against poverty and the irregularity of his birth, believed men to be fundamentally corrupt and only to be coerced into useful behavior by governmental pressure. Jefferson, secure on his estates and among his cultivated friends, believed in the common man; Hamilton, who knew the common man, sought out the society of the socially prominent. Jefferson, whose multifarious interests made him happy and unambitious, was of a forgiving disposition and high-minded in all his political campaigns; Hamilton, whose vanity needed the reassurance of success, was venomous as an enemy and unscrupulous in controversy. Both in a measure succeeded, and both in a measure failed: Jefferson made America the home of democracy, Hamilton made it the home of the millionaire.

In politics, the victory went to Jefferson; in economics, to Hamilton. Hamilton's party went to pieces, largely because he lost his head, but it could not have controlled the government much longer than it did, however ably it had been led. The expansion of America westward increased the number of voters who believed in Jeffersonian democracy; so did the foreign immigration, particularly of the Irish, since Hamilton and his party were pro-English. Later developments, by increasing the area devoted to agriculture, only increased the hold of democracy on American politics. Politically, Hamilton's attempt was a forlorn hope.

From an economic point of view, the history of his policies has been very different. For various reasons, at first more or less accidental, American manufactures enjoyed a gradually increasing measure of protection; as the tariff was frequently an issue in elections, employers and employed in industry had the same economic interests. Consequently, in spite of some sporadic movements in the '30's, there was little proletarian politics, and industrial regions tended to be solidly conservative. Corruption, deliberately introduced into the body politic by Hamilton, found increasing opportunities in the development of the West, first in connection with the allotment of new lands, and then in the financing of railways. The West, while it struggled against the power of Eastern capital, was invariably defeated, partly by corruption, partly by its inability to formulate a programme. The Western farmer's own convictions, like the Constitution of his country, forbade disrespect for the rights of property, and these very rights secured his subjection to the banks. The rich in America grew richer than any men had ever been before, and acquired a degree of power far exceeding that of the monarchs of former times.

Agricultural democracy of the Jeffersonian type can succeed in a country like Denmark, which offers little opportunity for large-scale capitalistic developments. But in a vast region such as the United States, where the agriculturist is in essential dependence upon the railway, an agrarian liberalism cannot hope to succeed. To master the great forces of modern capitalism is not possible by means of an amiable go-as-you-please individualism. By fastening this now inadequate philosophy upon American progressives, Jefferson unintentionally made the victory of Hamiltonian economics more complete than it need have been.

The philosophies of which these two men were the protagonists dominated American life until the year 1933.

CHAPTER XXII

THE SETTLEMENT OF THE WEST

THE optimism of the nineteenth century was caused by a very rapid progress in material well-being, which, in turn, was due to two correlated factors: the continual acquisition of new markets by industrialism, and the continual conquest of virgin soil by agriculture. Our planet being of finite size, this process could not continue for ever, but the Western portions of the United States, the British Dominions, and the Southern countries of South America, afforded such a vast field for expansion that there seemed no need to trouble about the distant time when all the empty spaces would have been occupied.

In the United States, the conquest of the West was made by men who believed in Jeffersonian democracy, and who caused its governmental forms to be established wherever the wilderness had come to contain sufficient inhabitants. The agricultural population which grew up in America was, in many ways, totally unlike any previously known in human history. In Europe, the division into feudal lords and serfs had existed everywhere, and still survived in Russia, Poland, Austria-Hungary, and parts of Germany. The agricultural worker, even where he was no longer a serf, was in practice tied to a particular plot of land, or at least to a certain neighborhood. He had little initiative, either technically or politically; even in France, after he had gained possession of his land through the Revolution, he sank into conservatism under the influence of the Church. In America, the agricultural settlers in the West were migrants, men of adventurous disposition, on the lookout for technical improvements in methods of production, deriving from self-government and an arduous life a self-respect and a self-confidence that made them incapable of regarding others as their social superiors. Throughout the West, democracy, triumphant and aggressive, was ready to challenge the world, and its amazing material success made it every day more convinced of its own rightness.

The first stage in the conquest of the land beyond the Alleghanies was a matter of war and diplomacy. In 1756, the French owned Canada and the whole Mississippi Valley, while the Spaniards owned Florida, Texas, and the Far West. In 1763, the English acquired Canada and the Eastern half of the Mississippi Valley, the latter being ceded to the United States in 1783. In 1803, Jefferson bought the Western half of the Mississippi Valley from Napoleon. Florida was bought from Spain in 1821; Texas, after a brief period of independence, was, by its own wish, annexed to the United States in 1845; the territory thence westward to the Pacific was conquered from Mexico in 1848.

Extensive occupation was sometimes much later than legal possession; but the trans-continental expansion was a continuous movement from the founding of the Union till the end of the nineteenth century. Even in the Colonial period the English had been unable to repress the natural wish of the Americans to explore and utilize the virgin land behind them; and, when they had shaken off the control of George III, the people of the seaboard States, exulting in possession, and partly also driven by hardship, moved in great numbers across the mountains towards the Mississippi Valley. Day by day, month by month, year by year, long trains of migrants, the richer families in wagons, followed by their flocks and herds, the poorer families on foot, carrying their property in wheelbarrows or bundles, passed along the Western highways on their way to found new States. Kentucky was admitted to the Union in 1792, Tennessee in 1796, Ohio in 1803. In the Northwest the advance was slow at first, as the English, remaining hostile, retained, under various pretexts, until the conclusion of Jay's Treaty in 1794, the forts which they had agreed to surrender in 1783, and the Indians, siding with them, made the country unsafe for settlers until after the War of 1812. From 1815 onwards, Indiana and Illinois, though still containing many Indians, rapidly acquired settlers, becoming States in 1816 and 1818 respectively. Parts of the further Northwest, where irrigation by combined effort was necessary, remained unsettled until a much later date. North and South Dakota, for example, were not admitted to the Union until 1889. But by 1820 there were in all more than two and a quarter million settlers west of the Alleghanies. In 1840 there were nearly seven millions.

The movement westward decreased in good times and increased in bad times, when the poorer people fled from unemployment, low wages, and high taxation. But many non-economic motives contributed, and migration never wholly stopped. Love of adventure, love of freedom, an almost romantic wish to be in the vanguard of the advancing army of civilization, made some men leave comfort to endure the risks and hardships of a pioneer's life. As de Tocqueville says:

I readily admit that the Americans have no poets; I cannot allow that they have no poetic ideas. In Europe people talk a great deal of the wilds of America, but the Americans themselves never think about them: they are insensible to the wonders of inanimate nature, and they may be said not to perceive the mighty forests which surround them till they fall beneath the hatchet. Their eyes are fixed upon another sight: the American people views its own march across these wilds—drying swamps, turning the course of rivers, peopling solitudes, and subduing nature. This magnificent image of themselves does not meet the gaze of the Americans at intervals only; it may be said to haunt every one of them in his least as well as in his most important actions, and to be always flitting before his mind. Nothing conceivable is so petty, so insipid, so crowded with paltry interests, in one word so anti-poetic, as the life of a man in the United States. But amongst the thoughts which it suggests there is always one which is full of poetry, and that is the hidden nerve which gives vigour to the frame.[1]

Western America came to consider itself, and to be considered by the world, as typical of democracy. There were, however, three important circumstances peculiar to the America of that day, which affected the character of the people and of social life, making both very different from what they would be in Europe under no matter what government. These three circumstances were: the free land, the Indians, and negro slavery. The last of these I shall reserve for a later chapter. On each of the other two there is something to be said at this point, if we are to understand the peculiarities of American democracy. I shall begin with the Indians.

The conflict with the Indians gave, from the first, a certain fierceness and social cohesion to life in America, which was not to be ex-

[1] Alexis de Tocqueville, *Democracy in America*, Vol. II, p. 67. (Longmans, Green & Co., 1875.)

pected in a less perilous environment. The Indians had many fine qualities, but they were exceedingly cruel; men whose wives and children were in constant danger of being scalped or tomahawked could hardly be expected to view them with fraternal affection. Nor could the Indians fail to resent the unscrupulous and savage aggression of the white men. James Truslow Adams, describing the Pequot War of 1637, says: [2]

It was the story of white aggression and racial hatred which was unhappily to be repeated on almost all of our frontiers for two and a half centuries. The chief incident of this first New England war was the surprise by the Puritans, under the lead of Captain John Mason, of the main village of the savages. In the dark, with a strong wind blowing, the two entrances to the stockade were guarded to prevent any escape, and then a torch was applied. Five hundred Indian men, women, and children were burned to death, the Puritan leader merely remarking that by the Providence of God there were 150 more than usual at home that awful night.

After this, we are not surprised to learn how these same colonists, on religious grounds, treated the Quakers: they hanged three men and one woman, others they imprisoned, beat, and tortured, while the children were sold as slaves in the West Indies.[3] Some element of persecuting zeal survived on the frontier even in the nineteenth century. It did not take a religious form except against the Mormons, but politically it still existed, particularly in connection with the slavery question.

The usual course of events in the Northwest was as follows. First came explorers, then, not long after them, traders in furs. After a lapse of time varying from two centuries to a decade, the reports of traders induced the Government—French, English, or American— to establish a military post in the wilderness. (The governing motive was usually the desire to secure the fur trade for one's own country.) In the course of war between white nations, the Indians would be incited to massacre these remote garrisons. This led to reprisals: the Indians would be defeated in a pitched battle, and induced to sign a treaty by which they "sold" their lands and removed to some new reservation further West. In the course of a war, settlers in remote places were massacred by Indians, and Indians were

[2] *The March of Democracy*, I, p. 25.   [3] *Ibid.*, p. 26.

massacred by settlers. Every white man in a frontier region was expected to be willing to serve against the Indians when called upon. Although the Indians were always defeated in the end, they won as many battles as they lost, and were almost always victorious if numbers were equal on the two sides.[4]

In early days the fear of Indians hung over the frontier at all times. Nicolay and Hay, describing the life of Abraham Lincoln's grandfather (also called Abraham), say:

Until the treaty of Greenville, in 1795, closed the long and sanguinary history of the old Indian wars, there was no day in which the pioneer could leave his cabin with the certainty of not finding it in ashes when he returned, and his little flock murdered on his threshold, or carried into a captivity worse than death. Whenever nightfall came with the man of the house away from home, the anxiety and care of the women and children were none the less bitter because so common.

The life of the pioneer Abraham Lincoln soon came to a disastrous close. He had settled in Jefferson County, on the land he had bought from the Government, and cleared a small farm in the forest. One morning in the year 1784, he started with his three sons, Mordecai, Josiah, and Thomas, to the edge of the clearing, and began the day's work. A shot from the brush killed the father; Mordecai, the eldest son, ran instinctively to the house, Josiah to the neighbouring fort, for assistance, and Thomas, the youngest, a child of six, was left with the corpse of his father. Mordecai, reaching the cabin, seized the rifle, and saw through the loophole an Indian in his war-paint stooping to raise the child from the ground. He took deliberate aim at a white ornament on the breast of the savage and brought him down. The little boy, thus released, ran to the cabin, and Mordecai, from the loft, renewed his fire upon the savages, who began to show themselves from the thicket, until Josiah returned with assistance from the stockade, and the assailants fled. This tragedy made an indelible impression on the mind of Mordecai. Either a spirit of revenge for his murdered father, or a sportsmanlike pleasure in his successful shot, made him a determined Indian-stalker, and he rarely stopped to inquire whether the red man who came within range of his rifle was friendly or hostile.

Lincoln himself served against the Indians in the Black Hawk War of 1832. Harrison owed his elevation to the Presidency to his defeat of the Indians at Tippecanoe, and President Jackson, while his chief claim to fame was the vanquishing of Wellington's brother-in-law,

4 Cf. M. M. Quaife, *Chicago and the Old Northwest.*

was also popular on account of his success against the Seminole Indians.

One of the most dramatic episodes in the warfare with the Indians was the massacre of most of the garrison of Fort Dearborn, on the site of Chicago, in 1812, as an incident of the war against England. Chicago, at that date, consisted almost entirely of a military post and a trader named Kinzie. Captain Heald, who was in command, was ordered to evacuate the fort, and did so. Two miles from the fort, his small force was attacked, and according to his own account 38 men, 2 women, and 12 children were killed. The few who survived had curious adventures.[5] There were, for example, Mrs. Simmons and her daughter, aged six months. Mrs. Simmons lost in the massacre her husband, and her two-year-old son. She endured six months of captivity among the Indians, most of the time on the march carrying her infant. She had to run the gauntlet between a double line of Indian women who beat her with sticks while she managed to shield the child from their blows. At last she was taken to Detroit, then in the hands of the English; this ended the worst of her troubles. Eight months after the massacre, she reached a blockhouse in which her parents had taken refuge. Even there, however, shortly after her arrival her sister and brother-in-law were killed by Indians. After this, her life and her daughter's were uneventful. The daughter married, and moved perpetually westward, living successively in Ohio, Iowa, and California, where she died in 1900.[6]

The trader Kinzie was treated by the Indians as a neutral, and was unharmed during the massacre. Nevertheless he and his sons and his daughters and his sons' divorced wives were compensated for their losses at this time in every subsequent treaty with the Indians.

At the time of the War of 1812 the Indians were stirred to unwonted unity of action by a chief named Tecumseh and his brother,

[5] See M. M. Quaife, *Chicago and the Old Northwest.*

[6] The minority who survived the massacre appear to have had remarkable vitality. One of them, named Kennison, asserted that he was born in 1736; he certainly fought in the War of Independence. After the War of 1812 he devoted himself to peaceful pursuits, which he found more dangerous than war: a falling tree broke his skull, collar bone, and two ribs, and a gun at a military review broke both his legs. Nevertheless he married four times and had 22 children. At the age of 109 he settled in Chicago, where he lived on his soldier's pension till 1852. His last years were spent in the Museum, and he was given a public funeral.

who was a Prophet, and received revelations from the Great Spirit. On one occasion the Great Spirit said to the Prophet:

I am the father of the English, of the French, of the Spaniards, and of the Indians. I created the first man, who was the common father of all these people, as well as yourselves; and it is through him, whom I have awaked from his long sleep, that I now address you. But the Americans I did not make. They are not my children, but the children of the evil spirit. They grew from the scum of the great water where it was troubled by the evil spirit, and the froth was driven into the woods by a strong east wind. They are numerous, but I hate them.[7]

If the Great Spirit specially loved the Indians, he had reason to hate the Americans. Yet, from the standpoint of civilized mankind, it is difficult to see what could have been done that would have been consistent with justice and humanity. We cannot regret that the territory of the United States is inhabited by civilized men; and if civilized men were to inhabit it, it was inevitable that the Indians should suffer. As de Tocqueville says:

From whichever side we consider the destinies of the aborigines of North America, their calamities appear to be irremediable: if they continue barbarous, they are forced to retire; if they attempt to civilise their manners, the contact of a more civilised community subjects them to oppression and destitution. They perish if they continue to wander from waste to waste, and if they attempt to settle they still must perish; the assistance of Europeans is necessary to instruct them, but the approach of Europeans corrupts and repels them into savage life; they refuse to change their habits as long as their solitudes are their own, and it is too late to change them when they are constrained to submit.

The Spaniards pursued the Indians with blood-hounds like wild beasts; they sacked the New World with no more temper or compassion than a city taken by storm: but destruction must cease, and frenzy be stayed; the remnant of the Indian population which had escaped the massacre mixed with its conquerors, and adopted in the end their religion and their manners. The conduct of the Americans of the United States towards the aborigines is characterised, on the other hand, by a singular attachment to the formalities of law. Provided that the Indians retain their barbarous condition, the Americans take no part in their affairs; they treat them as independent nations, and do not possess themselves of their hunting grounds

7 Quaife, *op. cit.*, p. 186.

without a treaty of purchase: and if an Indian nation happens to be so en-
croached upon as to be unable to subsist upon its territory, they afford it
brotherly assistance in transporting it to a grave sufficiently remote from
the land of its fathers.

The Spaniards were unable to exterminate the Indian race by those
unparalleled atrocities which brand them with indelible shame, nor did
they even succeed in wholly depriving it of its rights; but the Americans
of the United States have accomplished this twofold purpose with singular
felicity; tranquilly, legally, philanthropically, without shedding blood, and
without violating a single great principle of morality in the eyes of the
world. It is impossible to destroy men with more respect for the laws of
humanity.[8]

Independently of the Indians, the life of the pioneer was a very
hard one, in which, during the early stages, he was sustained only by
freedom and hope—the latter, as often as not, proving delusive. The
hardships were greater in the North than in the South, both on account of the severe winters, and because of the absence of slavery.
Nevertheless, for those who were too poor to own slaves, the North
was preferable, since in the South they were regarded as socially inferior to slave-owners. Lincoln's father, after Kentucky had ceased
to be on the frontier, removed in 1816 to Indiana, for which purpose he built a raft and loaded it with all his possessions, consisting
of his kit of tools and four hundred gallons of whisky. The raft cap-
sized, but he recovered most of his goods. From the house of the last
settler, he hewed a way through the forest to a site which pleased
him, deposited there the whisky and tools, and was joined by his wife
and two children with a little bedding and some pots and pans. For
a year they lived in a three-sided shelter, open to the wind and rain
and snow on the fourth side. During this time he cleared some ground
for cultivation and built a proper log cabin, without, however, thinking it necessary to provide it with doors or windows or floor. "His
cabin," say Nicolay and Hay, "was like that of other pioneers. A few
three-legged stools; a bedstead made of poles stuck between the logs
in the angle of the cabin, the outside corner supported by a crotched
stick driven into the ground; the table, a huge hewed log standing on
four legs; a pot, kettle and skillet, and a few tin and pewter dishes
were all the furniture. The boy Abraham climbed at night to his bed

[8] When de Tocqueville says "without shedding blood" he is not correct.

of leaves in the loft, by a ladder of wooden pins driven into the logs." Here Abraham's mother died of fever, along with many other settlers of the region.

Malaria and other fevers were very prevalent throughout the West. Nicolay and Hay regard Lincoln's melancholy as partly due to this cause. They say:

"This taint of constitutional sadness was not peculiar to Lincoln; it may be said to have been endemic among the early settlers of the West. It had its origin partly in the circumstances of their lives, the severe and dismal loneliness in which their struggle for existence for the most part went on. . . . Besides this generic tendency to melancholy, very many of the pioneers were subject in early life to malarial influences, the effect of which remained with them all their days. . . . Many died, and of those who survived, a great number, after they had outgrown the more immediate manifestations of the disease, retained in nervous disorders of all kinds the distressing traces of the maladies which afflicted their childhood." [9]

In the South, pioneering life was comparatively easy. Andrew Jackson, whom there is no reason to credit with business acumen, passed quickly and easily from a state of destitution to being the owner of a large landed estate and a number of slaves. This he achieved by practising law [10]—his qualifications for which did not include learning—and investing the fees in land. He went to Tennessee in 1788, a penniless youth of twenty-one, and "eight years after his arrival he was one of the wealthy men of that region." [11] The chief difficulties in the South were Indians, Spaniards, and fever. But there was not the same call upon a man's powers of independent physical endurance as in the North.

The conditions of life on the frontier necessarily produced, in the pioneers and their children, a temporary decay of culture. No schools, no churches, no men of education, the exhausting struggle with the wilderness, few books, and much whisky, made men forget what they knew and fail to pass their knowledge on to their children. Belief in witchcraft and omens revived; fences must be built when there

[9] *Abraham Lincoln: A History*, I, p. 189.
[10] "He doubtless knew little law," says his biographer. Bassett, *Life of Andrew Jackson*, p. 14. (The Macmillan Co., New York, 1916.)
[11] *Ibid.*, p. 17.

was a moon, but potatoes must be planted when there was none.[12] The pioneers, especially the women among them, were for the most part deeply religious, and were troubled by the absence of churches. Camp meetings, addressed by itinerant preachers, from time to time supplied the spiritual needs of sparsely populated districts. The gathering, assembled from fifty miles around, under the combined stimulus of emotional oratory and relief from solitude, would exhibit the most remarkable hysterical symptoms, rolling on the ground, uttering strange cries, and falling into trances. The whole phenomenon is characteristic of isolated agricultural populations; it existed in Germany in the sixteenth century, England in the seventeenth, and Rasputin's Siberia in the twentieth. But it astonished Mrs. Trollope, who gave a vivid and interesting description.[13]

What is surprising in the conquest of the West is not the fact that it involved a temporary loss of culture, but the fact that the loss was so quickly made good when the pioneering stage was passed. For this, in addition to the general character of the people, there were various causes, of which the most important seem to have been women, and law and politics.

The influence of women has been greater in the United States than in any other country, and in frontier communities their influence was on the side of civilization. This was due partly to the fact that they did not drink whisky, partly to a desire for social distinction, partly to maternal affection, and partly to the fact that they were less imbued than their husbands with the rough adventurer's desire to be rid of the trammels of an artificial society. On the frontier there were of course fewer women than men, and this helped them to command respect. In spite of the wildness of the camp meetings, religion was, in the main, a chastening force, and women were, on the average, more religious than men. For all these reasons, women kept alive the desire for an ordered existence even under conditions which, for the moment, made it impossible.

This civilizing influence may be illustrated by Lincoln's stepmother, whom his father married when Lincoln was ten years old. It will be remembered that the log cabin had been left without doors and windows; this was at once remedied. She brought beds and

[12] Nicolay and Hay, I, pp. 41–2.
[13] Mrs. Trollope, *Domestic Manners of the Americans*, Chap. XV.

clothes for the children; her husband joined the Baptist church, and Abraham was given such education as the neighborhood afforded, which was not much, as bears were commoner than schoolmasters. In the whole course of his life he had only a year of schooling, and as soon as he was old enough his father set him to work as a farm-hand. In the evenings he read the only books he could get hold of: the Bible, *Aesop's Fables*, *Robinson Crusoe*, *Pilgrim's Progress*, *The Life of Washington*, and the *Revised Statutes of Indiana*. For the rest, he made his way by his own efforts; but the first steps, when he was still too young to help himself, he owed to his stepmother.

It is interesting to observe that, in a letter to a newspaper serving as an election address, in the year 1836, he says: "I go for admitting all whites to the right of suffrage who pay taxes or bear arms (by no means excluding females)." A hundred years ago this was a remarkable opinion.

The movement in favor of women's rights first reached the stage of practical politics in Western America. In 1846 a Constitution was proposed for Wisconsin involving married women's right to their own property; this was rejected, but in Texas in the same year and California in 1849 the same right was enacted.[14] The first State to admit women to the vote was Wyoming in 1890. In the East, and in Europe, votes for women came only as a result of the Great War.

Law and politics were powerful influences in promoting contact between the Western settlers and the intellect of the East. The Constitution and the Ordinance of 1787 showed great prescience as regards future States and Territories. Owing to them, there was everywhere, as soon as sufficient population existed, self-government tempered by the Constitution as interpreted by the Supreme Court. Self-government provided political education, and Federal campaigns made men aware of the opinions of more settled regions on questions of national importance. Law-suits might, in certain circumstances, come before the Supreme Court; in any case, there were many that involved important rights, and required considerable legal skill for their adequate treatment. Most of the prominent men in frontier States were lawyers, and it was largely through the need for lawyers that men of education first established themselves on the fringe of civilization. The law played a great part in the life of the

[14] McMaster, *History of the People of the United States*, VII, pp. 184, 201, 611.

Western township, and was usually administered, in a rough and ready fashion, by the pioneers themselves. The court was often held in a log hut, from which the jury would retire to a neighboring glade to consider their verdict. The desire to participate in the management of local affairs was general, and was the chief incentive to acquiring knowledge.

The importance of schools and universities was early realized in America. In the year 1780, in the middle of the troubles of the War of Independence, the Legislature of Virginia endowed a university in Kentucky, "it being the interest of this commonwealth always to encourage and promote every design which may tend to the improvement of the mind and the diffusion of useful knowledge even among its remote citizens, whose situation in a barbarous neighbourhood and a savage intercourse might otherwise render them unfriendly to science." [15] This has a Jeffersonian ring; although it speaks of "useful knowledge," it is less utilitarian than the advocacy of education in a later age. But substantially the same policy has been pursued wherever possible, culminating in the system of State Universities in all States.

The problem of schooling was a difficult one, owing not only to sparseness of population, but also to foreign immigration. There were nearly twice as many white illiterates in the United States in 1850 as in 1840; in 1840, they formed one in 31 of the total population, in 1850 one in 24.[16] It is interesting to find that one of the most active agitators for universal education at this time was Owen's son, Robert Dale Owen.[17] Schools were better in the North than in the South, even in the less settled parts of the North. "Michigan was in many respects a typical north-western frontier State . . . yet she had, in 1850, more libraries, more newspapers and periodicals, more public schools, less white illiterates, than had Arkansas or Missouri." [18] There were schools in almost all villages, but the teachers were badly paid: men received $15 a month, women $1.25 a week. The schools were merely log cabins, but at any rate they sufficed to teach almost all the children to read and write.

There was, however, some permanent loss in the quality of cul-

---

[15] Nicolay and Hay, I, pp. 15–16.
[16] Channing, *History of the United States*, V, p. 271.
[17] *Ibid.*, p. 250.
[18] McMaster, VII, p. 199.

ture, as there always is when an interruption occurs. Revolution inflicted a blow upon French culture, from which it has never completely recovered, and in Russia the same effect is probable. The founders of the United States possessed a civilized attitude towards the things of the mind naturally and self-consciously; Franklin and Jefferson were respected in Paris in the most intelligent social milieu that has ever existed. The civilization that emerged in the West wherever the pioneering stage had been passed was more self-conscious, without sufficient roots in tradition, rather machine-made, and unduly utilitarian because it had to justify itself to a somewhat rude democracy. Education, such as can be demonstrated by diplomas or degrees, is eagerly desired, but professors are less respected than in Europe: they are subjected, in the State Universities, to the prejudices of the tax-payers, and in the others to the financial interests of a board of business men. The result is that theology in the former, and economics in the latter, cannot be treated with complete honesty. Similar evils, it is true, exist in other countries, but in America they ought not to exist because they are contrary to the Jeffersonian tradition, and they would not exist if the Jeffersonian belief in academic freedom had survived.

Another result of the pioneering period has been that the non-utilitarian parts of culture have come to be regarded as almost exclusively the concern of women. Since most women have not pursued painting or literature or philosophy professionally, but only taken an intelligent interest in all of them, there has come to be a certain superficiality in regard to all such subjects, which, from an early date, was ministered to by lectures. The East, almost as much as the West, left culture to women, because business absorbed Eastern men; but the business that absorbed them was very largely concerned with the opening up of the West. McMaster [19] quotes from the *Philadelphia Ledger* the following intellectual entertainments as having occurred in Philadelphia on three days in 1842:

A Sermon by a Mormon elder; a lecture on Geology by Lyell; a lecture on Courtship and Marriage, at the Wilber Fisk Literary Institute; on the Huguenots, at the William West Institute; on Socialism, in the Hall of the United Friends of Human Progress; on the Existence of Apparitions, in the Southern Lyceum; on Animal Magnetism before the

[19] *Op. cit.*, VII, p. 82.

Jefferson Library and Literary Association; on Napoleon, at the Richmond Institute; and at Carroll Institute, a discussion of the question, "Should Capital Punishment be Abolished?"

To this day, America has remained on the cultural side chiefly a nation of appreciators, mainly female, while on the utilitarian side it has achieved high excellence. America is good in medicine, in law, in architecture, in mechanical invention, but in such studies as mathematics and theoretical physics almost all the advances have been European, while in art there has been a world-wide deterioration. An English writer in 1821, describing American hopes for the future, says:

> Other nations boast of what they are or have been, but the true citizen of the United States exalts his head to the skies in the contemplation of what the grandeur of his country is going to be. Others claim respect and honor because of the things done by a long line of ancestors; an American glories in the achievements of a distant posterity. Others appeal to history; an American appeals to prophecy, and with Malthus in one hand and a map of the back country in the other he boldly defies us to a comparison with America as she is to be, and chuckles in delight over the splendors the geometrical ratio is to shed over her story. This appeal to the future is his never-failing resource. If an English traveller complains of their inns and hints his dislike to sleeping four in a bed he is first denounced as a calumniator and then told to wait a hundred years and see the superiority of American inns to British. If Shakespeare, Milton, Newton, are named, he is again told to "wait till we have cleared our land, till we have idle time to attend to other things; wait till 1900, and then see how much nobler our poets and profounder our astronomers and longer our telescopes than any that decrepit old hemisphere of yours will produce." [20]

The prophecy was right as to the inns and telescopes, which are now better in America than anywhere else, but not as to Shakespeare, Milton, and Newton. Shakespeare and Milton have no analogues in the modern world, and Newton's nearest analogue is a European.

The occupation of the free land in the West was not completed until about the year 1890—not counting Oklahoma, which for a long time remained Indian territory. But after the coming of the railways the hardships of frontier life were much diminished, and the pioneers were forced to face new problems. The Mississippi and its tributaries ran, broadly speaking, north and south, so that, so long as

[20] McMaster, V, 333.

transport was chiefly by water, the most important contacts of a western region were with regions to the south of it; but after the building of the railways the lines of transport ran east and west. This began even earlier, with the opening of the Erie Canal in 1825; but until the railway age most of the West continued to depend chiefly on the Mississippi.

The movement across the mountains and the plains had, in early days, a kind of blind instinctive quality such as must have belonged to the migrations of the ancient Germans. It was opposed by George III, and disliked, at first, by the Eastern States, which it drained of population. The early settlers did little in the way of trade; they produced what they required for their own needs—crops for their food, deerskins for their clothing, and logs for their habitations. They asked nothing of the world except to be let alone. A great change came when the frontier passed from the forest to the prairie; it became profitable to grow only grain, and to send it by rail to the East or to the hungry populations of Europe, in return for the necessaries of life and for a gradually increasing share of the luxuries. But at this stage economic problems arose for which the pioneers were not fitted by temperament, experience, or political philosophy. Through the railway they were brought into dependence upon Eastern capitalism. Their old freedom was gone, for though they could still grow wheat as they pleased, they could only export it by the favor of the railway. The great organized economic forces baffled them. Even before the railways, the banks presented them with the same problem. From Jackson's attack on the United States Bank to Bryan's free silver campaign, the West struggled, blindly and ineffectually, to master big business by the formulae of individualist democracy.

The men who conquered the West had courage, tenacity, hope, self-reliance, and a fundamental instinct towards civilized society. To understand their achievement, one should compare it with what happened in most parts of Latin America, where a thin stream of white blood was lost amid Indians and negroes, leaving most of the primeval jungle untamed, while the Government, such as it was, combined tyranny with anarchy. The Western settlers in the United States had certain collective purposes, of which it was not necessary to speak, because they were instinctive and common to all. They wished, first and foremost, to conquer the earth; that done, they desired a community of free equal citizens, submitting to the rule of the majority where rule was necessary, but as far as possible exempt from governmental interference. They succeeded in the conquest of the earth; they succeeded in preserving political freedom; but economic freedom was lost by a process which we can now see to have been inevitable. They did their work well, but their philosophy depended for its success upon the empty spaces, and cannot solve the problems of our more crowded world.

CHAPTER XXIII

JACKSONIAN DEMOCRACY

THE first conquest of political power by the West occurred when Andrew Jackson was elected to the Presidency in 1828. Under him a new type of democracy was inaugurated, more democratic than that of Jefferson. The Presidents up to that date had been four Virginians —Washington, Jefferson, Madison, and Monroe—and the two Adamses, father and son. All these were from the East, all were men of education and traditional culture; they were such men as might have governed the country under an aristocratic constitution. Madison and Monroe were close personal friends of Jefferson, and the "Virginia dynasty" had begun to seem an established power in the body politic. The dynasty, however, became extinct, and Jackson, himself a Southerner, was supported by the South as well as the West. In addition, the growing democratic sentiment of Pennsylvania and New York turned a majority in those States over to his side, as against J. Q. Adams, who was felt to represent tradition and New England conservatism. While no man could, at that time, have become President by the support of the West alone, Jackson introduced Western ideals and sentiments into the administration; but they were the ideals of the Southwest, where slavery existed, as opposed to those of the Northwest, which were subsequently embodied in Lincoln.

Jackson's father was an Ulster Presbyterian,[1] who emigrated to North Carolina with his wife and two sons in 1765. His efforts to make a living by farming were unsuccessful, and he died in 1767, his son Andrew being born shortly afterwards, but whether in North or South Carolina is not known. The widow, left destitute, became housekeeper to her married sister, who was comparatively prosperous, her husband being a farmer in a South Carolina community composed mainly of immigrants from Protestant Northern Ireland. Andrew's mother wished him to become a minister of religion, but his tastes

---

[1] The biographical facts in what follows are in the main derived from J. S. Bassett's *Life of Andrew Jackson*, 1916.

led him in a different direction. "Of all the wild youths of the neighbourhood he was the wildest," says his biographer; he was fond of
horse-racing, cock-fighting, and violent encounters with other boys.
As for education, he was "neither studious nor teachable"; he just
managed to master reading and writing and easy sums, but to the end
of his days could neither spell correctly nor write grammatically.

Meanwhile, the War of Independence was raging in his neighborhood. One of his brothers was killed in battle, the other died either
of smallpox or of his wounds; his mother died of a fever caught in
nursing invalided soldiers. All these deaths occurred in 1780 and
1781. In both these years the boy Andrew, though only thirteen,
fought against the British, and was captured in 1781. The British
Commanding Officer "ordered Andrew to black his boots. The boy
remonstrated, we may guess in what tone, that he was a prisoner-of-
war and not a servant. The reply was a sabre-blow aimed at the head
of the young prisoner: it was warded off by the arm of the recipient,
but hand and head carried the mark of it to the grave." Having
secured his freedom in an exchange of prisoners, he was left, at the
age of fourteen, completely dependent upon his own resources. He
went over the mountains to Charleston, where he made friends with
rich young men interested in horse-racing, and apparently made his
living by betting. His biographer does not say that he was a book-
maker, but that seems to be implied. It is also suggested that it was
by associating with the sporting élite of Charleston that he acquired
the stately manners by which, on suitable occasions, he subsequently
impressed Washington.

Charleston, however, was not to his taste, and ambition urged him
to adopt some serious profession. At the age of seventeen, he decided
in favor of the law, and became a law student in a town called
Salisbury, where, according to an acquaintance of the time, he was
"the most roaring, rollicking, game-cocking, card-playing, mischievous
fellow that ever lived in Salisbury." Three years later, in 1787, he
began practising law in North Carolina; but within twelve months he
decided to move further West, and established himself at Nashville,
Tennessee, which was his home during the remainder of his long
life.

The Cumberland Valley, containing the town of Nashville, was,
in 1788, still in an unsettled condition. The Indians, incited first by

the English and then by the Spaniards, attacked the Americans whenever opportunity offered. The Americans defeated them in two successive years, 1793 and 1794, and in 1795 a treaty with Spain opened the navigation of the Mississippi to the United States. These events caused Tennessee to prosper, and it became a State in 1796, after considerable opposition in Congress on the part of the Federalists.

Meanwhile Jackson's prosperity had increased with that of the region. When he arrived in Nashville, he found only one lawyer settled there before him; this one was permanently retained by the debtors of the neighborhood, with the result that creditors could not obtain justice. They turned to Jackson, who was successful on their behalf. His methods in his practice were somewhat different from those of eminent counsel in more sedate cities. "Offenders were apt to be turbulent and often they were supported by bands of associates who made the life of a prosecuting attorney both unpleasant and perilous. Jackson's physical courage was equal to his moral courage. . . . Bad grammar, bad pronunciation, and violent denunciation did not shock judge or jury nor divert their minds from the truth." His behavior in his leisure hours commanded equal admiration. "His horses were the fastest, his cocks were the most noted, he would quarrel with none but the men of distinction, and his great oaths became the despair of the young braggarts of the valley." In recognition of these various merits, his neighbors chose him as their first member of Congress in 1796. In the following year he became a Senator, and in the year after that he became a Justice of the Supreme Court of Tennessee. In this latter capacity he personally arrested a felon who had successfully defied the sheriff and his *posse*. It does not do to be too much of a specialist in a frontier town, and Jackson could do his own work, whatever it might be. His appearance was as commanding as his pistol: he was tall, erect, and pale, with eyes that were very blue and very intense.

The claims of his profession were not so great as to leave no leisure for romance. Cumberland Colony, which became Tennessee, had been founded in 1779 by two men, Robertson and Donelson, of whom the latter, when Jackson went to Nashville, "was already dead, a sacrifice to the red man's vengeance, and his widow was taking boarders." One of the boarders was Jackson. The widow had a daughter, and the daughter had a husband; the husband was a scamp, and the daughter had come to live with her mother. The husband became nominally reconciled with his wife, and settled in Nashville. But he grew jealous of Jackson, although Jackson assured him there was no cause. The husband departed, vowing vengeance; the lady was distressed, and Jackson fell in love with her. In 1791, hearing that her husband had obtained a divorce, Jackson married her; but in fact no divorce had been obtained, and when it was obtained, two years later, it was on the ground of her adultery with Jackson. When this became known, Jackson married her again. They were completely happy in each other until her death, which occurred just after his election to the Presidency. Throughout the electoral campaign, his opponents had spread the story that he was an immoral man who had lived with a married woman. He chivalrously kept this from her knowledge, but she discovered it by accident, and the discovery is said to have hastened her death.

In friendship he was less fortunate than in love. His character resembled King Lear's: he could not distinguish between true friends and flatterers, and fell into furious rages when he found that he had bestowed his affection upon traitors. He was at all times fond of quarrels, and by no means judicious in choosing the men upon whom to vent his irascibility. For example: having tired of the law and become a General, he was anxious for military advancement at a moment (1807) when war seemed imminent, but he chose this moment for telling home truths to the Secretary of War, Dearborn. He had been courted by Aaron Burr, who was engaged in a conspiracy which the Government considered treasonable; Dearborn wrote a letter to him on the matter, which he resented. He replied:

The first duty of a soldier or good citizen is to attend to the safety and interest of his country: the next to attend to his own feelings whenever they are rudely or wantonly assailed. The tenor of your letter is such and the insinuations so grating, the ideas and tenor so unmilitary, stories allude to, and intimations of a conduct, to stoop, from the character, of a general to that of a snarling assassin. (Then hereafter) I will sir enclose you, a copy of a letter from Governor Claiborne, that will shew you I never depart, from the true sense of duty to my country, whenever I am even suspicious of its injury.

Health and respect,
Andrew Jackson.

adding a postscript (which, however, was perhaps not sent):

Col. B. received, sir, at my house all that hospitality that a banished patriot from his home was entitled to. I then thought him a patriot in exile for a cause that every man of honor must regret, the violence with which he was pursued, all his language to me covered with a love of country, and obedience to the laws and your orders. Under these declarations and after his acquittal by a respectable grand jury of Kentucky, my suspicions of him vanished, and I did furnish him with two boats, and had he wanted two more on the same terms and under the same impressions I then had he should have had them. But sir when prooff shews him to be a treator, I would cut his throat with as much pleasure as I would cut yours on equal testimony.

This quarrel was patched up, but there were others that had tragic terminations. In 1806 he challenged a man named Dickinson, who was considered the best rifle-shot in the West. The weapons were pistols, the distance eight yards, and each meant to kill the other. Dickinson had the first shot; when he had fired, Jackson pressed his hand over his chest, but otherwise did not move. Dickinson exclaimed "Great God! have I missed him?" and for a moment was seized with terror. But Jackson's second sharply reminded him of the laws of "honor," and he stood awaiting his fate.

Jackson now had his opponent at his mercy. He stood glowering at him for an instant, and then his long pistol arm came slowly to a horizontal position. Dickinson shuddered and turned away his head. Jackson's eye ran along the pistol barrel, deliberately adjusting the aim, and then he pulled the trigger. But there was no explosion. A hurried consultation by the seconds revealed that the hammer stopped at half-cock, which by the rules agreed upon was not to count as a fire; and Jackson was given another shot. Again he took careful aim at the poor victim who all the time stood awaiting his fate, and this time the pistol fired. The ball cut a large artery, and Dickinson died that night. Jackson walked triumphantly from the field, carefully concealing from his attendants the fact that he was wounded; for he wanted his dying antagonist to think his shot failed. "I should have hit him," Jackson once said, "if he had shot me through the brain."

In this and some of his other quarrels, Jackson went too far even for the Tennessee of that day, with the result that, for a time, he had to retire into private life. He was rescued from this situation by the

War of 1812, which, it was thought, would give an opportunity for the conquest of Florida, then still Spanish. Florida extended along the coast immediately south of Tennessee, which was inconvenient; moreover the Spaniards and British were accused of inciting the Indians against the Americans. A proclamation to his troops on July 21, 1812, sets forth Jackson's sentiments:

You burn with anxiety to learn on what theatre your arms will find employment. Then turn your eyes to the South! Behold in the province of West Florida, a territory whose rivers and harbors, are indispensable to the prosperity of the western, and still more so, to the eastern division of our state. Behold there likewise the asylum from which an insiduous hand incites to rapine and bloodshed, the ferocious savages, who have just stained our frontier with blood, and who will renew their outrages the moment an English force shall appear in the Bay of Pensacola. It is here that an employment adapted to your situation awaits your courage and your zeal, and while extending in this quarter the boundaries of the Republic to the Gulf of Mexico, you will experience a peculiar satisfaction in having conferred a signal benefit on that section of the Union to which you yourselves immediately belong.

There were diplomatic and political difficulties, and Jackson was ordered to confine himself to the Indians, whom he duly defeated and pursued into Spanish territory. But the exploit which made him the idol of the nation was his defeat of the British at New Orleans on January 8, 1815, when peace had already been signed, though neither side knew it. This useless battle was typical of the futility of that war, which ended without deciding any of the controversies that had given rise to it, but revived for a hundred years the hatred of England generated during the War of Independence. The world lost by England's folly, but General Jackson profited.

When the United States acquired Florida in 1821, Jackson was appointed Governor. When he occupied Pensacola, Mrs. Jackson was pained by the Spanish custom of treating Sunday as a day of enjoyment, and saw to it that the inhabitants should become aware of the advent of a purer régime. "I sent," she wrote, "Major Stanton to say to them that the approaching Sunday would be differently kept. . . . Yesterday I had the happiness of witnessing the truth of what I said. Great order was observed; the doors kept shut, the gambling houses demolished; fiddling and dancing not heard any more on the Lord's Day; cursing not to be heard." As the American flag was hoisted, a Methodist began distributing tracts in spite of the protests of priests, and office-seekers besieged both the Governor and his wife in their eagerness for jobs in the new territory. Jackson had a terrific quarrel with the retiring Spanish Governor, in which both sides were absurd, but the Spaniard rather the more so of the two. After various other quarrels, Jackson resigned in disgust and retired to Nashville. His house, "The Hermitage," was large and comfortable; he had an adequate estate, with sufficient slaves; he drove about in "a fine carriage drawn by four handsome gray horses, with servants in livery."

Yet he was regarded as far more truly democratic than Jefferson, partly, no doubt, on account of his origin, but still more, I think, because of his lack of education.

Jackson just missed the Presidency in 1824, but achieved it by a great majority in 1828, and was re-elected in 1832. He is traditionally (though not with complete justice) credited with the introduction of the "spoils system," [2] according to which all Government appointments, even postmasterships, should go to party men, and be changed with a change of administration. Though he did not invent the system, he certainly intensified it. This was one example of his "democracy"; the other was his destruction of the United States Bank. Both sprang from the same theory of government—the theory that what is required is not skill, but honesty, and that honesty is proved by membership in the popular party. In a rough draft of his Inaugural Address, the newly elected President wrote:

It shall be my care to fill the various offices at the disposal of the Executive with individuals uniting as far as possible the qualifications of the head and heart, always recollecting that in a free government the demand for moral qualities should be made superior to that of talents. In other forms of government where the people are not regarded as composing the sovereign power, it is easy to perceive that the safeguard of the empire consists chiefly in the skill by which the monarch can wield the bigoted acquiescence of his Subjects. But it is different with us. Here the will of the people, prescribed in a constitution of their own choice controuls the service of the public functionaries, and is interested more deeply in the

[2] "President Washington began the spoils system." Channing, *op. cit.*, VI, p. 123.

preservation of those qualities which ensures fidelity and honest devotion to their interests.

The working out of this theory was not always fortunate. For example, the post of Collector of the Port of New York was given to a man named Swartwout, who appeared to the President to "unite the qualifications of the head and heart." This wise and good man, however, used his position, almost from the first, as an opportunity for peculation; when, after Jackson had ceased to be President, his depredations were discovered, they were found to have amounted to a million and a quarter dollars.

Jackson's belief in the spoils system was wholly sincere; it was by no means simply a matter of finding rewards for political friends. Two or three months after he became President, he wrote in his private journal:

There has been a great noise made about removals. This to be brought before Congress with the causes, with the propriety of passing a law vacating all offices periodically—then the good can be reappointed, and the bad, defaulters, left out without murmurs. Now, every man who has been in office a few years, believes he has a life estate in it, a vested right, and if it has been held twenty years or upwards, not only a vested right, but that it ought to descend to his children, and if no children then the next of kin. This is not the principles of our government. It is rotation in office that will perpetuate our liberty.

Americans had not at that time, and still have inadequately, the conception of a non-party civil service: if offices did not change hands with a change of government, it was held that they would come to belong by prescriptive right to an hereditary class of officials. The creation of a permanent civil service selected by examination is one of the things that England owes to the Philosophical Radicals, who reformed the aristocratic corruption of the eighteenth century without substituting the democratic corruption that resulted from Jackson's system. But Jackson, who held that governmental functions require virtue rather than intelligence, would have been horrified at the suggestion of giving jobs for proficiency in academic studies. After all, he had been a successful judge without knowing the law, and a successful General without studying strategy or tactics; it was therefore only natural that he should regard a good heart rather than a good head as affording the right qualification for public position.

The spoils system must not be attributed to Jackson as an individual; it was the inevitable outcome of democracy as understood in America. As Channing says: "The change from the old colonial system of permanent official tenure to the more democratic mode of political rotation in the public offices was inevitable." [3] In Illinois, when Lincoln was young, it was considered correct for the leading politicians of a party to take turns in accepting nominations for Congress or for any other particularly desirable position. It is true that this is within the domain of party politics, but it shows the same point of view as that which inspired the spoils system, namely, that the public service requires no particular skill, and that, therefore, it is only fair that its advantages should go to all "good" men in turn.

The ultimate result of the belief that the work of government is unskilled was to leave the skill in the hands of private enterprise. Instead of government by the people, government by financial interests was what frequently resulted from Jackson's system. The spirit of Hamilton lived on in America, and the more it was nominally defeated, the more it was really victorious. The conception of democracy was so individualistic that all enterprises (except war) which required the co-operation of large numbers were left to private initiative, and were so managed as to bring profit to their promoters in the first place, and benefit to the community only incidentally.

It must, however, be admitted that the system of a partisan civil service has merits from a governmental point of view, and is, in certain circumstances, almost unavoidable. During the presidency of John Adams, Jefferson found it necessary to be very careful in using the post, as he believed that his correspondence was tampered with.[4] Lincoln came across instances in which postmasters in Illinois had used their position for the benefit of the Democratic party, by omitting to deliver newspapers supporting the Whigs.[5] In such cases, the advantage to the Government is outweighed by the disadvantage to the public, though the existence of such a system hitherto makes it natural for a newly victorious party to dispossess officials who have obstructed it. A non-political civil service is only possible in com-

[3] Channing, *History of the United States*, V, p. 402.
[4] Tucker, *Life of Jefferson*, II, p. 64.
[5] Nicolay and Hay, I, p. 183.

paratively quiet times; it was wholly impossible, for example, in Russia in 1918. But except at the time of the Civil War party divisions in America have not been so deep as to make a non-partisan civil service impossible. What made it impossible in Jackson's day was unwillingness to admit that governmental functions involve skill. Skill is not universal, and to admit the need of it seemed, therefore, a treachery to the democratic faith.

A similar point of view inspired Jackson's attack on the United States Bank. There had been an earlier Bank of the United States, created in 1791 on the initiative of Hamilton, opposed by Jefferson, and sanctioned by Washington after some hesitation as to its constitutionality. This Bank had a charter which expired in 1811, and was not renewed, partly because three-fourths of its shares were held by foreigners, mainly English. The second Bank of the United States was created in 1816, largely as a means of rehabilitating the currency. Its charter, unless renewed, was to expire in 1836. From the first it was unpopular, and when Jackson, in the presidential campaign of 1832, appealed for a mandate in his fight against it, he was enthusiastically supported, especially in the South and West.

Banking in America had long been in a state of hopeless confusion. In addition to the United States Bank, there were State banks and private banks. These last, which were called "wild-cat" banks, usually failed. All the banks issued notes; the wild-cat banks often started with practically no other assets. In the West there was very little specie. During the interval between the first and second United States Banks, the currency in the West consisted either of notes issued by wild-cat banks or of notes on State banks. The value of the former was everywhere problematical; the latter lost some of their value as they travelled away from their place of origin. The Bank of the United States was intended to establish a uniform currency throughout the country; but there were bad times, and it appeared to be making them worse. Ohio attempted to tax it, whereupon the Supreme Court decided that the States could not tax it. Ohio declared that a State had as good a right to pronounce on the interpretation of the Constitution as had the Supreme Court; it collected the tax by force from the branches of the Bank in Ohio, and decreed that any one in Ohio might rob the Bank with impunity. In several other States there was similar trouble. Everyone in the West borrowed money to clear as much land as possible, and very many borrowers could not meet their obligations. The creditors, in the main, were in the East, and the Bank represented their interests. Debtors everywhere had reason to oppose the Bank, and Western debtors had, in addition, a geographical reason, since it seemed to be impeding the great work of Western development.

Western pioneers, including Jackson, were intellectually baffled by the operation of the credit system. All of them were only too anxious to make use of the banks to enable them to take up and develop more land, but it did not seem to them that the banks did anything substantial when they lent money. The whole thing was on paper: the banker did not sweat, like a man felling timber or ploughing virgin soil. In return for a mere document, without any work, the banker acquired rights by which industrious men could be ruined: if the crops were bad, or prices inadequate, or merely if there was a currency crisis in the East or in Europe, the banker could call in his loan, and if the farmer could not find the money, all the result of his labor became the property of the bank. Credit is a kind of reservoir filled by the labor of the whole community; it is a collective product, not an individual one. The collective aspects of economic life were unintelligible to the self-reliant Westerner, and therefore made him angry. Very unwisely, all civilized communities have allowed credit, although it is due to the community as an organized whole, to be appropriated by certain individuals, and used by them to extract money from those to whom credit is necessary. The opposition to the gains of these individuals became, in Jackson's time, an opposition to banking as such, and especially to its least harmful because most centralized form. There must be institutions for the control of credit in any civilized community which permits private enterprise; but these institutions, left in private hands, tend to become so powerful as to acquire an almost despotic control over all economic activities. Jackson and his supporters were all anxious to profit by the opportunities of growing rich that existed in the West: those who owned slaves saw nothing objectionable in appropriating the results of *their* labor, and those who speculated in real estate did not wish to lose the chance of gain when their land increased in value through the enterprise of their neighbors. So long as the kinds of gain that they desired for themselves are permitted, so long the banker's kind of gain must also be permitted. Jackson, therefore, could only decree that private banking should be badly done, not that it should cease altogether. Jacksonian democracy wished to give free play to the desire for wealth, and at the same time to envy of those who had succeeded in acquiring wealth. This made it logically incoherent, and therefore, from the nature of things, incapable of success.

Jackson could not destroy all banks, though he would have liked to do so. To Biddle, President of the United States Bank, he said: "I do not dislike your Bank any more than all banks. But ever since I read the history of the South Sea bubble I have been afraid of Banks." On another occasion he said: "Everyone that knows me, does know, that I have been always opposed to the U. States Bank, nay all Banks." When he says that he has been "afraid of Banks," he is expressing the kernel of his feeling. Banks are puzzling and mysterious; an honest citizen devoid of education cannot make head or tail of them. They have so much power that they are politically important, but in a democracy every sane adult citizen ought to be able to judge of all political questions. Therefore anything too difficult for the plain man to understand is anti-democratic, and consequently wicked. The United States Bank, being more powerful than any other, is more wicked than any other; since we cannot abolish *all* banks, let us at least abolish the most wicked of them. This, I think, fairly represents what Jackson thought on the subject, and in so thinking he was a faithful interpreter of the people's will.

Jackson, as was inevitable from his character and career, was an ardent nationalist, not merely in the sense of loving his country, but in the imperialistic bellicose sense. In 1829, speaking of the Mississippi, he said: "The God of the universe intended this great valley to belong to one nation." The Divine purpose had been fulfilled until the Seven Years' War, while the whole belonged to France, but since then it had apparently been forgotten until the Government of the United States brought the matter to the attention of the Government of the Universe. Jackson's hatred of the English was natural, in view of his sufferings in the War of Independence and his victories in the War of 1812; but his hatred of the Spaniards was less justifiable. All Southerners in his time wished to make conquests in the South. Louisiana, Florida, and Texas were successively acquired during his life-time; it was in spite of him that Florida was acquired by diplomacy and not by war. Long after he had retired from politics, in 1843, he wrote a vehement letter urging the annexation of Texas lest the English should acquire it:

Great Britain has already made treaties with Texas; and we know that far-seeing nation never omits a circumstance in her extensive intercourse with the world which can be turned to account in increasing her military resources. May she not enter into an alliance with Texas? And reserving, as she doubtless will, the North-western boundary question as the cause of war with us whenever she chooses to declare it—let us suppose that, as an ally with Texas, we are to fight her. Preparatory to such a movement she sends her 20,000 or 30,000 men to Texas; organizes them on the Sabine, where supplies and arms can be concentrated before we have even notice of her intentions; makes a lodgement on the Mississippi; excites the negroes to insurrection; the lower country falls, with it New Orleans; and a servile war rages through the whole South and West.[6]

His imperialism pleased the South, and his patriotism pleased the whole country—except, indeed, South Carolina when that State wished to secede and he stood vigorously for the preservation of the Union. His nationalism was of a sort which is generally popular in democracies provided they are powerful. But the love of Southern conquests became, towards the end of his life, unpopular in the North, owing to the slavery issue. While he was President, it was not slavery, but the tariff, that divided North and South, and on this issue compromise was possible. Political parties were only just beginning to be divided according to latitude; he was supported, not only by the South, but by the Northwest, by Pennsylvania, and by a majority in New York State. He was admired as a patriot and a military hero, quite as much as on account of his democracy. Under his guidance, the plain man in America learnt to despise, not only Europe, but much that was valuable in his own country. If his had been the last great influence in the formation of the American character, American democracy might have become associated with ignorance, recklessness, and violence. Fortunately in the next generation a new issue gave scope for a new influence, through which America became more worthy of its power over the destinies of mankind.

[6] Nicolay and Hay, Vol. I, p. 226.

CHAPTER XXIV

SLAVERY AND DISUNION

THE United States, as its name implies, is a federation, in which the powers of the Federal Government are determined by the Constitution as interpreted by the Supreme Court. The original thirteen States existed before they were united, and there were among them wide differences of religion, climate, and history. Their economic interests were different, and on many points mutually antagonistic; their important economic relations, for a long time, were with Europe rather than with each other. Puritan Massachusetts, which lived mainly by sea-faring and manufactures, had no natural affinity with Episcopalian Virginia, where large landed proprietors grew tobacco by slave labor. The War of Independence had produced the Union, but the War of 1812 nearly destroyed it, because the North disliked the interruption to commerce. When, in 1798, the Federalists passed the Sedition and Alien Acts, Kentucky passed Resolves, written by Jefferson, to the effect that that State regarded these Acts as unconstitutional, and refused to enforce them, and Virginia followed suit. It was not generally admitted, at that time, that the Supreme Court's interpretation of the Constitution must be accepted by all. In 1832, South Carolina almost seceded from dislike of the tariff. So late as 1843, thirteen northern Congressmen, headed by ex-President J. Q. Adams, threatened secession of their States if Texas was annexed. Throughout the older North and South, secession was regarded as an ever-present possibility.

As time went on, the chief disruptive influence came to be that of slavery. This question had a long history, without which it cannot be understood.

Slavery was introduced by the Europeans into all parts of the American Continent. Columbus, it is true, was imprisoned by the Spanish Government for making slaves of the Indians, but this phase did not last long. The Indians being unsatisfactory as slaves, negroes were brought from the West of Africa in large numbers.

In Colonial days, slavery was legal everywhere in America, but it never had any importance in the North. The Virginia Assembly passed measures abolishing the slave trade, which George III vetoed. In the original draft of the Declaration of Independence, this was one of the counts of Jefferson's indictment of that foolish monarch; but it was afterwards cut out as not affording a genuine ground of complaint. The slave trade, however, was abolished by agreement with the English in 1808.

In 1784, Jefferson proposed the prohibition of slavery in the Northwest, and, though defeated at the time, he was successful in 1787, when, by a unanimous vote, the Continental Congress prohibited slavery throughout the territory north and west of the Ohio. Before the end of the eighteenth century, slavery was abolished in all the Northern States. The Southern States, at that time, looked forward cheerfully to its gradual extinction, and there was, as yet, no bitterness between North and South on the question.

In America, as in contemporary England, the course of history was changed by the invention of labor-saving machinery. In England, inventions enabled one person to accomplish as much spinning or weaving as fifty persons could previously accomplish in the same time; the result of these "labor-saving" devices was that young children had to work fifteen hours a day. Another result was to stimulate the demand for raw cotton. Whitney's cotton gin, which was invented in 1793, enabled a negro to clean fifty pounds of fibre a day instead of only one. The result was the rapid extension of cotton cultivation in the most southern States. The cultivation was enormously profitable, and depended upon slave labor. The cotton belt, therefore, ceased to be indifferent on the subject of slavery. Moreover, the climate being very unhealthy and the slave trade having ceased, there was need of a constant importation of slaves into the cotton belt from the less southern slave States; consequently the price of slaves everywhere was increased, and Virginia and North Carolina became valuable as breeding grounds for the destined victims of hook-worm, malaria, and yellow fever. The sentiment and the economic life of the South were transformed, and the defence of slavery became the defence of a vital interest.

The first serious clash between North and South occurred in 1820, and issued in the Missouri Compromise. From the time when the

Northern States abolished slavery, the number of free and slave States had been equal, and had remained so, since, of the eight new States, four were free and four slave. Owing to the fact that the Senate consisted of two Senators from each State, it maintained the balance so long as the number of States on either side was the same. The admission of Missouri would tip the balance in favor of the South. There was a vehement controversy, causing alarm for the future; Jefferson described it as like a fire-bell in the night. At last it was decided that Missouri should be balanced by Maine, and that, in future, when new States were created in the West, those of latitude 36° 30′ should have slavery, and those north of this line should not. This compromise governed the policy of the Federal Government for a generation.

The ultimate effect was to drive the South into schemes of imperialist expansion. After the acquisition of Florida, no territory remained for the creation of new Southern States, while many free States could still be created in the Northwest. However, Mexico was weak, and it was said that "manifest destiny" demanded the acquisition by the United States of so much of its territory as might at any time be found convenient. American adventurers, with Southern encouragement, caused Texas to declare its independence of Mexico, and to re-introduce slavery, which the Mexicans had abolished. The Government of Texas, which consisted of immigrants from the United States, desired annexation, which occurred in 1845. This gave the slave States a majority of one.

Mexico, meanwhile, had ventured to protest, and thereby provided occasion for the Mexican War. This ended with the annexation of territory now covered by the States of California, Nevada, Utah, Arizona, with parts of New Mexico, Colorado, and Wyoming. The result, however, was less satisfactory than the South had hoped. The only part of the new acquisition that quickly acquired enough population for admission as a State was California, half north of the Missouri Compromise line, and half south of it, but determined to exclude slavery. This led to a difficult situation, which was ended— for a few years—by a new compromise, that of 1850. At the time of this compromise, the number of free and slave States had again become equal through the admission of Wisconsin in 1848. But the

"Wilmot Proviso," which proposed to exclude slavery from the newly acquired territories, was defeated.

The Compromise of 1850 was only arrived at after long and acrimonious debate, accompanied by threats of secession. There were three provisions pleasing to the North, and two that were pleasing to the South. To please the North, California, undivided, was admitted as a free State, although about half of it was south of the line of the Missouri Compromise; New Mexico and Utah were organized as Territories without slavery; and the slave trade was prohibited in the District of Columbia. To please the South, a new and stricter fugitive-slave law was passed, and Texas was given ten million dollars. As regards this last provision, Nicolay and Hay remark: "It has been gravely asserted that this indemnity of ten millions, suddenly trebling the value of the Texas debt, and thereby affording an unprecedented opportunity for speculation in the bonds of that State, was 'the propelling force whereby these acts were pushed through Congress in defiance of the original convictions of a majority of its members.'" They do not wholly endorse this view; but it can hardly be doubted that ten million dollars would have an effect upon some people's "original convictions."

For a number of reasons, the Compromise of 1850 broke down, although, for a few years, it was hoped that the slavery question had been finally settled. The two causes of the revival of controversy were: (1) that the North hated the fugitive-slave law and resisted its execution; (2) that the South, seeing no chance of creating new slave States south of 36° 30', was driven to repeal the Missouri Compromise. From these two sources, the disagreement gradually widened until no issue remained but war.

The question of fugitive slaves, more perhaps than any other, brought about the truth of Lincoln's doctrine that the Union could not persist half slave and half free. When he first stated this view publicly, in 1858, it surprised many people, and provided the staple of Douglas's arguments against him in their great debates. But when slaves fled into free States, or when free negroes in the North were falsely claimed as slaves, the inhabitants of regions in which slavery was detested were compelled either to break the law or to become accomplices in what they felt to be indefensible cruelty. Many men who would have been unmoved by abstract abolitionist arguments could not bring themselves to give up an actual negro whom they had before their eyes; the concrete example was irresistible, and the law brought it home to the Northern conscience as no anti-slavery oratory could have done.

United States legislation on the subject of fugitive slaves begins with the Constitution, which was framed by men who were very careful of all property rights. The Constitution provided that fugitive slaves should be delivered up to their owners wherever they might be within the United States; this was, at the time, one of the advantages which the South derived from consenting to the Federal Union. Effect was given to this provision of the Constitution by a law passed in 1793, according to which the owner, or his agent, could seize the alleged slave, take him before a magistrate, prove his ownership to the magistrate's satisfaction, obtain a certificate from him, and carry off his property. Any person who obstructed this procedure was liable to a fine of $500.

The negro, being supposed to be a slave, was not allowed to give evidence in his own case. Professional slave-catchers were employed, and often found it less trouble to take some free negro and swear he was the right man, than to hunt for the particular slave of whom they were supposed to be in search. The result was that no negro was safe until he reached Canada. Dickens, in his *American Notes*, has described the practical operation of the law as it was before 1850:

Public opinion has made this law. It has declared that in Washington, in that city which takes its name from the father of American liberty, any justice of the peace may bind with fetters any negro passing down the street and thrust him into jail: no offence on the black man's part is necessary. This justice says, "I choose to think this man a runaway": and locks him up. Public opinion empowers the man of law when this is done, to advertise the negro in the newspapers, warning his owner to come and claim him, or he will be sold to pay the jail fees. But supposing he is a free black, and has no owner, it may naturally be presumed that he is set at liberty. No: HE IS SOLD TO RECOMPENSE HIS JAILER. This has been done again and again and again. He has no means of proving his freedom; has no adviser, messenger, or assistance of any sort or kind; no investigation into his case is made, or inquiry instituted. He, a free man, who may have served for years, and bought his liberty, is thrown into jail on no process, for no crime, and on no pretence of crime; and is sold to pay the jail fees.

Dickens is speaking of what happened in the District of Columbia. Further north, the States passed Acts to prevent the kidnapping of free negroes, and to enable the State judicial authorities to demand proof that a negro was a slave before allowing him to be removed. The Supreme Court, which always endeavored to strengthen slavery so long as it existed, decided in 1842 that all interference by States with the operation of the fugitive-slave law was unconstitutional. The slave-owner, so it appeared from the Court's decision, could seize any negro anywhere, and did not have to offer evidence of ownership until he had brought him back to his own slave State.

Such was the state of the law in 1850, when the South demanded that it should be made more stringent. As a part of the compromise, this demand was granted. Under the new law, all the harsh features of the old laws were continued, and, in addition, the penalties for helping a fugitive slave in any way were increased to $1,000 together with imprisonment up to six months. Moreover a *posse comitatus* could be summoned to assist in capturing the alleged slave, so that all the neighborhood were liable to be involved in carrying out the unpopular law. When a Southerner's horse ran away, he had to catch it himself; but when his slave ran away, he could call upon all the inhabitants of a northern district to help him in recovering his property, and any who failed were liable to penalties.

The results of this law in the North were disastrous to the Southern cause. The arrest of a fugitive slave in Boston caused a riot, in which a whole regiment of soldiers had to be called out, between whose lines the captive was marched on to a U.S. frigate which took him by sea to the South. At Oberlin in Ohio, where a rescue had been effected, professors and ministers of religion had to be put in jail; and on other similar occasions eminent Quakers were involved. Southerners complained that they risked their lives in attempting to capture runaway slaves. The North, where most people had previously viewed Southern slavery with indifference, was led by the operation of the fugitive-slave law to regard the matter as one in which it was impossible to be neutral or indifferent. Abolitionist sentiment was still exceptional, but it was felt to be intolerable that respected citizens should be punished for helping unfortunate negroes to escape from bondage. The insistence of the South was the more unwise in view of the very small number of fugitive slaves. South Carolina, in 1860, lost 23 slaves, i.e. one in 17,501; the South as a whole lost one-fiftieth of 1 per cent. The outcry was loudest in the most southern States, where the loss was the smallest.[1]

Throughout the thirty years preceding the Civil War, Abolitionism in the North had been gradually increasing both in numbers and in fanaticism. As a force in public life, it may be taken as dating from 1831, when William Lloyd Garrison began the publication of his newspaper *The Liberator*. In the opening number he said:

I shall strenuously contend for the immediate enfranchisement of our slave population. . . . On this subject I do not wish to write, or speak, or think, with moderation. No! No! Tell a man whose house is on fire, to give a moderate alarm; tell him to moderately rescue his wife from the hands of the ravisher; tell the mother to gradually extricate her babe from the fire into which it has fallen; but urge me not into moderation in a cause like the present. I am in earnest—I will not excuse—I will not retreat a single inch—and I *will be heard*.

He *was* heard—in the South.

The Georgia Legislature offered a reward of five thousand dollars to any one who should kidnap Garrison, or who should bring to conviction any one circulating the *Liberator* in the State. Yet so little known in their own neighborhoods were these early workers in this great reform that when the Mayor of Boston received remonstrances from certain Southern States against such an incendiary publication as the *Liberator* he was able to say that no member of the city government and no person of his acquaintance had ever heard of the paper or its editor; that on search being made it was found that "his office was an obscure hole, his only visible auxiliary a negro boy, and his supporters a very few insignificant persons of all colors." [2]

President Jackson denounced anti-slavery propaganda, and wished Congress to prohibit agitation "calculated to stimulate the slaves to insurrection and to produce all the horrors of civil war." When Boston did hear of Garrison, it at first disliked him. He was on one

[1] Nicolay and Hay, III, 31.   [2] Nicolay and Hay, I, 148.

occasion attacked by a Boston mob, and his life was saved by his being put in jail. In Illinois, in 1837, an Abolitionist clergyman, Elijah P. Lovejoy, who edited a newspaper, was murdered by a mob. But gradually, especially in Massachusetts, the Abolitionists gained attention. It must be said that their fanaticism did more harm than good to their cause, and served as a goad to Southern violence. They urged that any one attempting to capture a fugitive slave should be killed. They called for dissolution of the Union, since they held it sinful to have any dealing with the accursed thing—though how the slaves would have benefited is not clear. Garrison in 1843 said that "the compact which exists between the North and the South is 'a covenant with death and an agreement with hell'—involving both parties in atrocious criminality, and should be immediately annulled." The extreme Abolitionists continued to demand the dissolution of the Union even after the outbreak of the Civil War—a demand which is difficult to understand if they genuinely desired the welfare of the negro. And by their fanaticism they helped to make the South aggressive.

The repeal of the Missouri Compromise in the interests of the South was the first definite political infringement of the Compromise of 1850. The question arose in connection with Kansas, which was north of the Missouri Compromise line, but next to the State of Missouri, some of whose inhabitants wished to occupy it as slave territory. In 1854, by the Nebraska Bill, it was enacted that Kansas and Nebraska should be slave or free as they themselves might decide. In regard to Nebraska, it was known that freedom would prevail, but in regard to Kansas there was uncertainty, and Kansas at once became a battle-ground. Southerners came in through Missouri, Northerners through Iowa. Each set up a government, and said theirs was the legitimate authority for deciding on slavery. Civil war raged, and each side appealed to Washington. Although Washington sided with the Southerners, the North won in the end by weight of numbers, and Kansas was admitted as a free State on the eve of the Civil War.

The aggressiveness of the South, as shown in the repeal of the Missouri Compromise, led to the formation of the Republican party, whose first National Convention met at Philadelphia in 1856. The platform of the new party aimed at excluding slavery from all Territories; on other points it revived the doctrines of the Whigs, the most important of which was high tariff. In the presidential election, the new party failed to win, but nevertheless did surprisingly well. The successful Democratic candidate, Buchanan, had 1,838,169 votes; Frémont, the Republican, had 1,341,264. Frémont's vote was entirely in the free States, and of them eleven voted for him while five voted for Buchanan. Lincoln's State, Illinois, was one of the five.

The Democratic party began its career with Jackson, and held power from 1829 to 1861, except for the breaks in 1841 when Harrison was elected, and in 1849 when Taylor became President. The break in 1841 came to very little, because Harrison died within a month of his inauguration, and the Vice-President Tyler, who thereupon became President, in the main went over to the Democrats. Until the slavery issue, the chief question on which parties were divided was the tariff. The Democrats stood for low tariff; their opponents, the Whigs, stood for high tariff. The South favored free trade; New England favored protection. New York State was usually democratic; the Northwest fluctuated. Owing to the fact that the tariff was the main issue, and that on this question the South was united while the North was divided, the South usually controlled the administration; from 1789 to 1861, there were only twelve years of Northern domination. This had given Southerners a feeling that they had a right to govern. As the North outstripped the South in territory, in population, and in wealth, it became increasingly clear that, in the end, the North must prevail. To men accustomed to power, this seemed monstrous. They thought of conquering Mexico and Cuba and Central America; they dreamed of introducing slavery throughout the Territories of the West. Their mentality was that of threatened aristocrats, and they felt that there was something unnatural in their being expected to submit to a mere numerical majority. Instead of becoming more conciliatory as the crisis approached, they became more blustering and bullying, and sought by blatant self-assertion to terrify the supposedly timid North.

The Supreme Court, which contained a Southern majority, celebrated Buchanan's inauguration by announcing, two days later (March 6, 1857), the famous Dred Scott decision, which reversed what had previously been supposed to be the law. It was judicially decided that negroes "cannot become citizens of the United States nor sue in the Federal courts. . . . That the Constitution of the United States recognizes slaves as property, and pledges the Federal Government to protect it; and that the Missouri Compromise Act and like prohibitory laws are unconstitutional." It was laid down explicitly that the words of the Declaration of Independence, concerning all men being born equal, had not been intended to apply to negroes.

The South welcomed this decision with acclamation; the North, which did not like to bring the Supreme Court into contempt, was perplexed. Lincoln, who never failed in respect for the Constitution, replying to a speech by Douglas, said:

And now as to the Dred Scott decision. That decision declares two propositions—first, that a negro cannot sue in the United States courts; and secondly, that Congress cannot prohibit slavery in the Territories. It was made by a divided court—dividing differently on the different points. Judge Douglas does not discuss the merits of the decision, and in that respect I shall follow his example, believing I could no more improve on McLean and Curtis, than he could on Taney. He denounces all who question the correctness of that decision, as offering violent resistance to it. But who resists it? Who has, in spite of the decision, declared Dred Scott free, and resisted the authority of his master over him? Judicial decisions have two uses—first, to absolutely determine the case decided, and, secondly, to indicate to the public how other similar cases will be decided when they arise. For the latter use they are called "precedents" and "authorities." We believe as much as Judge Douglas (perhaps more) in obedience to and respect for the judicial department of government. We think its decisions on constitutional questions, when fully settled, should control, not only the particular cases decided, but the general policy of the country, subject to be disturbed only by amendments of the Constitution as provided in that instrument itself. More than this would be revolution. But we think the Dred Scott decision is erroneous. We know the court that made it has often overruled its own decisions, and we shall do what we can to have it overrule this. We offer no resistance to it. Judicial decisions are of greater or less authority as precedents according to circumstances. That this should be so, accords both with common sense and the customary understanding of the legal profession. If this important decision had been made by the unanimous concurrence of the judges, and without any apparent partisan bias, and in accordance with legal public expectation, and with the steady practice of the departments throughout our history, and had been in no part based on assumed historical facts which are not really true; or, if wanting in some of these, it had been before the court more than once, and had there been affirmed and reaffirmed through a course of years, it then might be, perhaps would be, factious, nay, even revolutionary, not to acquiesce in it as a precedent. But when, as is true, we find it wanting in all these claims to the public confidence, it is not resistance, it is not factious, it is not even disrespectful, to treat it as not having yet quite established a settled doctrine for the country.

But while the immediate effect of the decision in the Dred Scott case was to give confidence to the South and to cause perplexity in the North, the ultimate effect was very different. It now appeared that, as things stood, there was no legal way by which slavery could be excluded throughout the Territories of the Northwest. There had been no need to repeal the Missouri Compromise Act, since it was unconstitutional; the Nebraska Act, against which the North had vehemently protested, conceded to the South less than was already granted by the Constitution. The Supreme Court said, in effect: "You may have come to dislike slavery, you may think more highly of the negro than men did in 1789, but your feelings and thoughts are of no avail against the words decreed at that time. You may think you live under a democracy, but you are mistaken: you are governed still by what was decided nearly seventy years ago, and you must remain in the grip of the dead hand until three-quarters of the States agree to release you." Lest this paraphrase should be supposed misleading, I will quote some of the actual words of the judgment:

No one, we presume, supposes that any change in public opinion or feeling in relation to this unfortunate race, in the civilized nations of Europe or in this country, should induce the court to give to the words of the Constitution a more liberal construction in their favor than they were intended to bear when the instrument was framed and adopted. . . It is not only the same in words, but the same in meaning, and delegates the same powers to the Government, and reserves and secures the same rights and privileges to the citizen; and as long as it continues to exist in its present form, it speaks not only in the same words but with the same meaning and intent with which it spoke when it came from the hands of its framers and was voted on and adopted by the people of the United States.

It was clear that a majority of the citizens of the United States did not desire the establishment of slavery in the Territories of the Northwest. The Supreme Court had declared that there was no way in which the majority could make its will prevail on this point. This was intolerable, and afforded an incentive to war. If the South had been less impatient, the North might have been forced into unconstitutional action in defence of majority rule; but the South, more aggressive and even more intolerant than the North, was the first to appeal to force, with the result that the North, while defending the Constitution, won more than it had ever claimed.

Externally as well as internally, the South, and the administrations which represented its interests, was imperious and indifferent to the rights of others. Jackson in his dealings with the Spaniards set an example which was followed, on a larger scale, in the Mexican War. Seeking for slave territory to annex, President Pierce thought that Cuba afforded a suitable opportunity. He endeavored to buy the island from Spain, but Spain had the effrontery to refuse to sell it. Thereupon, in 1854, the U.S. Ministers to London, Paris, and Madrid met and drew up what was known as the Ostend Manifesto, which declared that if Spain would not sell Cuba it should be annexed by force. Buchanan, the first signatory of this interesting document, succeeded Pierce as President. In that office he continued to seek an opportunity for the annexation of Cuba, and in this the whole Democratic party supported him. When nominated, he said: "If I can be instrumental in settling the slavery question upon the terms I have mentioned, and then add Cuba to the Union, I shall, if President, be willing to give up the ghost, and let Breckenridge take the government." The Democratic platform demanded "that every proper effort be made to insure our ascendency in the Gulf of Mexico," and applauded efforts to "regenerate" Central America.

When the South decided to secede, it did not abandon the plan of extensive conquests in Latin America. The slave-holders, said a pamphlet published in 1860, would carry out the designs of Providence and establish "a vast, opulent, happy and glorious slave-holding Republic, throughout tropical America—future generations will arise and call us blessed!" "This picture of a slave empire or republic," says Channing, "extending from Mount Vernon on the Potomac to the 'Palaces of the Montezumas' within sight of the mighty Popocatepetl comes again and again before one's eyes in Southern books." [3]

The outlook of Southern politicians was that to which, in England, we are accustomed in upper-class imperialists and the financiers who inspire them. Democracy fades into the background, and a predatory oligarchy increasingly dominates the scene. What is characteristic of America in world history is not to be found in the South of 1850 to 1860.

In personal relations, as well as in their larger political dealings, prominent Southerners were arrogant and brutal. In 1856, Senator Sumner of Massachusetts, a distinguished man, made the following speech, attacking Senator Butler of South Carolina:

> With regret I come again upon the Senator from South Carolina, who, omnipresent in this debate, overflowed with rage at the simple suggestion that Kansas had applied for admission as a State; and with incoherent phrases discharged the loose expectoration of his speech, now upon her representative and then upon her people. There was no extravagance of the ancient parliamentary debate which he did not repeat; nor was there any possible deviation from truth which he did not make, with so much of passion, I am glad to add, as to save him from the suspicion of intentional aberration. But the Senator touches nothing which he does not disfigure—with error, sometimes of principle, sometimes of fact. He shows an incapacity of accuracy, whether in stating the Constitution or in stating the law, whether in details of statistics or the diversions of scholarship. He cannot open his mouth but out there flies a blunder.

Two days later, a young Southern Senator named Brooks, a nephew of Butler, deliberately attacked Sumner while he was sitting at his desk, hitting him on the head repeatedly with a guttapercha cane. Sumner, for some time, could not get up because the desk was in his way. Brooks continued to beat him until he became unconscious and sank upon the floor; by this time the cane was shivered to pieces. Another South Carolina Senator kept would-be rescuers at bay. The Senate refused to censure Brooks in any way. In the House of Representatives, which had a Northern majority, he was censured; he resigned, and was immediately re-elected. Sumner, as a result of the attack, had an injury to the spine, from which it took him years to recover, during which he was incapacitated from

[3] Channing, *op. cit.*, VI, p. 260.

work. This was only one example of Southern violence, which made Washington unsafe for Northerners.

The leading spirits in the South aimed at a revival of the slave trade. A certain amount of it went on surreptitiously in the last years before the Civil War, but naturally the facts are difficult to ascertain. Senator Douglas stated in 1860 that more slaves had been imported in 1859 than in any previous year, even while the slave trade was legal. In 1858, the *Wanderer,* a yacht with a cargo of slaves from Africa, arrived in the Savannah River. She had pretended to be a pleasure yacht, and her owner had hobnobbed with the officers of the British warship *Medusa* which was on the lookout for slavers. After these mutual courtesies, her owner took her to the Congo, packed several hundreds of negroes into her, landed them in South Carolina, and distributed them over the South. The Captain and some of the crew were arrested, but acquitted; the yacht was confiscated, but bought back by the owner's partner, a man named Lamar. He "told those present that the vessel was his, that she had been wrongfully seized, and asked them not to bid. None save the keeper of the jail did, and for doing so he was assaulted by Lamar at the close of the sale." [4] The owner did not, however, escape unpunished: he was expelled from the New York Yacht Club.

. Another slightly earlier venture had ended less fortunately for the slave traders. The *Echo,* "with some three hundred naked Congo negroes on board," was seized by the *Dolphin* of the U.S. Navy and brought into Charleston. What should be done? The question was argued in the *Richmond Enquirer* of September 1, 1858:

The law required that the ship be confiscated, the owners fined double the value of the ship and cargo, that the captain be hanged, and that the negroes be sent back to Africa. Who knew from what part they came? Casting them loose on the coast was of doubtful humanity. Liberating them in South Carolina was impossible. Nothing remained, then, but the selection of good masters who could turn these useless barbarians into useful laborers. A citizen of Charleston asked, why send them back? They were wanted by the planters, by the mechanics, by the railroads. They had reached the threshold of civilization. Why return to barbarism? They had come within the influence of Christianity. Why return them to heathenism? There was no reason save that another section of the country looked with disgust on

[4] McMaster, VIII, 351.

the institutions of the South and called on her to make this sacrifice of interest to humanity.[5]

The President decided that the negroes must be returned to Africa, and meanwhile handed them over for a year to the care of the Colonization Society. But I find no record that the captain was hanged.

South Carolina's mouth watered at the sight of the booty of which she had been deprived. There were resolutions in the legislature maintaining that interference with the slave trade was unconstitutional. The legislature of Arkansas rejected a resolution against the slave trade. But the Governor of Florida, while repudiating "sickly sentimentality on the subject," reminded the American slave-breeding industry that foreign competition was opposed to its interests.

South Carolina, as always, was the leading spirit. A Grand Jury in that State spoke of the law against the slave trade as a "public grievance." The Governor pointed out the necessity of reviving the slave trade if free labor was to be avoided, and urged that only by slave labor could conflicts between labor and capital be prevented:

If, he said, the demand for slave labor could not be supplied, then the South must expect to receive a kind it did not want, a kind antagonistic to her institutions. That her drays should be driven by slaves, her factories worked by slaves, her hotels served by slaves, her locomotives manned by slaves, was far better than to be exposed to an inroad from any quarter of a population alien by birth, training, and education; a population which in time would lead to that conflict between capital and labor which made it so difficult to maintain free institutions in countries where slavery did not exist. In all slave-holding States the superior race should direct, the inferior race perform, all manual service.

The standpoint of the South was stated with admirable lucidity by W. B. Gaulden of Georgia, at the Charleston Democratic National Convention in May, 1860:

I tell you, fellow-Democrats, that the American slave-trader is the true Union man [cheers and laughter]. I tell you that the slave-trading of Virginia is more immoral, more unchristian in every possible point of view, than that African slave-trade, which goes to Africa and brings a heathen and worthless man here, christianizes him, and sends him and his posterity down the stream of time to enjoy the blessings of civilization. . . . It has

[5] McMaster, VIII, p. 349.

been my fortune to go into that noble old State to buy a few darkies, and I have had to pay from $1000 to $2000 a head, when I could go to Africa and buy better negroes for $50 apiece. . . . I advocate the repeal of the laws prohibiting the African slave-trade, because I believe it to be the true Union movement. I do not believe that sections whose interests are so different as the Southern and Northern States can ever stand the shocks of fanaticism unless they be equally balanced. I believe that by reopening this trade, and giving us negroes to populate the Territories, the equilibrium of the two sections will be maintained.

It must not, however, be supposed that the South was actuated by ignoble motives in defending slavery; on the contrary, it was carrying out the wishes of the Creator. As the Confederate Vice-President Stephens said at the beginning of the struggle:

The prevailing ideas entertained by him [Jefferson] and most of the leading statesmen at the time of the formation of the old Constitution, were that the enslavement of the African was in violation of the laws of nature; that it was wrong in *principle*, socially, morally and politically. . . . Our new government is founded upon exactly the opposite idea; its foundations are laid, its corner-stone rests upon the great truth, that the negro is not equal to the white man; that slavery—subordination to the superior race—is his natural and normal condition. This, our new government, is the first, in the history of the world, based upon this great physical, philosophical, and moral truth. . . . The substratum of our society is made of the material fitted by nature for it, and by experience we know that it is best, not only for the superior, but for the inferior race, that it should be so. It is, indeed, in conformity with the ordinance of the Creator. It is not for us to inquire into the wisdom of his ordinances, or to question them. For his own purposes he has made one race to differ from another, as he has made "one star to differ from another star in glory." The great objects of humanity are best attained when there is conformity to his laws and decrees, in the formation of governments as well as in all things else. Our Confederacy is founded upon principles in strict conformity with these laws.

The conflict between North and South was a clash between two radically different conceptions of the social organism. The North believed in political equality, the South believed in the essential subordination of the manual laborer, who should be of an "inferior" race. The Northern conception was modern, seeking prosperity for all through mechanical inventions; the Southern conception was antique, seeking prosperity for the few through the labor of slaves. To the Northern mind, slavery and democracy were incompatible, but an ancient Greek or Roman democrat would have agreed with the South. The South belonged to the past, the North to the future.

Economic interests determined the outlook of the different sections of the United States. The important sections, in the decade from 1850 to 1860, were four: the cotton South, the tobacco South, the old North, and the Northwest. The Far West, except in the matter of gold production, had not yet any great importance.

The cotton South was the moving spirit in Southern politics in the years before the Civil War. The demand for cotton, especially in England, grew with amazing rapidity, and was promoted by England's adoption of free trade.[6] The economic relations of the cotton belt were mainly with England by sea: British manufactures were imported in exchange for cotton. There was, consequently, a strong desire for free trade. In 1861, as in 1832, the tariff was assigned by South Carolina as a reason for leaving the Union. On the large cotton plantations, rich planters lived an isolated life, which did not promote the culture characteristic of Virginia in an earlier day. The poor whites followed the lead of the great landowners, and supported slavery both because they believed that the South would be ruined by its abolition, and because it was a pleasure to have inferiors to look down upon. South Carolina, though it produced cotton, was less successful than the Gulf States, and was rendered rather hysterical by the feeling of gradual failure.

Of the northerly group of slave States, Virginia had lost her former importance, largely owing to the exhaustion of tobacco-growing soils. Both Virginia and North Carolina had been drained of population by the westward emigration, and had not had their numbers replenished by immigrants from Europe. Kentucky was in much closer touch with free Ohio than with other slave States; Eastern Tennessee also was more bound to the North than to the South. Missouri, on the border, was pretty evenly divided in its interests. But there was one reason which made all the northerly slave States anxious to preserve slavery, and that was that they were the breeding-grounds for slaves. As the demands of the cotton belt increased,

---

[6] The cotton crop was valued at seventy-eight million dollars in 1850, and two hundred and thirty-six million in 1860. Channing, VI, 207.

the price of slaves was enhanced. The cotton South was unhealthy, and could not produce all the slaves that it needed. As Channing says:

The premium on the production of negro children in the northern tier of the Slave States was great, for each one born was worth in a very short time about two hundred dollars to its master. It is hardly necessary to go farther. One has only to think for another moment to arouse in his mind many unpleasant surmises as to the results of such a condition of affairs, however we may minimize it, upon both master and slave. Moreover, the traffic, great or small, established an economic bond between the northern region of "tolerated slavery," if one may use such a phrase, and the cotton South and thereby strengthened the political and social forces that bound the two sections of the Slave States together.

In the old North, New England prospered by manufactures, and continually advocated a high tariff. Agriculture was becoming unimportant, owing to the growth of the West. New York City lived by commerce, partly with the South, and was therefore more friendly to the South than was the rest of the North. All the big cities of the East contained large numbers of recent immigrants; the Irish preponderated, but the Germans were also numerous, though a larger proportion of them settled in the West.

The Northwest, by its history and economic interests, was more bound to national unity than either the South or the East. Its part in the struggle, which proved decisive, is bound up with the career of Lincoln.

CHAPTER XXV

LINCOLN AND NATIONAL UNITY

THE Northwest, the most rapidly growing region in the United States, and in some ways the most vigorous, had very definite economic interests, which were largely not identical with those of other parts of the Union. The export of wheat to Europe began to be important just before the Civil War. At this time, the disposal of the public lands, homestead acts, and railways, were matters as to which the West depended upon the Federal Government or Eastern capital. The desire to find a field for white labor on new lands caused opposition to the extension of slavery into Kansas and other Territories that bordered on the Northwest.

History, as well as present circumstances, produced a very different feeling in the West from that which existed either in the old North or in the old South: there was less loyalty to one's own State, and more to the Union. While the older States antedated the Federal Government, the Western States had been created by it. The immigrants by whom they were peopled came some from the North, some from the South; a great many were recent arrivals from Europe, seeking freedom and prosperity in a land of promise, but not interested in its local divisions. Moreover the West, instead of looking directly upon the sea, and thence to Europe, was separated from the sea by many hundreds of miles of American roads or rivers. It looked to the Federal Government to encourage the building of roads and to help in keeping them free from Indians, as well as to keep open the navigation of the water routes. The Northwest, more especially, was dependent upon national unity. The roads, and subsequently the railways, as well as the water system of the Great Lakes and the Erie Canal, ran east and west, while the Mississippi and its tributaries ran north and south. Apart from means of transport, the West was reminded of the need of a strong government by the Spaniards in the South, the English in the North, and the Indians wherever they were least wanted. In these circumstances, it is not surprising that patriotism towards the United States acquired in the West far more force than it had in the East while the old loyalty to one's own State still survived.

Abraham Lincoln, through whom the Northwest [1] first found effective political expression, was subject in youth to the external influences that operated upon most of the citizens of Illinois. As we have seen already, he was born in Kentucky in great poverty, but when he was seven years old the family moved to Indiana. "The social condition of Kentucky," say Nicolay and Hay, "had changed considerably from the early pioneer days. Life had assumed a more settled and orderly course. The old barbarous equality of the earlier time was gone; a difference of classes began to be seen. Those who held slaves assumed a distinct social superiority over those who did not. Thomas Lincoln, concluding that Kentucky was no country for a poor man, determined to seek his fortune in Indiana." But no fortune awaited him there, and in 1830, the year in which Abraham came of age, his father decided to move westward once more, this time to Illinois.

Lincoln's early years formed his character. In childhood, "he lived a solitary life in the woods, returning from his lonesome little games to his cheerless home. He never talked of these days to his most intimate friends. . . . Of all those advantages for the cultivation of a young mind and spirit which every home now offers to its children, the books, toys, ingenious games, and daily devotion of parental love, he knew absolutely nothing." Hard work, traditions of Indians, solitude, and the silence of the forest made up his environment; he loved human beings, partly, perhaps, because in the forest they were rare.

In Illinois, Lincoln gradually won his way, not by an obvious brilliancy, but by hard work, and by a character and disposition which made him popular. In 1831 he became a clerk and shop assistant, and took a cargo down the river to New Orleans. In 1832 he took part in the Black Hawk War. This gave him occasion at a later date (1848) to make fun of military glory as a political asset, when General Cass was being extolled for his somewhat obscure services in the War of 1812:

[1] The Northwest of Lincoln's time was the eastern portion of what is now called the Middle West.

"Did you know, Mr. Speaker," he said, "I am a military hero? In the days of the Black Hawk war I fought, bled, and came away. I was not at Stillman's defeat, but I was about as near it as General Cass was to Hull's surrender; and, like him, I saw the place very soon afterwards. It is quite certain I did not break my sword, for I had none to break, but I bent my musket pretty badly on one occasion. If General Cass went in advance of me picking whortleberries, I guess I surpassed him in charges on the wild onions. If he saw any live fighting Indians, it was more than I did, but I had a good many bloody struggles with the mosquitoes; and although I never fainted from loss of blood, I can truly say I was often very hungry. If ever I should conclude to doff whatever our Democratic friends may suppose there is of black-cockade Federalism about me, and thereupon they shall take me up as their candidate for the Presidency, I protest that they shall not make fun of me, as they have of General Cass, by attempting to write me into a military hero."

At the time of these military exploits, Lincoln was a candidate for the State Legislature of Illinois. He stood as a Whig, a supporter of Henry Clay. "I am," he said, "in favor of a national bank; I am in favor of the internal improvement system, and of a high protective tariff. These are my sentiments and political principles." At no period did Lincoln attempt to win votes by ambiguity as to his opinions. The State of Illinois was for Jackson, Lincoln was against him, and on this occasion he was defeated.

Having failed as a politician, he thought of becoming a blacksmith, but, more or less by chance, acquired a share in a grocery store. This came to grief, leaving him loaded with debt. For a while he was a postmaster, and then an official surveyor. We are told that he was popular wherever he went, sometimes for reasons we should not expect, such as that "he was the best judge at a horse-race the county afforded," and that "he could raise a barrel of whisky from the ground and drink from the bung." Whether for these or for other merits, he was at the head of the poll in the election to the Legislature in the year 1834.

His political actions at this time were correct but not remarkable, except on one occasion, that of the "Lincoln-Stone Protest" in 1837. This was his first individual public expression of opinion on slavery, which, after a period of semi-toleration, had been definitely excluded from Illinois by a popular vote in 1832. In spite of this vote, there was fierce hatred of Abolitionists, which extended itself to all New England. It was dangerous to avow oneself an opponent of slavery, and fierce laws prevented the entry of free negroes into Illinois. We have already seen how, at Alton in Illinois, the Rev. Elijah P. Lovejoy was murdered by a mob for his abolitionism in the very year, 1837, in which Lincoln and Stone made their protest. Their protest was against resolutions passed by the State Legislature, unanimously in the Senate, and with only five dissentients in the House, in support of the Southern view as to slavery. Their protest stated their belief "that the institution of slavery is founded on both injustice and bad policy, but that the promulgation of abolition doctrines tends rather to increase than abate its evils." They go on to say that Congress has no power, under the Constitution, to interfere with slavery in the States. It shows how rapidly opinion changed that, in 1837, even so mild a protest should have been an act of high courage. Lincoln shows already at this time the combination, which he always maintained, of dislike of slavery with respect for the Constitution.

In 1841 he began the practice of the Law, which he had been studying for years in his odd moments. As a lawyer he was successful and popular, though his income was never large. "The largest fee he ever got was one of five thousand dollars from the Illinois Central Railway, and he had to bring suit to compel them to pay it." [2] He was elected to Congress in 1846, the only successful Whig in Illinois. He thought the Mexican War unjustifiable, but nevertheless considered that, once begun, it ought to be supported and brought to a successful conclusion. In a speech in Congress he said: "If to say 'the war was unnecessarily and unconstitutionally commenced by the President' be opposing the war, then the Whigs have very generally opposed it. . . . But if when the war had begun, and had become the cause of the country, the giving of our money and our blood, in common with yours, was support of the war, then it is not true that we have always opposed the war." His position was always that a private citizen should not set himself in opposition, except argumentatively, to a democratically elected government. He was one of the few thoroughly consistent believers in democracy that have ever lived. He believed not only, like Jefferson, in government by the

[2] Nicolay and Hay, I, 308.

people, but in *government* by the people; he never lost sight of the need of authority and submission to the law.

His interest in politics was not increased by his term in Congress, and in 1849 he returned to Illinois and his practice at the Bar. "From 1849 to 1854, both inclusive, I practised law more assiduously than ever before," he says. "I was losing interest in politics, when the repeal of the Missouri Compromise aroused me again." It is notable that during the years of his retirement he studied logic and learnt by heart the first six books of Euclid. The effect of this may be perceived in some of his speeches, for instance: "One would state with great confidence that he could convince any sane child that the simpler propositions of Euclid are true; but nevertheless he would fail, utterly, with one who should deny the definitions and axioms. The principles of Jefferson are the definitions and axioms of free society." No doubt Jefferson himself took this view, and was influenced by Euclid, directly or indirectly, in his political thinking. The substitution of the inductive for the deductive method has been a slow and gradual process, in which intellectual advance has sometimes involved political retrogression. Perhaps we may rejoice that Lincoln, in spite of his close contact with human experience, still thought deductively on some points, since by doing so he gained in certainty and persuasive force.

Lincoln's hatred of slavery, deeply controlled as it was, and subordinated to his respect for the Constitution, brought him back into politics when it appeared that there was danger of an extension of slavery. The man who, by the Nebraska bill, had repealed the Missouri Compromise, was Senator Douglas of Illinois. In October, 1854, at the State Agricultural Fair in Springfield, Douglas and Lincoln for the first time met in public debate of the issues which Douglas's action had made acute. Douglas, defending his doctrine of popular sovereignty, said, as was his wont, that he was indifferent as to whether the new Territories voted for or against slavery; he was content to leave the issue to the wishes of the settlers. Lincoln, in a four hours' speech, set forth the doctrines which guided all his subsequent actions:

This declared indifference but, as I must think, covert zeal for the spread of slavery, I cannot but hate. I hate it because of the monstrous injustice of slavery itself. I hate it because it deprives our republican example of its just influence in the world; enables the enemies of free institutions with plausibility to taunt us as hypocrites; causes the real friends of freedom to doubt our sincerity; and especially because it forces so many really good men among ourselves into an open war with the very fundamental principles of civil liberty, criticizing the Declaration of Independence and insisting that there is no right principle of action but self-interest.

.   .   .   .

The doctrine of self-government is right,—absolutely and eternally right,—but it has no just application as here attempted. Or perhaps I should rather say that whether it has such just application, depends upon whether a negro is not, or is, a man. If he is not a man, in that case he who is a man may as a matter of self-government do just what he pleases with him. But if the negro is a man, is it not to that extent a total destruction of self-government to say that he too shall not govern himself? When the white man governs himself, that is self-government; but when he governs himself and also governs another man, that is more than self-government— that is despotism.

One passage is specially suggestive of Lincoln's later speeches:

Little by little, but steadily as man's march to the grave, we have been giving up the old for the new faith. Near eighty years ago we began by declaring that all men are created equal; but now from that beginning we have run down to the other declaration that for some men to enslave others is a "sacred right of self-government." These principles cannot stand together. They are as opposite as God and mammon.

Lincoln's criticisms of Douglas made a great impression in Illinois, and many Democrats joined the "anti-Nebraska" section in opposing any extension of slavery. Douglas, sensitive to the drift of public opinion, began to cool somewhat in his ardor for his Southern friends. When, in 1858, he and Lincoln stood against each other for the Senate, Lincoln drove him to make further concessions which lost him the support of the slave States in 1860, and thus led to the split in the Democratic party which gave the victory to Lincoln in the presidential election. The South had ruled by the help of Northern votes; it was Lincoln's catechizing of Douglas that made a continuation of this process impossible.

The inevitability of violent conflict on the slavery question was evident to Lincoln sooner than to other public men. He did not desire

the conflict; he was willing to leave the South in undisturbed possession of its slaves; but he felt that no peaceful issue would be acceptable to both sides. In 1855 he wrote to a friend: "Experience has
demonstrated, I think, that there is no peaceful extinction of slavery
in prospect for us." He continues: "So far as peaceful, voluntary
emancipation is concerned, the condition of the negro slave in America, scarcely less terrible to the contemplation of a free mind, is now
as fixed and hopeless of change for the better as that of the lost souls
of the finally impenitent. The Autocrat of all the Russias will resign
his crown and proclaim his subjects free republicans, sooner than will
our American masters voluntarily give up their slaves.

"Our political problem now is, 'Can we as a nation continue together *permanently—forever*—half slave, and half free?' The problem is too mighty for me. May God in his mercy superintend the solution." [3]

This was the first statement of the doctrine which he set forth publicly in 1858, in his senatorial contest with Douglas. Speaking of the
Nebraska policy, he said, on accepting nomination:

We are now far into the fifth year since a policy was initiated, with the
avowed object and confident promise of putting an end to slavery agitation.
Under the operation of that policy, that agitation has not only not ceased,
but has constantly augmented. In my opinion it will not cease until a crisis
shall have been reached and passed. "A house divided against itself cannot
stand." I believe this Government cannot endure permanently, half slave
and half free. I do not expect the Union to be dissolved—I do not expect
the house to fall—but I do expect it will cease to be divided. It will become
all one thing or all the other. Either the opponents of slavery will arrest the
further spread of it, and place it where the public mind shall rest in the
belief that it is in course of ultimate extinction; or its advocates will push it
forward till it shall become alike lawful in all the States, old as well as new,
North as well as South.

This doctrine seemed, at that time, astonishing and unwarranted.
In the debates between Lincoln and Douglas which made the most
interesting part of the campaign, Douglas found his most effective
arguments in attacking Lincoln on this point. He assumed that Lincoln was not merely, out of his curiously impersonal sagacity, perceiv-

[3] Nicolay and Hay, I, 391–2.

ing what the future inevitably had in store, but was urging a violent clash as something desirable. He accused Lincoln of stirring up Civil War, a war of North against South, a war of extermination, to be carried on till one or other should be subdued. The general view was that Douglas had the best of it, and even Republicans, in the East, regretted that he was being opposed. He had belatedly changed sides, to some extent, as to the affairs of Kansas, and on this ground, it was thought, he deserved support.

Douglas, though a clever debater, was in a very difficult position. If he satisfied the South, he would lose Illinois; and if he failed to satisfy the South, he could not hope to become President in 1861. Lincoln, in a debate at Freeport, compelled Douglas to make a definite pronouncement on a matter on which he wished to hedge. Among other questions, Lincoln asked: "Can the people of a United States Territory, against the wish of any citizen of the United States, exclude slavery from its limits, prior to the formation of a State constitution?" Douglas replied that they could do so, in spite of the Dred Scott decision; they could do so by "unfriendly legislation," since "slavery cannot exist a day or an hour anywhere, unless it is supported by local police regulations." This doctrine satisfied Illinois, and Douglas won his election to the Senate; but it offended the South, and split the Democratic party.

When Lincoln was nominated by the Republican party in 1860, there were a number of issues not directly connected with slavery. There were river and harbor improvements. There was the tariff; Lincoln had always favored a high tariff, and still did so. Another issue, which governed many votes, was the question of free homesteads. Parades of Lincoln's supporters demanded: "Homesteads for all actual settlers," "Lincoln and free homesteads," "Pass the homestead bill and that will settle the slavery question," "That 160 acres we must have," "The United States is rich enough to give us all a farm." [4] Emancipation was no part of Lincoln's programme in 1860. He knew the feelings of the West and of the Ohio Valley; he knew that the men of Illinois, Indiana, Ohio, and even Kentucky and Eastern Tennessee, would fight to preserve the Union, but would not fight to put down slavery. [5] Even so late as 1864, it is estimated

[4] McMaster, VIII, 460.　　　　　　[5] Cf. Channing, *op. cit.*, VI, 388.

that "not one man in ten in the North cared whether the negro was a slave or a free man." [6]

Opposition to the extension of slavery must not be confused with opposition to slavery where it had always existed. In the Northwest, and wherever the climate seemed suitable for white labor, there was, very naturally, an opposition on the part of labor to negro competition, whether slave or free. And on the part of small farmers there was no wish to be eclipsed by rich planters with hundreds of slaves, who would absorb land otherwise available for homesteads. If there had been *no* moral sentiment against slavery, perhaps the country could have continued peaceably on the lines of the Missouri Compromise. But fear of abolitionism, and resentment at being thought wicked, drove the South into aggression, and this, in turn, drove the North into defence of what it regarded as free territory. Even after Lincoln's election to the Presidency, compromise might have been possible if the South had been willing to return to the condition of affairs before 1850. But the South had the arrogance bred of a long tenure of power, it was maddened by the Abolitionists, and it mistakenly regarded Lincoln as one of them. It seceded, it fired the first shot at Fort Sumter, and Lincoln, as President, undertook the defence of the Union. Slavery had caused the conflict, but slavery was not the question at issue; the question at issue was the right of secession.

As a private citizen, Lincoln disliked slavery, but as a public man he stood always and consistently for the Constitution. During his debates with Douglas in 1858, he stated that, under the Constitution, the South had a right to a fugitive slave law, and he repeated this view in his first inaugural address, in which he also said: "I have no purpose, directly or indirectly, to interfere with the institution of slavery in the States where it exists."

To conduct a great war, through years of difficulty and ill success, resolutely, to a victorious conclusion, and to remain throughout conciliatory and calm and large-minded, is a feat which was accomplished by Lincoln, but, so far as I know, by no other historical character. In spite of secession, he would not have attacked the South if the South had not attacked him.

[6] *Ibid.*, 586.

"The power confided to me," he said, "will be used to hold, occupy, and possess the property and places belonging to the Government, and to collect the duties and imposts; but beyond what may be necessary for these objects, there will be no invasion, no using of force against or among the people anywhere. Where hostility to the United States, in any interior locality, shall be so great and universal as to prevent competent resident citizens from holding the Federal offices, there will be no attempt to force obnoxious strangers among the people for that object."

He goes on to say that he has no objection to a Constitutional Amendment providing that the Federal Government shall not interfere with the domestic institutions of the States. The only thing refused to the South was an extension of slave territory, a thing which the South could scarcely secure by seceding. Looking back, secession seems to have been illogical, unless viewed as a step towards foreign conquest in Latin America. Lincoln's pacific words, however, had no effect, and Civil War was forced upon him.

Although he was making the Union, not slavery, the issue in the war, the momentum of military events brought about abolition. He believed that "gradual, not sudden, emancipation is better for all," [7] and would have preferred a measure involving compensation to owners, and provisions closely similar to those of Jefferson's proposals for extinguishing slavery by degrees. He proposed such measures, first for Delaware, then for all the slave States that had remained loyal; he pointed out that compensation for the slaves in Delaware would cost less than half a day of the war, while for all the border States it would cost no more than eighty-seven days of the war. The border States, however, spurned his offer, preferring slavery to cash. In the District of Columbia, where the Federal Government was unhampered, the slaves were emancipated with compensation early in 1862.

As everyone knows, Lincoln issued a Proclamation on September 22, 1862, declaring that all slaves in States which should be in rebellion on January 1, 1863, should be thenceforth and for ever free; he offered compensation to loyal States which should agree to emancipation, and, after the war, to loyal citizens even in rebel States. He issued this Proclamation for military reasons, as Commander-in-Chief

[7] Nicolay and Hay, V, 209.

of the army. He had just told Greeley, in his famous letter, that he would deal with slavery in whatever way might best further the preservation of the Union, and that "my paramount object in this struggle is to save the Union, and not either to save or to destroy slavery." It was only as a military measure, and as directed against the enemies of the Federal Government, that the Emancipation Proclamation could be justified under the Constitution. There can be no doubt that Lincoln wished the slaves to be free, and was prepared to take any justifiable measure to that end; but he was in no circumstances willing to infringe the Constitution, or to allow the slavery issue to override that of preserving the Union. When he first proposed the Emancipation Proclamation to his Cabinet, Seward suggested the wisdom of waiting for a victory, and Lincoln acquiesced. After the battle of Antietam, he told his Cabinet that the moment had come. He had decided that "if God gave us the victory in the approaching battle, he would consider it an indication of the Divine will, and that it was his duty to move forward in the cause of emancipation. . . . God had decided the question in favor of the slaves." [8]

During the war, anti-slavery feeling was greatly strengthened, and even the Border States became, by a majority, favorable to abolition. When, in January 1865, the thirteenth Amendment (abolishing slavery) was, for the second time, before the House of Representatives, it was supported by one Member from Delaware, four from Maryland, three from West Virginia, four from Kentucky, and seven from Missouri.[9] The ratification of the Amendment, requiring the affirmative vote of twenty-seven States, was completed on December 18, 1865, eight months after Lincoln's assassination.

With Lincoln and the extinction of slavery, the political institutions of the United States reached their full growth; since that time, the most important developments have been economic, not political. Democracy, as embodied in the Declaration of Independence, was his guiding principle, and proved, in the end, sufficiently powerful to bring about the liberation of the negro. But, although Lincoln seemed unconscious of any divergence between his principles and Jefferson's, there was, in fact, a very important change which had come about by

---

[8] Nicolay and Hay, VI, 160. Lincoln never admitted the right of Congress to legislate as to slavery in the States. Compare his action on the Wade-Davis Bill, *ibid.*, IX, 120.
[9] *Ibid.*, X, 84.

imperceptible degrees. The power of the Federal Government as against the several States had become much greater than it was supposed to be at the time when the Constitution was adopted. This was due partly to practical exigencies; Jefferson himself, though an ardent supporter of States' rights, had to stretch the Constitution at the time of the Louisiana Purchase. Partly, also, the Federalist Marshall, safely entrenched in the Supreme Court, was able to give effect to the views of his party long after the ordinary voter had forgotten its existence. But in the main it was the westward expansion of America that strengthened the central government. Local patriotism could not grow up overnight in a new State, and with the spread of railways free mobility made men more conscious of the country as a whole. Jefferson might, perhaps, have regarded the Southern claim to the right of secession as on a level with the claim of the United States to secede from the British Empire. Lincoln could not take this view; to him, and to most of his countrymen, America was one country, for the unity of which they were prepared to fight.

Abraham Lincoln was an embodiment of Western sentiments, Western interests, and Western hopes. In his public capacity, he was almost as impersonal as a natural force, and it was from this quality that he derived his extraordinary power. As a private individual, he hated slavery, but in his public actions he opposed it only in so far as he perceived it to be a cause of disunion. Even after he had come to the conclusion that the Union could not persist half slave and half free, he favored gentle and gradual methods of emancipation, with compensation and with time for readjustment. But against disunion he was uncompromising. When the South seceded, a powerful section of Northern opinion favored peaceful acquiescence, but Lincoln never hesitated as to the necessity of asserting Federal authority. Like Mazzini and like Bismarck, he stood for national unity, and like most nationalists he found his justification in the association of his nation with a moral idea. But unlike most others, he was justified in making this association. America *had* been "dedicated to the proposition that all men are created equal." Slavery had made this seem a mockery; in the Civil War it became again a creative belief, molding facts more nearly into conformity with an ideal, and restoring to America its self-respect and the respect of other nations.

CHAPTER XXVI

COMPETITIVE CAPITALISM

WHILE idealists were killing each other in the Civil War, practical
men, from the highest to the lowest, were devoting themselves to
money-making. The Homestead Act, vetoed as subversive by President Buchanan in 1860, was passed in a more drastic form in 1862.
By this measure, any American, or any foreigner expressing his intention of becoming naturalized, could obtain 160 acres of public land
for nothing. In order to increase the amount of attractive public land
available, the Federal Administration, in the middle of the Civil War,
started a war against the Indians, to deprive them of the lands west
of the Mississippi which had been assigned to them by Jackson. There
was a great exodus to the new homesteads, not only from eastern
farms, but also from cities and factories. To compensate for the loss
of American labor, an Act was passed enabling employers to import
indentured labor from Europe. Meanwhile the war was financed
partly by loans, partly by a protective tariff, which rose from an average of 19 per cent to an average of 47 per cent during the war years.[1]

The first trans-continental railway, the Union Pacific from Omaha
westward and Central Pacific from California eastward, was authorized in 1862 by Congress, which gave to the two railway companies
about twenty-two million acres of land and government bonds amounting to over twenty-seven million dollars.[2] Various other railways received large grants of land or bonds.

The great fortunes of subsequent times owed their origin to the

---

[1] Beard, *Rise of American Civilization*, Vol. II, p. 108.
[2] Bogart, *Economic History of the American People*, p. 634.

conditions which existed during the Civil War, which afforded exceptional opportunities for corruption. Pierpont Morgan, for example, then a young man of twenty-four, bought, in combination with two other men, five thousand carbines, condemned as old and dangerous, from the Government in the East for three and a half dollars each, and sold them to the troops on the Mississippi for twenty-two dollars each. The matter was investigated by a Congressional Committee and (for the Secretary of War) by a commission of two, one of whom was Robert Owen's son, Robert Dale Owen. Although the facts were established, Morgan and his friends got their money.[3]

The success of the Republican party in 1860 brought about, not only the extinction of slavery, but also the victory of plutocracy. Until that time, the West had been allied with the South in favor of agriculture and free trade. But Southern desire for the extension of slavery and opposition to free homesteads caused the Northwest to ally itself with the East, and to acquiesce in a Hamiltonian policy as regards tariff and banking in return for a liberal policy in the matter of Western land. And the war, as was to be expected, brought great profit to the farmers: all agricultural prices rose, and wheat, at one time, was worth two and a half dollars a bushel. In spite of these high prices, the export of wheat, especially to England, increased with extraordinary rapidity, from seventeen million bushels in 1860 to fifty-eight million in 1863. No wonder the farmers forgot their Jacksonian allegiance, the more so as the new policy was bringing freedom to the oppressed negro. Never were virtue and self-interest so nicely united.

It was not only in agriculture that new natural sources of wealth were made available during the Civil War. The first flowing oil-well was discovered in Pennsylvania in 1861, and in the three years 1862–5 three hundred million gallons of oil were produced. Any man who had land in the Oil Regions, or could induce an ignorant farmer to part with land, might hope to become a millionaire overnight, if he happened to have luck. Just before the beginning of the war, gold in large quantities was found in Colorado and Nevada. The Lake Superior iron ores, the most profitable in the world, began to be worked at this period. Most of the immense mineral wealth of the West became known in the sixties.

The success of the system of national economy inaugurated by the

[3] Myers, *History of the Great American Fortunes*, III, 170–5.

Republican party in 1861 depended upon an inlet and an outlet: cheap European labor coming in at the East, and virgin land waiting for development in the West. Immigrant labor without Western land would have compelled the American wage-earner to lower his standard of comfort to that of the Old World; Western land without immigrant labor would have compelled Eastern employers to raise wages enormously, and would have made the rapid growth of American industrialism impossible. The system was thus not self-contained, but could endure only so long as the supply of surplus labor and surplus land continued. The surplus land came to an end first, and with its ending an agitation gathered strength which, in no long time, led to a stringent restriction of immigration. Without cheap labor and cheap land, the causes of the old prosperity were gone; this is the larger cause of the depression that began in 1929. An economic system which is self-contained cannot afford such lack of regulation as had accompanied the increase of wealth in America; but the mental habits generated during a hundred and fifty years of progress made it difficult to assimilate the ideas required by an epoch in which pioneering was at an end.

The gospel of America, as of industrial England, was competition. But whereas England, through the adoption of free trade, had proclaimed the doctrine in an international form, America, whose industries were still in their infancy, confined capitalistic competition, to a continually increasing extent, within national limits by means of the tariff. Cheap labor from Europe was admitted, but cheap goods from Europe, after the alliance of West and East in the Republican party, were taxed to an extent which gradually became prohibitive. It might have been thought that American labor would have objected to this one-sided form of competition, but American labor was intent on acquiring a homestead, and was content to leave wage-earning to foreigners. In the scramble for wealth that took place among those who were not fighting, the prizes were such as no one had ever won before, and even for those who stood outside the scramble, there were consolation prizes which were not to be despised: 160 acres of rich land in a region where the railways advanced at the rate of a mile a day, where towns grew up in a month, and where wheat could be grown with incredibly little labor for the continually expanding markets of Europe and America.

What was happening did not present itself to contemporaries as a scramble for wealth. The resources of the country were felt to be crying out for development, and a certain haste in responding to the cry was thought to be a proper homage to the great god Competition. A competitive spirit was inculcated in school, where boys were taught to recite:

> Oh where's the town, go far and near,
> That does not find a rival here,
> Oh where's the boy but three feet high
> Who's made improvement more than I?
> These thoughts inspire my youthful mind
> To be the greatest of mankind;
> Great, not like Caesar, stained with blood;
> But, like Washington, great in good.

Washington (according to Charles A. Beard) died the richest man in his country. Several of those who, during the Civil War, avoided becoming "stained with blood," succeeded, in this respect, in becoming "great like Washington."

The greatest fortunes in America, from the time of the Civil War onwards, arose out of railways, oil, and steel, which ultimately mingled in one great ocean of finance. Railways, oil, and steel all passed from an era of intense competition to one of more or less complete consolidation. During the Civil War, and for some time afterwards, railways were the most important of the three; and in the railway world, the greatest name was that of Commodore Vanderbilt.

Commodore Vanderbilt was already an old man of 69 when the war led him to take an interest in railways; until then, his triumphs had been on the water. When he died, in 1877, he was worth $105,000,000. He had begun in the days of sailing ships, building and owning schooners for the coasting trade. When steamers came, he sold his schooners and became captain of a steamer. By the year 1829, he had managed to save $30,000, which he invested in steamboats built by himself. As a competitor, he was ruthless; sometimes he ruined his rivals by cutting rates, sometimes he extorted large sums as the price of abstention from competition. For example: two nominally competing steamship lines (the public demanded the appearance of competition) were paid, between them, $900,000 a year for carrying the mails from New York to California, but out of this sum Vanderbilt extorted first $480,000, and then $612,000, on condition of not running his ships to California. Seeing that running ships was profitable, and not running them was even more so, it is no wonder that his fortune increased.

The war made steamships unprofitable, unless they could be sold to the Government. For this, however, an opportunity soon presented itself. In 1862, it was decided to send a military expedition by sea to New Orleans, and Vanderbilt was commissioned to purchase the ships. His agent exacted a commission before he would buy, but when he had his commission he would agree to exorbitant prices, sometimes for vessels built for the lakes and unsuitable for the open sea. Thus the sale of ships afforded a sound profit to Vanderbilt, and his farewell to the sea was not entirely melancholy.

The first of his railway operations, which was typical of many others, was concerned with a small suburban line, the New York and Harlem Railroad. In 1862, when the stock was selling at $9 a share, he began buying. After he had acquired control, the price suddenly rose to $50 a share. The reason was that he had obtained from the New York City Common Council, by corrupt means, permission to run a street railway from the terminus of his line all through the heart of the city. But he had a competitor, a man named Law, with whom he had formerly had battles concerning steamships. While Vanderbilt owned the City Common Council, Law owned the New York State Legislature, and the City Common Council discovered that this body alone had the legal right to grant the permission which Vanderbilt was thought to have obtained. Law thought that Vanderbilt was defeated, and the City Councillors thought so likewise. They saw no reason for being involved in his misfortune, and they foresaw that the stock of the railway would fall when the truth came out. The City Fathers therefore contracted to "sell short," that is to say, they undertook, at a specified future date, to sell Harlem stock to certain purchasers at the price of $50 or so, which was its price at the moment. They reckoned that, when the time came, Vanderbilt's defeat would have become known, and they would be able to buy the stock very cheap for the purpose of selling it dear. When the time came, however, it was found that Vanderbilt had discovered the plot, and owned so much that not enough could be obtained to enable the aldermen to fulfil their contracts. They therefore had to buy from him at what ever price he chose to ask; in fact, he sold at $179 a share. In a week, so his biographer states, he made a million dollars out of the Common Council, and other millions from others.

It cannot be denied that this was competition, but it was not quite what Cobden had in mind, or what American schoolboys were supposed to be taught to admire. It was not, however, the last time that Vanderbilt was engaged in competition for the purchase of legislatures, judges, and other commodities of that description. Indeed, so well had his schemes worked in the case of the New York and Harlem Railroad that he repeated them almost exactly with the New York and Hudson River Railroad. This time, however, the victims were not the City Common Council but the State Legislators at Albany. "We busted the whole Legislature," he boasted, "and scores of the honorable members had to go home without paying their board bills."

It would be unjust to the Commodore to treat him as merely a bold buccaneer. The New York Central, to which he next turned his attention, became a permanent possession of himself and his heirs, and a much more efficient railway than it had been before his day. In the process he made, of course, many millions by the usual tricks of finance, but incidentally he served public interests as well as his own.

Vanderbilt's next campaign is the classic model of competition between great capitalists. The battle-ground was the Erie Railroad, and his opponents were three men as astute as himself: Drew, Fisk, and Gould. In his contests with these three, for the first time, he failed of complete success.

The Erie battle occurred in 1868, when the Tweed ring were in control of politics both in the City and in the State of New York. Corruption had been prevalent in New York ever since the days of Hamilton, but was never so shameless as it was under Tweed. The city was full of immigrants, ignorant of America, not infrequently ignorant of the English language. Tammany had perfected the art of appealing to these men, who were not accustomed to democracy and by no means proof against demagogy. The well-to-do throughout the country were so busy getting rich that they had no time for combating professional politicians. When I first visited America in 1896, I asked a prosperous Philadelphia Quaker why he did nothing to purify the government of his native city. He replied that, at one period, he had taken an interest in reform movements, but he now found that, in the time he could make more money in business than he could save in taxes, so "of course" he had given up bothering about reform. This attitude, still fairly common in 1896, was typical in 1868. Immensely valuable rights were in the gift of the City and State governments, and professional politicians specialized in the art of inducing the voters to part with these rights for nothing. What was paid for the rights went to the politicians, not to the public. State judges, being elected, were creatures of the boss; while he lasted, therefore, he was above the law, and so were those whom he favored. This system reached its highest pitch of perfection just after the Civil War, and had much to do with the swaying fortunes of the Erie battle.

Drew, Fisk, and Gould are an interesting trio. Drew was an old man, a contemporary of Vanderbilt, with whom he had had many previous dealings when they were both steamboat captains, a position to which, by dubious means, he had risen after being first a cattle-drover, then, for a while, an employee in a circus, and then an inn-keeper. He was not, like Vanderbilt, bold and masterful, but timid and sneaking. Whenever one of his schemes went wrong, he would take to his bed and pretend to be ill. He was a man of great piety, and spent a large sum out of his ill-gotten gains in founding a theological seminary, apparently in the hope of taking the Lord into partnership. Gould was a young man, born in 1836. He concealed the lower part of his face behind a bushy beard. He was quiet and secret, capable, at a crisis, of snatching victory from defeat by skilful treachery to his confederates. Fisk, who was Gould's contemporary, was a gay fellow, a plausible talker, and a great ladies' man; he had begun as a peddler, but had subsequently risen, like Drew, to a post in an itinerant circus. Both Gould and Fisk had been poor, and owed their first great successes to Drew. In the end, Fisk was killed by a rival for the favors of one of his many ladies, while Gould succeeded in bankrupting Drew; but in their first struggles with Vanderbilt all three worked together in harmony.

The Erie Railroad had been in Drew's hands since 1857. He did nothing to keep up the permanent way or the rolling stock; in fact, when ordered to supply new steel rails, he merely turned over the old iron rails, with the result that accidents were frequent and serious.

He treated the property solely as a means of stock-exchange manipulation. He would set going rumors which would make the stock rise or fall as suited his interests, and by these means, in the course of nine years, he accumulated a very large fortune.

Vanderbilt's connection with the Erie Railroad begins in 1866, in which year, by the usual methods, he acquired control and prepared to put in directors of his own in place of Drew and his puppets. But for once he appears to have yielded to sentiment. Drew went to him and appealed to their old companionship during the early days of struggle, and reminded him that he (Drew) had called one of his sons after him: he was, he said, an old man, to whom failure now would be final; moreover, he was quite willing to carry out Vanderbilt's policies loyally and wholeheartedly. Such was his skill in pathos that the Commodore agreed to leave him as a director of the railroad. He agreed also when Drew recommended two young men who, he said, could be depended upon to obey Vanderbilt's orders; the two young men were Gould and Fisk. For a time, all three gave satisfaction to their employer, and he believed himself secure.

It was not long, however, before he was violently disillusioned. He set to work to corner Erie stock, and for that purpose bought all that came into the market. Drew, Fisk, and Gould, knowing his intentions, issued to themselves a mass of Erie bonds, which they had perhaps a legal right to do. They then bought a printing press, and proceeded, quite illegally, to convert the bonds into shares. These shares they sold to Vanderbilt's brokers, who bought them unsuspectingly as fast as they were issued. Naturally, the trick they had played was soon discovered, and Vanderbilt, filled with fury, set to work to wreak vengeance on the traitors. There was in New York a judge named Barnard, who was in the habit of taking orders from him, and from this worthy man he obtained an injunction prohibiting the issue of any more shares. The trio had a great number on hand which they were intending to issue, but they bowed to the majesty of the law. Drew and Gould put the unissued shares in a bag, and gave them to the office-boy to take away and lock up in a safe. To the boy's horror, as he was leaving the office he was set upon by a big man whom he did not know, and who robbed him of the precious bag; but Drew merely told him mildly to be more careful next time, for in fact the big man was Fisk. There were 100,000 new shares in the bag; they were sold immediately, the money was converted into cash, and with six or seven million dollars in currency the three men fled across the river to Jersey City, where they were no longer within the jurisdiction of Judge Barnard.[4] They were only just in time; two other directors were caught and imprisoned.

Vanderbilt had lost many millions, and felt the double rage of a clever man outwitted and a masterful man disobeyed. But, given time, the legal position of the trio was by no means desperate. True, they had disobeyed Judge Barnard's injunction; but he was not the only judge in New York State. Judge Gilbert had issued a contrary injunction, "restraining all the parties to all the other suits from further proceedings, and from doing any acts in furtherance of said conspiracy;—in one paragraph ordering the Erie directors . . . to continue in the discharge of their duties, in direct defiance of the injunction of one judge, and in the next, with an equal disregard of another judge—(for Barnard was not Vanderbilt's only judicial friend)—forbidding the directors to desist from converting bonds into stock." [5] The directors were thus able to plead that they were in the unfortunate position of being compelled to disobey the law, since one judge forbade what another commanded. Moreover, for men with six or seven millions in cash, the Legislature at Albany might prove tractable. They therefore set about to obtain a law regularizing their conversions of bonds into shares. There was a slight difficulty, because they were liable to arrest in New York State, but they decided to run the risk, and Gould went to Albany with $500,00 in cash. He was arrested but was released on bail, and set to work to purchase the Legislature. Vanderbilt tried to outbid him, but in vain: one representative of the Sovereign People, for example, after accepting $75,000 from Vanderbilt, obtained $100,000 from Gould, and voted for him. The outcome was that the bill legalizing the issue of stock was duly passed.

In this, as in all similar contests, each side tried to enlist public sympathy, either by blackening the character of the other side, or by alleging that it was endeavoring to secure a monopoly and deprive the public of the blessings of competition. Charles Francis Adams

[4] The whole story of the Erie battle is admirably told by Charles Francis Adams, grandson and great-grandson of Presidents, in his "A Chapter of Erie," published in the North American Review of July 1869, and reprinted by the Yale University Press in 1929, in a volume called High Finance in the Sixties.

[5] High Finance in the Sixties, pp. 47–8.

describes the tactics of the absconding directors in winning public opinion:

The moment they felt themselves settled at Jersey City they had gone to work to excite a popular sympathy in their own behalf. The cry of monopoly was a sure card in their hands. They cared no more for the actual welfare of commerce involved in railroad competition than they did for the real interests of the Erie Railway; but they judged truly that there was no limit to the extent to which the public might be imposed upon. An active competition with the Vanderbilt roads, by land and water, was inaugurated; fares and freights on the Erie were reduced on an average by one-third; sounding proclamations were issued; "interviewers" from the press returned rejoicing from Taylor's Hotel to New York City, and the Jersey shore quaked under the clatter of this Chinese battle. The influence of these tactics made itself felt at once. By the middle of March memorials against monopoly began to flow in at Albany.[6]

There was, of course, an investigation into the charges of bribery at Albany, at which Gould himself was obliged to give evidence, but nothing came of it.

If the official reports of investigating committees are to be believed, Mr. Gould at about this time underwent a curious psychological metamorphosis, and suddenly became the veriest simpleton in money matters that ever fell into the hands of happy sharpers. Cunning lobby members had but to pretend to an influence over legislative minds, which everyone knew they did not possess, to draw unlimited amounts from this verdant habitué of Wall Street. It seemed strange that he could have lived so long and learnt so little. He dealt in large sums. He gave to one man, in whom he said "he did not take much stock," the sum of $5,000, "just to smooth him over." This man had just before received $5,000 of Erie money from another agent of the company. It would, therefore, be interesting to know what sums Mr. Gould paid to those individuals in whom he did "take much stock." Another individual is reported to have received $100,000 from one side, "to influence legislation," and to have subsequently received $70,000 from the other side to disappear with the money; which he accordingly did, and thereafter became a gentleman of elegant leisure. One senator was openly charged in the columns of the press with receiving a bribe of $20,000 from one side, and a second bribe of $15,000 from the other; but Mr. Gould's foggy mental condition only enabled him to be "perfectly astounded" at the action of this senator, though he knew noth-

[6] *High Finance in the Sixties*, p. 67.

ing of any such transactions. Other senators were blessed with a sudden accession of wealth, but in no case was there any jot or tittle of proof of bribery. Mr. Gould's rooms at the Delavan House overflowed with a joyous company, and his checks were numerous and heavy; but why he signed them, or what became of them, he seemed to know less than any man in Albany. This strange and expensive hallucination lasted until about the middle of April, when Mr. Gould was happily restored to his normal condition of a shrewd, acute, energetic man of business; nor is it known that he has since experienced any relapse into financial idiocy.[7]

The situation was still, however, in some ways uncomfortable for the fugitives in Jersey City. They were liable to arrest if they returned to New York, except on Sundays, when sabbatarianism forbade the making of arrests. Gangs of roughs, whom Drew believed to be in Vanderbilt's employ, assembled round his hotel, and made him afraid of being kidnapped. But New Jersey felt itself honored by the presence of three such great men, with such considerable stores of cash; accordingly the State militia were placed at their service, and artillery was mounted at the ferries. Drew, nevertheless, still felt nervous, and perceived that Gould and Fisk distrusted him; in fact, they spied upon his correspondence, and saw his telegrams before he did. He therefore opened negotiations with Vanderbilt, and the others followed suit. At last a treaty of peace was arranged, by which Vanderbilt recovered some, but not all, of his losses, Drew obtained cash, while Fisk and Gould obtained undisputed control of the Erie Railroad. They secured the services of Boss Tweed as a fellow director and continued to enrich themselves, but no longer by pitched battles with Vanderbilt. Presently, as the result of a reform agitation, Boss Tweed was sent to prison. But Gould marched on from victory to victory, and when he died in 1892 the plutocracy, from Pierpont Morgan downwards, attended his impressive funeral.

As for the Commodore, he prospered more than Gould; the last years of his life were the most successful. His wife died when he was seventy-four, but he married again the next year. His final illness began when he was eighty-two, and outlasted two doctors, who died during its eight months' duration. But even his immense strength failed at last,

[7] *High Finance in the Sixties*, p. 72.

> nor did he 'scape
> By all his engines, but was headlong sent
> With his industrious crew to build in Hell.

In the 'sixties and early 'seventies, the popular demand for railways in the West was clamorous. Farmers, towns, and cities would take shares in a projected line; States and the Federal Government would give it huge grants of land, and vast sums of public money would be voted to facilitate construction. The financiers who controlled a railway had various devices for transferring the money of the small shareholders into their own pockets. One of the favorite schemes was to form a construction company for the actual work. The shares of the construction company would all be held by the directors of the railway and their friends. As directors of the railway company, they would make extravagant contracts with the construction company, which would grow rich as the railway approached bankruptcy. Then they would come to the Federal Government or the States governments, and explain that the work had proved more costly than was expected; the eager populations, which thirsted for the railway as men thirst for water in the desert, would vote fresh subsidies, which the construction companies would again absorb. By the time the line was finished, it would be on the verge of bankruptcy. A financial crisis would give the excuse, and it would be put into the hands of a receiver, thus finally transferring all the savings of the small men into the pocket of some magnate. Most American railways have been bankrupt at some time or another, but this is not a proof of incompetent management—quite the contrary, in fact.

The best example of this process was in connection with the first trans-continental railway, authorized, as we saw, in 1862. Construction westward from Omaha and eastward from California was pushed on rapidly, and in 1869 the line was completed. The eastern portion of the work had been done by a construction company called the Crédit Mobilier Company of America. There were allegations of bribery, and the matter was investigated by Congressional Committees, which decided that the line had cost fifty million dollars to construct, and that the Crédit Mobilier had charged $93,546,287.28. The difference, forty-three and a half million dollars, represented the plunder of the railway and ultimately of the public. In the case of the Central Pacific, the "profit" was even more exorbitant: for work costing fifty-eight million dollars, a construction company was paid a hundred and twenty million. In the attendant bribery many prominent politicians were involved, including one who subsequently became President and another who became Republican candidate for the Presidency.

From the wage-earners' point of view, the system established by the plutocrats was far from pleasant. In spite of democracy, in spite of protection, in spite of the rapidly increasing wealth of the country, hours were long, and wages, though better than in Europe, were infinitesimal as compared with the rewards of financial magnates. In 1872, when Commodore Vanderbilt was rapidly approaching his hundredth million, he lowered the wages of drivers and conductors on the surface line on Fourth Avenue from $2.25 a day to $2, and that for a fifteen-hour day. In steel, until well into the present century, the men who attended to the blast furnaces had to work twelve hours a day, and once a fortnight, when they changed from day to night work, they had to work for twenty-four hours on end. Trade unions were more difficult to establish than in England, because of the mixture of races; among the unskilled, they were almost nonexistent before 1900. Employers were able to refuse to treat with unions, and in some cases—for instance, Carnegie after the strike of 1892—they refused altogether to employ union men. In cotton mills, especially in the South, child labor was very prevalent, and attempts to prevent it were, until lately, declared unconstitutional by the Supreme Court. Child labor in the South, says Bogart, "brought up economic problems which were becoming burning questions in New England in the middle of the nineteenth century and in old England at the beginning." [8]

Nevertheless, wage-earners preferred America to Europe. Though hours were long, wages compared favorably with what the same men had earned before they emigrated. Democracy, with all its limitations, gave them a feeling of self-respect; they had not the sense of belonging to an inferior caste. And there was always hope. Many millionaires had begun as wage-earners. By saving a little, making a lucky investment of a few dollars, attracting the favorable notice

[8] Bogart, *op. cit.*, p. 581.

of the employer, a man might make the first step towards gigantic wealth. Many men in steel preferred the seven-day week and the twelve-hour day to the six-day week and the eight-hour day at lower wages, not because the lower wages would have meant actual hardship, but because they would have meant less opportunity to save and so to rise. The creed of competition and self-help existed throughout all classes, not only among those who profited by it. Trade unionism was weak, Socialism was practically non-existent. Some lived well on success, others lived meagrely on hope, but none wished to curtail the opportunity for spectacular success.

As the heroic age of railway construction came to an end, the railway magnates became less like buccaneers and more like aristocratic landowners; in about twenty years they passed from the stage of the Norman barons of 1066 to that of the House of Lords of the present day. Their power was immense. They owned much of the land, and except by their help no one could get his produce to market. The tyranny of the railways over the farmer is well portrayed in Norris's story, *The Octopus*. Naturally the farmers tried to hit back by political means. The Jeffersonian and Jacksonian tradition of agricultural radicalism revived, but memories of the Civil War made co-operation with the South difficult. Moreover, the old individualist democracy was powerless against a giant organization like a modern railway. The only remedy, according to the old order of ideas, was competition. But where there was (as at first in the West) scarcely enough traffic for one railway, it would be ridiculous waste to build another; and where there were two apparently competing railways, they usually had agreements, since otherwise both would have been ruined. The agrarians were furious whenever they discovered evidence of railway pools. The States made innumerable laws to restrict the powers of railway companies, and the Federal Legislature made some. The object was to compel them to compete; but when two cocks won't fight, there is nothing to be done.

The Radical who believes in competition is doomed to defeat in any contest with modern corporations. Their power is analogous to that of armies, and to leave them in private hands is just as disastrous as it is to leave armies in private hands. The large-scale economic organizations of modern times are an inevitable outcome of modern technique, and technique tends increasingly to make competition wasteful. The solution, for those who do not wish to be oppressed, lies in public ownership of the organizations that give economic power. For so long as this power is in private hands, the apparent equality conferred by political democracy is little better than a sham.

CHAPTER XXVII

THE APPROACH TO MONOPOLY IN AMERICA

A. OIL

AMERICANS in 1870 attributed a great part of their prosperity to free competition. But technical forces were at work which, against the will of almost all the inhabitants of the United States, transformed the economic system from one in which many small firms competed to one in which, in a number of important industries, one or two vast corporations were in almost complete control. The very men who were instrumental in bringing about this change accepted the prevalent competitive philosophy, and achieved their success by following its maxims. To the dismay of those who were not successful, the prevailing philosophy turned out to be self-defeating: the competitors competed until only one survived, and that one could then no longer use competition as its watchword. This happened in many industries, but I shall concentrate attention upon the most important, oil and steel. And of these two oil comes first in point of time.

Two men have been supreme in creating the modern world: Rockefeller and Bismarck. One in economics, the other in politics, refuted the liberal dream of universal happiness through individual competition, substituting monopoly and the corporate state, or at least movements towards them. Rockefeller is important, not through his ideas, which were those of his contemporaries, but through his purely practical grasp of the type of organization that would enable him to grow rich. Technique, working through him, produced a social revolution; but it cannot be said that he intended the social consequences of his actions.

Rockefeller was born on a farm in 1839, of a shiftless father and a pious mother.[1] His father kept his occupation secret: he was, in fact, an itinerant pill-doctor. He would arrive in some village or small town, and put up a sign: "Dr. William A. Rockefeller, the Celebrated

---

[1] On Rockefeller's parents, see John T. Flynn, *God's Gold*.

Cancer Specialist, Here for One Day Only. All cases of Cancer Cured unless too far gone and then they can be greatly benefited." During his long absences, his wife had to live on credit at the village shop, but whenever he returned he brought enough money to pay debts and to give each of his children a five-dollar piece. He was a big, jolly, vigorous man, who lived at least to the age of 96. (The date of his death is uncertain.) He was often in trouble with the police, and on one occasion the farm was sold for debt; owing to his escapades, the family had to make frequent moves. He was very proud of his shrewdness, and would boast of his skill in outwitting people. "He trained me in practical ways," said his son John. "He was engaged in different enterprises and he used to tell me about these things and he taught me the principles and methods of business." The father's own description of his teaching the "principles"of business is simpler: "I cheat my boys every chance I get. I want to make 'em sharp. I trade with the boys and skin 'em and I just beat 'em every time I can. I want to make 'em sharp."

John's mother was, in most ways, the opposite of his father. Her husband was vagrant, unreliable, unfaithful, viewed with disfavor by the neighbors; during his long absences, she had to do the work herself, in spite of a growing family; she had to struggle to make ends meet, and to preserve respectability in spite of all her husband did or was thought to do. Before marriage she had been full of merriment, but she became sad and turned increasingly to piety. She disapproved strongly of alcohol, and came to abhor all merry-making.

John, a careful, serious, shy boy, loved his mother and imbibed her virtues. He became deeply religious, a teetotaller, and a non-smoker; he never used profane language, however great the provocation. He is described as being, throughout his life, "low-voiced, soft-footed, humble." It may be doubted whether, in all his ninety-five years, he has ever done anything that would have been disapproved of in his Sunday School. When, in later life, he taught a Bible class, he would say: "Don't be a good fellow. I love my fellow-man and I take a great interest in him. But don't be convivial. Be moderate. Be very moderate. Don't let good fellowship get the least hold on you. If you do, you are lost, not only you but your progeny, your family for generations to come. Now I can't be a good fellow. I haven't taken my first drink yet."

Poverty, frequent moves, his mother's unhappiness, and the neighbors' hostility must have made a deep impression upon him as a child. Although he could be bold in business, he always feared the crowd, and sought secrecy instinctively, even when it served no purpose. The timid man who wants power is a very definite type. Louis XI, Charles V, and Philip II are instances: pious, cunning, unscrupulous, industrious, and retiring. But power, for Rockefeller, could only be obtained through money.

Two facts will illustrate his love of money in early youth. When a group photograph of all the boys in his school was taken, he and his brother remained outside, because their clothes were so shabby. Nevertheless, a year or so before this, at a time when he was only ten years old, he heard that a neighboring farmer wanted fifty dollars, for which he was prepared to pay 7 per cent interest. John had the money saved, and lent it, after inquiring what "interest" meant. "From that time onward," he said later, "I determined to make money work for me."

In spite of this acquisitive passion, he began giving to charitable objects as soon as he began earning. He got his first job in 1855, when he was sixteen; his salary was three and a half dollars a week. Out of this meagre sum, he gave away 10 per cent. And in proportion as he grew richer, his gifts grew larger.

There can be no doubt that he genuinely believes himself to be a virtuous man. The actions for which he has been criticized are not such as he was warned against in his youth, nor have they made him unpopular with Baptist ministers. He has not disobeyed the teaching of those whose moral authority he respects, and therefore his conscience is at rest. Speaking to his Bible class, he said:

"It is wrong to assume that men of immense wealth are always happy. If a man lives his life to himself and has no regard for humanity he will be the most miserable man on earth. All the money he can get will not help him to forget his discontent. . . . The kind of man I like is one that lives for his fellows—the one that lives in the open, contented with his lot and trying to bestow all the good he can on humanity."

He showed Christian forbearance under criticism. "Sometimes things are said of me that are cruel and they hurt, but I am never a pessimist. I believe in man and the brotherhood of men and I am confident that everything will come out for the good of all in the end." On another occasion he said: "They will know me better when I'm dead. There has been nothing in my life that will not bear the utmost scrutiny. . . . What advantages had I that every other poor boy did not possess?" And of Theodore Roosevelt, who was trying to use the "big stick" against him, he said: "A man so busy cannot always be right. We are all bound to make mistakes at times. I think he does not always grasp every side of a question. Sometimes I wish that he might be more fair. I do not mean that he is consciously unjust. He is often misinformed."

What he said, what he thought, and what he felt, came from his mother, but what he did came from his father, with the addition of a great caution generated by early unpleasantnesses. And it is what he did that makes him important.

Up to the end of the year 1871, Rockefeller's career was in no way different from that of other self-made men who have risen by industry and shrewdness. Throughout the Civil War he worked hard as a Produce and Commission Merchant, and at the end found himself moderately rich. He first invested in oil in 1862, and after the war he concentrated on refining oil, taking as a partner, in 1867, Flagler, who remained prominent in Standard Oil all his life. In 1870 they incorporated the Standard Oil Company, with a capital of one million dollars, of which Rockefeller held $266,700. They did well, but both thought they could do even better. Whether by their initiative or by that of other men, they entered into a combination with certain refiners in Philadelphia, Pittsburgh, and New York to form a company called the "South Improvement Company." The methods of this company first showed the distinctive abilities of Rockefeller and Flagler.

The most important problem for refiners was the problem of transport. Pipe lines, in those days, only conveyed oil to the nearest railway; long-distance pipes had not yet been constructed. The railways therefore controlled transport. The firms which could get their oil carried most cheaply on the railways had thus a great advantage. The South Improvement Company, in January, 1872, obtained contracts from the New York Central, the Erie Railroad, the Pennsylvania Railroad, and two other railroads, by which their oil was carried at a lower rate than that of outside firms. Not only so, but the extra that was paid by the outside firms was to go, not to the railways, but to the

South Improvement Company. And incidentally, in obtaining this payment, the South Improvement Company was to know exactly how much oil its various rivals shipped to and from all points on any of these five railways.

To give an illustration: the open rate on crude oil from the Oil Regions to New York was $2.56, but the South Improvement Company paid only $1.06. The lowering of the price to it was a "rebate." But the extra $1.50 which competitors paid, and which it received, was a "drawback." It had thus a double advantage over all other refiners.

Four railroad presidents made contracts of this nature with the South Improvement Company: William H. Vanderbilt (son of the Commodore) for the New York Central; Jay Gould for the Erie; Tom Scott for the Pennsylvania; General G. B. McClellan for the Lake Shore and Michigan Southern. It was verbally agreed that all refiners should be invited to come into the combine; until they had this promise the railways held off. But the promise was not embodied in the contracts,[2] and little attempt was made to carry it out.

The utmost secrecy was observed, and before entering into negotiations with anyone the person concerned was made to sign a pledge that he would reveal nothing, whether or not he came to terms.

As soon as he had the contracts with the railways, Rockefeller set to work on the other refiners in Cleveland, offering to buy them at his own valuation. Some, who had hitherto been successful, were at first indignant at what seemed to them effrontery. But Rockefeller, very gently, very kindly, and as if deeply concerned for their welfare, would strongly advise them to sell. "Take Standard Oil stock and your family will never know want," he would say; and if that argument failed, he would add, mysteriously: "I have ways of making money you know nothing about." One by one they yielded, in a kind of fascinated terror: "We felt a pressure brought to bear on our minds," as one of them expressed it. Another, named Hanna, who had been doing well, told Rockefeller that he had decided to refuse. "Rockefeller raised his eyebrows and shrugged his shoulders as if all were up with Hanna's firm."[3] "You will stand alone," he said, "your firm can never make any more money in Cleveland. No use trying to

[2] The contract with the Pennsylvania Railroad is printed in full in Ida Tarbell's *History of the Standard Oil Company*, Vol. I, p. 281 ff.

[3] John T. Flynn, *God's Gold*, p. 159.

do business in competition with the Standard Oil Company. If you do it will end in your being wiped out." Hanna sold.

Rockefeller's young brother Frank, the bad boy of the family, who continued through life to oppose John D., was treated more brusquely. He was told point blank that Standard Oil was going to buy all the refineries in Cleveland, while those who stood out would find their property valueless and be ruined. Frank was so angry that he wanted to fight, but his partners overruled him.

Within a month, the firm of Rockefeller and Flagler had acquired very nearly a monopoly of refining in Cleveland.

All was going merrily when, through the mistake of a railway clerk, the South Improvement Company's rebates and drawbacks came to be known to their competitors. Instantly there was a hullabaloo, especially in the Oil Regions, where indignation meetings were held. The railways began to be frightened and to consider backing out. Two telegrams were read to a mass meeting in the Oil Regions: [4]

Neither the Atlantic and Great Western, nor any of its officers, are interested in the South Improvement Company. Of course the policy of the road is to accommodate the petroleum interest.

G. B. McClellan.

Loud cheers. But the next telegram read to the meeting said:

Contract with South Improvement Company signed by George B. Mc-Clellan, president for the Atlantic and Great Western Railroad. I only signed after it was signed by all other parties.

Jay Gould.

Even the old Commodore was alarmed. "I told Billy [his son] not to have anything to do with that scheme," he said to a committee of the Producer's Union, a body formed to combat the combine. This body decided that no oil should be sold to the combine so long as its contracts with the railways remained in force. The producers were so united, and public opinion was so incensed, that the railways and the combine had to give way. In March, 1872, only two months after the signing of the contracts, they were cancelled; and shortly afterwards the South Improvement Company's charter was annulled.

It seemed a great victory for freedom. But Rockefeller retained

---

[4] Tarbell, op. cit., I, p. 89.

his acquisitions in Cleveland, and the knowledge of a method which could be revived when the storm should have died down—perhaps with more caution, and with more effective safeguards for secrecy, but with all the more certainty of success.

On April 6, the railroad presidents asserted that they no longer had any special contracts with Rockefeller or his group, and on April 8, Rockefeller confirmed this. But at a later date his partner, Flagler, swore that their firm had a rebate from April 1 to the middle of November 1872.[5] As a matter of fact, Rockefeller never ceased to profit by rebates, and at times by drawbacks also.

From the standpoint of the railways, it was reasonable to give cheaper rates to their largest customers, and to desire the concentration of refining in a few large firms. Rockefeller and Flagler, in 1872, could send enough oil from Cleveland to New York to make up one whole train of sixty cars every day. The railways explained that, if a car made the through journey without having to pick up freight on the way, it could be returned to Cleveland in ten days, whereas if it travelled by the ordinary freight trains it would not be returned for thirty days. Consequently Rockefeller's requirement of sixty cars a day could be met by 600 cars altogether, whereas the same amount of business distributed among smaller firms would have required 1,800 cars. As each car cost $500, this meant that Rockefeller's business cost the railway $600,000 less in cars than an equal amount of business distributed among many firms.[6] In this way, technical reasons worked on the side of concentration, which represented economies in production and distribution—economies which, of course, it was the object of the Standard Oil Company to retain in its hands as profits, and not to pass on to the consumer in the form of lower prices.

Rockefeller's enemies could be divided into three groups: the producers, the independent refiners, and the general body of consumers, The producers desired co-operation among themselves and competition among the refiners, who were their customers. The general public desired competition everywhere, both on principle, and in order to keep down the price of oil. The independent refiners were either men who were waiting for better terms to throw in their lot with Rockefeller, or men who objected to monopoly on principle and had a personal pride in their own business. Each of these groups had its

[5] Tarbell, *op. cit.*, I, pp. 96, 100.   [6] Tarbell, *op. cit.*, I, p. 278.

separate weakness. The producers endeavored to combine to limit output—a purpose which, oddly enough, writers hostile to Standard Oil regard as laudable in this instance. But their efforts constantly failed. Many of them had leases from the farmers who had been in the region before the rise of the oil industry; these leases were on a royalty basis, and the farmers could not be got to agree to the wells not being worked. The producers also formed associations for the specific purpose of resisting Rockefeller's group. But after their initial victory against the South Improvement Company, they repeatedly suffered defeat through the treachery of individuals, through Rockefeller's friends acquiring shares, or through bogus independents to whom they sold not knowing them to be acting for Standard Oil. By these various causes the producers' methods were always rendered ineffective.

The weakness of the refiners' position was that their economic interest was not necessarily opposed to that of Standard Oil. To the ablest of them, Rockefeller offered good terms if they would come in, and gradually they came in, with few exceptions. The men to whom he did not make attractive offers were those whom he thought inefficient, and these he ruined. There remained only a small group, actuated by an unusual degree of principle or obstinacy. Against these, Standard Oil adopted every conceivable competitive device. Wherever their oil went, spies reported the fact, and Standard Oil went to the same place at a lower price. Grocers who dealt in independent oil were threatened with competition, not only in oil, but in everything; if necessary, rival shops were established where all goods were so cheap that the disobedient grocers were ruined. When independents tried to escape the tyranny of the railways, which continued to favor the combine, by building a pipe line to the sea, they had to cross the Erie Railroad at a place called Hancock. They wished to cross by a river under a bridge, but the law was doubtful. Neither side appealed to the law:

The last Saturday night in November, 1892, the quiet of Hancock was disturbed by the arrival of one hundred armed men, railroad employés, by special train. They unlimbered a cannon, established a day and night patrol, built a beacon to be fired as an appeal for reinforcements, put up barracks, and left twenty men to go into winter quarters. Dynamite was part of their armament, and they were equipped with grappling-irons, cant-hooks, and other tools to pull the pipe up if laid. Cannon are a part of the regular equipment of the combination, as they are used to perforate tanks in which the oil takes fire. To let the "independents" know what they were to expect the cannon was fired at ten o'clock at night, with a report that shook the people and the windows for miles about. These opponents of competition were willing and ready to kill though their rights were dubious, and there could be no pretence that full satisfaction could not be got through the courts if any wrong was done.[7]

In this case the independent pipe line found a way round, and was completed. But in the end Standard Oil obtained control of it.[8]

The general public, as represented by lawyers and the State Legislatures, made many onslaughts on monopoly, and endeavored by various means to keep competition alive. As early as 1874, the Windom Committee of Congress, which investigated abuses on railways, went so far as to advocate a certain number of national or State railways, not, as might be supposed, to secure the advantages of monopoly to the general public, but, on the contrary, to make sure of the existence of competitors which would not agree to pools, rebates, drawbacks, etc.

"The only means," they reported, "of securing and maintaining reliable and effective competition between railways is through national or State ownership, or control of one or more lines which, being unable to enter into combinations, will serve as a regulation of other lines."

But this recommendation was never acted upon.

The Interstate Commerce Act of 1887 and the Sherman Anti-Trust Act of 1890 were attempts to prevent the evils of monopoly in railways and other corporations. These laws were useful to lawyers, since they involved rich men in complicated and expensive litigation; otherwise, they served little purpose. The Supreme Court decided that the Anti-Trust Act was not valid against the great corporations, but could be invoked against trade unions and used to put their leaders in prison. *Regis voluntas suprema lex.*

True, in 1892 the Standard Oil Trust was dissolved, nominally, as the result of an adverse judgment of the Supreme Court of Ohio. But six years later the dissolution had still not been carried out, and the Attorney General of Ohio brought a charge of contempt against

[7] H. D. Lloyd, *Wealth against Commonwealth*, pp. 161–2.
[8] Flynn, *op. cit.*, p. 324.

the Trust. The Court decided evenly—three to three—in its verdict, and the Trust escaped condemnation. But the Attorney General failed to be re-elected, and his successor was friendly to Standard Oil. It had had plenty of practice in managing the politics of Ohio. For example, it had made Payne, the father of its treasurer, one of the Senators from that State. The other Senator and the State Legislature charged that his election was corrupt, and demanded an investigation by the Senate. Payne showed no wish to have the charges investigated, and the Senate made no move in the matter.

Nevertheless, the Standard Oil Trust was at last dissolved, and replaced by the Standard Oil Company of New Jersey, which did the same business for the same men. This in turn was dissolved by order of the Supreme Court in 1910, as an illegal organization in restraint of trade. Since then, Standard Oil has consisted of nominally separate companies in the several States, but the change is scarcely noticeable.

The attacks of the public on the plutocracy, conducted from the standpoint of old-fashioned liberalism, were certainly not a brilliant success. The net result of forty years of continued agitation against the rich was the imprisonment of one Socialist leader, Eugene V. Debs. Meanwhile the Standard Oil magnates could commit perjury with impunity; Rockefeller, for example, swore on two occasions only a few months apart that he had been, and that he had not been connected with the South Improvement Company.[9]

More difficult than the fights with producers and public was the fight with rival refiners. In this, at first, the railways were the chief allies of the Standard and the causes of its victories. When new firms were brought in, they continued to operate as apparently independent concerns, and every possible care was taken to conceal the fact that they had been acquired by the combine. For example, when, in 1876, Rockefeller got control of the firm of Scofield, Shurmer and Teagle,

The making of this contract and its execution were attended by all the secret rites peculiar to Mr. Rockefeller's business ventures. According to the testimony of one of the firm given a few years later on the witness stand in Cleveland the contract was signed at night at Mr. Rockefeller's house on Euclid Avenue in Cleveland, where he told the gentlemen that they must not tell even their wives about the new arrangement, that if they made money they must conceal it—they were not to drive fast horses, "put

[9] Tarbell, *op. cit.*, II, pp. 132, 138. See also pp. 70–1, and I, p. 230.

on style," or do anything to let people suspect there were unusual profits in oil refining. That would invite competition. They were told that all accounts were to be kept secret. Fictitious names were to be used in corresponding, and a special box at the post-office was employed for these fictitious characters. In fact, smugglers and house-breakers never surrounded their operations with more mystery.[10]

Once, and only once, Standard Oil did battle with a railway, the Pennsylvania. This was in 1877, when pipe lines had become important and Rockefeller was trying to control them all. There was one system, however, the Empire Transportation Company, which belonged to the Pennsylvania Railroad. It seemed that it was in danger of becoming worthless through the acquisition of all the refineries by Rockefeller, who employed his own pipe lines and the railways that remained friendly to him. Scott, the president of the Pennsylvania, therefore decided to build refineries in New York to use the oil carried by his lines. When this became known, Rockefeller argued with Scott; so did the Erie and the New York Central. But Scott decided to fight, and a rate war began, in which, at one time, oil was carried from the Oil Regions to New York for eight cents less than nothing. Everybody concerned lost millions, but the issue was still in doubt when a strike— one of the most desperate in American history—began on the Baltimore and Ohio and spread to the Pennsylvania. There were pitched battles between strikers and soldiers, involving many deaths and much destruction of railroad property. This convenient strike gave the victory to Rockefeller. The Pennsylvania, which for the first time paid no dividend, could not face further losses; it sold the refineries and the Empire Transportation Company's pipe lines to Standard Oil. From that moment, the railway never listened to any suggestion hostile to Rockefeller, but always replied that he was the only man who could keep peace between the different lines. Not even the ablest and the richest men considered it possible to win in a contest with Standard Oil after Scott had been defeated. W. H. Vanderbilt, giving evidence before a committee of the New York Assembly in 1879, expressed this view:

Q. Can you attribute, or do you attribute, in your own mind, the fact of there being one refiner instead of fifty, now, to any other cause except the larger capital of the Standard Oil Company?

[10] Tarbell, op. cit., I, p. 166.

A. There are a great many causes; it is not from their capital alone that they have built up this business; there is no question about it but that these men—and if you come in contact with them I guess you will come to the same conclusion I have long ago—I think they are smarter fellows than I am, a good deal; they are very enterprising and smart men; never came in contact with any class of men as smart and able as they are in their business, and I think a great deal is to be attributed to that.

Q. Would that alone monopolize a business of that sort?

A. It would go a great way toward building it up; they never could have got in the position they are in now without a great deal of ability, and one man would hardly have been able to do it; it is a combination of men.

Q. Wasn't it a combination that embraced the smart men in the railways, as well as the smart men in the Standard Company?

A. I think these gentlemen from their shrewdness have been able to take advantage of the competition that existed between the railroads, for their business, as it grew, and that they have availed themselves of that there is not a question of doubt.

Q. Don't you think they have also been able to make their affiliations with railroad companies and railroad officers?

A. I have not heard it charged that any railway official has any interest in any of their companies, only what I used to see in the papers some years ago, that I had an interest in it.

Q. Your interest in your railway is so large a one that nobody could conceive, as a matter of personal interest, that you would have an interest antagonistic to your road?

A. When they came to do business with us in any magnitude; that is the reason I disposed of my interest.

Q. And that is the only way you can account for the enormous monopoly that has thus grown up?

A. Yes; they are very shrewd men; I don't believe that by any legislative enactment or anything else, through any of the states or all of the states, you can keep such men as them down; you can't do it; they will be on top all the time; you see if they are not.

Q. You think they get on top of the railways?

A. Yes; and on top of everybody that comes in contact with them; too smart for me.[11]

Rockefeller says that God gave him his money. If God works through economic forces, perhaps the old man is right. At any rate,

[11] Tarbell, *op. cit.*, II, p. 388.

after his retirement he made four times as much money as he made while he was working, and in half the time. At first, oil was wanted for lighting; as this use decayed, motor cars came in. Nothing can stop the torrent of wealth. He has given away so much that most of the intellectuals of America and China, and a great part of those of other countries, are profiting by his benefactions; yet he grows richer. In spite of all his efforts, the discovery of oil in other parts of the world has revived competition, bringing with it, not the blessings which his enemies expected from it, but wars and rumors of wars; yet he grows richer.

"I don't believe that by any legislative enactment you can keep such men as them down; you can't do it; they will be on top all the time." This was William Vanderbilt's opinion; and within the framework of the capitalist system it would seem that it is so.

B. STEEL

"The manufacture of iron and steel," says the economic historian, "is the nation's key industry, by which the progress of other branches is determined." [12] At the time of the Civil War, Great Britain was much ahead of all other countries in iron and steel; but in the year 1890 America caught up, and by 1900 produced more than twice as much steel as was produced in England and Scotland. In 1860, the production of crude iron and steel in America was half a million tons; in 1900 twenty-nine millions, in 1910 seventy-five, and in 1920 a hundred and fourteen millions. During the period from 1860 to 1920, while the quantity of iron and steel had increased two-hundred-and-thirty-fold, the value had increased almost exactly a hundred-fold. Moreover in 1860 America produced hardly any steel, whereas the production of 1920 was almost entirely steel. We may reckon, therefore, that a ton of steel in 1920 cost about half as much as a ton of iron in 1860. This gives some measures of the technical progress on those sixty years, but an inadequate one, since the general level of prices in 1920 was much higher than in 1860.

The most important figure in the development of the steel industry is Andrew Carnegie, a man whose life was a meeting-point of all the phases of industrialism, from the earliest to the latest. His family, for

[12] *Bogart*, p. 593.

generations, had been handloom-weavers in Scotland, and in 1835, when he was born, they were falling into poverty through the competition of the machines. Most of his male relations were fiery Chartists, with a bitter hatred of king, lords, and clergy. His mother was a Swedenborgian, but he himself was a freethinker—at first in the revolutionary manner of working-class Radicalism in the 'forties, and afterwards in a more mellow style which led to admiration of Herbert Spencer and friendship with John Morley. The family emigrated to America, and in that country he passed through all the phases of the competitive era, finally selling his business to form the nucleus of the most colossal of all combinations, the United States Steel Corporation. After his retirement in 1901, he devoted himself to giving away his fortune, and had got rid of nine-tenths of it when he died in 1919 at the age of eighty-three. He lived long enough to congratulate Wilson on the Treaty of Versailles, but not long enough to know that no congratulations were due.

Carnegie's uncle Lauder, whom the boy much admired, was, like most Chartists, enthusiastic about America, and took as his heroes Washington, Jefferson, and Franklin. Consequently when the boy arrived in America at the age of twelve he was favorably disposed to the new country. In a long letter to his uncle, written in 1852, he explains that he is a free-soil Democrat, that he hopes slavery will soon be done away with, that, most regrettably, both presidential candidates are military men, that the greatest reform of the age is the Homestead Bill, and that Maine, to his joy, has adopted prohibition—"a step in advance of you at any rate." He became a patriotic American; nevertheless, as soon as he could afford it, he spent almost all his spare time in Scotland.

Arrived in Pittsburgh, his family at first had a struggle to make a living, and he had to go to work in a cotton factory when he was thirteen, earning only $1.20 a week. He hated the work as much as if he had been a weakling. Although he tried to fortify himself by invoking the memory of Scottish heroes, the smells caused him to be sick, and he would wake in the night with nightmares that he had done the wrong thing with the engine which he had to run. "I never succeeded," he says, "in overcoming the nausea produced by the smell of oil. Even Wallace and Bruce proved impotent here." In later life he concluded that all boys ought to go through what he had endured. "As a rule," he said, "there is more genuine satisfaction, a truer life, and more obtained from life in the humble cottages of the poor than in the palaces of the rich." However that may be, he got out of the cottage and into the palace as quickly as he could.

Carnegie soon began to prosper. After nearly a year in the factory, he became a telegraph boy—the second in Pittsburgh, though the number was quickly increased. The life-long apostle of competition immediately set to work to stifle competition among telegraph boys. On messages to be delivered outside the city limits there was a ten-cent tip; he arranged that the tips should be pooled, and shared out equally at the end of each week. "The plan was adopted, competition was stifled, and the messengers lived amicably ever after," says his biographer.[13]

By 1851 he had risen to be an operator, at four dollars a week, and in the following year he was raised to twenty-five dollars a month. Early in 1853, when he was still only seventeen, he had the good fortune to attract the notice of Scott of the Pennsylvania Railroad, then himself a rising young man, and he entered the service of the railway at thirty-five dollars a month, remaining with it, in various capacities, for twelve years, that is to say, until the end of the Civil War.

It did not take him long to discover that work is not the only way to get money. One day Scott offered him ten shares in the Adams Express Company for $500; he raised the money by inducing his parents to mortgage their house. On another occasion Woodruff, the inventor of sleeping-cars, which were still in the experimental stage, offered him an interest in the venture. "But how I was to make my payments rather troubled me—my first monthly payment was to be two hundred and seventeen dollars and a half. I had not the money and I did not see any way of getting it. But I finally decided to visit the local banker and ask him for a loan, pledging myself to pay back at the rate of fifteen dollars per month. He promptly granted it." This is the secret of growing rich: be such that when you ask a banker for money, you get it. In the year 1863, his dividend on the shares he obtained was $5,050. His total income in this year was $47,860.67, of which only $2,400 was salary; the remainder resulted from prudent investments. His first investment, in Adams Express Company, had risen from $120 a year when he bought it to $1,440 a year. Out of

[13] Burton J. Hendrick, *The Life of Andrew Carnegie*, p. 51.

savings he and some friends had bought a farm in the Oil Regions, and it was now worth $5,000,000. But he was already beginning to turn his attention to iron.

After the Civil War, Carnegie left the employment of the railway and became a manufacturer of iron bridges, in which, from the first, he was very successful. His attention was turned from iron to steel by the Bessemer process, invented in 1856, which completely revolutionized the manufacture of steel. The adoption of the process was retarded, however, by the fact that it could only be used with ores containing less than four-tenths per cent of phosphorus, while most English ores, and most American ores in use at that time, contained a considerably larger percentage. But the Lake Superior ores, which had been shown to white men in 1845 by a superstitiously timorous Indian named Majigijig, with the words "Iron mountain, Indian not go near, white man go," proved to be suitable for the Bessemer process, and thus acquired a new importance. The ores and the process, together, caused American supremacy in steel. Bessemer and Majigijig enabled Carnegie to dispel the British dream of eternal industrial supremacy.

It was in 1872, as the result of meeting Bessemer and seeing his converter in action, that Carnegie entered upon the manufacture of steel rails. Bessemer first made steel rails for English railways in 1862; but in 1872 in America iron rails were still almost universally employed.

Carnegie established his works on the site of the battle-field where General Braddock had suffered disaster in 1755, and from the first he prospered. The crisis of 1873 caused prolonged depression in the steel industry, but his works steadily expanded. He made it a principle throughout his career to increase his producing capacity during bad times, so as to be ready for good times when they came. "The man who has money during a panic," he said at a later date, "is the wise and valuable citizen." He always was that man. Panics have played an important part in the concentration of capital, since they enable the strong firms to buy up the weaker ones or drive them out of business. Carnegie never speculated, and was never short of cash. As soon as he became his own master, he developed a strong hatred of finance, and would have nothing to do with the methods of the stock markets. He made it an absolute rule that none of his partners should speculate if he could prevent it, and with even his most trusted employees he was adamant on this point. He was a pure industrialist: he made his money by manufacturing and selling steel and steel products, not by financial manipulations.

Carnegie was a republican in politics but a monarchist in business. He was an autocrat in his own works, and would not enter into pools or agreements of any kind with rival firms. He enjoyed competition, and was completely ruthless in battle. Inside the firm, he kept his eye on all who showed promise, and made them compete for his favor; the most meritorious became partners. "Mr. Morgan buys his partners; I grow my own," he said.

The prosperity of his business depended upon its technical excellence. Steel rails, at the time when he began making them, sold for a hundred and sixty dollars a ton, whereas in 1898 their price was seventeen dollars a ton. In 1900, the last year that he was in business, his works produced four million tons of steel, nearly as much as Great Britain, and nearly half the total output of the United States. The profits of the business were forty million dollars, of which his share was just under twenty-five millions. Fifty thousand dollars invested in the business by a partner in 1883 brought eight millions in 1898. And the strangest thing is that all this was achieved without hard work on Carnegie's part. From 1865 onward, he always spent half the year in Europe, mostly in Scotland; yet the command never slipped out of his hands. "We are a happy family, all unanimous," he boasted once to a visitor who was being shown the works. "God help the man who is not unanimous," murmured one of the partners.

There was one person, and only one, of whom Carnegie stood in awe, and that was his mother. She was certainly a formidable old lady. When Matthew Arnold, under Carnegie's auspices, gave his first lecture in America, it was a dismal failure. Afterwards, every one began telling him so with varying degrees of tact. At last he turned to his host's mother, hoping that she would say something soothing, but all she said was: "Too meenisterial, Mr. Arnold, too meenisterial." Carnegie used to drive a four-in-hand through Scotland with a party of friends, and his mother would sit next to him to keep away designing young ladies. She died in 1886, when he was fifty-one; until she was dead, he would not marry, though he was engaged. After her death, for many years, he would not speak of her; he removed pictures of her which had been on his desk and on the wall. Finally his wife restored his mother's miniature to his desk, and after that he spoke freely of her.

In the summer of 1892, during one of Carnegie's seasonal absences, there was a terrible strike at his works, the Homestead. Frick, who was in charge, engaged Pinkerton men to protect blacklegs; there was a battle in which the Pinkerton men were ousted by the strikers; Frick was wounded severely, but not fatally, by the anarchist Berkman; eight thousand soldiers, with artillery, overawed the strikers and occupied the works; and from that moment no union men were employed by Carnegie. The strike had occurred as a protest against a reduction of wages amounting to between 15 and 18 per cent. By this time, Carnegie had begun to forget his Chartist uncle; his radicalism had reduced itself to chaffing the Prince of Wales and the Kaiser about the relative merits of monarchies and republics, and to writing essays on the delights of poverty.

Carnegie, from the first, had made bridges and rails, but in the main his business had consisted of making steel. Towards the end of his business career, however, a new watchword came into the steel industry: "integration." This meant that all the raw materials and all the processes of manufacture, down to the final product, should be united under one management. For this there were technical reasons; for instance, it was found best never to let the metal get cold, from the first moment of dealing with the ore down to the last stage. This new movement compelled Carnegie to come into contact with two men as powerful as himself: Rockefeller and Pierpont Morgan.

Carnegie had secured his supply of coke by the alliance and subsequent partnership with Frick, who controlled all the coke in the neighborhood. The iron ore, which came from the Mesabi region on Lake Superior, was more difficult to control. Rockefeller had acquired vast areas during the panic of 1893, when smaller men had to sell. For a time, it seemed that Rockefeller was going to challenge Carnegie's supremacy in steel. However, he decided to content himself with oil: he leased his ore lands to Carnegie and made contracts as to the transportation of the ore by his railway and his twelve lake steamers. Carnegie undertook to buy Mesabi ore only from Rockefeller so long as it could be obtained from him, and it was understood that Rockefeller would not produce steel himself.

At the other end, Carnegie was more vulnerable. He was sure of his raw material, and could manufacture steel cheaply enough to defeat any competitor. But those who, hitherto, had bought his steel for various manufacturing purposes began to think that it would pay them to make their own steel.

The changed situation became acutely manifest in June and July 1900. Mr. John W. Gates, head of Amereican Steel and Wire, informed Mr. Schwab that in future he could produce his own steel, and that the contract with the Carnegie Company was therefore cancelled. The Moore brothers, controllers of Steel Hoop and Sheet Steel, sent identical notifications. Contracts with the Carnegie works were at an end and a customer for 20,000 tons a month vanished into limbo. A far greater concern, the National Tube Company, an assimilation of about nineteen previously contending factories, all for years steady purchasers from Carnegie, had recently been created by J. P. Morgan and Co. In future this organization, too, could manage without the ministrations of the Carnegie works. A pageant of blast furnaces and converting plants, rising in McKeesport and other places, even more haughtily emphasized this declaration of independence. Another Morgan achievement, the American Bridge Company, had been little more than an assembling plant; structural steel had been purchased from Carnegie, riveted together, and in full panoply sent forth into the world. And now this ambitious infant was similarly displaying a cold shoulder to Pittsburgh salesmen. The time was approaching when Mr. Morgan's all enveloping creation could fabricate its own steel.[14]

Carnegie was tired of money-making, and wished to retire to his castle in Scotland, where he could enjoy the conversation of philosophers, and devote as much energy to getting rid of his wealth as he had to acquiring it. But his self-respect required that he should go out of business in a blaze of glory, not as a man afraid of formidable competitors. He possessed at Conneaut on Lake Erie an entire harbor, at the terminus of the "Bessemer Railroad," which he had built to keep the Pennsylvania Railroad in order. At this place,

. . . Carnegie's agents had purchased five thousand acres stretching a mile along the Lake front, and here the tube mill was to be built, at a cost of $12,000,000. This venture was only the beginning. Land in plenty had been acquired for other "Finishing" works—tin plate, barbed wire, nails, and the like. In other words, the Carnegie Company was preparing to manufacture those articles for which it had formerly turned out crude steel,

[14] Hendrick, *Life of Andrew Carnegie*, p. 477.

and thus regain the market which was slipping away. A great steel city, not unlike that which afterward rose at Gary, Indiana, was in process of incubation.[15]

By these preparations, Carnegie inspired respect in those who might think of fighting him. Morgan wished to organize the steel industry, and for this purpose he must buy out Carnegie; Carnegie wished to sell, but on terms which would make the strength of his position evident. The two men, through intermediaries, made cautious approaches to each other. Carnegie's young partner, Schwab, at last, at the end of 1900, obtained a statement from Morgan: "If Andy wants to sell, I'll buy. Go and find his price." Schwab went to Carnegie, who, after a few minutes' conversation, took out a piece of paper and wrote on it: $400,000,000. "That's what I'll sell for," he said. The paper was taken to Morgan, who at once accepted the price. After this, for the first time, they met.

One day, several weeks after the negotiations were ended, Carnegie's telephone rang. Would he not come down to Wall and Broad Streets for a little talk? As Carnegie was older than Morgan this invitation seemed unbecoming. "Mr. Morgan," he replied, "it is just about as far from Wall Street to Fifty-First as it is from Fifty-First to Wall. I shall be delighted to see you here any time." In a brief period Morgan appeared at Carnegie's home. The ensuing conversation was pleasant and satisfactory. Mr. James Bertram, Carnegie's secretary, timed the interview, taking out his watch. Morgan emerged after precisely fifteen minutes had elapsed. So little time did two great men require to discuss a matter involving $400,000,000!

The parting was good-natured. At the door Morgan grasped Carnegie's hand.

"Mr. Carnegie," he said, "I want to congratulate you on being the richest man in the world!" [16]

Carnegie's business, along with many others, went into Morgan's gigantic "United States Steel Corporation," formed in 1901. It was popularly known as the Billion-Dollar Corporation, but in fact its capital was even larger: $1,300,000,000. It did not possess a monopoly in steel, and was careful to conciliate public opinion by stating that it had no wish for a monopoly. At the time of its formation it controlled 50.1 per cent of the total production.[17] It was Morgan's affair; he

[15] Hendrick, *Life of Andrew Carnegie*, p. 481.   [16] *Ibid.*, p. 496.
[17] Ida Tarbell, *Life of Albert H. Gary*, p. 131.

chose the directors, and he made Judge Gary chairman. In Carnegie's day, finance had played no part in his business, but in the United States Steel Corporation finance made all the difference between success and failure. The technical processes of manufacture were no longer the centre of attention; it happened that steel was being made, but it might just as well have been anything else. A more abstract stage had been reached in the organization of economic activities. Finance was essentially similar, whether applied to one business or to another; and by a natural evolution, this all-pervading financial aspect had come increasingly to the fore. Through finance it became possible to unify not merely one business, such as oil or steel, but all large and developed industries. This was the next stage in capitalist development.

C. FINANCE

The power of finance is no new thing, but it has increased with every development of capitalist technique. As we have seen, it played only a minor part in the success of such leading men as Rockefeller and Carnegie; but with the retirement of Carnegie a new era begins, in which the dominant figure is J. Pierpont Morgan the elder. His father, J. S. Morgan, was prominent in England, and acted as intermediary between American business and British investors. Pierpont Morgan, through his father, had more connection with Europe than had any of his predecessors in American big business. Until the Great War, Europe, and especially Great Britain, invested very largely in American railways, but obtained, as a rule, a very poor return. All through the battles for the Erie Railroad between Drew and Gould and Vanderbilt, the British shareholders make periodic appearances, but are helpless to prevent what is being done to make their investments worthless. And what was true of them was true also of small investors in the United States: they could do nothing but look on while their savings were dissipated in the battles of giants.

Pierpont Morgan, who first utilized the power and defended the interests of the smaller investors, was a very different kind of man from the Commodore or Rockefeller or Carnegie. Unlike them, he was born in the purple, he was an Episcopalian and a New Englander of old family, and he had been familiar from early youth with governmental and financial Europe. He was a patron of the arts, and had something of the pomp of a Roman Emperor. He collected pictures, palaces, and women, employing (at least as regards the first of these) expert advice obtained at less than cost price. Even in his busiest moments, he could attend Church Conferences. He employed his spare time by going into empty churches and singing hymns in solitude. He despised Carnegie as a vulgar fellow, and winced when he was told that that impertinent upstart spoke of him as "Pierpont." He hated Rockefeller as a prig and a Baptist. While the Steel Trust was being formed, Gary said to him: "We ought to have the Rockefeller ores." "How are we going to get them?" asked Morgan. "You are to talk to Mr. Rockefeller." "I would not think of it." "Why?" "I don't like him." However, he went next morning, and ultimately bought the ores for five million dollars more than the outside price that Gary thought he ought to have given.[18]

Morgan's earlier career was almost entirely concerned with railways, not in attempts to wrest control from other powerful men, but rather in avoidance of cut-throat competition. He first made a reputation in 1869, by organizing the defence of the Albany and Susquehanna Railroad against Gould and Fisk, who were attempting to seize it on behalf of the Erie Railroad. This story is full of the picturesque incidents which those two gentlemen were apt to introduce into the dusty annals of finance. They attempted to invade a shareholders' meeting with a gang of roughs from the slums of New York, each armed with a proxy; but Morgan and Ramsey, the president of the railroad, were ready for them with a band of train-men. Ramsey threw Fisk downstairs, and at the bottom a "policeman" placed him under "arrest" and then disappeared. At a later stage, an Erie train and an Albany and Susquehanna train, each full of vigorous fighters, collided end-on at the mouth of a tunnel because neither would concede the other's right of way. The men leaped out and fought until the State militia arrived and imposed peace. Meanwhile there were the customary army of judges imposing contrary injunctions on all parties. In the end, Gould and Fisk were defeated. Morgan had proved himself a useful man on the side of respectable finance.

After Commodore Vanderbilt's death in 1877, his son, having to face a State Legislature less compliant than in Tweed's day, decided that it would be wise to dispose of a great part of his holdings in the

[18] Tarbell, *Life of Elbert H. Gary*, pp. 118–19.

New York Central, which amounted to 87 per cent of the whole. He consulted Morgan as to methods of doing this without loss. Morgan undertook to take the shares at the current price, and to dispose of them in England, on two conditions: that he should be a director, and that 8 per cent dividend should be guaranteed for the next five years. Vanderbilt accepted these terms, the shares were successfully sold in England, and the English shareholders gave proxies to Morgan. In this way, without any large personal investment, he gained influence on the railway as the champion of genuine investors—not, of course, as an act of pure benevolence, since his personal profit was three million dollars.

Competition between railway magnates, as Morgan perceived, was wasteful and ruinous. In 1885, the New York Central and the Pennsylvania Railroads—or rather, William H. Vanderbilt and George H. Roberts of the Pennsylvania—were about to wage war on each other. The South Pennsylvania Railroad, in Vanderbilt's interests, was working against Roberts, while the West Shore Railroad, with Roberts's blessing, was damaging the New York Central. Morgan took both men for a cruise on his yacht, and talked to them until they agreed: Roberts was to have the South Pennsylvania and Vanderbilt the West Shore, so that each would be freed from competition. Roberts had been hard to persuade, but two years later, Morgan did him an important service: he used his financial power to prevent the Baltimore and Ohio Railroad from entering New York.

In 1889, Morgan formed the "Interstate Railway Association," composed of eighteen railway presidents and representatives of the principal banks concerned in placing new issues. Here, again, the object was to prevent competition and to protect the genuine investor, whose interests were of importance to Morgan because of his European connection. After giving all these magnates an excellent dinner, he introduced business by a very short speech:

The purpose of this meeting is to cause those present no longer to take the law into their own hands when they suspect they have been wronged, as has been too much the practice heretofore. This is not elsewhere customary in civilized communities, and no good reason exists why such a practice should continue among railroads.[19]

[19] John Kennedy Winkler, *The Life of J. Pierpont Morgan*, pp. 126–7.

It was the power of finance that enabled him to take this tone with a set of masterful men by no means inclined to submit to dictation. One of them, McLeod, protested: "You can't dictate to me. I'd rather run a peanut stand than take orders from any banker." In a short time, he was reduced to poverty, but it is not known whether he kept a peanut stand.

Morgan's power depended upon a device called the "voting trust." When a railroad was in a bad way, it would come to him for help in reorganization, and he would consent on condition of holding the proxies of a sufficient number of shareholders. He would succeed in obtaining these because experience showed that he could make even the most unpromising railways pay. The panic of 1893 enlarged his opportunities, and in 1898 he controlled a sixth of all the railways in the United States, with a capital of $1,500,000,000. His power was not that of actual money in his own possession; it was more analogous to political power, since he was the chosen representative of the scattered votes of innumerable shareholders.

He now began to launch out into wider spheres. In 1895 he "saved the country" by an agreement with President Cleveland at a time when the Treasury was destitute of funds owing to a drain of gold. He undertook to provide sixty-five million dollars in gold, half of it to be procured in Europe, and to use all his financial power to keep it in the United States. "Saving the country" became a habit with him; he did it again in 1907. But by dying in 1913 he missed the opportunity to "save" the whole world, which came to his son during the Great War.

The United States Steel Corporation, formed at the beginning of 1901, was, financially, Morgan's biggest operation. His opposition to competition had long been fomenting public hostility, and his promotion of the most enormous of all Trusts increased the alarm among the enemies of Big Business. Just at this time, the Conservative McKinley was assassinated, and Roosevelt, with a Radical policy, became President. With the enthusiastic approval of ordinary citizens, he began actions against various corporations under the Sherman Anti-Trust Act. His first victim was the Northern Securities Company, formed by Morgan and Hill to control the railways of the Northwest. Morgan was furious; he went down to Washington and gave the President a piece of his mind. He was formidable in anger: when his eyes blazed, men quailed before him. But Roosevelt was his equal in force of personality, and they parted in mutual fury. "The man's a lunatic, he is worse than a Socialist," said Morgan. "Mr. Morgan," said Roosevelt, "could not help regarding me as a big rival operator, who either intended to ruin all his interests or else could be induced to come to an agreement to ruin none." "I'd even vote the Democratic ticket to get that man out of the White House," retorted Morgan.

The Supreme Court had previously, in the Knight case, given a decision which, if accepted as a precedent, would have protected the Northern Securities Company. But the Supreme Court is not above yielding to pressure, and pressure was applied. "It was necessary," says Roosevelt, "to reverse the Knight case in the interest of the people against monopoly and privilege just as it had been necessary to reverse the Dred Scott case in the interest of the people against slavery and privilege." The Supreme Court, by a majority of five to four, decreed the dissolution of the Northern Securities Company. It is interesting to note that Justice Holmes, the most Radical of all the Supreme Court judges, voted against the Government.

The Steel Trust escaped legal condemnation. Very wisely, Morgan had chosen as its chairman Elbert H. Gary, a pious methodistical lawyer, who was shocked by the doings of the great men with whom he came in contact. Gary, much against the wishes of his fellow-directors, made friends with Roosevelt, and frequently went to Washington to praise his public spirit. When the Trust wished to buy up the Tennessee Coal, Iron, and Railroad Company, he obtained the President's consent in advance. He gave out that the Steel Trust was not as other Trusts, so that Mark Twain, on meeting him, said: "Oh, I know who you are. You are the *good* Corporation." Morgan had his reward, and Roosevelt left the Steel Trust alone. But after Taft had been President long enough to quarrel with his predecessor, he decided to show his independence by a reversal of the Government's policy. Although in general far more friendly to big business than Roosevelt, he brought suit against the United States Steel Corporation in October, 1911. In April, 1915, the United States Circuit Court of Appeals decided against the Government, which took the case to the Supreme Court. In March, 1917, the Supreme Court was evenly divided, and the case was ordered to be reargued. But America's entry into the War, in which the Steel Trust had a great part to play, caused a postponement. In 1919, the

Supreme Court finally gave a verdict of acquittal, and Gary's virtue was vindicated.

The ramifications of Morgan's power were endless. He controlled Armour's of Chicago, through whom he held power of life and death over the cattle of the Argentine. His shipping Combine contained most of the Atlantic liners. Edward VII, the Kaiser, and the Pope, entertained him as if he were a visiting monarch. *Life* published a revised catechism: "Who made the world, Charles? Answer: God made the world in 4004 B.C., but it was reorganized in 1901 by James J. Hill, J. Pierpont Morgan, and John D. Rockefeller."

In spite of his immense power, he was by no means the richest man of his time; he died worth sixty-eight million dollars. It was not so much through his own money that he ruled the world of finance, as through his capacity for inspiring confidence in others. In him credit was personified. He first undertook the organization of the money power of America and of great sections of Europe, so as to promote harmonious working in the general interests of capital. Roosevelt and the reformers, following the Jefferson-Jackson tradition, endeavored, by the machinery of the law, to keep alive the old anarchy, but whether they won or lost in their colossal law-suits, begun in one era and finished in another, mattered little to the masters of wealth. And in fighting against the old anarchy these men were doing a useful and necessary work: they were diminishing waste, and by their vast fortunes they were giving spectacular evidence of the productivity of modern labor. In all that concerned the problem of production, they were in the right as against the devotees of competition. The problem of distribution they could not solve, but this problem was equally baffling to their opponents. They also could not secure any approach to equality: Carnegie had made his four hundred millions by free competition.

The United States began in an uneasy compromise between Jefferson and Hamilton. Gradually the Jeffersonian elements were pushed westward, while the Hamiltonians ruled the East. So long as the West worked in harmony with the South, it had considerable influence, but after the Civil War Grangers, Populists, and Bryanites were ineffective in spite of vigor and enthusiasm. In the end America became, in its economic life, an organized whole, ruled, for their own profit, by a handful of unprecedentedly rich men. The organization, as organization, was valuable; the defect was in its purpose, which was solely to make rich men richer. The plutocrats were right in wishing to eliminate competition, and their opponents were right in demanding consideration for the interests of ordinary citizens. The solution lay, neither in a more absolute plutocracy, nor in a return to economic anarchy, but in public ownership and control of the machine that the masters of finance had created.

To achieve this requires a new popular philosophy, a new civil service, and a new kind of democratic intelligence. An attempt is being made to create these in America at this moment.

PART FOUR

NATIONALISM AND IMPERIALISM

. . . thou knowst the magistrates
And princes of my country came in person,
Solicited, commanded, threatened, urged,
Adjured by all the bonds of civil duty
And of religion; pressed how just it was,
How honourable, how glorious to entrap
A common enemy, who had destroyed
Such numbers of our nation: and the priest
Was not behind.

———————————

There stood a hill not far, whose grisly top
Belched fire and rolling smoke; the rest entire
Shone with a glossy scurf, undoubted sign
That in his womb was hid metallic ore,
The work of sulphur. Thither, winged with speed,
A numerous brigade hastened: as when bands
Of pioneers with spade and pickaxe armed
Forerun the royal camp, to trench a field,
Or cast a rampart. Mammon led them on,
Mammon, the least erected spirit that fell
From Heaven, for even in Heaven his looks and thoughts
Were always downward bent, admiring more
The richest of Heaven's pavement, trodden gold,
Than aught divine or holy else enjoyed
In vision beatific.

MILTON

CHAPTER XXVIII

THE PRINCIPLE OF NATIONALITY

I. CONTINENTAL LIBERALISM

THERE were, in the years between 1815 and 1848, three different types of progressives in the world. There were the American agrarian democrats; there were the Philosophical Radicals; and there were the Liberals. On the Continent, the relations of the two latter groups were somewhat complicated: since both were progressive, they felt that they ought to co-operate, but they differed so profoundly in their outlook that co-operation was difficult from the first, and in the end impossible.

The Philosophical Radicals, whose opinions were largely derived from eighteenth-century France, believed men to be congenitally all alike, and attributed the differences between adults entirely to education and environment. As to religion, they were sceptics; in ethics, they regarded happiness as the sole ultimate good. They held self-interest to be the mainspring of action, reason to be the means of discerning self-interest, and government to be the art of harmonizing the interests of different individuals. They were cosmopolitan, they were rationalistic, and they were rather democratic. Prosperity and enlightenment were, in their view, the proper aims of government; and in practical affairs their chief emphasis was on economics.

The Philosophical Radicals, through Cobden, dominated England, and through England they had, for a time, great influence on the Continent.

From the time of Owen onwards, however, their theory had two forms, one for the employer and another for the wage-earner. Almost all their characteristic doctrines survive in Marxism: the belief in the innate similarity of all men, the belief in reason, the cosmopolitanism, the appeal to self-interest, and the emphasis upon material prosperity. International Socialism, just as much as international capitalism, has resulted from their teaching; and the Socialistic form of Philosophical

343

Radicalism has proved the more durable. Cobden's day is past; Lenin's is not.

The Liberals of the period following the fall of Napoleon were very different from the Benthamites. They also, it is true, had affiliations with the French eighteenth century, but to Rousseau, not to the *Encyclopédistes* and Physiocrats. They were men of feeling rather than of reason: they looked to sensibility to redress the sufferings of the weak and downtrodden. They were dominated by certain rhetorical words from antiquity, such as *tyrants, slaves, freedom*. They seem to have never heard such words without feeling the appropriate emotion. It is true that one could not always be sure who was a tyrant and who was not. In England, the epithet applied to Napoleon: "there came a tyrant, and with holy glee thou foughtst against him," as Wordsworth informs Liberty. But in Italy Napoleon was revered as a liberator, as appears in Manzoni's well-known ode on his death. In Germany, Liberal opinion was divided. Heine wrote *"Das Buch Le Grand"* to glorify him, while the patriots of 1813 abhorred him; Goethe, as became a sage, preserved an Olympian neutrality.

In Catholic countries, Liberals were anti-clerical. They were everywhere in favor of religious toleration, which still did not exist in large portions of the Continent. Many thought that God reveals Himself directly to the heart, especially when it is the heart of an illiterate peasant, but that theology is a folly created by priests to enslave the human spirit; this led them to a vague and undogmatic religion like that of Rousseau. Others were pantheists, especially those connected with freemasonry, which had begun its career of Liberalism before the French Revolution.

The typical Continental Liberal was a republican, if only because Athens and Rome in their great days were republics. But many Liberals were prepared to put up with kings, provided they would grant constitutions, emancipate serfs, and allow freedom of religion and the press. Some were opposed to aristocracy, but many were not, holding, with Tacitus, that Rome enjoyed freedom under the oligarchy of the Senate, but not under the personal rule of the Emperors. All, under the influence of Rousseau, held that riches have a corrupting effect, and believed in the simple virtues of the poor.

From the standpoint of practical politics, the outlook of the Liberals can best be defined by their loves and hatreds. They hated the Holy

Alliance, and regarded Metternich as the quintessential archetype of evil. They loved France because of its Revolution and because of the free thought of its *philosophes*. They hated the Bourbons in France, Spain, and Naples, as the symbols of the victory of reaction. They hated the Turks as the oppressors of Greece, and therefore did not greatly hate the Tsar until 1848. They cursed Castlereagh and the memory of Pitt, but admired Canning more, perhaps, than he deserves.

Above all, they worshipped Byron.

The admiration of Byron on the Continent has always been something of a mystery to his compatriots; English Radicals preferred Shelley, whose revolutionary poems were recited at Chartist meetings and read by Owenite working men. But abroad Byron was considered the greatest poet of the age, with the possible exception of Goethe. Everything about him suited the romantic temperament: he was a Lord and yet an outcast, a man of wealth and yet a champion of the oppressed, outwardly a cynic but concealing (very ineffectually) a bleeding heart. Greece was the most romantic cause of the age, and Byron died for Greece. He praised the Prisoner of Chillon, who suffered for republicanism in the sixteenth century. Of Washington, the successful enemy of England, he wrote:

> Where may the wearied eye repose
> When gazing on the Great,
> Where neither guilty glory glows,
> Nor despicable state?
> Yes—one—the first—the last—the best—
> The Cincinnatus of the West,
> Whom envy dared not hate,
> Bequeathed the name of Washington,
> To make man blush there was but one.

It was the fashion of the age to be world-weary and to be gnawed by a secret sorrow, to despise the world and seek freedom in solitude. His Corsairs and Giaours appealed to the mood of aristocratic rebellion; he supplied the formula for those who loved Man but hated men. Mazzini could not forgive the English for their neglect of him, and refused to believe that he had treated his wife badly. Bismarck, in his youth, was always reading him: "Sometimes he would go duck-shooting in a punt, his bottle of wine always ready to his hand; between whiles he would read Byron." [1] When he became engaged to be married, he sent copies of Byron's poems to his fiancée, but marked them "all nonsense"—probably for fear of shocking her pietism. He even contemplated a world tour in the style of Childe Harold.

Byron's poems did much to popularize the principle of nationality. When he wrote about "the isles of Greece, where burning Sappho loved and sung," he suggested, and perhaps believed, that if the Turks were turned out a new Sappho would love and sing. While Metternich was persuading Alexander to prolong the slavery of Greece, Byron was writing:

Spirit of Freedom! when on Phyle's brow
Thou satst with Thrasybulus and his train,
Couldst thou forbode the dismal hour which now
Dims the green beauties of thine Attic plain?
Not thirty tyrants now enforce the chain,
But every carle can lord it o'er thy land;
Nor rise thy sons, but idly rail in vain,
Trembling beneath the scourge of Turkish hand,
From birth till death enslaved; in word, in deed, unmanned.

In all save form alone, how changed! and who
That marks the fire still sparkling in each eye,
Who but would deem their bosoms burn'd anew
With thy unquenched beam, lost Liberty!
And many dream withal the hour is nigh
That gives them back their fathers' heritage:
For foreign arms and aid they fondly sigh,
Nor solely dare encounter hostile rage,
Or tear their name defiled from Slavery's mournful page.

Hereditary bondsmen! Know ye not
Who would be free themselves must strike the blow?
By their right arms the conquest must be wrought?
Will Gaul or Muscovite redress ye? No!
True, they may lay your proud despoilers low,
But not for you will Freedom's altars flame.
Shades of the Helots! Triumph o'er your foe:

[1] Ludwig, *Bismarck*, p. 51.

Greece! Change thy lords, thy state is still the same;
Thy glorious day is o'er, but not thy years of shame.

Freedom, as it appeared in Byron's verse and in the aspirations of Liberals, was a very different thing from what it was to the Philosophical Radicals. Bentham and his followers, being Utilitarians, did not believe in any absolute "rights of man," though in practice they thought it usually better, within limits, to let men do as they liked. They valued liberty of opinion, because they thought that, where every man was free to state his case, the man with the best case would conquer public opinion. They valued liberty of commercial exchange, because it increased the total produce of labor. They had a general bias against governments, because they were composed of aristocrats who could quote Horace but knew nothing about trade. The kind of freedom they wanted was the freedom of individuals to engage in economic activities of a modern kind about which Homer and Vergil were silent.

As conceived by Liberals, freedom was something more romantic than the right to exchange Manchester cotton goods for Polish corn, or to make the dales hideous with mines and smoky chimneys. Freedom was, for the Liberal, a right due to human dignity: he held, with the Protestants, that there should be no intermediary between the soul and God, and that no external authority could instruct a man as to his duty. If an Italian felt that he owed devotion to his country, not to the adventitious ruler of some small part of it, he should act as a patriot, even though it might involve rejection of the divine right of the King of Naples or of the theologically sacred claims of the Pope. Thus nations, like individuals, had a right to be "free," i.e. to be not governed by foreigners, priests, or absolute monarchs. The belief that nations should be free was, in practice, the most important item in the Liberal creed. It developed into the principle of nationality, or of self-determinism, which largely dominated the affairs of Europe from 1848 to 1919.

The principle of nationality is difficult to state precisely. Approximately, it asserts that any geographical group which wishes to be a governmental unit has a right to be a single independent State. In practice, however, there are limitations. When, in 1917, a single house in Petrograd, appealing to the principle, declared itself to be a nation rightly struggling to be free, it was felt to be going too far, and even President Wilson gave it no countenance. Ireland had a right to invoke the principle against England, and Northeast Ulster had a right to invoke it against the rest of Ireland, but the counties of Fermanagh and Tyrone were not allowed to invoke it against the rest of Northeast Ulster. Thus one limitation of the principle was that the area concerned must not be very small. Another was that the area must not be in Asia or Africa; this was clear to all right-thinking people until the Japanese defeated the Russians. Yet another limitation was that the area concerned must not be one of exceptional international importance, such as Suez or Panama.

To the Liberals up to 1871, these limitations were not obvious, because a nation to them was something mystical, possessed of a soul almost as definite as that of a single human being. To force people to live under a government not that of their own nation was felt to be like forcing a woman to marry a man whom she hates. Love of home and love of family both have an instinctive basis, and together they form the foundation of love of country considered as a sentiment. It was the existence of this sentiment that contributed what was valid to the principle of nationality.

A nation, unlike a class, has a definition which is not economic. It is, we may say, a geographical group possessed of a sentiment of solidarity. Psychologically, it is analogous to a school of porpoises, a flock of crows, or a herd of cattle. The sentiment of solidarity may be due to a common language, a supposed common descent, a common culture, or common interests and common dangers. As a rule all these play a part in producing national sentiment, but the sentiment, however produced, is the only essential to the existence of a nation. The devotees of nationalism tend to think of a nation as a race in the biological sense, to a much greater degree than the facts warrant. Shakespeare speaks of the English as "this happy *breed* of men," and subsequent nationalists have followed suit. Since nations were conceived as races, the differences between them were thought to be, at least in part, congenital; thus Liberals, unlike the Philosophical Radicals, were led to emphasize differences in men and races, and to attribute these to causes other than education and environment. This outlook was much encouraged by Darwinism, when it came—not, of course, by its scientific form, but by the form in which it was found useful by politicians.

Nationalism in its modern form began in England in the time of the Tudors, being invoked by Henry VIII in religion and by Elizabeth in commerce. It was made holy by Protestantism, glorious by the defeat of the Armada, and profitable by overseas trade and the loot of Spanish galleons. These three elements of a vigorous national sentiment, temporarily dissociated during the struggle with the Stuarts, were re-united after 1688, and brought victory under Marlborough, the elder Pitt, and Nelson. After Waterloo, the English settled down to a comfortable belief that they were superior to all other nations in virtue, intelligence, martial prowess, and commercial acumen. Above all, they felt that, as Milton says (speaking nominally of the Jews), they understood "the solid rules of civil government." The first inroad upon their self-complacency was made by the growth of American and German industry in the late nineteenth century, to which they reacted with the somewhat hysterical imperialism of Rudyard Kipling and Cecil Rhodes.

English nationalism was liberal until the French Revolution, since it stood for the defence of parliamentary government against the absolute monarchies of Spain and France. From 1793 till the death of Castlereagh, opposition to revolutionary ideas made England reactionary; but from the time of Canning until Gladstone's fall in 1886, foreign policy was liberal except during a few short periods.

French nationalism begins with the defence of the Revolution against the alliance of kings; its sentiment is expressed in the Marseillaise. France led Continental Liberalism in 1789, in 1830, and in 1848; even in 1870, after the fall of Napoleon III, men like Garibaldi and Bakunin felt it worth while to volunteer for the defence of France. The patriotism of France always appeared, even to those who were not Frenchmen, to be something not merely national, but a crusade for the universal victory of the ideas of the Revolution. The most liberal elements in France were the most patriotic, while the kings of the Restoration were the most willing to submit to foreign dictation.

German nationalism was created by Napoleon. It began after the battle of Jena, and found vigorous expression in the War of Liberation in 1813. Like all nationalism, it had its idealism: it aimed at freeing the world from French "immorality" and restoring the simple ideals of duty of a more wholesome age. The Italians, oppressed and divided by priests, Bourbons, and Hapsburgs, hoped, if they could achieve freedom, to lead the world again in humanism and the spiritual life, as they had done from St. Francis to Michelangelo. The Slavs, whose various nationalisms first came to the fore in 1848, claimed for themselves a mystic consciousness of God, imbibed from the depths of their dark forests, and giving them a wisdom surpassing that of more explicit races.

The true and perfect Liberal believed in all these various national excellences, and held that the nations, free themselves, and respecting the freedom of others, should develop each its own special virtue, producing together a fine orchestral harmony.

In practice, unfortunately, things worked out rather differently.

II. ITALIAN NATIONALISM

Italians, whose national life had been violently extinguished in the sixteenth century, welcomed Napoleon as a compatriot and a liberator. The whole of the Italian mainland came under his influence; Sicily alone, under the influence of Nelson and Lady Hamilton, remained loyal to reaction and barbarism. The French régime in Italy was accompanied by liberal reforms, and Murat encouraged a feeling for Italian unity, though this remained somewhat vague.

The Congress of Vienna put an end to governmental liberalism in Italy. The powers of the Church and the aristocracy were restored; but where, as in Venice and Genoa, republics had existed for a thousand years before the revolutionary era, the *status quo ante* was not revived. We have seen in an earlier chapter what Talleyrand thought of the claims of the Genoese. The more they wished to preserve their ancient independence, the more important it became, in the eyes of the Congress, to show by their example how little the wishes of the populations concerned should influence the distribution of territory. In spite of the explicit promises of Lord William Bentinck, the Genoese were handed over to the absolute rule of the House of Savoy.

From Genoa, very appropriately, came the man who did most to generate Italian patriotism and desire for unity—Giuseppe Mazzini, born in 1805. His father had welcomed the republicanism of the French, and kept hidden behind his books certain old Girondin newspapers, which, if found, would have got him into trouble with the police. The study of Roman history at school stimulated at once patriotism and republicanism: Mazzini learnt to admire the younger Cato and the elder and younger Brutus—too much, indeed, since they encouraged in him a life-long taste for conspiracies. The French Revolution of 1830 had echoes in Italy; Mazzini, who was involved, became an exile, and spent most of the rest of his life in England; nevertheless, he remained the leader and inspirer of revolutionary Italy.

"Mazzini was a man of genius, but too much under the influence of two abstract ideas, God and the principle of nationality." So said the Rev. Benjamin Jowett, to whom both these "abstract ideas," one must suppose, appeared unimportant. To Mazzini, they were closely connected: his principle of nationality was not exclusively Italian, and his God was not a merely tribal Deity.

"Nationality," he says, "is sacred to me, because I see in it the influence of labor for the good and progress of all men." "Humanity is a great army, marching to the conquest of unknown lands, against enemies both strong and cunning. The peoples are its corps, each with its special operation to carry out, and the common victory depends on the exactness with which they execute the different operations." "God has written one line of his thought on the cradle of each people . . . special interests, special aptitudes, and before all special functions, a special mission to fulfil, a special work to be done in the cause of the advancement of humanity, seem to me the true, infallible characteristics of nationalities." He proceeded to tell each nation what its function was. England's business was industry and colonies, Russia's was to civilize Asia, Poland's was to be the champion of the Slavs; Germany was to think, France was to act, and Italy was to unite thought with action. "While the German walks earth with his sight lost in the depths of heaven, and the Frenchman's eye rarely looks aloft but scours the earth's surface with its restless penetrating glance, the Genius that guards the destinies of Italy has ever been wont to pass swiftly from the ideal to the real, seeking from of old how earth and heaven may be joined together."

It is not quite clear what Mazzini would have done with a Frenchman who wanted to think or with a German who wanted to act; nor does it seem very probable that a non-Italian would acquiesce in the pre-eminent rôle which he assigned to Italy. He rejected the claims of the Irish to be considered a nation, because they did not "plead for any distinct principle of life or system of legislation, derived from native peculiarities, and contrasting radically with English wants and wishes." So, at least, he said. But it is to be observed that, as the enemy of the Pope, he was always opposed by the Irish; perhaps if they had been friendly to him they would have had a national mission.

He considered the Slav movement, next to the Italian, the most important in Europe, and rightly observed that it must prove fatal to Austria and Turkey. He aimed ultimately at a United States of Europe, governed by a League whose headquarters should be in Rome, and whose creation should be the result of Italy's leadership. His principle of nationality, apparently, did not apply outside Europe. Asia was to be a mere appendage to Europe, and in the international orchestra no instrument was assigned to the United States. Nations existed, for Mazzini, through their poets and philosophers; those of Poland were known to him, but not those of China.

Mazzini undoubtedly meant to be fair as between different nations, but his predilection for his own continually broke out. He spoke of Italy as "radiant, purified by suffering, moving as an angel of light among the nations that thought her dead." "The destinies of Italy," he said, "are the destinies of the world." We have already seen the predominant part assigned to Italy in creating and administering from Rome the United States of Europe. It was "the land destined by God to the great mission of giving moral unity to Europe, and through Europe to humanity." A nation was, to him, not a mere aggregate of individuals, but a mystic entity with a soul of its own. He blamed Carlyle for undue emphasis upon the individual hero, as opposed to the collective life. The life of a nation, he said, "is not her own, but a force and a function in the universal providential scheme." God "divided Humanity into distinct groups or nuclei upon the face of the earth, thus creating the germ of Nationalities. Evil governments have disfigured the Divine sign. Nevertheless you may still trace it, distinctly marked out—at least so far as Europe is concerned—by the course of the great rivers, the direction of the higher mountains, and other geographical conditions." It is unfortunate that he omitted to tell us what was God's design as regards the Danube, for knowledge on this point might have prevented the Great War.

Not only the nation, but also the family, had for Mazzini the sacredness of a natural group which is more than the sum of its individuals. "The Family," he said, "is the Heart's Fatherland. There is in the Family an Angel, possessed of a mysterious influence of grace, sweetness, and love; an Angel who renders our duties less arid, and our sorrows less bitter . . . this Angel of the Family is Woman." Mazzini was a bachelor. It was with an exile's idealization that he viewed both family and country. "The conception of the family is not human, but divine, and no human power can extinguish it. Like the country—even more than the country—the family is an element of existence."

The Philosophical Radicals viewed men as individuals, and took an interest in such groupings only as arose from identity of economic interest. Mazzini was interested in groupings that have biological, sentimental, or geographical sources. The social entities that result in this way—the family, the nation, and humanity as a whole—appeared to him supremely important, and the source of most of the excellences to be found in individuals. This made him profoundly hostile both to Cobden and to Marx.

Apart from more general grounds, he objected to Cobden for his principle of non-intervention in Continental politics. He held neutrality to be base when a moral issue was involved. Italian unity was brought about by the armed support of France in 1859 and of Prussia in 1866 and 1870, as well as by the diplomatic sympathy of England in 1860; Cobden's policy of pacifism, he felt, would have left Italy for ever enslaved. Although, like Cobden, he disapproved of the Crimean War, he still said "the peace-men have no principle." We ought, it seems, to have fought against both Russia and Turkey at once, since both were oppressors. It never occurred to him that a habit of crusading all over the world would soon develop into imperialism.

The philosophy of utilitarianism was wholly repugnant to him: men should live for duty, not for happiness. He praised Carlyle for opposing "the strong materialism that for a century and a half has maintained a progressive usurpation, one while in the writings of Locke, Bolingbroke, or Pope, at another in those of Smith and Bentham, and has tended, by its doctrines of self-interest and material well-being, to the enthronement of selfishness in men's hearts. All the movement of industrial civilization, which has overflooded intellectual and moral civilization, has not deafened him [Carlyle]." Those who accept the principle of utility, he thought, "are led away by degrees to neglect the development of what is highest, holiest, and most imperishable in man, and to devote themselves to the pursuit of what they call the useful. There is nothing useful but the good, and that which it produces; uesfulness is a consequence to be foreseen, not a principle to be invoked." "Our concernment here below is not to be happy, but to become better; there is no other object in human life than to discover, by collective effort, and to execute, every one for himself, the law of God, without regarding individual results." He deduced that, in universities, there should be no professors of philosophy except such as agreed with his doctrines; speaking of the Hegelians, whom he disliked, he said: "One fine day we will sweep out all that stuff." He deduced further that "there is no sovereignty in the individual or society, except in so far as either conforms itself to the divine plan and law . . . the simple vote of a majority does not constitute sovereignty, if it evidently contradicts the supreme moral precepts . . . the will of the people is sacred, when it interprets and applies the moral law; null and impotent, when it dissociates itself from the law, and only represents caprice." These doctrines have been accepted and carried out by Mussolini.

"To execute, every one for himself, the law of God" is, no doubt, an admirable principle. For a Catholic, who believes that the Church knows the law of God, it may even be made into a rule of government. The results, as seen in the Papal States, may not have been quite what most moderns would think desirable; for example, the Inquisition still practised persecution, and issued edicts so late as 1841 "commanding all people to inform against heretics, Jews, and sorcerers, those who have impeded the Holy Office, or made satires against the Pope and clergy"; [2] while in 1851 a railway across the Romagna was prohibited on the ground that "railways produce commerce, and commerce produces sin." [3] But although such principles may seem curious, they are at least not anarchic, so long as it is admitted that the law of God is revealed to the Church. Mazzini, however, did not accept the authority of the Pope; for him, as for a Protestant, the law of God was revealed directly to each individual conscience. Unfortunately, there were conflicting revelations. Mazzini's conscience told him that England ought to intervene on the Continent by force of arms to se-

[2] Bolton King, *A History of Italian Unity*, I, p. 79.
[3] Simpson, *Louis Napoleon and the Recovery of France*, p. 48 n.

cure freedom for oppressed nations; Cobden's conscience told him the exact opposite. Both were earnest and highly moral men. Two men who both accepted the principle of utility could argue about their practical differences, since they had a common standard; but two men who both followed the "law of God" and found that they differed could only accuse each other of wickedness and fight it out. Thus Mazzini's ethic, which sounds so much nobler than Bentham's happiness principle, becomes, in its application to practical affairs, nothing better than the rule of the big battalions. Men who believe themselves the recipients of divine revelation are apt to be inconvenient, and Mazzini's doctrines could only end in perpetual war or an iron tyranny.

His objections to Socialism were such as might be expected from the nature of his objections to Bentham. He hated Marx's materialism, and he believed in preaching duty rather than class-war. He had some dealings with the International at first, but only until he became convinced that he could not turn it from Socialism to the defence of oppressed nations. He regarded religion, not economics, as fundamental in the interpretation of history; so far from regarding men as the product of their environment, he held, on the contrary, that the social and industrial environment is "the manifestation of the moral and intellectual condition of humanity at a given period, and above all of its faith." Although he favored a good deal of semi-Socialistic legislation, his philosophical outlook was the very antithesis of that of Marx. In all things, he emphasized will; he objected to the fatalism of Hegel, and therefore all the more to that of Marx, which had the added vice of being materialistic.

Throughout a long life of agitation, Mazzini had only a brief moment of precarious power, in the Roman Republic of 1849, which was snuffed out, after a few months, by Louis Napoleon, as a first step to the acquisition of a halo of respectability. The later and more successful pursuit of Italian unity was guided by the skilful policy of Cavour, and new territory, as it was conquered, was added to the dominions of the House of Savoy. Mazzini remained all his life a republican, and derived no satisfaction from the creation of the Kingdom of Italy. But it was his propaganda that had generated the enthusiasm which Garibaldi led and Cavour utilized. What Italy has become, Mazzini's doctrines have made it.

III. GERMAN NATIONALISM

German Liberalism, during the sixty years between the battle of Jena and the Austro-Prussian War of 1866, was a somewhat confused mixture of three different elements. In the West, there was a pro-French element, which liked the reforms introduced by the revolutionary governments, considered Germany a backward country, regarded democratic republicanism as the goal, and held revolution to be the indispensable method. Among merchants and industrialists, and also among Prussian officials, there was a movement influenced by English ideas of *laissez faire,* called in early days *Smithianismus* and afterwards *Manchesterismus;* this movement was strongest in the early 'sixties, when Cobden was at the height of his fame. The third element in German Liberalism was the desire for national unity; this purely patriotic feeling was compelled to take a Liberal form owing to the fact that unity could, seemingly, only be won in opposition to the Princes, and to Austria. The German unity movement was anti-French, and therefore had difficulty in co-operating with pro-French Liberalism, which died out when Bismarck found a Conservative way of achieving unity and German patriotism ceased to be liberal. In the 'seventies, industry turned against free trade, and Cobdenite Liberalism had no further influence in Germany. What survived of Philosophical Radicalism was only what had been embodied, through Marx, in Social Democracy.

While the French and English forms of Liberalism thus failed to make any very deep or lasting impression upon Germany, the nationalistic form gradually conquered the whole country with the exception of the Socialists. Its first literary expression was in Fichte's *Addresses to the German Nation,* which were delivered as lectures in Berlin during the winter of 1807–8. The battle of Jena and the Peace of Tilsit had humiliated Prussia, while Napoleon, having won the friendship of Alexander, seemed unshakable. Fichte was an earnest and unworldly philosopher, the heir of Kant, the recognized leader of the transcendental metaphysicians. He had been accused of atheism for identifying God with the moral order of the universe, and had been compelled to resign his professorship at Jena. But the Prussian Government befriended him, he came to Berlin, and ultimately (in 1811) became Rector of the University. His philosophy, which was what is called "idealistic," emphasized the importance of the Ego, and his behavior was sometimes in accordance with his beliefs, so that Goethe and Schiller, who disliked him, nicknamed him "The Absolute Ego." His beliefs and his character combined to inspire the doctrines which made him the founder of German nationalism.

Fichte begins his Addresses by saying that he is speaking to the whole German nation, "setting aside completely and rejecting all the dissociating distinctions which for centuries unhappy events have caused in this single nation." From foreign sources, Germany has been infected by self-seeking; it must be built up again on a loftier moral plane, and for this purpose the first requisite is a new system of education. "By means of the new education we want to mold the Germans into a corporate body, which shall be stimulated and animated in all its individual members by the same interest." Will, he says, "is the very root of man," and he immediately goes on: "the new education must consist essentially in this, that it completely destroys freedom of will in the soil which it undertakes to cultivate, and produces on the contrary strict necessity in the decisions of the will, the opposite being impossible. Such a will can henceforth be relied on with confidence and certainty." We must make the pupils indifferent to their material welfare, and "mold men who are inwardly and fundamentally good, since it is through such men alone that the German nation can still continue to exist." This, apparently, is the sole reason for preferring good men to bad ones.

During education, there must be no contact whatever with the world outside the school. "From the very beginning the pupil should be continuously and completely under the influence of this education, and should be separated altogether from the community, and kept from all contact with it. He must not even hear that our vital impulses and actions can be directed towards our maintenance and welfare." This means, I suppose, that boys are to eat, not because they are hungry, but because food is necessary if they are to help in preserving the German nation.

The education of Germans is important for the world, and not only for their own country, for "it is first of all the Germans who are called upon to begin the new era as pioneers and models for the rest of mankind." This is proved by considerations of language. The French, Spaniards, and Italians are regarded by Fichte as of more or less Teutonic descent, and the Germans in Germany are admitted to have much Slav intermixture; it is not therefore racially, but linguistically, that the Germans, including the Scandinavians, are purer than the nations speaking languages derived from Latin: these have become worn down and degraded through owing their origin to the attempts of immigrants to talk low Latin. Latin and Greek were pure languages, and so is German; but the Romance languages are impure.

From this it follows that the German is more earnest and more profound than the foreigner; it follows also that there is less difference between educated and uneducated in Germany than in Latin countries, because in the latter only those who know Latin can understand the original meaning of words in common use.[4] Hence it comes that the conception of "culture" is un-German, and that the German who wishes to be thought cultured imitates foreign ways. But this love of foreign ways has proved disastrous: "all the evils which have now brought us to ruin are of foreign origin. Of course it was only when united with German earnestness and influence on life that such evils were bound to bring destruction in their train." The researches of foreigners, or of Germans who have fallen under their influence, are merely historical, whereas those of the unspoilt German are truly philosophical. The foreign genius may be compared to a bee, which gathers honey and "deposits it with charming tidiness in cells of regular construction. But the German spirit is an eagle, whose mighty body thrusts itself on high and soars on strong and well-practised wing into the empyrean, that it may rise nearer to the sun whereon it delights to gaze."

Fichte speaks of Germany as the mother-country, and regards the rest of the world as somewhat faithless colonies,[5] whose sole function is to transmit to Germany the culture of antiquity, which they themselves are too superficial to understand. If Germany were destroyed

---

[4] There is much truth in this. Compare, e.g., the word "armistice" with the word "Waffenstillstand," literally "weapon-still-stand."

[5] This view is scarcely intelligible except to those who know how history is taught in Germany. The German schoolboy learns that there was a corrupt and effete Roman Empire, but that the countries which it had drained of vitality were rejuvenated by an influx of noble Goermans: Ostrogoths in Italy, Visigoths in Spain, Franks in Gaul. The royal families and aristocracies of these Latin countries were of Germanic origin, and it was held that German blood had given them whatever merit they possessed in later centuries.

by the foreigners, "the hitherto continuous stream of the development of our race would be in fact at an end; barbarism would be bound to begin again and to go on without hope of deliverance, until we were all living in caves again like wild beasts, and, like them, devouring one another. That this is really so and must inevitably follow, only the German can see, of course."

As the lectures proceed, the superlative merits of Germany become increasingly evident. "The German nation," we learn, "is the only one among the neo-European nations that has shown in practice, by the example of its burgher class for centuries, that it is capable of enduring a republican constitution." "Belief in death, as contrasted with an original and living people, we have called the foreign spirit. When once this foreign spirit is present among the Germans . . . it will reveal itself as the confession . . . of a belief in the universal and equal sinfulness of all. This belief I have sufficiently described in another place —see the *Guide to the Blessed Life*, Lecture II." At last it appears that the word *German* is only accidentally a geographical or racial term; to Teutonic profundity it has another and more spiritual significance:

So, let there appear before you at last in complete clearness what we have meant by Germans, as we have so far described them. The true criterion is this: do you believe in something absolutely primary and original in man himself, in freedom, in endless improvement, in the eternal progress of our race, or do you not believe in all this, but rather imagine that you clearly perceive and comprehend that the opposite of all this takes place? All who either are themselves alive and creative and productive of new things, or who, should this not have fallen to their lot, at any rate definitely abandon the things of naught and stand on the watch for the stream of original life to lay hold of them somewhere, or who, should they not even be so far advanced as this, at least have an inkling of freedom and do not hate it or take fright at it, but on the contrary love it —all these are original men; they are, when considered as a people, an original people, *the* people simply, Germans. All who resign themselves to being something secondary and derivative, and who distinctly know and comprehend that they are such, are so in fact, and become ever more so because of this belief of theirs; they are an appendix to the life which bestirred itself of its own accord before them or beside them; they are an echo resounding from the rock, an echo of a voice already silent; they are considered as a people, outside the original people, and to the latter they are strangers and foreigners.

Mazzini allowed every European nation (except the Irish) to have its own legitimate patriotism, and its own contribution to the symphony of human progress. Fichte is more thoroughgoing: "only the German—the original man, who has not become dead in an arbitrary organization—really has a people and is entitled to count on one, and he alone is capable of real and rational love of his nation." In fact, "to have character and to be German undoubtedly mean the same."

Descending from these metaphysical heights to the mundane affairs of practical politics, we learn that Germany should not trade with the outer world, but should be a closed commercial State—a subject upon which Fichte wrote a book in 1800. The German will never want the freedom of the seas, because "the abundant supplies of his own land, together with his own diligence, afford him all that is needed in the life of a civilized man." It must not, however, be supposed that the German State will be pacifistic: peace is the ideal of those who love material comfort. The State has "a higher object than the usual one of maintaining internal peace, property, personal freedom, and the life and well-being of all. For this higher object alone, and with no other intention, does the State assemble an armed force. . . . What spirit has an undisputed right to summon and to order everyone concerned, whether he himself be willing or not, and to compel anyone who resists, to risk everything including his life? Not the spirit of the peaceful citizen's love for the constitution and the laws, but the devouring flame of higher patriotism, which embraces the nation as the vesture of the eternal, for which the noble-minded man joyfully sacrifices himself, and the ignoble man, who only exists for the sake of the other, must likewise sacrifice himself."

"The ignoble man exists only for the sake of the other." This principle contains the denial both of the Rights of Man and of Benthamism, for Bentham held all men's happiness to be of equal importance. Fichte considers that the ignoble man should be sacrificed. Who is to decide which is the ignoble man? Clearly the government. Hence every tyranny is justifiable, and the extirpation of political opponents can be carried out in the name of national nobility.

The *Addresses to the German Nation* became the Bible of German patriots, and even so late as 1919 the Social Democrat Ebert, first President of the German Republic, after announcing his policy, said: "Thus shall we realize that which Fichte has given to the German nation as its task." Nor was it only in Germany that he was admired. Carlyle extolled him, and T. H. Green taught a whole generation at Oxford to regard him as the perfection of ethical purity. Yet there is in the modern world no governmental cruelty, injustice, or abomination which this virtuous professor's principles fail to justify.

The monarchs, and "that base and bloody tool of tyranny, Wm. Pitt," tried to destroy the French Revolution, and instead produced Napoleon. Napoleon tried to destroy Prussia, but produced Fichte, who led to Bismarck. Bismarck, by trying to destroy France, made the *revanche* inevitable; and the *revanche* led to Hitler. Perhaps a lofty morality, backed by bayonets, is not the best way of advancing human happiness.

If German patriotism, as inaugurated by Fichte, appears somewhat more fierce and domineering than that of Mazzini, the reason is obvious. Italy could not hope to achieve unity without foreign help, and must, therefore, make its propaganda such as would appeal to liberal minds in other countries. Prussia, on the contrary, still remembered the glories of Frederick the Great's resistance to a world in arms, while forgetting England's part as his ally, and the sudden *volte-face* of Russia by which he was saved at the end. A united Germany, it was felt, would be strong enough to stand alone. Nationalist convictions are never more conciliatory to foreigners than is necessitated by diplomatic and military considerations. If Fichte claims more for Germany than Mazzini claims for Italy, that is solely because Germany was potentially a more powerful country.

When the Germans rose against the French in 1813, they were inspired partly by patriotism such as Fichte preached, and partly by a desire for Parliamentary constitutions in the English style. Stein, who represented the union of patriotism and Liberalism in Prussia, carried out important reforms, including the abolition of serfdom; the King of Prussia and most of the other German rulers promised to grant constitutions after the overthrow of Napoleon. Austria, however, opposed constitutionalism, and also the desire for German unity, which was especially strong in Prussia. Under Metternich's influence, all nationalism was frowned upon, and Fichte's *Addresses* became illegal.

For a time, the revolutions of 1848 brought a change. The men who came to the fore were constitutional Liberals and patriotic advocates of German unity. In the Frankfort Assembly they endeavored to draft a constitution for Germany, but they could not solve the difficulty of Austria. Austria proper was German, and should, they felt, be included in the new Germanic Federation; but the bulk of the inhabitants of the Austro-Hungarian Empire were Magyars or Slavs, whom patriotic Germans had no wish to include. The Frankfort Assembly, after defeating a republican minority, offered the crown of united Germany to the King of Prussia, but he refused it. Austria recovered humiliated Prussia, and set to work to destroy afresh all hopes both of unity and of democratic government.

It is remarkable how many Germans who became vigorous supporters of the Prussian Government after the removal of Austrian influence were exiles in the years following the failure of the movements of 1848. Not only Radicals such as Heine, Marx, and Liebknecht were compelled to live abroad, but such men as Mommsen and Richard Wagner, and the two men who were afterwards Bismarck's secretaries and closest confidants, Lothar Bucher and Moritz Busch. It was only through Bismarck that German patriotism became respectable and Conservative, with the result that many men who had been Liberal because they were patriots became Conservative for the same reason.

What may be called the myth of German nationalism was perfected, in the time of Bismarck, by a number of professors, among whom the most important, perhaps, was the historian Treitschke. In his *History of Germany in the Nineteenth Century*, he presented events in the way most calculated to stimulate national pride, without any narrow-minded prejudice in favor of accuracy. His point of view was an important element in forming the outlook of Germans in the time of William II; a few quotations will make it clear.

Of literature in 1813, he writes: "The poets of the great struggle of the nations sang of war, the only form of political activity directly suitable for artistic expression. Their patriotic enthusiasm awakened the eternal and characteristically human feelings of joy in battle and wrath in the fray, of hope for victory and delight in victory. They pursued a definite end, one readily comprehensible to simple folk, the liberation of the fatherland from the yoke of foreign oppressors."

He recognized with regret that in the 'forties a mania for railways and factories, and a tendency to prefer science to Greek and Latin, seized upon many Germans, especially such as had lived in England or America:

Amid the busy activities of the new political economy, there had rapidly come to the front a race of persons who were fanatics for utility and for universal progress, a breed which had been quite unknown to the quiet Germany of earlier days, types ridiculed by the Munich artists in their masked processions and comic papers under the nickname of "Mister Vorwärts." These persons had all paid a visit to England or America; they were interested in every new railway company or factory enterprise (which were often mere swindles); they prized nothing but what could be counted, weighed, and measured. From these circles first came the cry which was eagerly reechoed by ignorant journalists, that training in natural science must become the basis of general culture, and that linguistic and historical education, upon which for thousands of years all civilized nations had been nourished, must be straightway dethroned from its high estate.

Fortunately, Jakob Grimm made clear the error in this scientific outlook. "He showed that the spiritual sciences must necessarily be the foundation of general culture because they alone comprehend the whole of human life, including the world of the imagination and of the heart." And the greatest of the men of science, such as Mayer and Helmholtz, took the same line: "in all these pioneering intelligences of the new natural science, the old and splendid German idealism still remained active. . . . A lapse into the foolishness of materialism was left to the lesser men who succeeded them."

Treitschke traces to its origins the struggle between protection and free trade, which, on the theoretical side, was inaugurated in 1841 by List's *The National System of Political Economy*:

The Scottish sensualist philosophy had never secured much vogue in our country, and it had been effectively refuted by Kant. Yet in the field of economic science there continued to prevail in Germany the doctrine of Adam Smith, which stands or falls with sensualism. By Ricardo and Say this doctrine had been reconstituted with one-sided rigidity, and had been popularised by the vigorous writings of Bastiat. When the need of the hour had been the overthrow of the feudal order of society, this doctrine had proved a liberating force, but it now lingered in German universities as nothing better than a sterile tradition. Following this petrified method of the teachers of the old law of nature, a method which every efficient jurist had long since abandoned, the political economists were accustomed to deduce their propositions as logical inferences from the abstraction of the economic man who buys in the cheapest and sells in the dearest market. The harmony of all interests, the just and rational ordering of society, were to issue from the struggle between the conflicting egoisms of such individual economic men, were to be the outcome of the free interplay of social forces; the animal impulse of selfishness was to work a miracle, was to lift men above the status of the beasts. Persons of refined sensibilities, able to realise that this doctrine was ungerman, were none the less willing to ascribe such a miraculous power to enlightened selfishness, for they failed to realise that selfishness cannot possibly be enlightened, cannot from the low levels upon which it perforce exists gain an extensive outlook across the wide vistas of national life. The theory rested upon an unhistorical optimism which completely ignored the two great forces of universal history, the force of stupidity and the force of sin.

There is truth in this criticism. The Benthamites took too little notice of "the force of stupidity and the force of sin," both of which had their revenge in the production of such men as Treitschke and in the growth of the nationalist movement throughout the world. But when he goes on to say that it was a mistake to suppose that "increasing understanding of self-interest would suffice to put an end to crime," it may well be doubted whether there is any other force likely to have this effect. In politics, there are powerful forces other than self-interest, but in the main they are worse: they are forces of envy, pugnacity, cruelty, and love of domination. All these may be called "stupidity and sin." But in fact they are the very forces to which "idealists" give noble names such as patriotism, national spirit, contempt for merely material ends, and so forth. Undoubtedly there are large crimes of enlightened selfishness, such as King Leopold's administration of the Congo; but their possibility depends upon absence of enlightenment in their victims. Undoubtedly, also, there are better motives than self-interest, but these are seldom sufficiently widespread to be politically powerful.

Treitschke appears to hold that, while Germans should never consider anything but the interest of Germany, men of other countries are wicked if they pursue national aims. He speaks of a Franco-Russian alliance as an "unwholesome political design," and of Slav nationalisms as "fantastic dreams." But what he hates most is a rationalistic utilitarian outlook. He complains that in England the landed gentry, when free trade lessened the value of their land, took to commerce instead of starving in a genteel manner:

Now that landed property ceased to furnish sufficient return, the land-owners began to interest themselves in railways, banks, and industrial enterprises of all kinds. Ere long a son of the duke of Argyll could run a lucrative wine business without suffering social ostracism. While the German gentry remained poor but knightly, in England old conceptions of honour and prejudices of caste were undermined by the potency of money. A mercantile breeze stirred the entire life of the nation. The duel, the indispensable and ultimate resource against the degradation of society, passed into disuse, and soon became altogether unknown.

Cobden, he says,

regarded the state as an assurance society founded by the arbitrary will of individuals. The sole function of this corporation was, he considered, to protect business and labour against violent disturbances, and to make its premiums to the assured as low as possible. For him, economic interest made up the entire content of human life, while quick journeys for commercial travellers and the cheap production of cotton were the supreme aims of civilisation. He was perfectly serious when he declared that Stephenson and Watt had enormously more significance in history than Caesar or Napoleon.

Not that Cobden was wholly bad: he "had more understanding of foreign nations than had most of his fellow-countrymen; he admired Prussia." Nevertheless his influence on Germany was to be deplored.

Treitschke is even more anti-French than anti-English. He describes the French literature read in Germany as "a compost of filth and blood," which has an apparent worldly wisdom derived from turning the old ideas topsy-turvy, and saying "God is sin, marriage is unchastity, property is theft." Some French writers, we are told, even go so far as to suggest that there may be virtuous prostitutes.

He is not much better about the Jews. He tells how the Elector of Hesse, because of his intimacy with Amschel Rothschild, granted equality of rights to the Jews in 1833, before any other ruler had done so.

"The results of this experiment were most unsatisfactory. It was made plain that the sins of usury and cheating were not merely the consequences of lack of freedom, but were deeply inracinated national failings of the Jews, vices whose extirpation would be far from easy. In Hesse, where the Jews could now adopt any profession they chose, they showed themselves to be cruel bloodsuckers upon the poor countryfolk, with the result that the cradle of Jewish emancipation in Germany became the focus of an utterly fanatical hatred of the Jews."

Who could guess, from such a passage, that the ancient Prussian nobility, whom Treitschke admires above all mankind, obtained every penny of their incomes by being "cruel bloodsuckers upon the poor countryfolk," and only began to emancipate serfs as a result of defeat at the hands of the French? In 1807–8, after Jena, the gradual emancipation of serfs was decreed; in 1816, after Waterloo, this measure was limited to those peasants who had plough oxen and a share in the village fields. And so the law remained until 1850.

In judging Germany, it is difficult to remember that the Germans, who have led the world in science, who are ultra-modern in art and in industrial technique, began their political development later than France and much later than England. Frederick the Great was more absolute than Henry VIII, and the status of the peasantry was less free at his death than it had been in England since the Black Death in 1349. Parliamentary institutions, which were established gradually during the nineteenth century, had in 1914 about as much power as in Elizabethan England. Prussia, the most important of German States, was also the most militaristic, and had in its Eastern Provinces a feudal nobility of Squire Westerns, who had come originally as alien conquerors of the native Slavs. Moreover, in England, Squire Western, as a Jacobite, had no influence upon the Government, which was divided between high finance and the great Whig families, both liberal influences; whereas in Prussia Squire Bismarck and his neighbors were the main support of the throne.

Another reason for the weakness of Liberal ideas in Germany as compared with England was the comparative unimportance of commerce. The Hanse Towns, which lived by commerce, retained throughout the nineteenth century a Cobdenite outlook; in 1871, Hamburg and Bremen remained outside the Zollverein because they clung to free trade. Liberalism is essentially an offspring of commerce; it existed in the commercial cities of ancient Greece and mediaeval Italy, and in the commercial States of Holland and England. Fichte, as we have seen, wished Germany to have no foreign commerce, and his modern followers retain this view as far as the times permit. What seems to us belated in the German outlook is connected with this depreciation of commerce.

The characteristic doctrines of German nationalism are all to be found in Carlyle: belief in the importance of will rather than knowledge, faith rather than reason, and duty rather than happiness; worship of the State and admiration of vigorous despotism; emphasis on race and on heroic individuals; dislike of industrialism disguised as pity for the industrial proletariat. Much of this is also to be found in Disraeli. And in British imperialism as practised in Asia and Africa, all the impulses that seem repulsive in German nationalism have found vent. The Empire has been a cesspool for British moral refuse; Germany had no such outlet, and had to endure its despots at home. "I wanted to take service in India under the English flag," said Bismarck in his youth; "then I thought, after all, what harm have the Indians done me?" The self-righteous Englishman will do well to ponder this reflection.

CHAPTER XXIX

BISMARCK AND GERMAN UNITY

LIBERALISM and the principle of nationality suffered joint defeat in 1848, but soon revived. In Italy, in 1859 and 1860, they won, in alliance, a spectacular victory in the unification of almost the whole country, with parliamentary government under the constitutional rule of Victor Emmanuel. (Venetia was won in 1866, and Rome in 1870.)

A similar liberal-nationalistic development was to be expected in Germany, where the victory of reaction after 1848 did not seem likely to be permanent. But the course of events in Germany was not according to the preconceived pattern. The principle of legitimacy, a hampering legacy of the Congress of Vienna, was thrown over by the Conservative Government of Prussia, which found satisfaction for German nationalism with only a few concessions to Liberalism. The separation of nationalism from liberalism, and of conservatism from the principle of legitimacy, was an important achievement, which profoundly affected European development. It was mainly due to the personal influence of Bismarck, who, on this account, must be reckoned one of the most influential men of the nineteenth century.

Bismarck was a country gentleman, and remained all his life somewhat bucolic. His ancestors were aristocratic landowners in Brandenburg, where they had lived for five hundred years or more—much longer than the Hohenzollern, as he remarked on one occasion. They had been proud and unbending; his grandfather, a disciple of Rousseau, had incurred the serious displeasure of Frederick the Great. His father, who was good-tempered and lacking in ambition, was in youth an officer in the army, as was almost inevitable; but he retired to his estates as soon as he could, and took no part in the campaigns of 1806 or 1813. The many generations of his ancestors, vigorous and sturdy, had eaten voraciously and drunk liberally, cultivated their fields and shot their game, begotten children and grown old and died, with an unchanging rhythm like that of the seasons. These centuries of stable existence among obedient serfs formed the unconscious background of Bismarck's thoughts and feelings, giving to conservatism a hold over him which nothing could shake. "I love great trees, they are ancestors," he said. When a visitor was about to drive through the forest in a top-hat, he exclaimed: "Spare my trees the sight of that object!" He did not like the thought of being buried in a coffin underground; pointing to two huge pines, he said: "There, between those trees, up in the free air of the forest, is where I should like to have my last resting-place, where the sunlight and the fresh breeze can get at me."

It was from his mother, not from his father, that he derived his intelligence and his restlessness. His mother's family, the Menckens, were not aristocratic; they were professors and civil servants. Her father was a minister under Frederick the Great, was dismissed by his successor as a Jacobin, and was recalled by Frederick William III as an ally of Stein. She herself was intellectual, urban, ambitious, and fashionable. She found her husband unsatisfactory because of his indifference to success. They lived in Berlin in the winters, and in the summers, when he would have preferred his estates, she would develop ailments and insist upon a fashionable watering-place, a custom which deprived her sons of their summer holidays in the country. Discontented, clever, and worldly, she made everybody uncomfortable, and could not put up with the manner of life that had satisfied the Bismarcks for five centuries.

The boy Otto, born in 1815, loved his father and the country, and hated Berlin and his mother. In his early childhood, he was happy at his father's estate at Kniephof in Pomerania, making friends with cowherds and gamekeepers, horses and dogs. And when his father took him down to the village, he would explain that it all belonged to them. However, the time came for him to go to school, and his mother, who was up-to-date, selected an establishment which boasted that it was conducted according to the principles of Pestalozzi. Here he suffered from the bad food and the harsh discipline, of which he continued to complain all his life, saying that he used to be waked in the morning with a rapier thrust. In adolescence, his school reports accused him of "pretentious arrogance" and of having "no thought of proper respect for his teachers." Respect was never his strong point.

At the age of seventeen, full of Byronic romance, believing himself to be a republican and an atheist, he became a student at the University of Göttingen, where he soon won the respect of his fellow-students by his extreme readiness to fight duels and his victories when his challenges were accepted. He made friends with Motley the historian, also at that time a student at Göttingen, who said that he never spoke sense except when they were alone together. For the rest, he spent most of his time in drinking and brawling. "There is the substance of a hero running to seed here," said Motley at the time. As might be expected, he ran up debts, and there were, he wrote to his brother, "very disagreeable scenes between myself and the old man [his father], who refuses to pay my debts. . . . Not that it matters very much, for I have plenty of credit, so that I can live a thoroughly dissolute life. The result is that I look pale and ill, and my old man, when I come home at Christmas, will naturally ascribe this to lack of victuals. Then I shall take a strong line, saying that I would rather be a Mohammedan than go on suffering hunger, and then I shall get my way." "The Kniephof court," he told his brother, "is more accessible to diplomatic cunning and to lies than to swashbuckling."

At the age of twenty-one, he obtained a diplomatic position in Aix-la-Chapelle, but the duties did not seem to him worth performing, and he went posting over Europe in pursuit of an English girl whom he wished to marry. Naturally, when he returned, it became necessary to resign. He was given another chance, but could not settle down to the routine of official life. For financial reasons—including his debts—his family decided that he should live at Kniephof and manage the estate. He himself felt no objection to this course, for reasons which he explained in a letter to a cousin:

Affairs and official service are utterly uncongenial to me; I should not think myself fortunate to become an official or even a minister of State; I deem it quite as respectable to grow corn as to write despatches, and in certain circumstances as more useful; I have more inclination to command than to obey. These are facts for which I can give no reason beyond my own tastes. . . . A Prussian official is like a player in an orchestra. No matter whether he be the first violin or the triangle, . . . he has to play his instrument as the needs of the concerted piece dictate. . . . But for my part, I want to play music such as I regard as good—or else not play at all.

For a few renowned statesmen, especially in countries with an absolute constitution, patriotism has been the motive driving them into the public service; much more often, the mainspring has been ambition, the wish to command, to be admired, to be famous. I must admit that I myself am not free from this passion. Many distinctions, such as those which accrue to a soldier in wartime, or to a statesman under a free constitution, to such men as Peel, O'Connell, Mirabeau, etc.—men who had their part to play in energetic political movements—would exert on me an attractive force which would override every consideration, would lure me as a flame allures a moth.

I am less attracted by successes which I might secure along trodden roads, by examinations, influence, the study of documents, seniority, the favour of my superiors. Still, there are moments when I cannot think without regret of all the gratifications to vanity which awaited me in the public service; the satisfaction of having my value officially recognised by swift promotion; . . . the pleasing sensation of being regarded as a capable and useful person; the glamour which would surround me and my family—all these considerations dazzle me when I have drunk a bottle of wine. I need careful and sober reflection to convince me that they are but cobwebs spun by foolish vanity, and are on the same footing as a dandy's pride in the cut of his coat and a banker's delight in his money; that it is unwise and useless for us to seek our happiness in the opinions of others, and that a reasonable man must live his own life in accordance with what he himself recognises to be right and true, and must not be guided by the impression he makes on others or by the thought of what people will say about him before and after his death.

In a word, I am not free from ambition, though I regard it as just as bad as any of the other passions, and even more foolish, because ambition, if I give myself up to it, demands the sacrifice of all my energy and independence without guaranteeing me, even in the most fortunate event, any permanent satisfaction. . . . An income sufficient for my needs and enabling me to set up house in town would not be mine, even if I were eminently successful, until I was about forty years old and had been raised to a presidency. By that time I should have become a dryasdust, should have grown hypochondriacal, should have had my health undermined by a sedentary life, and should only need a wife as a sick nurse.

These moderate advantages, the tickling of my vanity by hearing myself addressed as "Herr Präsident," the consciousness of rarely helping the country as much as I cost it, and of occasionally working it hindrance and doing it harm—do not allure me. I have therefore made up my mind to preserve my independence, and not to sacrifice my vital energies as long as there still remain thousands of persons (some of them highly distinguished), to whose taste such prizes seem precious, so that they are delighted to fill the place that I leave vacant for them.

From 1839 to 1847, Bismarck lived the life of a young country squire. He hunted, he drank (a mixture of champagne and porter, usually), he had innumerable love affairs, and he acquired a reputation for recklessness, so that mothers kept their daughters away from him. But he studied agriculture seriously, both theoretically and practically, and read poetry and history widely, French and English as well as German. When he was twenty-seven he made a journey to England, which he liked because people were polite, because peers returned from the House of Lords on horseback, because Hussars' remounts had rations of a bushel of oats and twelve pounds of hay, and because in restaurants he was allowed to carve the joint and take as much as he wanted.

When he returned from his travels, country life no longer seemed satisfying.

In the mornings I am out of humour, but after dinner I am accessible to kindlier feelings. My associates are dogs, horses, and country squires. Among the latter I enjoy a certain prestige, because I can read easily, always dress like a human being, can carve game with the accuracy of a butcher, ride easily and boldly, smoke very strong cigars, and am able to drink all my guests under the table—for, unfortunately, I can no longer get drunk, although my memory tells me that this condition used to be an extremely happy one. I therefore vegetate, very like a clock, without any special wishes or fears; an extremely harmonious and very tedious condition.

In this mood, he came in contact with a young and charming pietist lady, Marie von Thadden, who was engaged to his friend Moritz von Blanckenburg. She set to work to convert her fiancé's friend: she and Blanckenburg told him of a consumptive girl who was dying and who loved him, but must know of his conversion if she was to die happy. When she died, they told him that she had "received inner assurance that your soul will not be lost. . . . Oh if you only knew how the deceased had prayed for you!" He was moved to tears, but still not converted. However, after Marie and Blanckenburg were married, he met at their house a friend of hers, Johanna von Puttkamer, who pursued the work of reclaiming him with more success: he saw the light and married the lady. He was a model husband, affectionate, tender, and masterful, with an almost feminine attention to detail, passionately fond of his children and seriously troubled by their slightest ailments.

His conversion was perhaps not so complete as he allowed his fiancée to suppose. He wrote to his brother:

In matters of faith we differ somewhat, more to her distress than to mine. Still, the difference is not so great as you might imagine, for many external and internal happenings have wrought changes in me of late, so that now (a new thing in me, as you know) I feel justified in numbering myself among those who believe in the Christian religion. Although in respect of some of the doctrines, perhaps those which Christians as a rule consider the most important, I am—so far as I am clear concerning my own views—by no means fully reconciled with the Christian outlook, nevertheless, tacitly as it were, a sort of Treaty of Passau has been signed between myself and Johanna. Besides, I like pietism in women, and detest members of the female sex who make a parade of enlightenment.

He was at all times superstitious, but hardly religious. He made use of religion, almost unconsciously, when it was politically convenient. "If we withdraw the religious foundation of the State," he said on one occasion, "then the State remains nothing more than a chance aggregate of rights, a sort of bulwark against the war of all against all. . . . It is not clear to me how, in such a State, the ideals of the communists, for instance, concerning the immorality of property could be disputed." This sort of argument made him feel religion useful. But his own personal religion, in so far as he had one, was a vague pantheism connected with big trees and the country.

His engagement and marriage were in 1847. At this time, both for public and private reasons, his ambition revived. He became a member of the Landtag, and throughout the revolutionary period upheld the extreme Conservative views appropriate to a particular Prussian Junker, even going so far as to deny that in 1813 patriotic Prussians had had any thought for Germany as a whole.

The years from 1851 to 1862 were spent in acquiring official experience. From 1851 to 1858, he was Prussian envoy to the Federal Diet at Frankfort; from 1859 to 1862 he was ambassador at St. Petersburg; in 1862, for a few months, ambassador in Paris, and then, in the same year, Minister-President of Prussia. From that date until 1890, Prussia's policy was Bismarck's.

The situation in 1862 was one of acute conflict between King and Parliament. By the Constitution of 1851, which lasted until the Great War, the balance of power in the Prussian Landtag was held by the middle class. The electorate was divided into three sections, rich, medium, and poor, each section contributing an equal amount to the revenue. The sections, each separately, elected equal numbers of electors, and the electors, all together, elected the Landtag. Thus the middle class and the poor could overpower the rich, while the middle class and the rich could overpower the poor. In the early 'sixties, Anglophile liberalism dominated the middle class, while neither Lassalle nor Marx had yet incited the working class to Socialism. In these circumstances, the Diet was overwhelmingly Liberal. It possessed the power of the purse, but the Ministry was only responsible to the King. Liberal leaders, having studied English constitutional history, believed that, through the power of the purse, they could acquire control over the executive. Bismarck's task was to defeat them in this attempt.

The conflict had arisen over the army. The army, it was admitted, was the King's affair, but it was the affair of the Landtag to vote the money for it. King William wanted a larger army; the Landtag was willing that he should have part, but not the whole, of the increase that he demanded, but in return the Liberals wished all the taxes to be voted by an annual Budget, and they hoped, by this means, to force the King to choose a Ministry agreeable to the majority in Parliament. After a dissolution, the Liberals had come back stronger than ever; the King was frightened, and much inclined to yield. If he had yielded, Prussia would have become a Parliamentary democracy, and the history of the world would have been quite different from what it has been. But the Conservatives persuaded him to try one more expedient before yielding: perhaps Bismarck, who was known as a bold and resolute reactionary, who had counselled stern measures in 1848, would be able to find some way of defeating the Liberals. He was summoned from Avignon, and had a momentous interview with King William. When he advised resistance to Parliament, William expressed fears that he would have his head cut off, like Charles I. Bismarck replied that he, for his part, was willing to share the fate of Strafford, and appealed to Prussian pluck. The King, only half persuaded, gave Bismarck a tentative permission to see what he could do. Events proved that there was no Cromwell among the Liberals of the Landtag, and that the King's fears were groundless.

Bismarck began by telling the Diet that he was going to prolong the former taxes by decree, trusting to the future for an Act of indemnity. In his first speech in the Landtag, he produced an olive-branch which he had gathered at Avignon, but observed that the time was not yet ripe for presenting it to the Opposition. He went on to say:

Germany has its eyes not on Prussia's Liberalism, but on its might. . . . Prussia must reserve its strength for the favourable moment which has already more than once been missed. The great questions of the day will not be decided by speeches and resolutions of majorities—that was the blunder of 1848 and 1849—but by blood and iron.

This was a kind of language to which Parliament was unaccustomed. In reply there were "speeches and resolutions of majorities," but the Prussians continued to pay the taxes that were being illegally collected, the King introduced his army reforms, and Parliament was shown to be impotent. Meanwhile Bismarck decided to give the country something else to think about.

Most opportunely, the question of Schleswig and Holstein came up just at this time. These two duchies had belonged to the King of Denmark since 1460, but were not part of the kingdom of Denmark, and were subject to a different law of succession. Holstein had been part of the Holy Roman Empire, and was German in sentiment; Schleswig, at any rate in its northern portion, was predominantly Danish in feeling. Owing to the different law of succession, the legitimate heir to the Duchies was not the King of Denmark, but the Duke of Augustenburg; his father had renounced his rights in return for a money payment, but perhaps they could be revived. There were endless complications: Palmerston said that only three people had ever understood the question—the Prince Consort, who was dead; a German professor, now in a lunatic asylum; and himself—but he had forgotten about it. One thing was quite clear, in spite of the tangle, and that was that Prussia had no right to Schleswig and

Holstein. But Bismarck decided that Prussia should have them, and by means of two wars Prussia acquired them. In 1863, when Bismarck first suggested annexation, the King said: "But I have no rights in the Duchies." Bismarck replied: "Had the Great Elector, had King Frederick any more rights in Prussia and Silesia? All the Hohenzollern have been enlargers of the State." The King was shocked, as often by Bismarck; but the Minister had his way in the end.

The first step was an alliance with Austria, by which the two powers, Austria and Prussia, ostensibly in the interests of the Duke of Augustenburg, agreed to settle the question jointly. Then, in 1864, a short war with Denmark gave them possession of the Duchies, of which, provisionally, Austria took Holstein and Prussia took Schleswig, both now recognizing that the Duke of Augustenburg's claim was invalid. The other Powers, especially England, were furious but impotent.

The next step was to deal with Austria, and here Bismarck had to overcome the pan-German feeling which regarded war with Austria as "fracticidal." There were two parties among those who sought German unity, those who desired the "Great Germany" which included Austria, and those who desired the "Lesser Germany" which excluded it. But unity including Austria was an impracticable policy, because of the non-German Hapsburg dominions. Ever since 1815, Austria had been the main obstacle to unity, and to drive Austria out of the Germanic Federation was a necessary preliminary. Bismarck saw this, but many German patriots did not. Therefore in bringing about the war with Austria in 1866, he had to make sure of whatever support was available.

On April 8, 1866, Bismarck concluded an alliance with Italy, by which Italy undertook, at any time within the next three months, to go to war with Austria if Prussia did so; they were to make peace jointly, Italy was to have Venetia, and Prussia was to have some equivalent at Austria's expense. Next day, Bismarck had a resolution brought forward in the Federal Diet, according to which a Parliament elected by manhood suffrage from all Germany (implicitly excluding Austria) was to frame a German constitution in consultation with the Princes. Austria, of course, rejected this proposal, the purpose of which was only to conciliate the sentiment for unity on a democratic basis. Prussian troops were ordered into Holstein, from which the Austrians retired without fighting. As this step had not provoked war, Bismarck brought before the Federal Diet a proposal for a new organization *explicitly* excluding Austria. Austria declared that Prussia had violated the Federal Constitution, and demanded a mobilization against Prussia of all the other members of the Germanic Confederation. Prussia replied by an ultimatum, and the war began.

The King, as usual, had had to be managed. For his benefit, Bismarck kept a certain style of pious language which he found effective. At the crisis, he wrote:

Your Majesty will rest assured that it is opposed to my sentiments, I can even say to my faith, to attempt, in any urgent way, to influence your exalted and sovereign decisions in matters of war and peace. I am content to leave it to Almighty God to guide Your Majesty's heart for the welfare of the fatherland, and I am more inclined to pray than to advise. But I cannot hide my conviction that if we keep the peace now, the danger of war will recur, perhaps in a few months, and under less favourable conditions. Peace can only be lasting when both parties want it. . . . One who, like Your Majesty's most faithful servant, has for sixteen years been intimately acquainted with Austrian policy, cannot doubt that in Vienna hostility to Prussia has become the chief, I might almost say the only motive of State policy. This motive will become actively operative as soon as the cabinet of Vienna finds that the circumstances are more favourable than at the present moment. Austria's first endeavour will be to mould circumstances in Italy and France, so that they will become more favourable.

The Crown Princess (afterwards the Empress Frederick) wrote to her mother Queen Victoria calling Bismarck "the wicked man," and expressing the general sentiment of German Liberals. But Bismarck realized that victory would cause him to be forgiven, and he was assured by Moltke, the Chief of Staff, that victory was certain. Moreover, when he consulted the Bible in search of an oracle—so he wrote to his wife—he came upon the text: "When mine enemies are turned back, they shall fall and perish at thy presence. For thou hast maintained my right and my cause; thou satst in the throne judging right." However, even this left room for doubt: "We have good confidence," he wrote, "but we must not forget that Almighty God is very capricious."

The war was brief, and Prussia was completely victorious. Bismarck, who knew that he would need a benevolent Austria later on, insisted on peace at the first moment at which his purposes became realizable. The King and the Generals desired a triumphal entry into Vienna, but Bismarck pleaded and wept and in the end had his way. Italy obtained Venetia, Prussia obtained Schleswig-Holstein, Hanover, Nassau, Frankfort, Hesse-Cassel, and the northern portion of Hesse-Darmstadt. The old German Confederation, in which Austria had been predominant, was dissolved; in its place, a North German Confederation was formed, in which there was to be a Reichstag elected by manhood suffrage, and the King of Prussia was to be President. From this to the completion of German unity was only one more step. Fiscally, Germany had already been united in the Zollverein, except for the Hanse Towns, but the renewal of the Customs Union after the war, in which most of South Germany had sided with Austria, needed a new treaty, to which Bismarck would only consent if it were coupled with a military alliance in which Prussia had the upper hand. South Germany accepted his terms, though with some reluctance, and the Zollverein was renewed by a "Customs Parliament" which represented the whole country.

During the war of 1866 a new Landtag was elected in Prussia. By the time it met, Prussia had won, and Bismarck had become a national hero. Now was the time for the olive branch that he had brought from Avignon: the new Landtag indemnified the Government for having collected taxes unconstitutionally since 1862, and still more readily for having created the army that was bringing such delicious victories. The Liberals split into two factions, of which the larger, calling itself the National Liberal Party, became Bismarck's most loyal support. He had more difficulty, oddly enough, with the Conservatives, who were outraged by his alliance with the Italians against the Germans of Austria. His differences with them on foreign policy began during the Crimean War, when he favored friendship with Russia rather than with Austria. From the time when he had gone to Frankfort in 1851, he had felt the necessity of Prussian self-assertion as against the traditional arrogance of Austria. In the meetings of delegates at Frankfort, it was a custom that only Austria smoked, but Bismarck boldly lit his cigar. When the Austrian envoy once received him in shirt-sleeves, Bismarck remarked, "yes, it is hot," and took off his own coat. These acts were prophetic.

Bismarck had no respect for the principle of legitimacy. He stood simply for Prussian interests, and was quite willing to make friends with Napoleon III, "the man of sin" as Conservatives called him, if that would help him to make Prussia great. Writing to his arch-Conservative friend and former patron Gerlach, in 1857, he says:

How many entities are there left in the political world to-day that have not their roots in revolutionary soil? Take Spain, Portugal, Brazil, all the American Republics, Belgium, Holland, Switzerland, Greece, Sweden, and England, the latter with her foot even to-day consciously planted on the glorious revolution of 1688. Even for that territory which the German princes of to-day have won partly from Emperor and Empire, partly from their peers the barons, and partly from the estates of their own country, no perfectly legitimate title of possession can be shown, and in our own political life we cannot avoid the use of revolutionary supports.

At an earlier date, in 1848, he had exclaimed: "What the devil do I care about the petty States? My only concern is to safeguard and increase the power of Prussia." This was, in fact, his outlook through his whole career; he took up German unity only when he found a way of combining it with the increase of Prussian power. Unlike the upholders of legitimacy, he had no international principle. How the French chose to be governed was no concern of his; whether they had a Bourbon, a Bonaparte, or a Republic, whether they were well governed or badly governed, whether they were happy or unhappy, were, in his view, not questions that concerned a patriotic Prussian, except in so far as they affected France's power for mischief. In this he differed from Conservatives and Liberals alike, but he taught the world to adopt his principles. Following his precepts, the Tsar, at a later date, was not afraid to ally himself with the atheistical republican government of France.

There remained one more task to be accomplished before German unity could be completed, and that was to combine North and South in a war against France, which must appear as forced upon Germany by French arrogance. Nothing else, Bismarck was convinced, would produce the state of feeling necessary for union under Prussian hegemony. For war with France, the ground had to be carefully prepared. The military preparation could be safely left to Moltke; for although the two men often wrangled, Bismarck took care that his diplomacy should only produce wars that Moltke felt confident of winning. With the help of the military alliances with South German States, and after the experience of two wars, Moltke was ready to promise victory if he was allowed two or three years of preparation. The other problems were diplomatic. It was necessary to insure the neutrality of the other Great Powers. Russia was secured by the promise to support revision of the Treaty of 1856 as regards the closing of the Straits. England might have sympathized with her ally of the Crimean War, but Napoleon was tricked by Bismarck into an expression, in writing, of his desire to annex Belgium, which, published at the crucial moment, effectively prevented English assistance to France. Austria and Italy remained doubtful to the end, and were only converted to the German cause by Napoleon's military misfortunes. Italy would have sided with France if the Emperor had consented to Victor Emmanuel's occupation of Rome, but he refused, under the influence of Eugénie's ultramontane fanaticism. Thus it was left to Luther's countrymen, at Sedan, to end the temporal sovereignty of the Pope.

The final stages leading up to the rupture with France were managed by Bismarck with consummate skill. Both he and Napoleon were rogues, but one was as clever as the other was silly, and the clever rogue made the other's roguery apparent to all Europe, while successfully concealing his own. At the last moment, he was almost defeated by the simple honesty of King William, but by his "editing" of the Ems telegram he just succeeded in getting his war at the very moment when all was ready for it.

The war, as every one knows, resulted, for Germany, in the annexation of Alsace-Lorraine and the formation of the Empire; for France, in the payment of a huge indemnity, the establishment of the Third Republic, and the Paris Commune—extirpated with inconceivable barbarity by the new government of Liberty, Equality, and Fraternity.

The Empire, which embraced all Germany except German Austria, had a Federal Constitution very similar to that of the North German Federation established in 1867. The King of Prussia was German Emperor, the Prime Minister of Prussia was Imperial Chancellor; he and the other Ministers were responsible to the Emperor alone, not to Parliament. There was a Federal Diet (Bundesrat), consisting of delegations appointed by the several States; and there was a Parliament (Reichstag) directly elected by manhood suffrage. The Reichstag had control of finance, and laws required its assent, but the initiative in legislation belonged to the Bundesrat. Bismarck was Chancellor until 1890, and in practice the Constitution scarcely limited his omnipotence. The middle classes had been tamed, and he never again encountered difficulties like those of 1862. The sullen hostility of France suited his purposes, since it gave an obvious reason for keeping German militarism alive. But he had no occasion for further wars; the world had come to the conclusion that it was not a good plan to fight Bismarck.

His achievement in the years 1862 to 1871 is perhaps the most remarkable feat of skill in the history of statesmanship. He had to manage the King, whose wife and son and daughter-in-law were all bitterly hostile. He had to convert the nation, which at first hated him and his policies. He had to make nationalism Conservative instead of Liberal, militaristic instead of humanitarian, monarchical instead of democratic. He had to secure the victory of Prussia against the Danes, the Austrians, and the French, in spite of the fact that none of the Powers wished him to succeed. He could not allow the King to understand his policy, because it was not such as an honest old soldier could approve. He could not let the world understand it, because the world would have defeated it if it had understood it. At every moment he was liable to grave disaster. Fortunately for him, there was not in any country another statesman who understood the diplomatic game as he did. Even Disraeli, as subsequently appeared, was a child in his hands. Throughout the crucial years, Austria, France, England, and Russia danced to his tune. Everywhere he roused passionate resentments, but they died down except in France. And in the end Germany was so strong that resentment came to seem futile.

Bismarck's work bears the impress of his character, which was Titanic, complex, and divided. He wrote to his wife during their courtship in reference to a poem he had quoted to her: "Most congenial to me is the wish to become, in such a night, a sharer in the delight, a portion of the tempest of night; mounted on a runaway horse, to gallop down the rocks into the thunder of the Rhinefall." In his youth he preferred Byron to all other poets, and although he

professed to have discarded Byron after his marriage, his letters to
his wife show that that side of his nature still survived. "That which
is imposing here on earth," he tells her, "is always akin to the fallen
angel; who is beautiful, but lacks peace; is great in his plans and
efforts, but never succeeds; is proud, and melancholy." He was a
mixture of brutality and tenderness: tenderness to those who in no
way thwarted his will, wife, children, horses, and dogs; brutality to
all who opposed him. During the war with France, he showed unbelievable callousness in his dealings with the French. "Every village in which an act of treachery has been committed should be
burnt to the ground, and all the male inhabitants hanged." At Com-
mercy, a French woman came to intercede for her husband, who had
been arrested. "The minister [Bismarck] listened to her very ami-
ably, and when she had done he replied in the kindliest manner
possible, 'Well, my good woman, you can be quite sure that your
husband (drawing a line round his neck with his finger) will be
presently hanged.' " [1] When it was rumored that Garibaldi and
13,000 volunteers had been made prisoners, he said, "Why have they
not been shot?" On another occasion he said that, if Garibaldi were
caught, "We will exhibit him for money, and hang a placard round
his neck bearing the word 'Ingratitude.' " He maintained that no
black prisoners should be made. He had no feeling for the French in
their misfortune, but jeered at them all; when Favre looked ill, he
suggested that he was made up with a view to exciting sympathy.
But he felt the most acute anxiety as to the fate of his own sons. Riding among the corpses after the battle of Königgrätz, he said: "It
makes me feel sick at heart to think that Herbert may be lying like
this some day." His feelings were primitive, and divided mankind
rigidly into friends and others; the others aroused no sympathy,
whatever might happen to them.

The world that he created was of a piece with his emotions. It
was divided into Germany, which was to be cherished, and the rest
of the globe, which was to be either used or subdued. He was himself
harsh, restless, and heroic, and he sought to re-mold the world in
his own image. Unfortunately, he was largely successful.

[1] Busch, *Bismarck*, p. 305.

CHAPTER XXX

THE ECONOMIC DEVELOPMENT
OF THE GERMAN EMPIRE

THE growth of industry in Germany during the forty-three years from the inauguration of the Empire to the outbreak of the Great War was extraordinarily rapid, and presented certain features which were new. In England and America, industrialism was a haphazard affair, created by individual enterprise. In England until 1846, and in America until 1861, the Government was more favorable to agriculture than to industry. The principle of *laissez faire* led to an absence of central direction as regards economic life: it was thought that the most profitable enterprises were the most socially beneficial, and that enlightened selfishness was a better guide than governmental interference.

In the Germany of 1871, which had abandoned the Liberal philosophy, these maxims no longer inspired policy. It was held that economic activity should be such as to promote national well-being, and that, where natural forces failed to secure this result, the Government should intervene. The consequence was a development which was, to a considerable extent, centrally planned, which was nationalistic, skilful, and intelligent, and in which the State felt itself a partner in all approved enterprises.

Various old motives were thus put to new uses. Loyalty to the State, co-operation with compatriots, desire for national greatness, were all used in economic life as they had not been by Cobden and his followers, who, as Treitschke pointed out, "ignored the two great forces of universal history, the force of stupidity and the force of sin." Cobden thought of nationalism as an aristocratic vice, from which manufacturers ought to be exempt; he thought that they should ask little of the State, and give little in return. Nor did the merits of combination appeal to him: the cotton spinners of Manchester had no wish to own plantations in the Southern States, or ships for the transport of their raw material. It was only in the later stages of industrial development that it was found useful to combine what had been quite distinct kinds of industry, as happened, for example, in the formation of the Steel Trust in America. Germany, starting later, was able to profit by the previous experience of others. By means of nationalism, the competitive motive was directed outwards, against the foreigners, while internally the advantages of co-operation were facilitated by loyalty to the State. Loyalty is an old-fashioned sentiment, directed, in the first place, to the person of the sovereign. In Prussia, loyalty easily attached itself to the State, because the State was still the sovereign; but in England and America revolution and republicanism had made this impossible. This motive was especially important in facilitating the creation of an able and honest bureaucracy, without which German economic development could not have been what it was.

Economic nationalism was not a new doctrine. It had been taken for granted in the seventeenth century and in the first three-quarters of the eighteenth. Adam Smith, who first effectively challenged it, showed its influence by calling his book *The Wealth of Nations*. But his doctrines, followed by those of the Philosophical Radicals, produced an economic cosmopolitanism which reached its height in the 'sixties. The free-trade anti-national outlook, it is true, was never universal. Alexander Hamilton, in the age of Adam Smith, remained true to the older view, and by his "Report on Manufactures" caused the industrial part of America to adhere to a nationalistic form of economics. Friedrich List, who lived in America from 1825 to 1832, imbibed the Hamiltonian doctrine,[1] and taught it to the Germans in his *National System of Political Economy*, which was published in 1841. At the time, the Cobdenite current was too strong. Even List only advocated protection for "infant industries," while believing in ultimate free trade. But when Bismarck had defeated Liberalism and made nationalism triumphant, List was remembered, and was found to have supplied a theoretical argument in favor of what Germans of the 'seventies wished to do. What made him important was that he viewed economics from a national standpoint.

---

[1] In his *Outlines of American Political Economy* List says: "I found the component parts of political economy to be (1) individual economy; (2) national economy; (3) economy of mankind. Adam Smith treats of individual economy and economy of mankind. . . . He has entirely forgotten what the title of his book, *Wealth of Nations*, promised to treat."

It is curious to note that, at almost the same time, Japan embarked upon a very similar development, combining militarism, industrialism, and loyalty to the State with skilful modern technique, and producing an even more rapid change in the habits and ways of thought of the people.

The difference between Prussia and the Western democracies is illustrated by the contrast in railway policy. State ownership of railways, which, in England and France, is a measure advocated by Socialists, was adopted and carried out by Bismarck as part of a Conservative policy. He wished the railways to belong to the Empire, but particularism prevented this except in Alsace-Lorraine, where the railways became imperial property by the Peace Treaty. In Prussia, however, he was able to buy the lines for the Prussian State; by the time he left office, in 1890, there were only a few private lines surviving in Prussia. The policy of public ownership, not only in Prussia, was continued after his fall; in 1909, there were 60,000 kilometres of railways in Germany, of which, apart from a few narrow-gauge lines, only 3,600 were privately owned. The management was admirable, and the profits very considerably lightened the taxes. Railway tariffs were so arranged as to stimulate exports. The State, naturally, was alive to military considerations, and was able to construct whatever railways were strategically desirable without having to discuss the matter with bodies of unofficial capitalists.

Bismarck's bureaucratic Socialism was, in part, designed as a safeguard against the proletarian Socialism of the Marxists. In the case of the railways, the policy was thoroughly successful. As Clapham says:

The rigid military discipline enforced on the railway personnel should be noted. "Post and railway," a German wrote, were "only the civil sections of the army." Their directors, at any rate in Prussia, were not infrequently Generals. And there were few facts more significant than that in these two services were placed "three-quarters of a million men who stood stiff at attention when their superior spoke to them." These facts explained in part the excellent method and punctuality of the service. They were responsible also for the complete absence of any railway labour movement, comparable with those which were developing in France and England during the early years of the twentieth century. A four years' war, that was lost, and a political revolution were necessary before the Prussian railwayman struck.[2]

In tariff policy, as in the matter of railways, Bismarck abandoned the theory of *laissez faire*. Prussia was traditionally in favor of virtual free trade, and the Zollverein, before 1866, had kept duties low in order to exclude Austria, which considered a high tariff indispensable. Germany was predominantly agricultural, and as an exporter of food-stuffs was naturally against protection. Bismarck, until some years after the establishment of the Empire, paid no attention to economic matters, but left them to Delbrück, who was a free trader on principle.

For the first two years, all went well. But the world-wide crisis of 1873 was everywhere attributed to local causes, as crises always are; in Germany many people considered that free trade was to blame. Delbrück had, in that very year, abolished the duties on iron, and decreed that the duties on manufactures of iron should cease at the beginning of 1877. Throughout the intervening period complaints increased, and in 1876 Bismarck decided that Delbrück's health was no longer equal to the onerous duties of his office.

It was not only the industrialists who wanted protection. Russian competition was beginning to injure the grain-growers of the northeast, the Junkers, Bismarck's own class, and the firmest support of the Prussian monarchy; to them the Government was willing to show special consideration. The result was that, in 1879, a tariff was enacted giving moderate protection both to agriculture and to manufactures. Duties were further raised by Bismarck later, then slightly lowered by Caprivi; but in 1902 they were again considerably increased except upon raw materials. Even then, Germany remained less protectionist than any other great country except the United Kingdom.

It was calculated in 1904 that the average *ad valorem* equivalent of the import duties levied by Germany, on the principal manufactures exported from the United Kingdom, was 25 per cent. The corresponding figure for Italy was 27; for France 34; for Austria 35; for the United States 73; and for Russia 131. The figures are rough; but they illustrate tolerably well the relative intensity of protective tariffs.[3]

[2] Clapham, *The Economic Development of France and Germany*, p. 349.
[3] Clapham, *op. cit.*, p. 322.

Whether because of the tariffs or not, German industry grew rapidly and continuously from 1879 to 1914. To begin with the most important: iron and steel. This industry depended chiefly upon the ore of Lorraine and the coal of Westphalia. Before the war of 1870, the ore belonged to France, which, in the 'sixties, still surpassed Germany in the production of iron. By 1875, Germany produced two million tons of pig iron and France a little less than one and a half million. Then came a depression, partly due to the world-wide slump, partly to the fact that German ores were not suitable for the Bessemer process. This trouble was remedied by the invention and adoption of the Thomas-Gilchist process, which synchronized with the new tariff of 1879. From that moment, the German production of steel about doubled every ten years; from one and a half million tons in 1880, it rose to thirteen millions in 1910, passing that of the United Kingdom in the year 1900. German exports of iron and steel and manufactures thereof were over £100,000,000 in 1913. Only the United States surpassed Germany in iron and steel production at the outbreak of the war.

In Germany, as in America, the industry approached monopoly as it developed. There were not, in Germany, the picturesque incidents of competition between individual magnates which enliven the economic history of the United States; in the absence of a belief in free competition, monopoly was brought about by decorous agreements not frowned upon by the Government as their analogues were by Theodore Roosevelt. The Steel Union (*Stahlwerksverband*), formed in 1904, came to embrace practically the whole industry, Krupps, for instance, being merely one of the constituent companies. Meanwhile, the Rhenish-Westphalian Coal Syndicate had acquired control of half the coal production of Germany. Clearly the power of these two giant organizations, when they co-operated, was practically irresistible. In other industries, a looser form of combination, called a Cartel, was commoner than a Trust after the American model. A Cartel was often no more than an agreement as to selling-prices.

Union in a Trust or Cartel had certain advantages in addition to the ordinary economies of large-scale production. Taking advantage of the tariff, producers raised home prices as much as was compatible with defeating foreign competition, while they sold abroad at a lower price. This is what, in England, came to be called "dumping." It was an avowed part of the regular policy of all Cartels that had an export trade.

Another advantage was in relation to political action. For example, the steel industry of the world profited by war scares, and Liebknecht in 1913 scandalized the Reichstag by revelations of the corrupt machinations of the great Trusts in stirring up rival nations to arm against each other. Huge combines could do this work much more effectively than a number of smaller firms.

The manufacture of dye-stuffs and chemicals is an industry in which Germany led the way, chiefly owing to a higher standard of education than that of other countries, though natural advantages contributed something. The latter are exemplified by what Clapham calls "Germany's peculiar treasure, crude potassium salts," of which, in 1861, only two thousand tons were produced, while in 1911 the production had risen to nine and a half millions. Of sulphuric acid, which is useful chiefly for chemical fertilizers, Germany produced in 1878 a little over a hundred thousand tons, but in 1907, more than twelve times as much. The export of dye-wares, which depended upon the chemical industry, increased rapidly, and amounted in 1913 to about ten million pounds sterling.

The electrical industry "was the greatest single industrial achievement of modern Germany. The world had before it a new group of scientific and economic problems. In the handling of those problems Germany, now a fully equipped industrial nation, took the lead. She led too in all the specialized applications of electricity during the early years of the current century; electrical furnaces for steelwork and other branches of metallurgy; electrification of railways; electrical driving of agricultural machinery, including even ploughs; and the electrical method of producing nitrogen from the air." [4]

This industry afforded an example of concentration; after a period of competition, agreements were effected during the first years of the present century, and in the end there were only two groups, Siemens and the Allgemeine Elektrizitäts-Gesellschaft (A.E.G.), which no longer competed against each other.

In Germany, developments which in England were spread over a century and in America over forty years took place in a decade or so.

[4] Clapham, op. cit., p. 308.

We saw how, in America, power passed ultimately from industrialists to bankers; in Germany the banks had power almost from the beginning of modern industry. Men like Carnegie and Rockefeller had been able to pay off whatever they had borrowed, because their profits were so colossal; in Germany, where industrialists were content with a smaller reward, they usually remained indebted to the banks. The power of the Deutsche Bank, in particular, was very great, not only in Germany, but wherever German finance had penetrated. It had branches in most countries from China to Peru. It financed the Northern Pacific Railway in the United States until 1893. It controlled the Turkish railways, and was interested in promoting the Berlin-Bagdad scheme. As time went on, the Deutsche Bank came to have more and more influence on German policy. But the influence was reciprocal: if the Bank invested money in Turkey, that was partly because Turkey was important for German diplomacy. Patriotism and finance were in harmony, and the interests of the plutocracy could be furthered without any disloyalty to the State.

With the development of Cartels and the growing power of the big banks, economic direction became more and more concentrated. The Austrian Consul in Berlin, reporting officially in 1906, said:

Never before was economic Germany so entirely under the absolute rule of a group of men, barely fifty in number; in no former period of industrial expansion was the old formula of "the free-play of forces" abandoned to such a degree as in 1906, when the momentous decisions as to the extent of production, sales abroad, prices, the granting of credit, the raising of new capital, and the fixing of wages and rates of interest lay in the hands of a few persons found at the head of the large banks, mammoth industrial undertakings, and great cartels. The lion's share of the industrial boom has fallen to these great combinations of interests, whose gains have been the larger the more their industries were ruled by syndicates." [5]

At the time when this report was written, the process of concentration had not gone so far as it had in 1914; and since the War it has gone further still. Unless checked by political action, there is no reason why it should stop until all economic power in Germany is concentrated in the hands of a single man; it is even said [6] that that stage

[5] Quoted in Dawson, *The Evolution of Modern Germany*, p. 170.
[6] *Hitler Over Europe?* by Ernst Henri. Dent, 1934.

has now been reached, that the man is Thyssen, the head of the Steel Trust, and that Hitler is merely his megaphone.

The ultra-modern development of large-scale industry in Germany during the present century contrasts strangely with the survivals of mediaevalism which still existed when Bismarck came into power. Guilds still survived in 1848, when the revolutionary movement, for the moment, tried to sweep them away; but in the very next year the reaction restored them. A Prussian law of 1849 enacted, among other things, that goods such as were produced by skilled handicraftsmen could be sold only in shops belonging to qualified masters of the craft in question. In Mecklenburg, until 1869, "the old soke-mill retained the exclusive right of corn-grinding. The towns of the duchy could require rural alehouse-keepers to buy their beer within a radius of two miles, and to buy the beer used at baptisms, marriages, and burials at the nearest towns, while private brewing in the country might be prohibited by the towns." [7]

The most backward part of Germany was Prussia east of the Elbe, where the Junkers had their big estates; and the Junkers were politically the most influential class. Although serfdom was abolished, its abolition was accompanied, in 1810, by the "Servants' Ordinance," which applied not only to servants in the ordinary sense, but to all laborers permanently employed and living on the employer's estate. By this ordinance, "labourers are bound to render obedience to a degree which differs little from unrestricted compulsion; the right to cancel a contract of service is limited to such an extent that it can hardly be said to exist at all; in addition they are expressly forbidden by law of April 24, 1854, to strike collectively under any circumstances whatever on pain of imprisonment; so that, in effect, though the name of serfage is no longer used, this condition exists in spirit and almost in fact." [8] This ordinance remained in force in the East down to the Great War.

By a law of 1854, which also remained in force, "Servants (Gesinde) who are guilty of obstinate disobedience or contumacy against the orders of their employers or persons having oversight of them, or who without legal ground refuse or leave service are, on the application of the employers, yet without prejudice to their right to

---

[7] Dawson, *Bismarck and State Socialism*, p. 88.
[8] Dawson, *Evolution of Modern Germany*, p. 281.

dismiss or retain them, liable to a fine not exceeding 5 thalers (15s.) or imprisonment up to three days." [9] And it must be realized that the magistrates who tried such cases were the employers themselves or their friends.

In these circumstances it is not surprising that the agricultural East became depopulated. Men at the end of their military service refused to return to such semi-servile conditions, and sought employment in industry. The labor shortage grew increasingly serious, and was only met by a large seasonal immigration of Russian and Austrian Poles, who worked under contract, receiving 1s. 6d. for a twelve-hour day.

From 1849 to 1910, the rural population of Germany remained almost stationary, while the urban population was quadrupled. In 1871, just over one-third of the inhabitants of the German Empire lived in towns of 2,000 and upwards, while in 1910 the proportion had increased to three-fifths. Not only had the towns grown, but the big towns had grown most, and in the big towns there had been a more rapid change than elsewhere towards a modern way of living. This may be illustrated by the changes in the birth-rate. In 1876, the birth-rate in the country as a whole was 41, while in Berlin it was higher, being 45.4. But in 1905 it had fallen, for all Germany, to 33, while in Berlin it was only 24.6, as against 27.1 in London.[10] Ever since 1904, the birth-rate throughout Germany has been falling fast.

The industrialization of Germany brought with it an increase of Socialism and trade unionism. The first movement that appealed definitely to the working class was that led by Lassalle during the last two years of his life (1862–4). He aimed at the elimination of the capitalist by co-operative production, and he considered that the first step towards such a programme must be manhood suffrage. He advocated this measure in interviews with Bismarck, who saw in him an instrument against his enemies the Liberals, and spoke of him as "one of the cleverest and most agreeable men I ever met." Bismarck and Lassalle had a certain temperamental affinity, and the Chancellor, as he proved in 1867, had no objection in principle to manhood suffrage, and was not without sympathy for Lassalle's rather aristocratic Socialism. But after Lassalle's death the working-class movement came more under the influence of Marx, with the result that the

[9] *Ibid.*   [10] Dawson, *Evolution of Modern Germany*, p. 309.

German Social Democratic party was founded in 1869, under the leadership of Bebel and the elder Liebknecht. This party did not share the patriotic enthusiasm of the period, and its two representatives in the Reichstag of 1871 voted against the annexation of Alsace-Lorraine. The party had in its first twenty-five years a whole-hearted Marxist character, which caused it to be bitterly attacked as being against God and Fatherland. Nevertheless it grew.

In 1878 Bismarck, taking advantage of two attempts to assassinate the Emperor (with which the Socialists had no connection whatever), passed a law making Socialism liable to various penalties. This law remained in force until 1890, and in the meantime the Chancellor tried to reconcile wage-earners by his measures of insurance against sickness, accident, and old age, which were the models upon which Lloyd George's Insurance Act was based. A number of professors invented a doctrine which they called State Socialism, and which its enemies called *Kathedersozialismus* (professorial Socialism); this theory was to extract what was good in Socialism and reject what was bad; it was supposed to represent the principles upon which Bismarck was working. What was bad in Socialism was its atheism, its republicanism, its internationalism, its desire to deprive the rich of their well-gotten gains, and its wish to transfer power to the proletariat. What was good in it was that State action could do much to promote national efficiency; also that, in general, one ought to be kind to the poor wage-earner; also that many people on the Stock Exchange, especially Jews, speculated in an unscrupulous manner which it would be well to stop. This last point was taken up, with more emphasis, by the Christian Socialists, who tried to turn anti-capitalism into anti-Semitism. All these doctrines have since borne fruit, but remained, at the time, somewhat sterile.

Neither Bismarck's blandishments nor his threats interfered with the growth of Social Democracy. It must be said that, by post-war standards, the persecution of Socialism was rather mild. The party was still allowed to elect members to the Reichstag, and in 1880 it was allowed to hold a Congress, at which it voted for the establishment of Communism "by all means"—not, as hitherto, "by all legal means." In 1890, just before the Exceptional Law expired, 1,427,000 votes were given to the Social Democrats in the Reichstag elections. William II, who was posing as the inaugurator of a new era, allowed the law to lapse; but mildness proved as ineffectual as severity as a method of discouraging Socialism. The Reichstag of 1912, which was in being at the outbreak of the War, contained 112 Social Democrats out of a total of 397. In the election, four and a quarter million votes, more than a third of the total, went to the Social Democrats; and the increase of the Socialist vote since the previous election in 1907 was nearly a million. This was one of the facts that terrified the Government into thinking that something catastrophic must be done.

The rapid development characteristic of the last period before the War was very markedly illustrated by the growth of trade unionism. The trade unions in Germany were, from the first, connected with politics: there were Social Democratic trade unions, Liberal trade unions, and Christian trade unions. In effect, only the Social Democratic trade unions could be reckoned as part of a genuine working-class movement. Until the new century, union organization was weak. In 1895, there were only 269,000 unionists of all kinds; but in 1902 the number had reached a million, in 1906 two million, and in 1909 three million, of which about five-sixths were in the Socialist unions.

The growth of trade unionism synchronized with a change in the character of the Social Democratic party. It had been rigidly Marxist, looking forward to a revolutionary overthrow of the capitalist system, and inclined to frown upon such ameliorative efforts as occupied the British trade unions. But the amazing prosperity of Germany had penetrated, to some extent, to the working class; wages had risen; revolution seemed remote; and after all, it was difficult not to rejoice in one's country's successes. The more uncompromising features of the party programme were smoothed over by those who were called "revisionists," the first of whom, Bernstein, had lived in England and become impressed by the mildness of British labor. In spite of the opposition of Bebel and the older men, revisionism won the day, and the Social Democrats became, for all practical purposes, little more than a party of Liberal reform. Nevertheless, from old habit the Kaiser and the Junkers continued to feel terror at the thought of the Socialists in power.

The growth of Socialism was only one of the problems brought about by the growth of industry; another was the question of food supply. In 1871, Germany still had a surplus of food for export, but with the growth of population the situation was reversed about 1874, though it did not begin to be serious until after the fall of Bismarck. Caprivi, his successor, lowered the duties on grain, which had been greatly increased since 1879 (e.g. those on wheat and rye had been raised from 10s. a ton to 30s. in 1885, and in 1887 to 50s.): agricultural protection was not only disliked by the industrialists, but was bound, by increasing the price of food, to promote the spread of Social Democracy.

Caprivi's policy, however, was reversed by Bülow's tariff of 1902, which restored, and even augmented, the earlier duties. By the joint operation of the tariff and of a highly scientific agriculture, Germany became, in the last years before the War, more nearly self-supporting than in 1900. In 1911–12, about a third of the wheat consumed was imported, but of rye (which is more important than wheat in Germany) there was actually a small export balance. The main purpose of the tariff on food-stuffs, apart from favoring the politically influential Junkers, was to keep Germany able to feed itself in time of war. When the test came, it was found that the dependence on foreign sources of supply was greater than had been thought, particularly as regards fats. The problem was not easily soluble. High protection would manufacture Socialists; a foreign food supply made it necessary to challenge the British navy if successful war were to be possible. The compromise which was adopted combined some of the evils of both courses.

The economic development of Germany in the years from 1871 to 1914 showed collective energy and skill such as no nation had ever previously displayed. The Germans were better educated than the French or the English or the Americans; they had a larger number of technical experts of all kinds; and they had the organization that made expert skill quickly available where it was most wanted. But, admirable as were the merits which caused their advance, there were factors that made it unstable. The sudden change in habits of life—from East Prussian agricultural subjection to the comparative emancipation of modern industry in the case of large numbers of wage-earners, from traditional respectable poverty to sudden precarious luxury among business men, from Lutheran God-fearing piety to the freedoms of plutocratic Berlin in countless hitherto simple families—all this came about too quickly, too overwhelmingly, to be adequately assimilated. The result was, not infrequently, a kind of hysterical intoxication, a belief in boundless possibilities of power such as led Napoleon to his downfall. And before the holders of power there were two opposing spectres: Socialism, and the need of foreign food. The system, successful as it was, could not continue to succeed much longer: an explosion of some kind was necessary.

CHAPTER XXXI

IMPERIALISM

I. THE PARTITION OF AFRICA

THE new type of economic organization which, during the Napoleonic wars, existed only in the North of England and on the Clyde, spread, as we have seen, throughout Western Europe and North America, and reached in two countries—Germany and the United States—a stage of development more advanced than that achieved in Great Britain. Its expansive force, moreover, was not limited to the parts of the world inhabited by white men, but extended rapidly over the whole of Asia and Africa. Contact with less developed communities somewhat altered its character. On the one hand, there was need of governmental assistance where conquest was a necessary preliminary to capitalism. On the other hand, colored races, especially those of Africa, could be subjected to a more ruthless exploitation than the worst that was politically possible in countries with homogeneous white populations. Modern economic technique gave a new character to imperialism, and imperialism, in turn, gave a new political complexion to industrialism.

Imperialism had already a long history when the industrial epoch began. Ignoring antiquity, its origin in modern times was due to Christopher Columbus and Vasco da Gama, who guided the energies of Spain and Portugal respectively to the West and East Indies. Love of adventure and thirst for gold drew explorers and ruffians to the realm of the Incas and the Court of the Great Mogul. But the monopoly of new lands granted by the Pope to Spain and Portugal was not respected by the English, the Dutch, and the French, all of whom acquired wide empires. As a result of many wars, the English gained supremacy in the East, while the American Continent ceased, after 1824, to be a field for imperialism. From that time until about 1880, the British were the only nation possessed of a large distant empire. But under the influence of free-trade doctrine they became indifferent to the acquisition of colonies. Bentham, as we have seen,

396

considered them a useless expense, and his view became, in time, that of the Government. In 1850, when the Orange River was annexed, the Privy Council urged that there should be no further "additions whether permanent or provisional, however small, to the existing dominions of Your Majesty in the African Continent." The general policy of the British Government was opposed to extensions of the Empire until 1886, but Cabinets were repeatedly overborne by the force of circumstances.

The first signs of a change occurred during Disraeli's Government of 1874 to 1880. Disraeli loved the East, and enjoyed the pomp and splendor of our Indian Empire; Queen Victoria, with much relish, accepted from him the title of Empress of India. The Near East (especially the neighborhood of Palestine) always fascinated him: he bolstered up the Turk at the Congress of Berlin in 1878, and was glad to get a say in the affairs of Egypt. He showed considerable skill in dovetailing finance and politics. Turkey being unable to pay the interest due to British shareholders, he leased Cyprus from the Porte for an annual tribute, but paid the tribute, on behalf of the Sultan, direct to that potentate's British creditors. When the Khedive, owing to his extravagance, was obliged to sell his Suez Canal shares, Disraeli bought them on behalf of the British Government. Gladstone, with intense moral fervor, thundered against him for his support of the "unspeakable Turk," whose atrocities shocked that generation more than they would shock ours, which has "supped full of horrors." Nevertheless, when Gladstone became Prime Minister in 1880, he found himself compelled to carry on and develop some of his predecessor's policies, particularly as regards Egypt.

There were two motives which led Gladstone's Government to occupy Egypt in 1882: the Suez Canal and the bondholders. Both were threatened in that year by a nationalist mutiny, which the British suppressed in the interests of the Khedive. These interests—so they thought—obliged them to stay in the country and tell him how to govern it; and no one can deny that the Government was better under British influence than it had been before. The same may be said for the French occupation of Algeria (1830) and Tunis (1881). In these cases, imperialism is seen at its best: its effect has been good on the whole, in spite of the questionable motives by which it was inspired.

From 1884 onwards, the Western Powers entered upon what was known as the Scramble for Africa. It came to be a recognized principle of the diplomatic game that, whenever two countries were rivals, any territorial gain to the one should be balanced by an equal gain to the other, with the result that, by 1912, the whole of Africa was partitioned among the Western Powers, except the negro State of Liberia and the Christian Kingdom of Abyssinia—the former because it was small and of interest to the United States, the latter because it had inflicted a sanguinary defeat on the Italians. The partition of Africa was effected by diplomatic methods, but not without engendering bitternesses that did much to bring on the Great War.

II. THE CONGO

The Slave Trade having been abolished, and slaves having been emancipated, the easiest way to exploit black labor was to occupy the countries in which the black men live, and it conveniently happened that these countries contained various valuable raw materials. Greed was only one, though the most important, of the motives to African imperialism, but there was one case, that of the Congo "Free" State, in which it appears to have been the sole motive. Some of the Philosophical Radicals thought that pecuniary self-interest, rightly understood, should be an adequate motive for useful activity. The example of the Congo will enable us to test this theory.

The Congo is a vast river, draining an area about as large as Europe without Russia, flowing through dark forests, and passing through territory almost entirely inhabited by savages. Although the mouth had long been known, the upper reaches were first discovered in 1871 by the virtuous Dr. Livingstone, who combined in equal measure a love of exploration and a desire to convert Africans to the Christian faith. Stanley, who discovered him at Ujiji on Lake Tanganyika, was less interested in the Gospel than in some other aspects of Christian civilization. His first journey was undertaken on behalf of the *New York Herald,* his subsequent journeys (which established the whole course of the Congo and of several tributaries) were made at the expense and in the interests of Leopold, King of the Belgians, of whom Stanley spoke always in terms of the highest praise.

King Leopold was the son of Queen Victoria's Uncle Leopold, whose advice she valued in the early years of her reign. He was moreover, as Sir H. H. Johnston puts it, "grandson of Louis Philippe, husband of an Austrian Archduchess, a devoted upholder of the Roman Church, and a very rich man." He was a promoter of scientific research, particularly in Africa, and a patron of missionary efforts. The Berlin Conference of 1884, convened for the partition of Africa, decided that this high-minded monarch should be entrusted personally with the government of a territory which extended over about one million square miles, and contained the greater part of the Congo basin. He was respected by diplomats, extolled by travellers, and generally believed to be a model of philanthropy in his attitude to the negroes. In 1906, when he offered £12,000 for scientific research as to the prevention of sleeping sickness, he declared in a manifesto:

If God gives me that satisfaction (victory over sleeping sickness) I shall be able to present myself before His judgement-seat with the credit of having performed one of the finest acts of the century, and a legion of rescued beings will call down upon me His grace.[1]

When King Leopold took over the Congo, he announced that his purpose was purely philanthropic. Stanley, who conducted propaganda for him in England, explained how much he loved the black man, and feared that English people could not "appreciate rightly, because there are no dividends attached to it, this restless, ardent, vivifying, and expansive sentiment which seeks to extend civilizing influence among the dark places of sad-browed Africa." The Prince of Wales (Edward VII), whose help was invoked by King Leopold as early as 1876 in calling a conference to discuss "the settlement by Europeans of unexplored Africa and the encouragement of exploration with a view to spreading civilization," became dubious when assured that the sole motive was philanthropy. He wrote to Sir Bartle Frere:

The question is whether the public who represent money will take the same interest that he does. Philanthropy is all very well, but unless it is practical and gives a practical result it will not find that favour in the eyes of the English public that it deserves.[2]

---

[1] Quoted by E. D. Morel, *Red Rubber*, p. 151.
[2] Sidney Lee, *King Edward VII*, I, p. 629.

However, Leopold's emphasis on philanthropy served his purpose. The other Powers showed little enthusiasm for an enterprise that was represented as involving expenditure without hope of pecuniary recompense, and when he offered to bear all the expense himself, they allowed him to assume the burden (as they supposed it) on condition of his preserving freedom of religion, freedom of trade, freedom of the Press, and so on.

After winning the approval of the world by suppressing Arab slave-raiders, the royal philanthropist set to work to introduce orderly government into his dominions. Being thoroughly up-to-date, he established a system of State Socialism, the most thorough-going that has ever existed; and in agreement with much modern opinion, he seems to have held that Socialism should involve no nonsense about democracy. He issued decrees by which all the land, all the rubber, and all the ivory was to be the property of the State—which was himself. It was made illegal for natives to sell rubber or ivory to Europeans, and for Europeans to buy either from natives. He next sent a secret circular to his officials, explaining that they "must neglect no means of exploiting the produce of the forests," and that they would receive a bonus on all rubber and ivory, which would be great when the cost of collection was small, and small when it was great. For example, if the cost of collection was thirty centimes or less per kilo, the official received fifteen centimes per kilo; while if the cost was over seventy centimes per kilo, the official received only four centimes. The financial results were all that could have been hoped. Parts of the Congo were worked directly for the King, parts for companies in which he was a large shareholder. Take, for example, the Anversoise Trust, which exploited a region to the north of the river. The paid-up capital, of which the State had half, was £10,000, and the net profits in six years were £370,000. Another company, in four years, made a profit of £731,680 on a paid-up capital of £40,200. The orginal value of the shares—of which the King held half—was 250 francs, but in 1906 their value had risen to 16,000 francs. It is more difficult to discover what were the profits of the vast areas which were reserved as the King's private domain, but it is estimated by Professor Cattier that they amounted to £300,000 a year.[3]

The methods by which these vast profits were accumulated were

[3] Morel, *op. cit.*, p. 145.

very simple. Each village was ordered by the authorities to collect and bring in a certain amount of rubber—as much as the men could collect and bring in by neglecting all work for their own maintenance. If they failed to bring the required amount, their women were taken away and kept as hostages in compounds or in the harems of Government employees. If this method failed, native troops, many of them cannibals, were sent into the village to spread terror, if necessary by killing some of the men; but in order to prevent a waste of cartridges, they were ordered to bring one right hand for every cartridge used. If they missed, or used cartridges on big game, they cut off the hands of living people to make up the necessary number. The result was, according to the estimate of Sir H. H. Johnston, which is confirmed from all other impartial sources, that in fifteen years the native population was reduced from about twenty million to scarcely nine million.[4] It is true that the sleeping sickness contributed something to this reduction, but the spread of this disease was greatly accelerated by King Leopold's practice of moving hostages from one end of his dominions to the other.

Enormous pains were taken to keep secret the large-scale systematic murder by which the royal capitalist obtained his profits. The officials and law-courts were both in his pay and at his mercy, private traders were excluded, and Catholic missionaries silenced by his piety. Belgium was systematically corrupted, and the Belgian Government was to a considerable extent his accomplice. Men who threatened disclosures were bought off, or, if that proved impossible, disappeared mysteriously. The only men in the Congo who could not be silenced were the Protestant missionaries, most of whom, not unnaturally, supposed that the King was ignorant of the deeds done in his name. To take one instance out of many, Joseph Clark, of the American Baptist Missionary Union, wrote on March 25, 1896:

This rubber traffic is steeped in blood, and if the natives were to rise and sweep every white person on the Upper Congo into eternity there would still be left a fearful balance to their credit. Is it not possible for some American of influence to see the King of the Belgians and let him know what is being done in his name? The Lake is reserved for the King—no traders

[4] Sir H. H. Johnston, *The Colonization of Africa* (Cambridge Historical Series), p. 352.

allowed—and to collect rubber for him hundreds of men, women, and children have been shot.[5]

But it was easy to suppose that the missionaries exaggerated, or that these were merely isolated instances of officials who had been turned to cruelty by fever and solitude. It seemed incredible that the whole system was deliberately promoted by the King for the sake of pecuniary gain. The truth might have remained long unrecognized but for one man—E. D. Morel. Sir H. H. Johnston, an empire-builder untainted with eccentricity, thoroughly familiar with Africa, and originally a believer in King Leopold, after describing his influence in stifling criticism throughout the civilized world, says:

Few stories are at once more romantic—and will seem more incredible to posterity—than that which relates how this Goliath was overcome by a David in the person of a poor shipping clerk in the office of a Liverpool shipping firm which was amongst the partners of King Leopold.

This shipping clerk—E. D. Morel—was sent over to Antwerp, and Belgium generally, because he could speak French, and could therefore arrange all the minutiae of steamer fares and passenger accommodation, and the scales of freights for goods and produce, with the Congo State officials. In the course of his work he became acquainted with some of the grisly facts of Congo maladministration. He drew his employers' attention to these stories and their verification. The result was his dismissal.

Almost penniless, he set to work with pen and paper to enlighten the world through the British press and British publishers on the state of affairs on the Congo.[6]

From that day to the moment of his death, Morel was engaged in ceaseless battle—first against inhumanity in the Congo, then against secret diplomacy in Morocco, then against a one-sided view of the origin of the War, and last against the injustice of the Treaty of Versailles. His first fight, after incredible difficulties, was successful, and won him general respect; his second and greater fight, for justice to Germany, brought him obloquy, prison, ill health, and death, with no success except in the encouragement of those who loved him for his passionate disinterestedness. No other man known to me has had the same heroic simplicity in pursuing and proclaiming political truth.

[5] Morel, *op. cit.*, p. 54.   [6] *Op. cit.*, p. 355.

Morel's difficulties in the Congo Reform agitation were such as most men would have found overwhelming. The French, impressed by the magnitude of Leopold's profits, had established a very similar system in the French Congo, where it was producing the same results; they were, therefore, by no means anxious that the world should know the inevitable consequences of his economic methods. The British Foreign Office, needing the friendship of France and Belgium for reasons of high politics, was very loath to be persuaded, and at first suppressed consular reports tending to confirm the accusations of Morel and the missionaries. The Roman Catholic Church—acting, according to Morel, under orders from the Vatican—represented that the whole movement for reform was a disguised attack upon Roman Catholicism emanating from the Protestant missionaries; but later, when the evidence proved irresistible, this defence was abandoned. King Leopold and his agents, of course, stuck at nothing in the way of vilification and imputation of discreditable motives.

Nevertheless, Morel and the Congo Reform Association succeeded in rousing public opinion, first in England, and then throughout the civilized world. The British Government was forced to admit that the accusations had been confirmed by our Consuls, especially Casement (who was hanged during the War). The King, to keep up the pretence that the atrocities had occurred against his wishes, was compelled to appoint a commission of three impartial jurists to investigate the charges, and, although he published only a fragment of their report, what was allowed to appear made it evident that the charges were well founded. At last, in 1908, Europe, using the authority conferred by the Berlin Congress, deprived him of the Congo and handed it over to Belgium, on the understanding that the King's system of exploitation should cease. By this time King Leopold had come to be avoided by his brother monarchs, on account both of his cruelty to negroes and of his kindness to ballet-girls.

Against King Leopold, it was possible for the conscience of mankind to be victorious, for he was, after all, a minor potentate. Against France, agitation has proved powerless. Except in the coastal regions, from which travellers are not easily excluded, large-scale atrocities occurred, and probably still occur; but "an impenetrable mist still lies upon the forest of the middle and upper Congo, shutting them out from the observation of men." [7]

III. GERMAN SOUTHWEST AFRICA

Germany's governmental participation in the scramble for Africa was tardy and reluctant. Bismarck's interests were European, and he did not wish to embark upon adventures in distant regions, believing with Frederick the Great that "All distant possessions are a burden to the State. A village on the frontier is worth more than a principality two hundred and fifty miles away." His conservatism made him slow to realize the importance of new movements or understand their necessity. Beginning his official life with the narrow outlook of a particularist Prussian Junker, he was forced by degrees to include in his care for Prussia, first, the rest of Germany, then industrialism, then colonies. His political life was dominated by two desires: one that Prussia should be great; the other that it should consist of Junkers, peasants, fields, and trees. Step by step he was forced to sacrifice the second of these desires to the first.

There had been a vigorous colonial party in Germany since the 'forties, when Greville was surprised to hear Germans talking of the need for colonies and a navy. Supported by traders and missionaries, by List, and later, Treitschke, this party kept up a constant propaganda. But Bismarck was pre-occupied with the consolidation and extension of Germany in Europe. His success in this self-appointed task did much to drive the other Powers further afield in search of territory and prestige, but this did not trouble him. The colonial adventures of other nations pleased him, since they left him a freer hand in Europe and were also a source of useful international friction. Gradually, however, he realized that the game of Power Politics could be played on a wider field than Europe and that in an industrial age the maxim of Frederick was no longer valid.

In 1879 a traveller, Ernst von Weber, had published an article urging Germany to obtain Delagoa Bay from Portugal, fill the Transvaal with Germans, and gradually acquire a German-African empire extending to the Zambesi. In spite of governmental aloofness,

[7] Morel, *The Black Man's Burden* (1920), p. 147.

such schemes were receiving considerable support, and in the previous year Treitschke had written:

"In the South of Africa circumstances are decidedly favourable to us. English colonial policy, which has been successful everywhere else, has not succeeded at the Cape. The civilization which exists there is Teutonic, is Dutch. If our Empire has the courage to follow an independent colonial policy with determination, a collision between our interest and those of England is unavoidable." [8]

These large projects did not bear fruit, as Bismarck was not willing to antagonize the British. But difficulties arose as to German missionaries and traders settled in Damaraland and Namaqualand. They found themselves in conflict with the natives and asked for British protection; in 1881 the missionaries made a request for a British gunboat, which was refused. The British had annexed Walfish Bay, the only good harbor in the region, but refused to accept responsibility for any further territory. At last, in 1883, Lüderitz, a Bremen trader, asked the German Government whether he would be supported if he hoisted the German flag at Angra Pequena (subsequently Lüderitzbucht). Bismarck politely inquired of the British whether they had claimed sovereignty or a protectorate over this region, and signified his intention of claiming it for Germany if they had not. The British Foreign Office professed that it was necessary to consult the Cape Government before giving a reply. The Cape Government refused, on grounds of expense, to take any responsibility. Lord Granville then told Bismarck, who had waited nine months for an answer to a purely formal inquiry, that though his government did not claim sovereignty over Angra Pequena, it would regard such a claim by any other Power as an infringement of its legitimate rights. Bismarck asked for proofs of the existence of these "legitimate rights," received none, waited four more months, and then, on April 24, 1884, proclaimed a protectorate over the whole coast between the Orange River and Angra Pequena. At this, too late, the British became annoyed, and in May the Cape Government announced its intention of taking over the whole coast from the Orange River to Walfish Bay, including the area now claimed by Germany. In June, however, the British Government gave in, and in common with the other Powers,

[8] Quoted by Dawson, *The German Empire*, Vol. II, p. 178.

recognized the annexation, which developed into the considerable colony of German Southwest Africa.

Financially, the new colony was not a success. The Hereros, a vigorous and warlike race, were deprived of lands and cattle with impolitic suddenness. Finding themselves faced with the alternative of starvation or semi-servile labor, they rebelled. A long and difficult war ensued, conducted on both sides with much ferocity. Writing in 1913, Sir H. H. Johnston concludes his account of the war, in which the Germans were ultimately successful, with the reflection:

There are said to be only about 20,000 Herero people now living in Damaraland. It would be a great pity if this intelligent, strong race of Bantu negroes disappeared. . . . The long war in these deserts and bare, rocky mountains had cost the Germans the lives of over five thousand soldiers and settlers, and an expenditure of 15 millions sterling! So that it would have been cheaper at the commencement of this colony's history to have contented the natives and still have left more than half the area of South-West Africa at the disposal of the white men.

During the War it became customary to instance the Herero campaign as a proof of the cruelty of German colonial policy. The general policy of the Germans, however, was, as we shall see, exactly the same as that of the British in Matabeleland. General von Trotha, it is true, was unduly fierce, but he was not supported by the Home Government and was obliged to resign. Before the War, competent authorities thought well of German colonizing efforts in Africa. "They are," says Sir H. H. Johnston in 1913, "quick to realize their own defects, and equally quick to amend them. As in commerce, so in government, they observe, learn and master the best principles. The politician would be very short-sighted who underrated the greatness of the German character, or reckoned on the evanescence of German dominion in strange lands."

As a result of the War, Germany lost the whole of her possessions in Africa, amounting to over a million square miles.

IV. THE GROWTH OF BRITISH IMPERIALISM

The British Empire had grown up almost entirely without the help of deliberate governmental policy or the assistance of imperialistic doctrine. Gladstone, as a disciple of Cobden, disliked the acquisition of new territory, but with the victory of the Conservatives in 1886 a new epoch began. From that year until the end of the century the passion for empire continually grew, taking forms which were sometimes criminal, often ridiculous, and always disgusting. For this change of outlook there were many reasons. The growth of industrialism abroad, especially in America and Germany, made it no longer possible to feel a Cobdenite pride in being the workshop of the world; the need of boastfulness therefore demanded a different philosophy, which would enable us to rejoice in having the largest of all empires. Overseas possessions came to be more highly valued by the British when they found that other nations had come to desire them. Gladstone had tamely accepted defeat at the hands of the Boers and the Mahdi, but the average Englishman felt humiliated by Majuba and the death of Gordon. Home Rule for Ireland, which was the logical outcome of Gladstone's politics, was disliked by a majority, and resistance to it bred a taste for dominion. Queen Victoria's two Jubilees, in 1887 and 1897, were made the occasion for displays designed to increase this sentiment.

In addition to these political reasons for imperialism, there were others, some economic, some of a more idealistic kind. Missionaries were urged to consider that the conquest of the heathen by a Christian Power was calculated to further the diffusion of true religion. At the annual meeting of the Society for the Propagation of the Gospel in 1900, Lord Hugh Cecil, son of the Prime Minister and one of the most devout men of our time, set forth this argument:

A great many people were most anxious to go with their whole hearts into what might be called the imperial movement of the day, but had, as it were, a certain uneasiness of conscience whether, after all, this movement was quite as unpolluted by earthly considerations as they would desire it to be. He thought that by making prominent to our own minds the importance of missionary work we should to some extent sanctify the spirit of Imperialism.

Seeley's *Expansion of England,* an appeal to what in America is called "manifest destiny," had a great effect on the more educated classes. Ruskin, a Socialist, a moral leader, and the idol of progressive youth, in his inaugural lecture at Oxford, set forth the creed of imperialistic nationalism in its most extreme form:

There is a destiny now possible to us, the highest ever set before a nation to be accepted or refused. We are still undegenerate in race; a race mingled of the best northern blood. We are not yet dissolute in temper, but still have the firmness to govern and the grace to obey. . . . Will you youths of England make your country again a royal throne of kings; a sceptred isle, for all the world a source of light, a centre of peace; mistress of learning and of the Arts, faithful guardian of time-tried principles, under temptation from fond experiments and licentious desires; and amidst the cruel and clamorous jealousies of the nations, worshipped in her strange valour, of goodwill towards men? This is what England must either do, or perish: she must found colonies as fast and as far as she is able, formed of her most energetic and worthiest men; seizing every piece of fruitful waste ground she can set her foot on, and there teaching these her colonists that their chief virtue is to be fidelity to their country, and that their first aim is to be to advance the power of England by land and sea; and that, though they live on a distant plot of ground, they are no more to consider themselves therefore disfranchised from their native land than the sailors of her fleets do, because they float on distant seas. . . . If we can get men, for little pay, to cast themselves against cannon-mouths for love of England, we may find men also who will plough and sow for her, who will behave kindly and righteously for her, and who will bring up their children to love her, and who will gladden themselves in the brightness of her glory, more than in all the light of tropical skies.

This lecture, in particular, had importance as an inspiration to Cecil Rhodes, who came up to Oxford shortly after its delivery, and regarded it as expressing the guiding principles of his life.

The chief literary influence on the side of imperialism throughout the 'nineties was Rudyard Kipling. Beginning with stories of the lives of Anglo-Indians, he set forth the view that Englishmen went to India solely for the good of the Indians, and endured untold sufferings from mere devotion to duty. But he soon became interested in other parts of the Empire, more particularly in South Africa. He had an unshakable belief in the superior virtue and virility of the Anglo-Saxon race, and represented England as saying to the cities of Greater Britain, including such centres of British racial purity as Calcutta and Hong-Kong:

Truly ye come of The Blood. . . . So long as The Blood endures,
I shall know that your good is mine: ye shall feel that my strength is yours:
In the day of Armageddon, at the last great fight of all,
That Our House stand together and the pillars do not fall.

He thought of the Christian God as primarily a British tribal deity
and was

> . . . well assured that on our side
> The abiding oceans fight.

He exclaimed, in *A Song of the English:*

> Fair is our lot—O goodly is our heritage!
> (Humble ye, my people, and be fearful in your mirth!)
> For the Lord our God Most High
> He hath made the deep as dry,
> He hath smote for us a pathway to the ends of all the Earth!

The imperial sentiment of the Jubilee of 1897 found its most complete expression in Kipling's *Recessional:*

> God of our fathers, known of old,
> Lord of our far-flung battle-line,
> Beneath whose awful hand we hold
> Dominion over palm and pine—
> Lord God of Hosts, be with us yet,
> Lest we forget—lest we forget!
>
> . . . .
>
> If, drunk with sight of power, we loose
> Wild tongues that have not Thee in awe,
> Such boastings as the Gentiles use,
> Or lesser breeds without the Law—
> Lord God of Hosts, be with us yet,
> Lest we forget—lest we forget!

This lofty mood, however, was only for a great occasion. Though it involved some genuine idealism, in daily life imperialism was usually a more mundane affair, with straightforward economic motives. These were somewhat different in those who emigrated and in those who merely invested money. Various reasons caused the upper and professional classes to favor extensions of the Empire. Young men of no great ability, brought up in habits of social superiority, and finding society at home becoming democratic, were glad of the chance of earning a living and exercising command in regions inhabited by "inferior" races. Overcrowding, industrialism, and legality made England seem dull to adventurous dispositions, and hateful to those who loved solitude and beautiful surroundings. A considerable number of men went to the colonies only to escape from the ugliness and cramped conditions of modern English life, and found themselves unintentional empire-builders. The contrast between their desires and their achievements has been described by Kipling in one of his better poems, *The Voortrekker:*

> The gull shall whistle in his wake, the blind wave break in fire.
> He shall fullfil God's utmost will, unknowing his desire.
> And he shall see old planets change and alien stars arise,
> And give the gale his seaworn sail in shadow of new skies,
> Strong lust of gear shall drive him forth and hunger arm his hand,
> To win his food from the desert rude, his pittance from the sand.
> His neighbours' smoke shall vex his eyes, their voices break his rest.
> He shall go forth till south is north sullen and dispossessed.
> He shall desire loneliness and his desire shall bring,
> Hard on his heels, a thousand wheels, a People and a King.
> He shall come back on his own track, and by his scare-cooled camp
> There shall he meet the roaring street, the derrick and the stamp:
> There he shall blaze a nation's ways with hatchet and with brand,
> Till on his last-won wilderness an Empire's outposts stand!

The "thousand wheels," however, were impelled by different motives. The commerical classes, impressed by the growth of tariffs everywhere except in the United Kingdom, were anxious to secure markets from which foreign governments could not exclude them. Industrialists welcomed acquisitions in the tropics as affording sources of valuable raw materials and food-stuffs. But what was more important than either markets or raw materials was the opening for investment.[9] The making of roads and railways, the development of plantations and mines, the building of dams, and all the multifarious work of developing regions hitherto untouched by civilization, afforded a welcome outlet to capital which could no longer be invested in home industries with the same profit as in the days when factories were new or when railways were being introduced in England. More-

[9] See J. A. Hobson, *Imperialism: A Study*, p. 60.

over, old capital as well as new capital led to imperialistic ventures. We have already seen how the British holders of Turkish and Egyptian bonds secured their interest. This shows the advantage of armies and navies where they are available: English investors in the Erie Railroad had no redress when Mr. Drew swindled them, while those who lent money to the Khedive could employ the armed forces of the Crown (at no expense to themselves) to collect their debts, and could even win admiration as patriots for desiring the British occupation of Egypt.

In the case of South Africa, to which we must now turn our attention, there was added a force which has done more than any other to promote foreign conquest ever since the dawn of history: the lure of gold and precious stones.

V. BRITISH SOUTH AFRICA

The Cape of Good Hope, from which the British Empire in Africa has extended gradually northward until it has joined the extension southward from Egypt, was discovered by the Portuguese in 1488, but was not by them made the site of a settlement. It was the Dutch in 1652 who founded Cape Town. They colonized the surrounding country, and gave asylum, after the repeal of the Edict of Nantes, to large numbers of French Huguenots. Cape Colony was annexed by the English during the Napoleonic wars, to punish the Dutch for having been compelled to side with France; it was restored to them in 1802, but reconquered by the British and retained by them in 1815. Many of the Dutch disliked British rule so much that in 1836 they trekked northward into the wilderness, establishing first the Orange Free State and then the Transvaal. The status of these two republics was somewhat indeterminate: we claimed suzerainty, but they were unwilling to acknowledge it. In 1877, Sir Bartle Frere proclaimed the annexation of the Transvaal, but after three years of friction it rebelled, and Gladstone, who had meantime succeeded Disraeli, let it have its independence, while leaving the question of suzerainty once more somewhat vague.

For the next twenty years, the history of South Africa is the history of Cecil Rhodes.

Cecil Rhodes was born in 1853, and was the son of a country parson. He was the third son, and though his eldest brother had been sent to Winchester and his second to Eton, the money gave out by the time it came to his turn, and he was sent to a local day-school. The father hoped, with each son in turn, that he would take orders, but all refused: four became soldiers, and two became empire-builders. Cecil was threatened with consumption, and was therefore sent, when he was just seventeen, to join his oldest brother as a farmer in Natal. They had some measure of success in cotton-planting, but at the end of a year or so both were attracted to the new diamond fields. Cecil started from his farm in October, 1871, with "a few digger's tools, some volumes of the classics, and a Greek lexicon," and reached the diamond fields in about a month.

It was at that time only four years since the discovery of the first stone in what turned out to be the region most prolific in diamonds of all that are known to history. A Dutch farmer named Schelk van Niekerk went to call on a friend in the year 1867, and observed the friend's children playing marbles with stones they had picked up. One of the stones seemed to glitter, so he asked if he might show it to experts. The result was that it was sold to the Governor for £500. For two years after this, no big diamond was found. Then a native witch-doctor, who had a stone that he used for magic (probably the use for which diamonds were originally sought), showed it to van Niekerk, who bought it for 500 sheep, 10 oxen, and 1 horse. A trader, in turn, bought it from van Niekerk for £11,000, and sold it to Lord Dudley for £25,000. It was awarded the distinction, reserved for great gems, of a name, "the Star of South Africa."

The place where the diamonds had been found was just north of the Orange River, and in the territory of the Orange Free State, but taking advantage of some obscurities of title, the British successfully claimed it. To satisfy their conscience they paid an indemnity of £90,000, and secured a diamond field worth many hundreds of millions.

When Rhodes arrived at the place which afterwards became Kimberley, it was in the confused and disorderly condition typical of a new mining settlement. He quickly began to make money, and bought up claims as fast as his means permitted. It is curious that, in 1873, after less than two years of success, he abandoned South Africa for Oxford. The climate made him ill again, and he was obliged to interrupt his undergraduate career repeatedly to return to South Africa. Academically he was undistinguished, but during his enforced rustications he became a millionaire and a successful politician. In his last term, when he was twenty-eight, he must have been a rather odd undergraduate. On the whole, however, his time at Oxford served its purpose, since it helped him to enlist the support of the British governing class on various crucial occasions.

It must not be supposed that Rhodes was a mere money-grubber; on the contrary, he meditated much on profound problems of human destiny. He decided, after some hesitation, that the existence and non-existence of God are equally probable; anticipating William James's *Will to Believe,* he felt that hesitant indecision on such an issue would not do, and determined to adopt, in action, the hypothesis that there is a God. The next step was to determine God's purpose in creating the universe. As to this, Rhodes found less difficulty. "God was obviously trying to produce a type of humanity most fitted to bring peace, liberty, and justice to the world and to make that type predominant. Only one race, so it seemed to him, approached God's ideal type, his own Anglo-Saxon race; God's purpose then was to make the Anglo-Saxon race predominant, and the best way to help on God's work and fulfil His purpose in the world was to contribute to the predominance of the Anglo-Saxon race and so bring nearer the reign of justice, liberty, and peace." [10]

Rhodes proceeded to help on God's purpose of bringing "peace, liberty, and justice" by the Matabele wars, the Jameson Raid, the Boer War, the subjection, first of the northern negroes and then of the Boers, to British domination, and the creation of a vast system of political corruption both in England and in South Africa. Throughout, quite sincerely, he regarded himself as the agent of God.

The basis of Rhodes's success, throughout his career, was his control of the Kimberley diamonds. After 1888, the De Beers Consolidated Mines, in which he was the leading partner, owned all the South African diamond fields known at that time, amounting to 90 per cent of the world's total supply. In Transvaal gold mining he was important, but not a monopolist. His company, the Consolidated Gold Fields of South Africa, paid dividends which rose rapidly from 10 per cent in 1892 to 50 per cent in 1894–5, and brought him an

[10] Basil Williams, *Life of Cecil Rhodes,* p. 50.

annual income of three or four hundred thousand pounds. Nevertheless his interests in gold were never as important as in diamonds.

Meanwhile Rhodes determined, on imperialist rather than personal
grounds, that the British Empire must be extended northwards into
the region which was subsequently christened Rhodesia. The southern
part of this country, consisting of grassy uplands, inhabited by the
warlike and pastoral Matabele, was ruled over by a remarkable
potentate named Lobengula. He was tall and very stout, erect and
majestic, "completely naked save for a very long piece of dark blue
cloth, rolled very small and wound round his body, which it in no
wise concealed." He exercised a restraining influence on public opinion in his tribe, which was bellicose; within the limits of his experience, he was wise and politic, but a vigorous fighter when war seemed
necessary. As Wlliam Plomer says in his admirable little life of
Rhodes, he was "every ounce a king."

Unfortunately for himself and his subjects, he could not read,
but he could drink champagne. He did not like concession hunters,
who "come like wolves without my permission and make roads into
my country." But provided they sought his permission in a suitable
manner, he was affable and amenable. As it became known that his
country contained much gold, Rhodes, in 1888, sent three of his
friends, one of them a Fellow of All Souls, to secure his favor.
They were completely successful, obtaining all the mining rights
in his dominions in exchange for £100 a month, 1,000 rifles, 100,000
rounds of ammunition, and an armed steamer on the Zambesi. This
agreement was known as the Rudd concession.[11]

Rhodes's next step was to form a Chartered Company, with powers
analogous to those of the old East India Company. This required
action by the British Government, which was secured by means of
support in high quarters. Among those who applied for and obtained
the Charter were the Duke of Fife (Edward VII's son-in-law), the
Duke of Abercorn, Albert Grey (afterwards Earl Grey and Governor-
General of Canada), and other eminent persons. The Duke of Fife
was particularly useful, since through him the Royal Family became
implicated in Rhodes's doings. The Charter, which was granted in
1889, insured the protection of native rights, freedom of religion,

[11] The best account of Rhodes's dealings with Lobengula is in Morel's *The Black
Man's Burden*, Chap. IV.

and freedom of trade, and among the grounds on which it was given was that "the condition of the natives inhabiting the said territories will be materially improved and their civilizaton advanced." Incidentally, the Rudd concession was recognized, and the Company became the government of a vast area unbounded on the North except by the possessions of other European Powers.

Meanwhile Lobengula had discovered that the document to which he had set his mark was more far-reaching in its effects than he had supposed. He dictated a letter to Queen Victoria, saying, among other things:

Some time ago a party of men came into my country, the principal one appearing to be a man called Rudd. They asked me for a place to dig for gold, and said they would give me certain things for the right to do so. I told them to bring what they would give and I would show them what I would give. A document was written and presented to me for signature. I asked what it contained, and was told that in it were my words and the words of those men. I put my hand to it. About three months afterwards, I heard from other sources that I had given by that document the right to all the minerals of my country. I called a meeting of my *Indunas,* and also of the white men and demanded a copy of the document. It was proved to me that I had signed away the mineral rights of my whole country to Rudd and his friends. I have since had a meeting of my Indunas and they will not recognize the paper, as it contains neither my words nor the words of those who got it. . . . I write to you that you may know the truth about this thing.

And a few months later he sent another letter, in which he complained that "the white people are troubling me much about gold. If the Queen hears that I have given away the whole country it is not so."

The Queen, through her Colonial Secretary, replied to her brother monarch that it was impossible for him to exclude white men, and that, having made inquiries as to the persons concerned, she was satisfied that they "may be trusted to carry out the working for gold in the chief's country without molesting his people, or in any way interfering with their kraals, gardens, or cattle." There were occasional troubles connected with cattle-lifting, but for some years nothing was done. The Chartered Company was concerned with developments further South, and with financial operations in England. Its capital was £1,000,000 in one-pound shares, which made it possible to enlist as shareholders people who were far from rich, so that Rhodes's supporters were to be found even among wage-earners. De Beers took 200,000 shares, the promoters took 90,000, and Rhodes personally took a large number; moreover the United Concessions Company, of which he was an important part, was to have half of any future profits. While the world was getting used to these arrangements, it was desirable to give no handle to criticism.

In July, 1893, Dr. Jameson, who was the Chartered Company's manager, decided that the time had come to deal with the Matabele, and called for volunteers to help him in the "smashing of Lobengula." He offered every trooper who volunteered 3,000 *morgen* (nearly nine square miles) and twenty gold claims; he provided further that "the loot shall be divided, one-half to the B.S.A. Company, and the remainder to officers and men in equal shares." It is estimated that these various items together amounted to at least £10,000 per trooper. At this rate, it was not difficult to find men willing to help God in bringing about "peace, liberty, and justice." By October, the preparations were completed. Lobengula, still hoping for peace, sent three envoys to negotiate. The British gave a pledge of safe conduct, but on the day on which the envoys arrived at the camp, two of the three were "accidentally" killed. This was the beginning of the war, which lasted three months and realized all the hopes of the white men. Lobengula disappeared, his men fled or were killed, 900 farms and 10,000 gold claims were granted in what had been his kingdom, and about 100,000 cattle were looted, thus leaving the native survivors without means of livelihood.

In the "civilizing" of black Africa, it is always necessary to deprive the population of land and cattle, and other traditional sources of food, in order that they may be compelled to work for the white man. In Matabeleland, however, these methods were too slow, and forced labor was introduced. In 1896, after Jameson had been captured by the Boers, the Matabele made a desperate attempt to regain their freedom by rebellion, but they were, of course, defeated, and since then they have given no trouble. A tax of £2 a year was imposed on every native, who had to earn it by working for wages. Thus the two problems of revenue and wages were solved together. The

Matabele, however, according to a well-known missionary, Mr.
Carnegie, are not grateful, but say:

Our country is gone, our cattle are gone, our people are scattered, we
have nothing to live for, our women are deserting us; the white man does
as he likes with them; we are the slaves of the white man, we are nobody
and have no rights or laws of any kind.

It is comforting to think that all this suffering achieved a great and
beneficent purpose: the transfer of bits of yellow metal from certain
underground places to certain others, namely the vaults of the great
banks.

Jameson, the hero of the Matabele war, was Rhodes's lieutenant
and his most intimate friend. His next enterprise was less successful,
but more important.

The Transvaal outside the goldfields was still inhabited by the
descendants of those among the Cape Dutch who had found British
rule intolerable. On their isolated farms they preserved the simple
piety of the seventeenth century and regarded the modern capitalistic
world with horror. When gold was discovered on the Rand, they
realized that it brought sudden wealth to the farmers on whose land
it had been found, but beyond receiving rent and exacting revenue
they refused to have anything to do with the horde of international
adventurers who swarmed into their hitherto quiet country. Although
the Uitlanders (as the foreigners were called) came to outnumber
them by five to one, the Boers refused to allow them to vote, and for
a long time prevented the construction of railways connecting their
country with the Cape. Moreover they set up a high customs tariff,
which made everything dear that the Uitlanders had to import, and
almost destroyed trade with Cape Colony. The Uitlanders felt themselves the most important people in the country: many of them were
very rich, and their district produced most of the world's supply of
gold. This made them indignant at their exclusion from political power.

It was hoped by Rhodes, and also by the British Government, that
the Uitlanders would rebel against President Kruger on the old cry
of "no taxation without representation" which (this time) sounded
good in English ears. During 1895, the military authorities took to
bringing troops to and from India by way of the Cape instead of by the

Suez Canal, so that they might be on hand if trouble occurred. Rhodes was, at this time, not only in control of the Chartered Company, but also the Prime Minister of Cape Colony. Using both these sources of authority, he brought Jameson, with an armed force, to the borders of the Transvaal at the point nearest to Johannesburg, nominally to protect a railway which was being constructed. He endeavored to concert a rising on the Rand with a supporting movement by Jameson's troops. At the last moment he failed to agree with the "Reformers," many of whom wanted independence, whereas he insisted on annexation to the British Empire. At this point, he would have given up the enterprise, at least for a time. But Jameson, more hot-headed, set off on December 29, 1895; on January 2nd he and all his troop were ignominiously captured by Kruger's burghers.

The consequences of this event were surprisingly far-reaching. Rhodes's Dutch friends, naturally, turned against him, and he had to retire from Cape politics, though not from the control of Rhodesia. The British Government, or at any rate Joseph Chamberlain, the Colonial Secretary, was supposed to have been implicated, and, although this was probably not the case, there had indubitably been very culpable negligence. The German Emperor telegraphed his congratulations to President Kruger, which caused such indignation in England that most people forgot to blame the raiders. Jameson and his men were handed over to the English for punishment, and when they arrived in London all Society fêted them. Jameson was sentenced to a short term of imprisonment, but released almost at once "on grounds of health." Relations between England and Germany never again became cordial. The British Government took up the cause of the Uitlanders, and pressed it ruthlessly to its outcome in the Boer War. From the moment of the Raid, South African affairs exerted a disastrous influence upon the history of the world.

In Cape Colony, Rhodes's influence was at an end, but he retained his importance elsewhere. He wished to construct a telegraph line from the Cape to Cairo; Rhodesia touched Lake Tanganyika, but from that point to Uganda it was necessary to pass either through the Congo State or through German East Africa. In 1899, he visited the two monarchs concerned, to see which would grant him the best terms for permission to construct his line across their territory. He loathed King Leopold: "as he came out of the room he caught hold of our military attaché, who happened to be passing, and hissed in his ear: 'Satan, I tell you that man is Satan.' " [12] With the Kaiser, on the contrary, he got on admirably. He began by some arch remarks about the Kruger telegram: "You see, I was a naughty boy, and you tried to whip me. Now my people were quite ready to whip me for being a naughty boy, but directly *you* did it, they said, 'No, if this is anybody's business, it is *ours!*' The result was that Your Majesty got yourself very much disliked by the English, and I never got whipped at all."

The Kaiser was amused, and granted Rhodes's request.

From 1896 onwards, Rhodes's place in dealing with the Transvaal was taken by Joseph Chamberlain, who after Radical beginnings, had become as imperialistic as Rhodes himself, and had chosen the Colonial Office in order to give scope for his policies. "The Providence that shapes our ends intended us (he said) to be a great governing power —conquering, yes, conquering, but conquering only in order to civilize, to administer, and to develop vast races on the world's surface, primarily for their advantage, but no doubt for our advantage as well." During 1898, imperial sentiment in England had been greatly strengthened by Kitchener's conquest of the Sudan and the humiliation of the French in forcing them to abandon Fashoda. In 1899 it seemed to Chamberlain that the time had come to take up the other end of the Cape-to-Cairo Empire, and deal with the Boers once for all. It was, of course, a "war for democracy." "We seek no goldfields, we seek no territory," said Lord Salisbury; but cynical foreigners noted that we nevertheless got both goldfields and territory.

The Boer War was doubly disgraceful to England, in that our cause was unjust and our arms were at first unsuccessful. Continental feeling was bitterly anti-English, and our defeats at the hands of the Boers caused us to be thought decadent. There was talk of a Franco-Russo-German combination to force England to make peace with the Transvaal. The English realized, for the first time since the fall of Napoleon, that it might be advantageous to them to have allies on the Continent; Chamberlain offered an alliance to the Germans, but his offer was rejected. A considerable section of British opinion was opposed to the war throughout its whole course. Lloyd George, in Chamberlain's Birmingham, had to escape from the mob disguised as a policeman, but in Wales he never lost his popularity. Campbell-Bannerman, the

[12] Williams, *Life of Cecil Rhodes*, p. 310.

Liberal leader, spoke of "methods of barbarism" in connection with the burning of farms and the concentration camps for women and children. As soon as the war was over, the country turned against the party that had made it and the whole imperialist philosophy that had inspired it.

Two things helped to cause this reaction. The first was that Chamberlain embarked on a campaign for taxing food as the only way of cementing the Empire, but memories of the hungry 'forties made wage-earners think that an imperial Zollverein could be too dearly bought. The second was more directly connected with the South African War. The mine-owners, on whose behalf the war had been fought, wanted cheap labor. British working men had been told, throughout the fighting, that at the end there would be a great opening for them on the Rand, but their wages were too high for the Johannesburg magnates. The supply of black labor was considered inadequate, and it was decided to import Chinese coolies under semi-servile conditions. Trade-union feeling and anti-slavery sentiment were alike outraged. The Rector of Johannesburg pointed out what a kindness it was to bring these poor heathen to a Christian land, but this argument, somehow, fell flat. Anti-governmental moralists pointed out that there were ethical dangers in keeping 10,000 men without any women; the Government announced that it had imported a certain number of the coolies' wives, and the Archbishop of Canterbury said that the interests of morals were now safeguarded. But still skeptics shook their heads when they learnt that there were only two women.

In the end the nation gave a record majority to Campbell-Bannerman, in spite of his talk about "methods of barbarism." Simple folk imagined that imperialism and war had been voted down, and that the new Government would pursue the paths of peace. Unfortunately a small minority of the Liberal party had favored imperialism throughout, and in this minority was Sir Edward Grey, who became Foreign Secretary. While the nation was voting enthusiastically for peace, he, without the knowledge even of the Cabinet, sanctioned the military conversations with France which, if they did not make the Great War inevitable, at least made it certain that England would take part in it if it came.

And so, though Rhodes died just before the end of the war, and Chamberlain two years later, though Parliament repented of the evil it had done in their day, a few men, by dark and secret ways, kept

England's policy tied to the old bad courses, and led their country blindfold along the road to universal disaster.

VI. ASIA

European imperialism in Asia has been less successful than in Africa, and has pursued a very different course. Asiatic Russia must be regarded as a colony, not a conquered empire; the indigenous population was sparse, and offered less opposition to Russian immigration than the aborigines offered to the white men in the United States. The British position in India was already well established in 1815, and underwent no important change during our period. Gradually, however, contact with Western political ideas, in India as well as in other parts of Asia, generated a nationalist movement, which began to impress Anglo-Indians shortly before the outbreak of the Great War.

The regions open to imperialist competition were the Turkish Empire, Persia, and the Far East. The decay of Turkey had stimulated the lusts of the Great Powers ever since Napoleon and Alexander bargained about Constantinople, Syria, Moldavia, and Wallachia, but mutual jealousies had prevented a partition such as was successfully accomplished in Africa. The Russians, the French, and the English all had interests in the Near East, but gradually Germany took the place of England as the Sultan's friend. Asia Minor came to be a field for German capital, and the scheme for a Berlin-Bagdad railway excited German imperialists in the same sort of way as the Cape-to-Cairo excited those of England. (It would seem that imperialists in all countries are stirred by alliteration.) Both England and Russia objected to the plan of through railway communication between Berlin and the Persian Gulf, but a compromise favorable to Germany had just been reached when the War broke out.

Persia, the most intellectual and the most artistic of Mohammedan countries, after many centuries of misgovernment adopted Liberal ideas and instituted a Parliament. This did not suit either England or Russia. In virtue of the Entente of 1907, England seized a region in the South, containing oil fields of great value to the Admiralty, which had just decided to substitute oil for coal in the navy, while Russia seized a much larger region in the North, and suppressed the constitutionalists with the customary barbarity of the Tsarist régime. Normal independence was left to a territory in the centre, embracing less than a quarter of the country.[13]

More important than these events in the Near East were the repercussions of the white man's intrusion upon China and Japan. In the sixteenth and seventeenth centuries, the Portuguese from Macao and the Spaniards from Manila had sent missionaries and firearms to both countries. The Japanese, after they had learnt to make firearms, exterminated the Christian converts and closed their country to Europeans, except for one annual Dutch ship. The Chinese, though they took a Voltairean view of Christianity, had to admit that the Jesuits surpassed them in the power of predicting eclipses, and on this ground continued to tolerate them. Neither supposed that the white men could defeat them in war.

On this point, China and Japan, respectively, were enlightened by England and America. The English went to war with China in 1840, because the Chinese authorities objected to the importation of opium. The resulting Treaty laid the foundation of the system which continued in China until after the War, and in many respects is still in force. Chinese Customs were administered by a staff responsible only to its head, who was to be an Englishman as long as England had the largest share of China's foreign trade; and import duties were not to be above 5 per cent *ad valorem* even on such things as alcohol and (for a long time) opium. A gradually increasing number of "Treaty Ports," many of them hundreds of miles from the sea, were claimed by the Foreign Powers collectively, and ceased to be, except formally, under Chinese sovereignty. Foreigners in China were subject to their own law, and could only be judged by their own nationals. But still the Chinese, who had been supreme throughout their world since the third century B.C., retained their imperial pride, and regarded the foreigners as a nuisance rather than as a menace.

In Japan the course of events had been very different. Commodore Perry's squadron, which, in 1853, demanded the opening up of trade relations with the United States, made them aware that armaments had progressed since their last contact with Christian civilization in the early seventeenth century. For the moment they gave way to him, and

[13] I have dealt more fully with the Anglo-Russian partition of Persia in my essay "The Entente Policy, 1904–1915," included in *Justice in War-Time*, pp. 171–92.

to the British, who soon followed. Commercial agreements were concluded, Treaty Ports opened to trade; no Westerner doubted that the whole process would proceed according to plan. So it did—but the plan was that of the Japanese, not of the white men. They rapidly acquired whatever parts of European civilization contribute to military and naval efficiency; the Treaty Ports were resumed, foreigners submitted to Japanese laws and law-courts, and trade, though it continued, came to be conducted as between equals, not for the exclusive benefit of the white men.

When, in 1894, the Japanese and Chinese quarrelled over the suzerainty of Korea, which both claimed, the world was astonished by the rapidity and completeness of China's defeat. The result was a scramble for China. The French claimed a sphere of influence in the South, the British claimed one in the Yangtse. The Russians seized Manchuria, and rejoiced to think that, at Port Arthur, they at last had free access to the warm water. The Germans, in 1897, had the good fortune to have two missionaries murdered in Shantung; they extorted, as indemnity, the harbor of Kiaouchau with valuable railway rights in the hinterland. Finally ignorant Chinese reactionaries, the Boxers, encouraged by the Empress Dowager, attacked the "foreign devils" wherever they were to be found, especially in missions and in the legations at Peking. An international expedition was sent in 1900 to punish the country; Peking was sacked, a heavy indemnity was imposed, and the legation quarter henceforth had the right to garrison itself with foreign troops, while the Chinese were forbidden to build houses in the neighborhood of its walls. China was cowed—for the benefit of Europe, it was supposed at the time.

The Russo-Japanese War, four years later, changed everything. Since the war with China, the Japanese had considered their rights in Korea established. But Russian Grand Dukes had timber concessions in that country, which, moreover, seemed necessary in order to round off the new acquisitions in Manchuria. The newly constructed Siberian Railway made a war in the Far East seem feasible to the Russian military authorities. The Japanese, however, proved the stronger. At sea, they destroyed the Russian navy; on land, they conquered Port Arthur and South Manchuria up to Mukden. It was the first time since the great days of the Turks that Europeans had been defeated by non-

Europeans. In China, from that time onwards, the only important imperialism has been that of Japan, while Europeans, especially since the Great War, have survived only on sufferance.[14]

The effect of the Russo-Japanese War was as important in Russia as in China. It led first to the Revolution of 1905 involving a constitution with the beginnings of Parliamentary government. It next caused a complete change in Russia's foreign policy. Far Eastern adventure was no longer possible. The Anglo-Japanese Alliance made it impossible for the French to come to the help of the Russians. For the same reason, as well as the Anglo-French Entente in 1904, the year when the war with Japan began, the French could not be expected to help Russia against England. This made a forward policy in Asia impossible, and removed the reasons for enmity between England and Russia which had subsisted ever since the Russian advance in Central Asia made us nervous concerning our Indian Empire. The result was that Russian ambitions were directed to the Balkans and the Near East, where they came into conflict with Turkey, Austria-Hungary, and therefore Germany. This policy nowhere conflicted with British interests, but, on the contrary, made British friendship both possible and desirable. Hence arose the Anglo-Russian Entente of 1907, which completed the grouping of the Great Powers that persisted until the Great War.

Japan's rise to supremacy in the Far East put an end to the ambitions of European Powers in China, and thus removed from the sphere of their mutual bargaining the last important region that they had left unappropriated. Henceforth, the planet was mapped out, and a gain to one State could only be secured at the expense of some other. This intensified rivalries, and made adjustments more difficult; the expansive forces which had found their outlet in imperialism were compelled to operate, no longer in distant undeveloped regions, but nearer home, and in direct competition with neighboring nations. Though statesmen foresaw the result, they lacked the will and the intelligence to prevent it; impotently, though not blindly, they drifted to catastrophe.

[14] I have dealt more fully with imperialism in China and Japan in my book *The Problem of China.*

CHAPTER XXXII

THE ARBITERS OF EUROPE

IT was in the year 1907 that the division of the Great Powers of Europe into two camps received the final form which persisted until the Great War. The world had changed since the Congress of Vienna more than in any previous century: freedom and organization had both increased, and had increased in about equal measure. As to freedom: serfdom had disappeared; parliamentary institutions had been introduced where none existed before, and had been made more democratic where they came from an earlier time; trade unions had been legalized, and had given wage-earners some approach to equality of bargaining power in dealings with employers; emigration was everywhere permitted by governments, and was beginning to have a great effect upon Southern and Eastern Europe; religious toleration had been established everywhere except in the Russian Empire; the criminal law had become less ferocious; Press censorship had been abolished or mitigated, and in politics there was a nearer approach to free speech than at any previous period.

The change as regards organization was quite as remarkable. Large-scale economic organizations were made necessary by the invention of railways, and possible by the laws of limited liability. Both in Europe and America, aggregations of capital continually increased in size, and thus concentrated economic power in the hands of a few great men. Governments, which had had comparatively few functions in 1815, had come to be active in many new directions. The most important of these was education: the existence of a literate democracy in Western countries made possible a new intensity of national co-operation, such as had only previously existed in small city States. Railways, telegraphs, and telephones enabled men at the centre to give rapid instructions to men at a distance, and thus augmented the effective powers of governments. Outside Europe, where Red Indians had hunted, and where African chiefs had led their braves to battle, modern cities and modern machinery now brought men within the orbit of the Stock Exchange.

In spite of the fact that the world had been transformed since 1814, there was one respect in which there had been no change of importance, and such change as had occurred was of the nature of a retrogression. The external relations of the Great Powers were still, as at the time of the Congress of Vienna, in the hands of single individuals, whose power might be subject to theoretical limitations, but was in practice almost despotic. In spite of the establishment of Parliaments in the three Eastern Empires, their foreign relations were still as completely controlled by their Emperors as in the time of Alexander I and Metternich. In England, the tradition of continuity in foreign policy removed external relations from the effective control of Parliament; whichever party had the government, the Foreign Office was in the hands of members of the same Whig families that had come into office in 1830. In France, the Minister for Foreign Affairs was less absolute than elsewhere in Europe; but an alliance between permanent officials and certain business interests led to results very similar to those produced elsewhere by autocracy.

While the relations between States remained thus completely unmodernized, their power of injuring each other had been immeasurably increased. Science and industrialism had transformed the art of war, and had made it possible to devote to fighting and the production of munitions a far larger proportion of the population than had been available for destruction in the campaigns of Napoleon. More rapid mobility and transmission of orders made it possible to invade an enemy country far more quickly than at any previous time. Hence nations feared each other more than formerly, and this fear bred more intense nationalism, which, in turn, created still more fear, and therefore still more nationalism, on the other side of the frontier. Nationalism and fear, in disastrous interaction, continually increased each other, and promoted national organization for war, especially for sudden war, since the Power that mobilized most quickly could insure that the armies should meet on enemy territory. Army, navy, and diplomacy had to work in close co-operation, and always in the state of mind of men waiting for the last signal to begin a race.

The lack of organization in international relations was connected with a lack of organization in one aspect of economic life, namely the investment of new capital. We have seen the immense profits which Rhodes and King Leopold derived from the investment of capital in

Africa; and similar profits were sought by imperialistic ventures in many parts of the world. Sometimes these profits were obtained by conquest, sometimes by diplomacy. In the leading industrial countries, the iron and steel industry was bound up with the armament industry, and was perpetually endeavoring to sell armaments to more backward States. When the Tsar's ships had been sunk by the Japanese, the Kaiser repeatedly urged him to place orders for new ships with German firms, but the Tsar preferred to trust his allies the French. When Sir Basil Zaharoff wished to make a fortune out of submarines, he failed, at first, with all the Great Powers. But at last he got his compatriots the Greeks to take one; this led to the Turks taking two, another Power three, yet another four, and so on to the loss of the Lusitania—a progression wholly agreeable to shipbuilders, from first to last. In such ways the investment of new capital came to be bound up with the diplomatic game, and its profits often depended upon the danger of war.

Foreign affairs were treated everywhere as a mystery, which it would be against the national interest to lay bare before the eyes of the profane. Fortunately for the historian, the revolutions in the three Eastern Empires have caused State documents to be published at a much earlier date than would have been permitted if the old governments had remained in control. We can now judge, as accurately as if they had lived a hundred years ago, the supermen who wielded the immense forces of their States in the last years before the Great War.

Among the most important of these men were, as in 1814, the Tsar, the Austrian Emperor, and the King of Prussia, who had become the German Emperor. But as between these three Eastern Powers there had been great changes of relative importance. Germany now stood first, Austria last; and Russia, though still very prominent, had lost to Germany the supremacy that had belonged to Alexander I. England, still powerful through the Navy and the Empire, felt itself threatened by Germany. The external power of England, from the end of 1905, was in the hands of Sir Edward Grey, almost as absolutely as that of Germany was in the hands of the Kaiser. In France, there were alternations of policy; but the decisive men in the finally victorious policy were Delcassé and Poincaré. All these men were not *mere* embodiments of impersonal forces, but influenced events through their personal idiosyncrasies.

In the diplomatic map of Europe, some elements were fixed through-out the whole period from 1871 to 1914, while others varied. The most important fixed element was French hostility to Germany. Bismarck accepted this as inevitable, and dealt with it, on the one hand, by cultivating good relations with Russia, and on the other hand, by encouraging England, France, and Italy in imperialistic ventures which brought them into conflict with each other. After Bismarck's fall, the French, bit by bit, improved their diplomatic situation, first by the Franco-Russian alliance, then by the Entente with England, and finally by the weakening of Germany's and Austria's position in the Balkans as a result of the Balkan wars. Moreover, the financial and industrial resources of the United States, it was understood, would be more available to France and England than to Germany in the event of a war; the firm of Morgan, especially, could almost be regarded as a partner in the Entente. As the position of France improved, the hope of recovering the lost provinces—especially the iron ore of Lorraine—revived in the minds of French statesmen and industrialists. The hopes of other Powers might have been realized in minor wars, but the recovery of Alsace-Lorraine was only possible in the general European war. The interest and policy of France, therefore, more than of any other Great Power, pointed towards a first-class conflict, as soon as the support of England had been assured by the Entente of 1904.

The most important man in Europe, judged by his influence on events, was the Emperor William II. His youth had been passed under the shadow of his grandfather William I and his grandmother Queen Victoria. His mother, Queen Victoria's eldest daughter, was the wife of the Crown Prince Frederick, who, after waiting for the throne until he was fifty-seven, ascended it as a dying man, incapable, during his few months' reign, of taking any part in government. William II, born with a withered arm, was never loved by his mother; she told an Austrian (who, of course, repeated the words) how much she admired the Austrian Crown Prince as compared with her own "uncouth, lumpish son." She was an ambitious, masterful woman, longing for the succession, hating Bismarck, hating Germany, never troubling to conceal the fact that she felt herself English. The old Emperor lived on and on—he was ninety when he died—and gradually her hopes faded. She foresaw that her reign (her husband was under her thumb) would be short, and this added envy to her previous dislike of her son, with whom she quarelled irrevocably during her husband's last hours. William's hatred of his mother was the source of his hatred of England.

England, however, was to him not merely an object of hate, but also, and equally, of admiration. There was, in those days, a Royal International, much more influential than the Red International or the Black International. There was, in Northern Europe, only one Royal Family, of which different members governed different countries, and of this August House Queen Victoria was the recognized head. Not only was the Kaiser her grandson, but the Tsar had married her granddaughter—"I am to call her Granny," Nicholas records proudly in his diary at the time of his engagement. Since Versailles had come into the keeping of republicans, no royal palace was so grand as Windsor. Whenever William II was invited to stay there during the lifetime of "Grandmama," he felt a snobbish satisfaction, and boasted of its splendors on his return. He could not resist trying to ingratiate himself with the English, though his efforts were so clumsy that his Ministers had to keep on warning him against excessive effusiveness. His admiration for the English was bound up with Queen Victoria, just as his hatred was bound up with his mother.

At Kiel, in 1904, in the presence of King Edward, the Kaiser offered a defence of his big-navy policy which was psychologically true, though not perhaps politically wise: "When, as a little boy, I was allowed to visit Plymouth and Portsmouth, hand in hand with kind aunts and friendly admirals, I admired the proud English ships in those two superb harbours. Then there awoke in me the wish to build ships of my own like these some day, and when I was grown up to possess as fine a navy as the English." Bülow, his Chancellor, tried to prevent publication of this speech, saying that if the fleet was described "so sentimentally, as the outcome of your own personal inclinations and juvenile memories," the Reichstag might refuse to pay for it. But the Kaiser was irrepressible. He had insisted on showing "Uncle Bertie" his whole Navy, although he had been warned that the more the King was impressed the worse would be the political effect. All the time, he was wishing to feel as grand as "Grandmama."

The Kaiser's withered arm had as bad an effect on his character as his mother and grandmother. His uneasy vanity made it necessary for him to shine, and his position as head of the Hohenzollerns made it inevitable that he should be a soldier. But it was only with great difficulty and by heroic efforts that he learned to ride a horse, and his horses always had to be quiet. On crucial occasions, for instance when he landed at Tangier to please Bülow and vex France and England, he was agitated if his mount was too spirited. A long time after his visit to Tangier he wrote a complaining letter to Bülow: "I landed because you wanted me to, in the interest of the Fatherland, mounted a strange horse in spite of the impediment that my crippled left arm caused to my riding, and the horse was within an inch of costing me my life, which was your stake in the game!" Bülow comments on this: "Among the many lovable human qualities of the Kaiser, scarcely one was more appealing than the truly stoical manner in which he bore and overcame the paralysis of his left arm. Without in any way concealing this physical defect, he had by iron determination developed into a bold rider, a brilliant shot and a skilful tennis-player." This is very just, but the effort caused his vanity to develop in unfortunate ways.

His apparent bellicosity, his readiness to challenge combat, his swashbuckling boastfulness, were a cloak for nerves, for the fear of being thought not quite manly. If he had been born a rich man in a private station, he would have been perfectly happy as a patron of the arts: he would have surrounded himself with painters and musicians, who would have been expected to praise his pictures and his tunes. His need for applause would have been satisfied at the cost of a little insincere admiration of amateurish artistic productions, instead of compelling him to adopt a course which was one of the factors leading to the ruin of Europe. His natural disposition is shown by the friends he chose voluntarily, of whom Count Philip Eulenburg was the most intimate. Eulenburg was effeminate, sentimental and subtle, a homosexual like most of the Emperor's inner camarilla. Even in military circles, a reaction against the manly virtues of Old Prussia had set in. The Chief of the Military Cabinet, Count Hülsen-Haeseler, on several occasions dressed as a ballet-dancer; on the last of these occasions he danced before the Kaiser, and at the end fell down dead—to the scandal of His Majesty's subjects.

William II's masterfulness was not, like Bismarck's, that of a man of inflexible will, but rather that of an actor who is afraid of not having the best part. This did not make it any the easier for him to get on with the old Chancellor, who for twenty-six years had been the absolute master of Prussia. The old man had in his favor the fact that the Empress Frederick hated him, and he remained in office for the first two years of the new reign. But in 1890 the inevitable breach came, and Bismarck was dismissed.

It happened that, at this very moment, a matter of vital importance to Germany had to be decided, namely, the question of the renewal of the Re-insurance Treaty with Russia. The Austro-German Alliance, concluded in 1879, involved a danger of alliance between France and Russia; to obviate this, Bismarck, in 1887, concluded for three years a secret treaty with Russia, by which the two Powers mutually agreed not to join any third Power in an attack upon the other. Austria and Russia had conflicting interests in the Balkans, but Bismarck was determined to be friends with both. Except for a few weeks in 1866, the three Eastern Powers had been friends since 1813; their friendship both preserved the peace of Europe and prevented France from finding allies. By means of the Re-insurance Treaty (which, however, had to be concealed from Austria), Germany did what was possible to preserve harmony between the three Emperors.

This policy had been Bismarck's, and he was in disfavor; therefore the policy must be a bad one. In the confusion of the interregnum, there was only one man who understood the intricacies of German diplomacy, and that was the permanent head of the Foreign Office, Baron Holstein. He advised against renewal of the Treaty, because the Russian Government hesitated to renew it with any one but Bismarck, and he did not wish Bismarck to return to power. It was allowed to lapse, and Russia turned to France, concluding an Entente in 1891 and an Alliance in 1894.

Holstein, who in this matter first acquired important influence on German foreign policy, was a most singular character. When he was a child, a barn full of sheep belonging to his father had caught fire, and his father had been trampled to death by the sheep while he was trying to save them. This made such an impression on the boy that, throughout his life, the sight of sheep produced nervous prostration. However, he showed little eccentricity until, under Bismarck's orders, while he was Secretary of the Embassy in Paris, he procured evidence against his Chief, Count Arnim, whom Bismarck had decided to ruin, and against whom Holstein was compelled to appear as a witness in open court. Arnim was popular in Berlin society, and Holstein was ostracized for having played the part of a spy under the guise of friendship. From that moment he lived the life of a recluse; even the Kaiser only succeeded in meeting him once, after repeated invitations, generally refused by Holstein on the ground that he possessed no court dress.

The Kaiser, after his fall, said that the dismissal of Bismarck was like rolling away a granite block and revealing the vermin underneath. Perhaps he was thinking of Holstein, though at the time of Holstein's power he spoke of him as "a down-right good fellow." This "good fellow" consoled himself for social shipwreck by the joys of secret power. He made friends with Eulenburg, and at the same time collected evidence by which he could send his "friend" to prison whenever he chose. It is said that one night, taking refuge from the rain in a somewhat disreputable beer-house used as a rendezvous by homosexuals, he saw (himself unseen) two men, dressed as sailors and obviously disguised, who spoke to each other as "Krause" and "Hoffman." He recognized "Krause" as Eulenburg. Years afterwards, on meeting Bülow for the first time, he recognized the voice: Bülow was "Hoffman." The knowledge which he undoubtedly possessed, and of which this incident was said to be the beginning, enabled him to control both these eminent men, and made him, therefore, favorable to their advancement. But however high they rose, they had to adopt the policies that he recommended, and make the appointments that he favored. From 1890, when Bismarck fell, till 1906, Germany's foreign policy was Holstein's. He advised the rejection of Chamberlain's offers of alliance; he inspired the Morocco policy which Bülow forced upon the unwilling Kaiser. He did not recommend the Kruger telegram, which was the Kaiser's own doing, but he took care to be out of the way while it was being discussed, as he foresaw that the responsibility would fall upon the Foreign Secretary, Marschall, whom he wished out of the way in order to make room for Bülow. Almost everybody feared him, because of his knowledge of shady secrets and his skill in intrigue. When he fell, it was owing to a totally unpredictable accident. In 1906, Bülow fainted in the Reichstag, and all his papers were temporarily put in charge of his subordinate Tschirsky. Among them was Holstein's resignation, intended, like ten earlier ones, merely as a means of bringing pressure to bear. But Tschirsky, unlike many others, had no guilty secrets, and at once obtained the Kaiser's signature to the resignation. Holstein supposed Eulenburg to blame, and brought about his ruin, as well as that of other eminent men, by giving information as to the Kaiser's intimates to the Radical journalist Harden, who printed it in his newspaper. He died in 1909, old and poor and nearly blind, in the small apartment in an unfashionable part of Berlin in which he had lived throughout his years of power. The *Daily Mail* obituary spoke of him as "the prototype of the Prussian official of the old school." He was learned, he was indefatigable in work, in a sense he was patriotic. But his suspicious nature made him, on all crucial occasions, give the wrong advice, and his twisted hatreds did much to bring about the atmosphere of war.

The Kaiser's dealings with Eulenburg and his friends show one side of his character, but a quite different side is shown in his letters to "Dearest Nicky," the Emperor of Russia. Nicholas II, who ascended the throne in 1894, was younger than his cousin William, less intelligent, and less forceful. It seemed, therefore, that it should be possible to establish a personal ascendancy over him, and so make Russian policy such as would suit Germany. Even when the Triple Alliance and the Triple Entente had become well-defined mutually hostile groups, the Kaiser could not abandon this hope. Nor did he ever learn that what he said to his dear cousin against the French or the English was liable to be repeated to them. When the Russo-French Alliance was just concluded, he told "Nicky" to "keep those damned rascals [the French] in order and make them sit still." He was pained that an Autocrat could treat republicans with respect. The hobnobbing of Grand Dukes with the head of the Republic "makes Republicains [sic] [1] believe that they are quite honest excellent people, with whom Princes can consort and feel at home." Besides, "don't forget that Jaurès—not his personal fault—sits on the throne of the King and Queen of France. . . . Nicky take my word on it the curse of God has stricken that People forever!"

This line of argument failed to open the Tsar's eyes to the wickedness of France. William had more success—or at least so it seemed to him—when he wrote about the Yellow Peril, and incited the Tsar to go crusading for the Cross against Buddha. He was delighted by the outbreak of the Russo-Japanese War, and full of assurances of his moral support—provided that Russia would agree to a Commercial Treaty such as Germany needed. But when the Tsar refused to make a political

[1] The correspondence of the two Emperors was in English.

agreement without the knowledge of France, he wrote to Bülow that "we must now cultivate Japan and 'give Paris one in the eye.' "

Hatred of the English appears on every mention of them. The Kaiser spoke of them as "a certain meddlesome Power." Nevertheless, when Chamberlain suggested an Alliance, he wrote at once to "dearest Nicky" exaggerating the offer, apparently asking advice, and really hinting that he could not refuse unless the Tsar would make a better bid for his friendship. He continued, down to 1906, the hope that the Tsar would induce France to join in a Continental block against England, and felt that he and Nicholas, personally, could control the world. In September, 1902, he wrote: "As the rulers of the two leading Powers of the two great Continental Combinations we are able to exchange our views on any general question touching their interests, and as soon as we have settled how to tackle it, we are able to bring our Allies to adopt the same views, so that the two Alliances—i.e. 5 Powers—having decided that Peace is to be kept, the World must remain at peace and will be able to enjoy its blessings." That is to say, he wished to revive the Holy Alliance policy, by means of which Europe had had an international government, of a reactionary sort, from 1815 to 1830. It was a policy by which peace had been preserved in the past, but in 1902 it had become impossible. France, after the fall of Napoleon, was reactionary and not dismembered; after 1871, France was Liberal and not reconciled to the loss of Alsace-Lorraine. Russia and Austria were estranged by their divergent interests in the Balkans and Constantinople, which were exacerbated by the growth of Slav nationalism. The German Navy made England hostile, and anxious to fan the flames of French resentment against Germany. The Kaiser's policy, therefore—unfortunately, perhaps—was no longer possible, owing to the aggressive imperialism and nationalism of the epoch, both in Germany and elsewhere.

The best hope of winning Nicholas—so it seemed to the Kaiser—was through his fear of Liberalism and Revolution. Metternich had used this argument successfully to turn Alexander I against the Greeks; Nicholas I disliked the French after 1830, and fought against them in the Crimean War; Nicholas II's grandfather had been assassinated by revolutionaries, whose pernicious doctrines might be considered to come from France. From the standpoint of an autocrat, England was little better. For a moment, in 1905, these arguments prevailed. The

Tsar had suffered defeat in the Far East, and was faced with revolution at home. He was furious with England for resenting the Dogger Bank incident, in which his Baltic Fleet, on the way home from Japan, had fired upon English fishing smacks under the impression that they were Japanese torpedo boats. He telegraphed to the Kaiser: "I have no words to express my indignation with England's conduct." William took advantage of the favorable moment, met the Tsar yachting at Björkö on the Baltic, and, without the presence of Ministers, surprised Nicholas into signing a treaty. The day of its signature, he said to the Tsar, "is a cornerstone in European politics and turns over a new leaf in the history of the world." He sent equally triumphant paeans to Bülow: "The morning of July, 1905, at Björkö is a turning point in the history of Europe, and a great relief for my beloved Fatherland, which will at last be emancipated from the Gallic-Russo strangle-grip."

Alas, Bülow declared the Treaty worthless, because his draft had had two words added by the Kaiser; and the Russian Foreign Minister, Lamsdorf, refused to ratify it on the ground that it was incompatible with Russia's obligations to France. Bülow threatened to resign, but William sent him a long telegram of protest, ending: "The day after I receive your resgination, the Emperor will no longer exist! Think of my poor wife and children!" This thought (or some other) caused the Chancellor to consent to remain in office, but the Treaty was dead.

Nevertheless, Willy continued to write to Nicky as if their personal decision had made it a valid document. He maintained that the Anglo-French Entente, then new, had a Liberal purpose: "The French and English Liberal Press quite openly and in conjunction denounce all monarchical and energetic actions in Russia—the 'Zardom' as they call it—and openly espouse the cause of the Revolutionaries for the expansion and maintenance of liberalism and 'enlightenment' against the 'Zardom' and 'Imperialism' and 'certain' backward countries. That is yours and mine. The phrase which the French are always retaught by England is 'to uphold in common the interests of Liberalism in the world and to propagate it in other countries.' That means to foster and help revolutions all over Europe especially in countries which are happily not yet under the absolute domination of those infernal parliaments."

In the same letter, forgetting the wickedness of the French, he urged a coalition against England: "The 'Continental Combine' flanked by

America is the sole and only manner to effectively block the way to the whole world becoming John Bull's personal property, which he exploits at his heart's content after having, by lies and intrigues without end, set the rest of the civilized nations by each other's ears for his own personal benefit. We see this pernicious principle at work now in the Morocco [sic] question, in which John Bull is equally doing his best to set the French dead against us."

But nothing came of it; the Tsar composed his differences with England, and became gradually less friendly to William. In the interest of Emperors as a class, it would seem that Willy was more in the right than Nicky, and perhaps with more tact he might have proved more persuasive.

The German Navy, which determined British policy from 1902 onward, was the Kaiser's personal creation. We have seen how he asserted that his desire for battleships was inspired by the sights kind aunts showed him at Portsmouth and Plymouth when he was a boy. There were, however, more serious motives. He envied England's power in distant places: there was trouble at Koweit, and British ships were on the spot; there was a dispute about Samoa, and the King's Navy took a hand; owing to English Admirals, the bombardment of Crete was less ferocious than he could have wished. When he went cruising in the Mediterranean, he could not prevent himself from admiring Gibraltar, or from letting Nicky know of his enthusiasm: "Gibraltar is simply overwhelming! It is the grandest thing I ever saw. Words are utterly inadequate to give the slightest idea of what it is. Grand in its nature and by the military Power that is stored on and around this mighty Rock." He felt that, with an adequate Navy, he too might come to possess "mighty Rocks." It is quite consistent with his admiration of England that a few months later he was writing to the Tsar: "An excellent expedition to cool British insolence and overbearing would be to make some military demonstrations on the Persio-Afghan frontier," since "I am aware and I am informed that this is the only thing they are afraid of and that the fear of your entry into India from Turkestan and into Afghanistan from Persia was the real and only cause that the guns of Gibraltar and of the British Fleet remained silent 3 weeks ago!" [After the Dogger Bank incident.] This advice, as also the suggestion that the Tsar's Black Sea Fleet should suddenly force the Straits and set out to join his Baltic Fleet in the voyage to the Far East, must be regarded as proceeding from admiring envy of England. But such counsels, under the pretence of friendship, show perfidy to the Tsar, whose troubles from Japan and revolution could hardly be lightened by a war with England.

The Emperor William, in his building of the Navy, was supported, against his other Ministers, by an honest technical enthusiast, Tirpitz, who never understood anything of diplomacy. First Bülow, and then Bethmann-Hollweg, were alarmed by the isolation of Germany that resulted from England's hostility, and realized that, if Germany were ever involved in a serious war, England was sure to intervene on the other side. They wished for a naval agreement, which the British Government was constantly suggesting. At first, the Kaiser replied furiously that any such proposal, made by England officially, would mean war; and in this he was supported by Tirpitz, not on the ground that Germany was ready to fight, but because both thought that a firm tone would frighten the English. Admiral Fisher, a man very similar to Tirpitz, whom he greatly admired,[2] advised that the German Navy should be "Copenhagened," i.e., sunk without previous warning, as the Danish Fleet had been sunk by us a century earlier. And the Civil Lord of the Admiralty, Arthur Lee (afterwards Lord Lee of Fareham), in a speech, told his audience that if there were war, the German Navy would be sunk before the Germans knew that war had been declared. These amiable proposals did not make subsequent negotiations any easier.

Although both Tirpitz and William II, in 1912, ceased to oppose a naval agreement wholly and in principle, they remained so reluctant that they imposed impossible conditions, more especially a promise of neutrality in any war in which the other Power might be engaged, which would have been incompatible with England's obligations to France and Belgium. And so the hostility and the naval competition continued, although German statesmen saw that it would inevitably lead to a war which must be dangerous and might well prove disastrous. For naval policy, the Kaiser alone was responsible, since he supported Tirpitz against all his other advisers. The doctrine was that, after a few years, which were described as the danger-zone, the German Navy would be so strong that the English would not dare to attack it. When the Eng-

[2] In 1916, Fisher wrote a letter to Tirpitz beginning "Good old Tirps," and ending "Yours till Hell freezes."

lish announced their Two-Power policy, according to which they would always build enough to prevent Germany from reaching even approximate equality, Tirpitz assured William that fear of taxation would soon make them stop. Neither understood that naval supremacy was a fixed point of British policy, for which no financial sacrifices would be deemed excessive. Let us have peace for a few years more, they said, and we shall be able to stand up to the British Navy. As might have been expected, the War broke out before Tirpitz's "few years" had come to an end.

William's naval policy was unrealistic. He could not hope to catch up the British, since battleships cannot be built secretly. He caused England to join France and Russia, thereby encouraging Germany's enemies everywhere, awaking in France renewed hope of the "revanche," in Russia an intensified craving for Constantinople, and in the Balkans a new readiness to flout Austria. All the diplomatic upheavals from 1904 to 1914 derived their seriousness from British anxiety as to the German Navy. And in the end, when the time came for using his ships, William treated them as precious toys, to be kept safely in harbor. In war, as in peace, he loved his Navy too much.

The Russian Empire, even more completely than the German, was an autocracy. Nicholas II, who came to the throne in 1894, was compelled, it is true, to grant a sort of constitution in the following year; but England and France, whose Liberalism the Kaiser held up before the Tsar as a bugbear, helped their Ally to reduce the Duma to impotence, by lending him money when he wished to dissolve it. They did this in spite of the fact that the recently enacted Constitution forbade loans not sanctioned by the Duma. From 1907 to 1914, the Government of Russia was a ruthless despotism tempered only by assassination.

Nicholas married very soon after his accession, and fell completely under the influence of his wife. His politics, which were hers, were directed by certain fixed purposes. He wanted to plant the Cross on Saint Sophia in Constantinople; he wanted to preserve autocracy; he wanted to prevent any approach to religious toleration. When Stolypin (who was not exactly a Radical) suggested removing some of the disabilities of the Jews, the Tsar replied:

Up to now my conscience has never led me astray, or been mistaken. On that account, I am going, once more, to obey its dictates. I know that you, as well as myself, believe that the heart of the Tsar is in the hands of God. Let it therefore remain so. I am bearing in the sight of the Almighty a terrible responsibility in regard to the power which I possess and wield, but I stand always ready to render Him an account. I only regret that you and your Colleagues have wasted so much time over a matter which I absolutely refuse to approve or to sanction.

He was equally adamant about the Old Believers, but they, it must be admitted, were desperate characters: they disagreed with the Government about the spelling of the name of Jesus, and at a certain point of the liturgy they said Alleluia twice instead of three times.

When a boy fired at an Admiral and wounded him slightly, the Admiral interceded for the would-be assassin on the ground of his youth, and ventured to suggest that the death sentence might be commuted. The Tsar refused, saying:

I am neither cruel or vindictive. What I am writing to you is my belief and my deep-rooted conviction. Sad and hard as it is to have to say so, it is absolutely true, albeit to our sorrow and shame, that only through the execution of a few misguided people can we prevent the spilling of torrents of blood. I wish you health and complete peace of the soul; and I thank you for everything that you have done for Russia, as well as for me.

In 1895, when there was a movement for some participation of the zemstvos in the Government, a movement not at that time in any degree revolutionary, he made, against his Minister's advice, a fiercely autocratic speech:

It has come to my knowledge that during the last months there have been heard in some assemblies of the zemstvos the voices of those who have indulged in a senseless dream that the zemstvos could be called upon to participate in the government of the country. I want everyone to know that I will devote all my strength to maintain, for the good of the whole nation, the principle of absolute autocracy, as firmly and strongly as did my lamented father.

Nicholas continued to speak in the same tone down to the moment of his deposition.

It is not in such matters, however, that the Tsar's true character appears. Politics bored him; he loved his wife and children, he liked bicycling up and down the garden paths, and he had a passion for dominoes. When his dear Alix had a pain in her feet he was perturbed, but when he lost an Empire he hardly noticed it. On February 23, 1917, while he was at G.H.Q. in a last attempt to escape from the Revolution, he was worried by learning that his children had measles. He telegraphed to the Tsarina: "What a nuisance! I was hoping they would escape measles. Sincerest greetings to all. Sleep well. Nicky." On the same day he wrote: "I greatly miss my half-hourly game of patience every evening. I shall take up dominoes again in my spare time!" The day after his abdication, he telegraphed: "Hearty thanks for telegram. Mother arrived, for two days; it is so cosy and nice; we are dining together in her train. Another snowstorm. In thought and prayer I am with you. Nicky." Whatever happened, he never failed to note the weather.

Nicholas was an affectionate husband and a kind father. The rest of his character, what little there was of it, was a compound of cruelty, perfidy, and feeble arrogance.

What the Tsar lacked in firmness was fully supplied by the Tsarina, a woman who closely resembled Lady Macbeth, and in her letters to her husband repeated almost that vigorous woman's very phrases. "I do fear thy nature; it is too full of the milk of human kindness," says Lady Macbeth; "Forgive me, precious One," says the Tsarina, "but you know you are too kind and gentle." She goes on: "Do, my love, be more decided and sure of yourself. You know perfectly well what is right, so when there is any disagreement bring your opinion to the front and let it weigh against the rest." The particular question at issue when this was written was whether the plan of campaign in Galicia in 1915 should be decided by the military authorities or by the Man of God, Rasputin, who received inspiration on the subject from On High. The Empress, imperious to everyone else, was humble before "Our Friend," whom she believed to possess miraculous powers of preserving her son's health. Next month the Russian forces in Galicia suffered a series of appalling disasters in the middle of which the Tsar telegraphed from Headquarters: "Have just arrived safely. Lovely weather. The woods are now quite green and smell delightfully. I am just off to church. Thanks for telegram. I embrace you tenderly. Nicky."

The Empress, whose masterful will had come up against obstacles that seemed incapable of being overcome by human means—the German armies, the desire of all classes in Russia for revolution or reform, and the Tsarevich's haemophilia—turned more and more to supernatural sources of assistance, and believed, with increasing fervor, that she had found them in "the Saint." Late in 1916 she wrote to the Tsar: "All my trust lies in our Friend, who thinks only of you, Baby and Russia. And guided by HIM, we shall get through this heavy time. It will be hard fighting, but a Man of God is near to steer your boat safely through the reefs." A few days later, when there was a question of changing some of the Ministers who owed their appointment to Rasputin, she adopted a tone of gentle affectionate pleading: "Oh, Lovey, you can trust me. I may not be clever enough—but I have a strong feeling and that often helps more than the brain. . . . Keep the papers and names back, Lovey, dear, for Wifey's sake."

Rasputin, who, meanwhile, was rioting, drinking, and feathering his nest, was only the last and worst of a series of impostors—pretended mystics and spiritualists—who had influenced the Imperial policy for many years. The power of charlatans was a natural result of the unreality of the Tsar's position, which, in the modern world, could only be justified by a habit of believing in absurdities. Having rejected all reform, the august couple could only escape self-condemnation by living in a world of illusion.

William II and Nicholas II were the two most powerful individuals in the world during the twenty years preceding the Great War. It is a mistake to suppose that their policy was not their own, but that of their Ministers. Both chose men who would do their bidding, though on occasion they could be persuaded into some course that they would not have adopted if left to themselves. For example, Germany's Morocco policy in 1905 and 1906 was Bülow's, and never greatly pleased the Kaiser. But broadly speaking, Germany and Russia, the two most powerful nations of the Continent, allowed their diplomacy and their armies and navies to be directed by these two men.

Two other monarchs played a part of some importance, namely the Austrian Emperor Francis Joseph, and King Edward VII.

Francis Joseph, who had come to the throne during the troubles of 1848, was a very old man, and had lived through so many sorrows, both public and private, that he had come to accept misfortune as his natural lot. Publicly: he had been defeated by Prussia, he had lost his Italian provinces, he had been compelled to grant complete equality of status to Hungary, and he had been totally unable to check the dangerous growth of Slav disaffection in important parts of his dominions. Privately: his brother, the unfortunate Emperor Maximilián of Mexico, had been executed by his rebellious subjects; his wife had been assassinated by an Italian anarchist; his son had come to a violent end, which was probably suicide; his nephew and heir, whose murder was a signal for the war, had made a morganatic marriage, the children of which could not inherit. The old man lived long enough to know the inefficiency of his armies, but not long enough to suffer the disappearance of the Hapsburgs and the dissolution of his Empire. In the last years before 1914, he left matters mainly in the hands of his nephew the Archduke Francis Ferdinand, who made the army hustle and robbed the Emperor of his former pleasure in stately manoeuvres. At the end of a day's marching the men would be too tired even to salute, which caused the poor gentleman to deplore the hurry of modern life. His nephew, meanwhile, had schemes for giving autonomy to the Slavs, and transforming the Dual into a Triple Monarchy. It was partly the fear lest this policy should reconcile the South Slavs to the Hapsburg dominion that led Serbian nationalists to plot his assassination.

The importance of Edward VII was exaggerated on the Continent, but unduly minimized in England. He hated his nephew William II, and loved the French both *"gaîment et sérieusement,"* as Gambetta said. The French reciprocated his sentiments. He had considerable tact, and was well known in all European Courts. While always strictly constitutional, there can be no doubt that he did more to further his Government's policy after it had begun to be friendly with France than before. He had three reasons for being anti-German, connected, respectively, with his mother, his wife, and his sister. Queen Victoria passionately favored both Prussia and Austria; she was furious with Palmerston and Lord John Russell for favoring Italian unity at the expense of Austria, while in 1870 she wished that we were allied with Prussia, which (so she said) represented "civilization, liberty, order, and unity," as opposed to France, which stood for "despotism, corruption, immorality, and aggression." [3] The Prince, as is the nature of heirs to thrones, tended to disagree with his parent, and acquired, by reaction, a bias in favor of France. The Prusso-Austrian attack on Denmark, the year after his marriage to a Danish Princess, was a motive for disliking Prussia which was intensified by the annexation of Schleswig-Holstein. From this time on-

[3] Sir Sidney Lee, *King Edward VII*, I, p. 303.

wards he had the worst possible opinion of Bismarck, which was shared by his sister the Crown Princess (afterwards the Empress Frederick), who even called him "the wicked man" in a letter to her mother. Edward had a strong affection for his sister, and took her side when she quarrelled with her son. Queen Victoria, when the Kaiser annoyed her, treated him like a naughty boy in the nursery. When he complained of Lord Salisbury, she replied: "I doubt whether any Sovereign ever wrote in such terms to another Sovereign, and that Sovereign his own Grand Mother, about her Prime Minister. I should never do such a thing, and I never personally attacked or complained of Prince Bismarck, though I knew well what a bitter enemy he was to England, and all the harm he did."

Even an Emperor cannot resent this tone from his "Grand Mother," but "Uncle Bertie," though his feelings might be the same, had to express them differently. He was not so irrepressible as his nephew, but had an attitude of calm superiority which the Emperor found exasperating. "I know," Edward VII wrote to Lord Knollys, "the German Emperor hates me, and never loses an opportunity of saying so (behind my back), whilst I have always been kind and nice to him." Although he had been so "kind and nice," the Kaiser, when the War broke out, exclaimed "The dead Edward is stronger than the living I!" There was a larger element of truth in this view than Englishmen, complacently confident in their Parliamentary Constitution, have been inclined to believe.

Although the King liked the Entente policy, and helped by his diplomacy to make it successful, it was the Government that decided upon its adoption. The British, during the Boer War, had had reason to fear a Continental coalition against them, which could best be prevented by joining one or other of the two groups, the Triple Alliance and the Dual Alliance. There had been friction with France in Africa and with Russia in Asia; it therefore seemed, at first, more feasible to make friends with Germany. Efforts in this direction were made by Joseph Chamberlain in 1898 and 1900, but Germany held aloof. Holstein advised that delay would be advantageous, since England would find an Entente with France and Russia impossible, and would then be obliged to accept whatever terms the Germans chose to exact in return for their alliance. Moreover William II was just beginning to build his Navy, which he would have to keep small if he was to have England's friendship. Evasive answers were given by Bülow, who discovered, too late, that the formation of the Entente was not so impossible as Holstein believed.

The Entente with France (1904) was the work of Lord Lansdowne; that with Russia (1907) was the work of Sir Edward Grey. But both were really dictated by the permanent officials of the Foreign Office, about whom, since there has been no revolution in England, we know less than we do about Holstein. Their secret power, especially in the time of Grey, was almost unbounded. Grey was a high-minded man, a sincere patriot, a perfectly honorable gentleman in his dealings with those whom he regarded as equals, and an enthusiast for fly-fishing. On these grounds Englishmen entrusted their lives and fortunes to his keeping, although he knew no foreign language, had hardly ever been out of England, and had too little industry to verify what his officials told him. Moreover his belief in honorable dealing did not extend to the House of Commons, since he held the aristocratic opinion that ordinary mortals could not understand foreign politics. He allowed the Generals to prepare a joint plan of campaign with the French, and the Admirals to undertake the defence of the North Sea while the French Navy was concentrated in the Mediterranean. He told the House of Commons nothing of all this, and repeatedly asserted that we were not committed to France in the event of war. At last, on August 3, 1914, he blurted out the truth. By then the nation was excited, and applauded his foresight; but it would not, in the eight years during which he had held office, have sanctioned in advance the policy which had created such dangerous obligations. There was, in fact, in the years from 1906 to 1914, no more popular control over foreign policy in England than in Germany or Russia. British foreign policy was what Sir Edward Grey decided that it should be, and what he decided was what the permanent officials secretly advised. Not that their advice was unwelcome: he hated the Germans for their bad manners, whereas the suave Russians, while they ruthlessly exterminated all the best elements in Poland, Finland, Persia, and even Russia itself, preserved such perfect courtesy that he never noticed what use they were making of his support.

It must not be supposed that all Europe acquiesced quietly in the rule of its few autocrats. In Russia there was actual revolution in

1905, and a near approach to revolution in subsequent years. In Austria-Hungary Slav discontent made a break-up imminent. In Germany the Socialists, who formed, in 1912, over a third of the voters, were totally opposed to imperialism, and seemed likely, before long, to control the Reichstag and dictate policy. Unfortunately, in the three Eastern Empires, the defence of religion and property became bound up with the defence of autocracy, with the result that capitalists, even those who would be ruined by war, found themselves compelled to support the champions of an adventurous diplomacy, and earnest Christians had to support militarism in order to prevent the spoliation of those who taught Christ's doctrine.

In France and England, owing to democracy, the tactics of militarists were different in detail, though the large forces were almost the same as in Eastern Europe. France had recently emerged from the *Affaire Dreyfus*, in which an innocent man, because he was a Jew, had, by means of forged documents, been convicted of treason and sentenced to Devil's Island. Until the last shred of evidence had been destroyed, he was believed guilty by all good Catholics except those who had actually concocted the forgeries. The nation was convulsed: the Church, the Army, and the rich were against Dreyfus, while his defenders were atheists, Socialists, and proletarians. The victory of the pro-Dreyfus party seemed a victory for peace, and so it would have been but for the Anglo-French Entente, the conflict of French and German mining interests in Morocco, and the truculence of Delcassé under the stimulus of British encouragement. The peace party were strong enough to secure Delcassé's fall and the Conference of Algeciras; but the patriots, with the help of Bülow's blunders, established the legend that Delcassé had been offered up as a sacrifice to the Kaiser by poltroons who cared nothing for the honor of France. By means of this legend, when the time came, Delcassé and Poincaré were able to make the policy of France bellicose in spite of the extreme pacifism of the Socialists, the *Confédération Générale du Travail*, and large sections of the South. Indeed the pacifism of Socialists and anti-clericals was the chief reason for the warlike proclivities of priests and plutocrats.

In England, the techinque by which the reactionaries controlled foreign policy was more subtle than elsewhere. They allowed the friends of peace to suppose themselves in victorious control, while they quietly secured the key positions—foreign affairs, army, and finance—for their few friends in the Liberal party. The attention of progressive people was concentrated on home affairs; very few among them, before the War, realized the far greater importance of foreign policy. But their number was increasing, and they would soon have become formidable.

In every European country there were powerful and rapidly growing forces in favor of a radically new method in international relations. A few more years would have produced a transformation in Russia and Germany, with repercussions everywhere else. Meantime, the old system continued, unchanged since the Congress of Vienna except for the disappearance of the Concert of Europe. And before the new forces could gain control, the old system brought Europe to disaster.

The conception of "war-guilt," which flourished during the War and is enshrined in the Treaty of Versailles, is wholly unscientific. Every nation allowed its external affairs to be conducted by a small number of men, and the leading men of every Great Power could, by greater wisdom, have prevented the War from coming when it did. Perhaps postponement would have given time for a change of system, and so have prevented the War altogether; but given the system, or rather lack of system, a Great War sooner or later could only have been avoided by a greater degree of statesmanship everywhere than there was any reason to expect. None of the governments (with the possible exception of France) desired the War, any more than drunken motorists desire an accident. But they all desired various national advantages more than they desired peace. To ask who was to blame is like asking who is to blame for a motoring accident in a country which has no rule of the road. The absence of an international government made each nation the ultimate judge in its own cause, and still renders the occurrence of great wars from time to time almost a certainty. Unlimited sovereignty of each State was favored both by the pride of monarchs and by the Liberal belief in the principle of nationality; yet this anarchic exaltation of national self-assertion led logically to the outbreak of war in 1914, and must continue to lead to wars from time to time until some super-national authority is strong enough to command obedience.

CONCLUSION

THE nineteenth century was brought to its disastrous end by a conflict between industrial technique and political theory. Machine production, railways, telegraphs, and advances in the art of war, all promoted organization, and increased the power of those who held economic and political command. Pierpont Morgan and William II could direct human energy more rapidly and more massively than Xerxes or Napoleon or any of the great men of past times. But effective political thought had not kept pace with the increasing concentration of authority: theory, in so far as it had succeeded in molding institutions, was still divided between monarchy and competitive democracy, the first essentially pre-industrial, and the second appropriate only to the earliest stages of industrialism. Plutocracy, the actual form of government in Western countries, was unacknowledged and as far as possible concealed from the public eye.

The principle of legitimacy, which controlled Europe in 1815, continued to be accepted by the governments of the three Eastern Empires until their fall in 1917 and 1918. In alliance they were strong enough to enforce their system upon Europe, which enjoyed peace and endured despotism from 1815 to 1848. Then came a period when they could no longer enforce peace, though they remained friends. At last, through a variety of causes, of which the chief was Slav nationalism, they fell into conflict, with the result that legitimacy disappeared from the world as a political principle at the end of the Great War.

Political change throughout the century was inspired by two systems of thought, Liberalism and Radicalism. Of these, Liberalism was eighteenth-century in origin, and had inspired the American and French Revolutions. It stood for liberty, both individual and national, with as little government as possible; indeed, the functions of government were reduced by many Liberals to the prevention of crime. In agricultural communities it was successful in producing

447

stable conditions and a fairly contented population; but it had little
to offer to industrial wage-earners, since its philosophy suggested no
way of curbing economic power in the hands of individuals. It succeeded in establishing Parliaments, with a greater or less degree of
power, in every country of Europe and America, as well as in Japan
and China; but the resultant benefits were, in many parts of the
world, not very noticeable.

The most effective part of the Liberal creed was the principle of
nationality. States were viewed, by those who upheld legitimacy, as
the private estates of monarchs; but Liberals urged that the wishes
of the inhabitants should determine frontiers. In reaction against the
suppression of revolutions by the Great Powers which had taken place
while Metternich was dominant, Liberals held that each country
should be completely free, and should not be expected to tolerate
any interference from without. They thus destroyed the beginnings
of international government that had been established at the Congress
of Vienna.

The principle of nationality, after leading to the unification of
Germany and Italy, penetrated into the Balkans, where it raised
problems too difficult for the united wisdom of European statesmen.
And by a natural transition—considerably hastened by Bismarck—it
passed over into the principle of nationalism. The advocates of nationality said: *Every* country must be free to achieve its legitimate
ambitions. The advocates of nationalism said, or at least thought:
My country must be free to achieve its ambitions, whether legitimate
or not. By this transition, Liberalism was transformed into imperialism.

Radicalism, unlike Liberalism, was a doctrine inspired by economic
considerations, especially such as were suggested by nascent industrialism. Radicals were even more individualistic than Liberals, since
they took no interest in nations. As individuals they may have been
liable to patriotism, but as theorists they were cosmopolitan. They
believed in free trade, free competition, free individual initiative
within the limits of the criminal law. They did not object to the
power of property, so long as the property had been acquired by personal effort, not by privilege or inheritance. Their philosophy was
appropriate to the self-made first generation of industrial capitalists,
but the later generation, even when they owed everything to inherited

wealth, continued to speak of themselves as shining examples of the success to be achieved by self-help. In America, where most of the economic power was in the hands of a few monopolists, these very men still continued to praise competition as the motive force of progress.

The Philosophical Radicals, as a school, had certain important merits which, in our day, are apt to be overlooked. They applied to all existing institutions the test of utility, and accepted nothing on the mere ground of historical prescription. By this test, they found no justification for monarchy, aristocracy, religion, war, or empire. Liberals had a rhetorical and sentimental objection to some of these, but the objections of the Philosophical Radicals were argumentative, calm, and apparently derived from the inexorable voice of Reason. Prejudices such as those that had led to religious persecution and the disabilities of Jews could not survive their scrutiny, and those who had come under their influence were not likely to be led away by the glamour of martial heroes or royal personages. In economic questions, as in other matters, they reasoned carefully, assuming self-interest as the mainspring of individual action and the general happiness as the purpose of the legislator. When their bias led them astray, as it often did, the result was fallacious argument, which is far less persuasive than sophistical rhetoric. Consequently they had more influence when they were right than when they were wrong, and were more useful than might have been expected in view of the large admixture of error in their doctrines.

The outlook of the Philosophical Radicals was very largely shared by the Socialists, who differed from them chiefly in the fact that they regarded the world from the standpoint of the wage-earner rather than from that of the employer. Owen was a friend of Bentham; Marx was, in many important respects, a disciple of Ricardo. But Marx perceived what his Radical predecessors had not suspected, the tendency of capital to vast aggregations having immense economic power; he was also aware of the influence of capitalists on governments, which had not been obvious while governments were still in the hands of semi-feudal aristocratic landowners. There was one respect, however, and that a very important one, in which Marx inherited the limitations of the Philosophical Radicals. The organizations against which, in his opinion, it was necessary for proletarians to contend, were economic and voluntary, not, like nations or families, sentimental and biological. He assumed that the proletarian, having no property, would have no patriotism, or at any rate not enough to stand in the way of his opposition to the capitalists. In this respect, he underrated the strength of non-economic motives.

Economic nationalism, the dominant force in the modern world, derives its strength from the fact that it combines the motives of self-interest, to which Marx and the Radicals appealed, with those less rational motives that inspire patriotism. Cool heads can be won over by dividends, hotheads by rhetorical appeals. By this means, a sinister synthesis is effected between the watchwords of different schools. Competition, yes, between nations; co-operation, yes, within the nation. Self-interest, yes, for the nation as a whole; sacrifice, yes, to the nation on the part of the individual who has no share in the plutocratic plunder. Wealth, yes, in the service of the national glory; money-grubbing, no, since the industrial magnate in all he does is helping to make his country great.

This was the prevalent creed throughout the civilized world in the years preceding the War, and is still more so at the present day. Organization to the utmost within the State, freedom without limit in the relations between States. Since organization increases the power of States, and since their external power is exerted by war or the threat of war, increase of merely national organization can only increase disaster when war occurs. And while the danger of war is a constant terror, freedom within the nation is felt to be dangerous. By accepting national organization from the Socialists, and international freedom from the Liberals, the world brought itself to a condition threatening to the very existence of civilization. Organization, with modern industrial and scientific technique, is indispensable; some degree of freedom is a necessary condition both of happiness and of progress; but complete anarchy is even more dangerous as between highly organized nations than as between individuals within a nation. The nineteenth century failed because it created no international organization. It inherited States from the past, and thought the problem solved when it made them into national States. In a haphazard way, as a result of technique unguided by thought, it created economic organizations which its philosophy did not teach it to control. Their alliance with national States made international anarchy a far graver danger than it had ever been before. Liberals and Radicals alike failed to understand the part played by organization in a world ruled by scientific technique. Through this one failure, in spite of a great increase in wealth, intelligence, and happiness, the century which they attempted to guide ended in disaster.

America, throughout the period with which we have been concerned, remained to a considerable extent cut off from Europe. Owing to remoteness from the other Great Powers, the United States did not become part of the military and diplomatic system which had grown up in Europe, until two and a half years after the outbreak of the Great War; and the unification of America and Europe, when it came, was brought about mainly by the influence of finance.

The Great War was, in some respects, the end of an epoch, while in other respects it was a mere incident in a continuing process. It made an end of the doctrine of Divine Right, for which, in the countries where that doctrine had prevailed, has been substituted the naked rule of armed force. It refuted and extinguished the Liberal hopes and the creed of inevitable progress which expressed themselves in the optimism of the nineteenth century. But in those aspects of politics that depended upon modern economic developments, the War was the first large-scale expression of forces which had been operative for fifty years, and are still growing continually stronger. The development of nationalistic monopolies, particularly in iron and steel, and still more particularly in connection with the ore of Lorraine, was, and is, a more important factor in world politics than most men know or statesmen will admit. The same causes that produced war in 1914 are still operative, and, unless checked by international control of investment and of raw material, they will inevitably produce the same effect, but on a larger scale. It is not by pacifist sentiment, but by world-wide economic organization, that civilized mankind is to be saved from collective suicide.

BIBLIOGRAPHY

The following is a list of those books which we have found particularly useful. The dates given are those of the editions used.

PART I

Alexandre Ier et Napoléon d'après leur correspondance inédite.
> Serge Tatistcheff. Paris. 1891.
Correspondance de l'Empereur Alexandre Ier avec sa Souer La Grande-Duchesse Catherine, 1805–1818.
> Edité par le Grand-Duc Nicolas Michaelovitch. St. Petersburg. 1910.
L'Empereur Alexandre Ier.
> Par le Grand-Duc Nicolas Michaelovitch. St. Petersburg. 1912.
Memoirs of the Emperor Alexander and the Court of Russia.
> Comtesse Choiseul-Gouffier. London. 1904.
Modern Russian History.
> Kornilov. London. 1916.
Life and Letters of Mme. de Krüdener.
> Clarence Ford. London. 1893.
Memoirs of Prince Metternich.
> Edited by Prince Richard Metternich. London. 1880–82.
Metternich.
> Sandeman. London. 1911.
Mémoires de Talleyrand.
> Edités par le Duc de Broglie. Paris. 1891–92.
Memoirs and Correspondence of Castlereagh.
> London. 1848–58.
The Congress of Vienna.
> C. K. Webster. London. 1919.
Les Dessous du Congrès de Vienne.

PART II

The Creevey Papers.
> Edited by Sir H. Maxwell. London. 1903–4.
Leaves from the Greville Diary.
> Edited by Philip Morrell. London. 1929.

Economic History of Modern Britain.
    Vol. I. The Early Railway Age. 1926.
    Vol. II. Free Trade and Steel. 1932.
    J. H. Clapham. Cambridge.
The Town Labourer. 1932.
The Village Labourer. 1932.
The Skilled Labourer. 1919.
Lord Shaftesbury. 1923.
The Age of the Chartists.
    J. L. and Barbara Hammond. London. 1930.
Essay on Population.
    Malthus. London. 6th edition. 1826.
Malthus and His Work.
    James Bonar. London. 1924.
Works of Bentham.
    Edited by Dr. Bowring. London. 1843.
The Education of Jeremy Bentham.
    C. W. Everatt. Columbia University Press. 1931.
Jeremy Bentham: His Life and Work.
    C. M. Atkinson. London. 1905.
Life of Francis Place.
    Graham Wallas. London. 1898.
Autobiography.
    John Stuart Mill. London. 1873.
Principles of Political Economy and Taxation.
    Ricardo. London. 1817.
A Fable of the Bees.
    Bernard de Mandeville. London. 1724.
History of the Chartist Movement.
    R. G. Gammage. London. 1894.
Political Writings of Richard Cobden.
    2nd edition. London and New York. 1868.
Life of Richard Cobden.
    John Morley. London and New York. 1908.
Life of John Bright.
    G. M. Trevelyan. London. 1913.
Robert Owen: A Biography.
    Frank Podmore. London. 1928.
Life of Robert Owen.
    G. D. H. Cole. London.
A New View of Society.
    Robert Owen. London. 1813.
History of Trade Unionism.
    Sidney and Beatrice Webb. Revised edition. 1920.

James Mill: A Biography.
    Alexander Bain.   London.   1882.
Oeuvres de Saint-Simon et d'Enfantin.
    Paris.   1865–78.
Le Nouveau Monde Industriel.
    François Fourier.   Brussels.   1840.
Revolution and Reaction in Modern France.
    G. Lowes Dickinson.   London.   1892.
The Growth of Philosophical Radicalism.
    Elie Halévy.   London.   1928.
Thomas Hodgskin.
    Elie Halévy.   Paris.   1903.
The Communist Manifesto.
    Karl Marx.   London.   1888.
The Condition of the English Working Class in 1844.
    Friedrich Engels.   London.   1892.
Karl Marx: His Life and Work.
    Otto Rühle.   London.   1929.
Socialism Utopian and Scientific.
    Engels.   London.   1892.
Über Historischen Materialismus.
    Marx and Engels.   Berlin.   1930.
Revolution and Counter Revolution.
    Marx.   London.   1896.
The 18th Brumaire of Louis Bonaparte.
    Marx.   London.   1926.
Misère de la Philosophie.
    Marx.   Paris.   1922.
Capital.
    Marx.   Chicago.   1932–33.
Materialism and Empirio-Criticism.
    Lenin.   London.

PART III

The Digger Movement in the Days of the Commonwealth.
    Lewis H. Berens.   London.   1906.
Life and Letters of Thomas Jefferson.
    F. W. Hirst.   London.   1926.
Life of Jefferson.
    George Tucker.   1836.
Jefferson and Hamilton.
    Claude G. Bowers.   New York.   1929.

Works of Thomas Jefferson.
    Edited by W. C. Foord. 1904–5.
Economic Origins of Jeffersonian Democracy.
    Charles A. Beard. New York. 1927.
An Economic Interpretation of the Constitution of the United States.
    Charles A. Beard. New York. 1925.
Democracy in America.
    Alexis de Tocqueville. London. 1875.
Chicago and the Old North-West. 1673–1835.
    M. M. Quaife. Chicago. 1913.
The Frontier in American History.
    Turner. New York. 1920.
Abraham Lincoln: A History.
    Nicolay and Hay. New York. 1890.
The March of Democracy.
    James Truslow Adams. New York and London. 1932–33.
A History of the People of the United States.
    McMaster. New York and London. 1913.
A History of the United States.
    Channing. New York. 1925.
The Rise of American Civilisation.
    Charles A. and Mary R. Beard. New York and London. 1927.
An Economic History of the United States.
    G. S. Callender. New York and London. 1909.
An Economic History of the American People.
    E. S. Bogart. New York. 1930.
The History of the Great American Fortunes.
    Gustavus Myers. Chicago. 1908–10.
High Finance in the Sixties.
    Edited by Frederick C. Hicks. Yale and Oxford. 1929.
God's Gold.
    John T. Flynn. London and New York. 1933.
History of the Standard Oil Company.
    Ida M. Tarbell. London and New York. 1904.
Wealth Against Commonwealth.
    H. D. Lloyd. London. 1894.
The Life of Andrew Carnegie.
    Burton J. Hendrick. New York and London. 1933.
The Life of Elbert H. Gary: A Story of Steel.
    Ida M. Tarbell. New York and London. 1926.
The Life of J. Pierpont Morgan.
    John Kennedy Winkler. New York and London. 1931.
Life Story of J. Pierpont Morgan.
    Carl Hovey. New York. 1912.

Trusts, Pools and Corporations.
    Edited by William Z. Ripley.   New York and London.   1905.
Problems in Railway Regulation.
    H. S. Haines.   New York.   1911.
The Gospel of Wealth and Other Essays.
    Andrew Carnegie.   New York.   1900.

PART IV

Addresses to the German Nation.
    Fichte.   Chicago.   1922.
Life and Writings of Mazzini.
    London.   1864–70.
A History of Italian Unity.
    Bolton King.   London.   1899.
Life of Mazzini.
    Bolton King.   London.   1902.
The Rise of Louis Napoleon.
    F. A. Simpson.   London.   1909.
Louis Napoleon and the Recovery of France.
    F. A. Simpson.   London.   1923.
Bismarck: The Story of a Fighter.
    Emil Ludwig.   London.   1927.
Bismarck.
    C. Grant Robertson.   London.   1918.
Bismarck.   Some Secret Pages of His History.
    Dr. Moritz Busch.   London.   1898.
Life of Friedrich List and Selections from His Writings.
    M. E. Hirst.   London.   1909.
Reflections and Reminiscences of Otto Prince von Bismarck.
    London.   1898.
Bismarck and State Socialism.   London.   1890.
The Evolution of Modern Germany.   London.   1914.
The German Empire.   London.   1919.
    William Harbutt Dawson.
The Economic Development of France and Germany.
    J. H. Clapham.   Cambridge.   1921.
Red Rubber.
    E. D. Morel.   London.   1906.
The Black Man's Burden.
    E. D. Morel.   Manchester and London.   1920.
History of the Colonization of Africa.
    Sir H. H. Johnston.   Cambridge.   1913.

Cecil Rhodes.
 Basil Williams. London. 1921.
Life of Benjamin Disraeli, Earl of Beaconsfield.
 Monypenny and Buckle. London. 1910–12.
Life of Queen Victoria. 1902.
King Edward VII.
 Sir Sidney Lee. London. 1927.
Imperialism: A Study.
 J. A. Hobson. London. 1902.
Life of Joseph Chamberlain.
 J. L. Garvin. London. 1932–33.
The War of Steel and Gold.
 H. N. Brailsford. London. 1914.
Joseph Chamberlain: An Honest Biography.
 A. Mackintosh. London. 1914.
Nicholas I: the Last of the Tsars.
 Princess Catherine Radziwill. London. 1931.
The History of the Russian Revolution.
 Leon Trotsky. London. 1932.
The Kaiser's Letters to the Tsar.
 London. 1921.
Memoirs of Prince von Bülow.
 London. 1931–32.
Records.
 Lord Fisher. London. 1919.
Memories.
 Lord Fisher. London. 1919.
The Origins of the World War.
 Sidney B. Fay. New York. 1932.
Fifty Years of Europe.
 J. A. Spender. London. 1933.
Bismarck and the World War.
 Brandenburg. London. 1933.
Kaiser William II.
 Emil Ludwig. London. 1926.
His Excellency the Spectre: the Life of Fritz von Holstein.
 Joachim von Kürenberg. London. 1933.

GENERAL WORKS

History of Germany in the Nineteenth Century.
 Treitschke. London. 1919.
Histoire Générale di IVe Siècle à Nos Jours.
 Lavisse et Rambaud. Paris.

History of Modern Europe.
    C. A. Fyffe.   London.   1892.
British History in the Nineteenth Century, 1782–1901.
    G. M. Trevelyan.   London.   1922.